MW00471083

MORNING & EVENING
DEVOTIONAL

Then
Sings
My
Soul

BroadStreet
PUBLISHING

BroadStreet Publishing Group LLC
Savage, Minnesota, USA
Broadstreetpublishing.com

Then Sings My Soul: A Morning & Evening Devotional

© 2018 by BroadStreet Publishing

ISBN 978-1-4245-5627-4 (faux leather)
ISBN 978-1-4245-5719-6 (ebook)

Entries composed by Robert Campbell, Kathy Castor, Ken Castor, Chris Folkestad, Rob Mapstone, John Mulholland, Tony Myles, Kelly Nelson, Phil Petersen, Rachel Riebe, Tony Roos, and Jared Van Voorst.

Design by Chris Garborg | garborgdesign.com

Compiled by Ken Castor.

Printed in China.

18 19 20 21 22 23 24   7 6 5 4 3 2 1

Bless the Lord,
O my soul,
and all that is
within me,
bless his holy name!

Psalm 103:1 NASB

Introduction

God deserves our wonder and praise from morning to evening. Each day may bring us our predictable routines, testing trials, or unexpected experiences. But how great God is! Even in the midst of our circumstances, God is to be praised.

This unique devotional helps your soul begin and end each day in concert with God. Imagine bookending your days in awe of the Lord. Imagine how your soul will sing when each day is saturated with praise, gratitude, and wonder toward our great God.

Next Step

We should make plans—counting on God to direct us.

PROVERBS 16:9 TLB

At the beginning of any new year you'll likely find yourself reflecting on your life more than you might on a daily basis. This is especially true if you spend your energy "trying to get through the day" because of how overwhelming your schedule feels. When the thought of making massive changes freezes us, we tend not to make any.

Proverbs 16:9 clarifies that there are only two ways to live—by default or by design. The former focuses on letting life in our cubicles, classrooms, or carpools lead us while the latter is us reclaiming with God the most important priorities in the universe. It's the difference between doing what feels good versus doing what is good. Amazingly, these two options are only one decision away from each other—to believe we call the shots or recognize God does. If you want to make the most of what can happen in the next moment, invite him into this one.

I'm all in with you, God. May this year reflect that as I take my next step with you each day.

A man's mind plans his way [as he journeys through life],
But the Lord directs his steps and establishes them.

PROVERBS 16:9 AMP

Life is not measured in decades, years, months, or even minutes;
it's measured in eternity. This means that while it may be
popular to set a big New Year's resolution, it makes more sense
to discern the design of what's happening in your life right now
so you can better respond to it. This takes place moment by
moment as you keep taking your next steps with God.

In financial terms, it might mean asking God to guide you
as you develop a budget. In your marriage or singleness,
it involves you becoming a whole person to contribute to
wholeness in relationships. In your hurts, it is allowing
God to heal you while empowering you to forgive. Instead of
letting the length of the journey discourage you, focus on one
simple change through Jesus that when repeated day in, day
out, can make a massive difference in your life.

Lord, I don't want to live a small life, so guide me into my next
big step. May I do this not in my power but in yours, for in you all
things are possible.

What is one next step or decision that would move you from
"default" to "design"?

Who Goes before Us

The Lord is the one who goes ahead of you; He will be with you. He will not fail you or forsake you. Do not fear or be dismayed.

DEUTERONOMY 31:8 NASB

God is calling you to follow him. He stands in front of us, leading us toward the life that he has set before us. For many though, we are afraid to follow. We are afraid of where God might be leading us. We are afraid that we aren't hearing God correctly, or that we will fail if we step out of our comfort zone. It's so much easier to stay where we are or to continue with what is familiar.

In this morning's verse though, God is reminding us that not only has he prepared the way for us, but he has gone before us! He's blazing the path for us to follow. He's giving us a promise that where we are leading, he is already there. God is not just calling for us from a distance, he's walking with us each step of the way.

God, thank you that you have a plan for me. Help me to follow after your leading in my life.

The Lord himself will go before you. He will be with you; he will not leave you or forget you. Don't be afraid and don't worry.

DEUTERONOMY 31:8 NCV

What do these words teach you about who God is? How do they help build your confidence in him? These words are Moses' as he speaks to the Israelites. He told them that his leadership is coming to an end and that Joshua will now be leading them. He is imploring the Israelites to not lose courage or give up. Moses reminds them that it is God who is leading and that he can be trusted.

These words of Moses are for you too. You can trust where God is leading; he's already been down the road. God is with you! He's not blindly calling from above saying, "Follow the sound of my voice." He's saying, "I am right here with you, follow me." You can trust that God is not going to leave you stranded or forget you. He loves you. He's leading you. He's with you. You can trust him.

Lord, thank you for your active leadership in my life. Help me to confidently follow where you lead.

Which promise in today's verse brings you the most confidence in God?

God's Immeasurable Love

> How great is God's love for all
> who worship him?
> Greater than the distance
> between heaven and earth!
> How far has the Lord taken
> our sins from us?
> Farther than the distance
> from east to west!

PSALM 103:11-12 CEV

When little kids describe their love for their parents, they'll often spread their arms as wide as they possibly can, and say, "Daddy, I love you this much!" If that doesn't get the point across they will continue with, "Mom, I love you to the moon and back five times!" They want their mom and dad to know just how much they are loved.

This morning's verse is reminding you that you are loved by God. His love for you is seen in the immeasurable mercy that he has for you. He loves you so much that he's forgiven you for all your sins. It's as if he's standing here in the room with you this morning with his arms spread wide saying, "I love you this much." Can you hear him? Do you believe him? He loves you so much!

God, thank you for your immeasurable love for me. Thank you for not just loving me a little, but for loving me completely.

Measure how high heaven is above the earth;
God's wide, loving, kind heart is greater for those who revere Him.
You see, God takes all our crimes—our seemingly inexhaustible
sins—and removes them.
As far as east is from the west, He removes them from us.

PSALM 103:11-12 VOICE

One of the hardest things for many to accept about God's
love for us is his promise to blot out our sin. It's not how we
operate, so it's difficult for us to wrap our heads around it.
When someone wrongs us, it's not natural for us to forgive
them. If we do forgive them, it's still very difficult to not
continue to hold their sin against them. When we see the
person who hurt us, we are reminded about what they did.

God is different. In his immeasurable love, he not only
forgives us (along with making it possible through Jesus), but
today's verses remind us that he also removes that sin from
us completely. He doesn't see an asterisk next to us denoting
our sin history. Praise God!

Heavenly Father, your forgiveness is so perfect. Thank you for
perfect, immeasurable love.

In what ways have you experienced God's love in your life?

Give Thanks

Thank the Lord for all the glorious things he does; proclaim them to the nations. Sing his praises and tell everyone about his miracles.

PSALM 105:1-2 TLB

We have so much to be thankful for. Stop, right where you are, and think about all the different things that you have to be thankful to God for. How have you seen God working in your life this week? How has God blessed your family? How many things can you think of that you are thankful for in the next thirty seconds?

Don't just keep your thankfulness to yourself though. Tell others about your thankfulness, and start with God. Take some time right now to say thank you to God for some of the ways that you are grateful for his work in your life.

Heavenly Father, thank you. I don't say it enough, but I am thankful for your work in my life. Help my life reflect my thankfulness to others in the way that I act and the things that I say. May I never grow weary of telling others all that you have done for me.

Oh give thanks to the Lord; call upon his name;
make known his deeds among the peoples!
Sing to him, sing praises to him;
tell of all his wondrous works!

PSALM 105:1-2 NIV

Did you know that your thankfulness is not just pleasing to
God's ears, but that it helps others around us know of his
goodness as well? Our thankfulness is a declaration to others
that God is good and he is working in our lives.

When we share what God is doing in our lives with others,
God becomes real to them. He's no longer just a character
in the Bible. He is living and active, and they know it's true
because they've seen him in you and heard your testimony of
his goodness.

God, thank you for using me to bring the message of the gospel to
the people in my life. Help me to reflect on all the ways I have to be
thankful tonight.

How can you share God's good work in your life with others
this week?

Search Me, Oh God

Search me, God, and know my heart;
test me and know my anxious thoughts.
See if there is any offensive way in me,
and lead me in the way everlasting.

PSALM 139:23-24 NIV

How well do you receive evaluation, especially thorough evaluations? If you are like many, the answer is, "not well." We want to know when things are going good, and we love to hear other people sing our praises; but we don't like hearing about things that need changing in us. That's what makes David's prayer in Psalm 139 so interesting.

David understands something very important about God. He knows that he's on David's side. He trusts that God's examination will help to guide him down the right path. He believes that God isn't going to respond in anger, but in love. Start today with David's prayer as well as his understanding of who God is.

God, search my heart and my thoughts this morning. Help me to see areas of my life that don't live up to your standard for my life. Help me to know and follow the path that you have created for me.

Search me, O God, and know my heart;
test me and know my anxious thoughts.
Point out anything in me that offends you,
and lead me along the path of everlasting life.

PSALM 139:23-24 NLT

One of the most dreaded parts of air travel is the long security lines that now fill every major airport. It seems with every trip, there are further security measures that have been put in place. And with each new step of the security process, a little more of our privacy is gone. Full body digital scans, the dreaded pat down, and searches of our bags and computers are now common practice. But if we want to travel, we need to participate in the process.

This prayer is voluntarily inviting God to search your life, to look in every corner and crevasse. It's asking him to look for anything that doesn't honor him, and then to report his findings to us. That's a vulnerable prayer, but one that leads to us growing closer to God.

Heavenly Father, I am giving you full access to my life. If there is anything in my attitude, in my heart or in my life that does not please you, bring that to light. Help me to experience the joy of walking in everlasting life.

What is God revealing to you about your life?

Praise Him

Let everything alive give praises to the Lord! You praise him!
Hallelujah!

PSALM 150:6 TLB

The book of Psalms is filled with psalms that help us wrestle through the realness of life. Psalms of gratitude and thanks to our creator, psalms of doubt and question, psalms of pain and hurt, and so many more. As readers, we can relate to the wide array of joy, pain, wonder and doubt, the frustration, and the contentment. Many times, the psalms put to words what our lips cannot say. This is why so many are drawn to the psalms. The psalms help us to walk through some of life's lowest lows and highest highs.

One thing is sure though, psalms always lead us back to a position of praise. That's what makes the final words of the book of Psalm so impactful. They remind us through it all, the good and the bad, that our creator is worth our praise. It's not profound or complex, in fact, it's quite simple: "Let everything that has breath praise the Lord. Praise the Lord!" Allow these words to lead you to praise throughout your day today.

God, you are worthy of our praise! You have given me breath; help
me to use it today to give you praise.

Let everything that has breath praise the Lord.
Praise the Lord!

PSALM 150:6 NASB

What did you use your breath for today? It brought you oxygen
to fill your lungs and keep you alive. It most likely helped
you to communicate with co-workers, your friends and your
family. It may have helped you cheer on your favorite sports
team, share a simple greeting with a stranger on the street, or
place your order at your favorite restaurant.

What if our praise for God was as natural as breathing to us?
What if, when we woke up, the first thoughts on our minds
were thoughts of praise to God? What if, as we communicated
with others, we used our breath to share of God's goodness
to us? What if we used our breath to praise God as loudly and
passionately as we do to cheer on our favorite sports teams?

God is certainly worthy of our praise.

God, may my praise for you become as natural and consistent as
my breathing.

How can you use your breath to praise God tonight?
Tomorrow?

God Is Faithful

Lord, you are my God.
I honor you and praise you,
because you have done amazing things.
You have always done what you said you would do;
you have done what you planned long ago.

ISAIAH 25:1 NCV

"Lord, you are my God." Stop and think about that for a second this morning. God, the creator of the universe, is your God. He spoke the world into existence and he is your God. He formed us out of the dust, breathed a breath of life into mankind, and he is your God. His faithfulness has been evident throughout time, and he is your God.

Before you begin your day today, take some time to thank God for being your God. He's your provider, your protector, your sustainer, your God. Honor him and praise him by telling him how thankful you are for his work and his faithfulness in your life.

Lord, you are my God and I am so thankful for that reminder this morning. Help me to never forget that you are a personal God who loves and cares for me, not just for humanity. Thank you, Lord, for being my God.

O Lord, you are my God;
I will exalt you, I will praise your name;
for you have done wonderful things,
plans formed of old, faithful and sure.

ISAIAH 25:1 NRSV

You started this morning praising God that he is your God. This evening, take some time to praise him for his faithfulness to complete the plans that he has for you that were created long before we were ever born. Throughout Scripture we see God's faithfulness on display in his people. His faithfulness continues in your life today.

Isn't it comforting knowing that God is not absent, distant or uninvolved in our lives? He has a track record of faithfulness that stretches to the beginning of time, and if there's one thing that we can be sure of, it's that his faithfulness will continue.

Heavenly Father, I praise you this evening for your faithfulness. I thank you for the faithfulness that I have seen in my own life. Thank you for the faithfulness that you have displayed that has gone unnoticed by others and even by myself.

How has God been faithful to you? Start a list of the ways God has answered your prayers.

Persevering Joy

Count it all joy, my brothers, when you meet trials of various kinds, for you know that the testing of your faith produces steadfastness. And let steadfastness have its full effect, that you may be perfect and complete, lacking in nothing.

JAMES 1:2-4 ESV

The words joy and trials don't usually go together. Typically, when we think of trials, joy is one of the last emotions we would associate with it. But James is not saying that he wants us to enjoy the trials. He is not saying that we are supposed to like what we are going through.

The joy that James is talking about here relates more to the end result than to the current situation. We have joy because we recognize what the Lord is accomplishing in us through the trials. He is developing perseverance and maturity in our lives, and that is good. So, looking forward to the end result, we can consider the trials to be good even though we might not enjoy them.

Heavenly Father, I don't enjoy the trials in my life, but I see your purpose in the midst of them. Help me to trust in you.

My friends, consider yourselves fortunate when all kinds of trials come your way, for you know that when your faith succeeds in facing such trials, the result is the ability to endure. Make sure that your endurance carries you all the way without failing, so that you may be perfect and complete, lacking nothing.

JAMES 1:2-4 GNT

What do you think the end result of this verse might look like? James refers to being mature and complete not lacking anything. What would a Christian who lacks nothing look like? Maybe it would be someone who completely reflects the fruit of the Spirit that we find in Galatians 5. Do you know anyone like that? If so, then they have probably gone through trials well.

It is possible to go through trials and not mature and become more complete. Some people go through trials and all they have to show for it is bitterness. That is not what James has in mind. He doesn't want us to just endure the trials, but to embrace them. He wants us to recognize Gods work and yield ourselves more fully to him.

God, help me to go through trials well. Help me to trust in you and yield myself to you in the midst of those trials. May you complete your good work in me.

Are you embracing the trials you face and letting God use them to his honor and glory or are you just becoming bitter?

There Is Rest in Jesus

"Come to me, all of you who are tired and have heavy loads, and I will give you rest. Accept my teachings and learn from me, because I am gentle and humble in spirit, and you will find rest for your lives."

MATTHEW 11:28-29 NCV

For some of you, your morning started with an alarm clock that went off too early and you are just now getting a chance to enjoy the cup of coffee. You are awake, but already you are tired. Tired not because you didn't sleep last night, but tired because you are carrying a heavy load. The stress of work, family life, relationships, expectations, and a busy schedule has left you tired and stressed, and you haven't even checked your email yet.

Jesus is inviting you this morning to rest in him. Even with everything that is going on in your life, and all the tasks that are calling for your attention, Jesus is inviting you to pause and spend time with him. What a beautiful picture of Jesus this paints for us.

Jesus, thank you for knowing my need for rest, and inviting me in. My mind is filled with to-do lists and deadlines, but this morning, help my mind instead to be filled with your thoughts. Help me to experience the rest you offer.

"Come to me, all you who are weary and burdened, and I will give you rest. Take my yoke upon you and learn from me, for I am gentle and humble in heart, and you will find rest for your souls."

MATTHEW 11:28-29 NIV

The analogy of a yoke loses some of its impact in our world today, because it's not a tool that we are familiar with. A yoke was a large wooden plank that when put around the neck of two oxen that allows them to work side by side, sharing the workload. Though the imagery is not as familiar to us today, the invitation from Jesus still remains.

Jesus is inviting us to allow him to share our workload. He knows how difficult life can be for us, and he's willing to help us through it. When we take his yoke, it allows us to not have to feel the full weight of our burden. It also allows us to walk where Jesus is leading. As we do, he promises that we will find rest for our souls. We are not meant to walk this life alone, and Jesus is inviting us to walk alongside him.

Jesus, thank you for walking alongside of me. Forgive me for the times when I feel like I need to carry the burdens of life alone. I want to connect to your yoke and learn from you. Thank you for the rest that you provide.

What are some burdens that you've been carrying that you need to allow Jesus to help with?

Priceless

"The kingdom of heaven is like a treasure hidden in the field, which a man found and hid again; and from joy over it he goes and sells all that he has and buys that field."

MATTHEW 13:44 NASB

Following Jesus does not come without its costs. For some of us, it has cost relationships, friendships, jobs, reputation, and preferences. For others, it has cost them their lives. So why are we so willing to make such great sacrifices for the kingdom? Because the benefit far outweighs the cost.

In the kingdom of heaven, we have forgiveness of sin, we are a new creation, we have fellowship with God, and we have the power of the Holy Spirit to live the lives that God has created us to live. Trading everything that we have for the kingdom of God is a bargain!

Heavenly Father, I want my life to be marked as one who lives for you, no matter the cost. Help my decisions I make today reflect the value I place on following you. You are worth my everything.

"The kingdom of heaven is like treasure hidden in a field, which a man found and covered up. Then in his joy he goes and sells all that he has and buys that field."

MATTHEW 13:44 ESV

Have you ever been hard up for cash? Are there times when you are scrambling around looking for loose change between the cushions of the couch, checking the pockets of the jackets in the closet, and looking for any other money around the house, but still come up short? Have you ever had to decide to sell some of your possessions in order to make necessary purchases? If so, was it done out of need and desperation?

Notice that in our verse this evening, it was "in his joy" that he went and sold everything that he had in order to be able to purchase the field that included the newly discovered treasure. He knew that what he was trading in paled in comparison to what he was receiving. As a follower of Jesus, this should reflect our attitude towards the kingdom in heaven.

Jesus, the kingdom of heaven is available to us because you gave up everything and died on the cross on our behalf. Help me to joyfully serve you, no matter the cost.

How does your life reflect the joy of the kingdom of heaven?

Seeing through God's Eyes

He called a little child to him, and placed the child among them.
And he said: "Truly I tell you, unless you change and become
like little children, you will never enter the kingdom of heaven.
Therefore, whoever takes the lowly position of this child is the
greatest in the kingdom of heaven."

MATTHEW 18:2-4 NIV

It's human nature to want to be the best. We often jockey for
positions of power and authority. It was no different with the
disciples. These were Jesus' closest friends, who seemingly
were already in a rather powerful position. One day, they
asked Jesus who would be the greatest in the kingdom of
Heaven. His unlikely response gives us a glimpse into how he
views success.

Jesus reminds us that it's is not about our earthly
accomplishments or achievements that makes us great in
the kingdom of heaven, but our ability to put our faith in
him. Follower of Jesus, you don't need to perform to grab
the attention of Jesus. He knows you and sees you. You are
valuable and loved!

Jesus, thank you that I don't need to earn your attention. Your love
is perfect.

Jesus called a little child to him and put the child among them. Then he said, "I tell you the truth, unless you turn from your sins and become like little children, you will never get into the Kingdom of Heaven. So anyone who becomes as humble as this little child is the greatest in the Kingdom of Heaven."

MATTHEW 18:2-4 NLT

Babies are cute and cuddly. But once you have one of your own, you begin to realize how hard they are! They rely on others for their every need. Food, clothing, shelter, changing—they are helpless on their own. This is the word picture Jesus uses to describe the greatest in the kingdom of heaven. Encouraging huh?

But what if the picture that Jesus was painting was one of grace. What if he was reminding us that it isn't about what we have to offer him that makes us great, but that it's all about our ability to recognize our complete dependence on him? Jesus is reminding us that it is his work in us that brings us greatness in the kingdom.

Jesus, thank you for the grace that you show me in my life. May I live my life in total dependence on you.

In what ways are you trying to earn God's attention on your own ability?

Just as He Said He Would

"Jesus is not here. He was raised, just as He said He would be. Come over to the grave, and see for yourself."

MATTHEW 28:6 VOICE

Can you imagine what it must have been like to discover the empty tomb of Jesus? As Mary and Mary went to pay their final respect to Jesus, that's exactly what they found. They were met by an angel that said to them, "Jesus is not here. He was raised, just as he said he would be."

Picture the strange mix of their confusion and excitement. They were at the tomb to grieve, but instead, they were suddenly faced with the reality that what Jesus had been teaching them all along had come true. Jesus was and is who he said he was! His resurrection was proof that he was the Son of God, proof that he had victory over sin, and proof that he had come to fulfil the Old Testament prophecies. The ladies at the tomb went from mourning to celebration! Jesus was not dead; he was alive and still is today!

What is your response to the empty tomb? How can you celebrate Jesus today?

Jesus, you are alive! Because you live I have hope and forgiveness. Thank you!

"He is not here; he has risen, just as he said. Come and see the place where he lay."

MATTHEW 28:6 NIV

Throughout Jesus' life and ministry, he faced many who doubted and questioned him. There were those who doubted his claims of being the Son of God. Those who questioned his power to heal the sick and bring sight to the blind. There were those who called him a blasphemer for claiming he could forgive sins. Yet he rose from the dead, just as he said he would. He provided all the proof that was needed that he was who he said he was.

Still today, there are those who doubt and question Jesus. But we can draw confidence in knowing that Jesus proved who he was by coming back from the dead. Jesus has never backed out of a promise that he made. This is the Jesus we serve, the Son of God, who came to take the sins of the world upon himself. One day soon, Jesus will return, just as he said that he would.

Jesus, thank you for always following through on your promises. You are worthy of my trust and praise.

How do you respond to those who question your faith in Jesus?

I Am with You Always

Then Jesus came to them and said, "All authority in heaven and on earth has been given to me. Therefore, go and make disciples of all nations, baptizing them in the name of the Father and of the Son and of the Holy Spirit, and teaching them to obey everything I have commanded you. And surely I am with you always, to the very end of the age."

MATTHEW 28:18-20 NIV

"Therefore, go and make disciples of all nations." Not only is Jesus challenging his followers to go and spread the message of the Gospel, but he is commissioning them to go to all nations. Can you imagine what must have been going through their minds as they heard these words from Jesus? Jesus was commissioning them into something that was much bigger than themselves.

Jesus didn't leave them to figure it out on their own though. His commission came with a promise: "I am with you always." Jesus doesn't send us somewhere or give us a task that he's not also going to empower us to accomplish. It would have been easy for the disciples to be overwhelmed with their new responsibility, and there are times when we can be overwhelmed with this same responsibility, but Jesus' promise of his presence remains true today.

Jesus, thank you for the promise of your presence in my life today and forever. Help me to remember your presence is with me, empowering me to accomplish your plan.

*Jesus came and told his disciples, "I have been given all authority
in heaven and on earth. Therefore, go and make disciples of all
the nations, baptizing them in the name of the Father and the
Son and the Holy Spirit. Teach these new disciples to obey all the
commands I have given you. And be sure of this: I am with you
always, even to the end of the age."*

MATTHEW 28:18-20 NLT

It's easy for us to feel like we are unqualified to do Jesus'
work. We are quick to look at all the reasons that there are
better, more qualified people. It's why we are sometimes slow
to volunteer at church and why we don't share our faith as
often as we could. We simply don't feel qualified.

But just as we see in these verses, Jesus is sending us authority
and is promising that he will be with us. We are commissioned
with authority, and we are promised that we are not alone.
That's a great confidence builder to step out and serve Jesus.
You are called and qualified—Jesus' presence is our promise.

*Jesus, forgive me for feeling unqualified. You have called me to be
a disciple-maker; help me to have the confidence that is found in
your presence to serve you faithfully.*

What is Jesus calling you to that can only be accomplished
with his strength?

The Good News

"The time promised by God has come at last!" he announced. "The Kingdom of God is near! Repent of your sins and believe the Good News!"

MARK 1:15 NLT

These are the first words that Jesus spoke in the book of Mark. With these words, the good news of the gospel went from something spoken about as sometime yet to come, to something that was now at hand. Previously, John the Baptist spoke about the one who would come after him, but now, Jesus spoke as that person.

This is a big deal because Jesus came to fulfill the prophecies of the Old Testament. This is a big deal because Jesus came to reconcile us to God. It's a big deal because Jesus came as the ultimate and final sacrifice for sin. No longer was the good news sometime yet to come. No longer was animal sacrifice necessary for the forgiveness of sins. Jesus came to point people to the good news. In fact, he was it! Today, remember that Jesus, the Good News, is living, that Jesus has reconciled you to God, offered forgiveness for your sins, and is ruling in your heart today.

Jesus, you are the Good News! Thank you for the hope that is found in you.

"The time has come," he said. "The kingdom of God has come near. Repent and believe the good news!"

MARK 1:15 NIV

Can you hear the tone of Jesus' voice as he says these words? It isn't out of judgment or damnation. He is proclaiming that the good news is here! The kingdom of God is near! It's no longer far off and unreachable! He's imploring people to turn from their sinful ways, and to instead believe in the good news that is standing in front of them. There's excitement in his voice, care in his tone. This is good news indeed.

In a sense, this is Jesus' pregame speech. He's saying it is go time. He knows that he is here for a purpose and he's not going to waste time. His message is simple; the far-off kingdom of heaven is now among the people. Turn from your sinful ways and believe in Jesus. His message is the same today. What is our response to the good news?

Jesus, thank you that you are not distant, but here with me. Help me to share the good news with just as much enthusiasm.

Spend some time tonight thanking Jesus for being the Good News in your life.

Father Knows Best

He withdrew from them about a stone's throw, and knelt down and prayed, saying, "Father, if you are willing, remove this cup from me. Nevertheless, not my will, but yours, be done."

LUKE 22:41-42 ESV

Jesus had just finished revealing his impending death to his disciples in what we now know as the Last Supper. He knew that his time was running short, so he made his way to a familiar place of prayer on the Mount of Olives. His disciples followed after him. He instructed his disciples to pray so as to not fall into temptation, and then he went to find a place alone to pray. As Jesus thought through what he knew was about to happen, he prayed, "Father, if you are willing, remove this cup from me. Nevertheless, not my will but yours, be done."

Jesus knew that his father's plan was much greater than his own. He knew that the benefit of his father's plan was for the good of not only him, but all of mankind. Incredibly, even in his darkest moment, Jesus shows us how to focus our hearts when we pray. Let's remember that our father always knows best.

Heavenly Father, thank you that your ways are good and perfect. Thank you that you have a plan for our lives! Help me to know your plan and to boldly and faithfully follow you. May it be your will be done in my life, not my own.

He was withdrawn from them about a stone's throw, and He knelt down and prayed, saying, "Father, if it is Your will, take this cup away from Me; nevertheless not My will, but Yours, be done."

LUKE 22:41-42 NKJV

We have a tendency to think about what we want; about what's best for us. Have you noticed that? Often our prayers are filled with what we want and what we want God to do on our behalf, and on behalf of those that we know. We are good, it seems, at telling God how to do his job.

It's not wrong to let the Lord know our desires in prayer. The Bible is filled with invitations to bring our requests to the Lord. But sometimes we are so busy telling God what our will is, that we forget to ask him for his will. It's a subtle shift in thinking, but it makes a world of difference. What if we asked him what he wanted more than we told him what we wanted?

God, I want what you want. I'm really good at telling you what I want, but I want to change that. I want to know what you want so that I can be a part of what you doing.

What if our prayers always included, "God what do you want?"

35

The Mark of Jesus

"A new commandment I give to you, that you love one another: just as I have loved you, you also are to love one another. By this all people will know that you are my disciples, if you have love for one another."

JOHN 13:34-35 ESV

The love that Jesus is commanding is not a love based on feelings or emotion, but instead a love that reflects the perfect love we have already received from him. It may seem like an obvious command, but it certainly isn't always an easy one to live out. That's why Jesus said to follow his example that he has given us.

In fact, this command was given towards the end of what is now called "The Last Supper." This is where Jesus revealed to his closest disciples that his time was coming to an end. Before the supper began, Jesus, of all people, got down and washed the disciples' feet. In doing so, set an example of what true love looks like. This is the love that we are called to. We are to love one another, just as he has loved us. Jesus' life was marked by his love for others, and he's commanded us to follow his lead.

Jesus, thank you for your love that you have given me. Help me to love others the same way. Help me to love when it isn't easy. Help me to love the way that you have loved me.

"A new commandment I give to you, that you love one another; as I have loved you, that you also love one another. By this all will know that you are My disciples, if you have love for one another."

John 13:34-35 NKJV

Jesus was marked by his love for others. His love motivated him to live differently. Out of love, he healed the lame and sick, interacted with outcasts, ministered to the masses, and ultimately gave his life all of humanity. His love caused him to live differently than what was normal.

Jesus' command to follow his example in love is an invitation to take on the mark of Jesus' love. As we love others, it marks us as one of his disciples. As we love others, our actions tell a story not of ourselves, but of the one who has shown us what true love looks like. Bearing the mark of Jesus through our love is both a command and a privilege.

Jesus, your love is perfect. I want to love the way that you love others. I want my actions to tell your story.

What message did the love you displayed today tell?

Turn Your Eyes

"Repent and turn back, so that your sins may be wiped out, that seasons of refreshing may come from the presence of the Lord, and that He may send Jesus, who has been appointed for you as the Messiah."

ACTS 3:19-20 HCSB

The Lord is so good to us. Our verses today remind us of our need and dependence on Jesus our savior. We know that our sin has separated us from him. But we are reminded that the Lord is pursuing us! He's calling us to repent of our sins, to turn away from them, and come to him. We come to him, not for punishment but for forgiveness and refreshing found his presence and Jesus' work on the cross. This is the grace, mercy, and love of the Lord for you today! As you go through your day today, remember the words of the old hymn, "Turn Your Eyes Upon Jesus" which say:

Turn your eyes upon Jesus,
Look full in His wonderful face;
And the things of earth will grow strangely dim
In the light of His glory and grace.

Lord, thank you for your forgiveness from sin! Help me to find refreshing through your presence today.

"Repent of your sins and turn to God, so that your sins may be wiped away. Then times of refreshment will come from the presence of the Lord, and he will again send you Jesus, your appointed Messiah."

ACTS 3:19-20 NLT

We often focus on the forgiveness that the Lord offers us through Jesus, and rightfully so. Without it, we are hopeless and lost. But sometimes we don't remember that when we are forgiven, that the Lord no longer sees our sin. He has wiped it out! The all-knowing God forgets our sin. What an amazing display of his grace and mercy to us!

Allow these verses to spring up a well of thanksgiving and joy for the Lord within your heart! Tell him of your thankfulness! You can approach the Lord in confidence and without guilt. You are forgiven in Jesus. Come to the Lord and be refreshed. Come to the Lord and find the hope that is found through our coming Jesus!

Lord thank you for not holding my sin against me. Thank you that I can experience your presence.

Plan a date with the Lord. Mark it off on your calendar and spend an hour with him.

The Solid Rock

Salvation is found in no one else, for there is no other name under heaven given to mankind by which we must be saved.

ACTS 4:12 NIV

When using the GPS on your phone, it will often give you several route options for your desired destination. The GPS will give you estimated times of travel and any possible causes for delays such as accidents or road construction on a specific route. With this information, you can then choose which route looks the fastest and easiest and make your selection. Whatever route you choose, you'll get to where you want to go.

The road to eternal life with the Lord is not the same. As you look at the Bible, it is clear that there is only one path to God. That path is Jesus Christ. There is no amount of money that you could gain or fame that you could attain that would save you from the penalty of sin. But there is an answer. Jesus is our salvation. Through Jesus, we are forgiven of our sins, reconciled to God and given the hope of eternity. Praise God today that Jesus has made a way for you!

Heavenly Father, thank you that I am saved through Jesus.

Salvation is to be found through him alone; in all the world there is no one else whom God has given who can save us.

ACTS 4:12 GNT

When we call on the name of Jesus to be saved, we are calling on the only name that can save, and the only name that ever has saved. We are calling on the same name that Paul called on as his life was dramatically transformed. We are calling on the same name that saved the disciples, and the same name that saved the criminal who hung alongside Jesus on Calvary. Jesus has always been, and will always be the only one who can save us from our sins. There are no other ways.

May we continue to stand firm in Jesus, knowing that salvation is found in him alone. May our claim be similar to that familiar hymn, "My hope is built on nothing less than Jesus' blood and righteousness; I dare not trust the sweetest frame, but wholly lean on Jesus' name. On Christ, the solid Rock, I stand; all other ground is sinking sand."

Jesus, it is you alone who save. All other ways are incomplete and insufficient. Thank you for your continued faithfulness throughout all generations.

Who in your life Jesus' gift of salvation with this week?

The Inseparable Love of God

I am convinced that nothing can ever separate us from God's love. Neither death nor life, neither angels nor demons, neither our fears for today nor our worries about tomorrow—not even the powers of hell can separate us from God's love. No power in the sky above or in the earth below—indeed, nothing in all creation will ever be able to separate us from the love of God that is revealed in Christ Jesus our Lord.

ROMANS 8:38-39 NLT

When Jesus died on the cross, he revealed the depth of his perfect love. His love is not based on what we have done for him, or even on our potential to love him. His love for us is based on who we are as his creation. He has loved us from the beginning, and we are reminded today that nothing can separate us from that love.

God's love was not going to allow him to do nothing about the sin that separated us from him, so he sent his son to take our penalty. His love for you has not changed. There is nothing that is going to change God's love for you. God's love for you does not change.

Heavenly Father, thank you that I can always count on your love in my life. Help me to hold onto this promise.

I am certain that nothing can separate us from his love: neither death nor life, neither angels nor other heavenly rulers or powers, neither the present nor the future, neither the world above nor the world below—there is nothing in all creation that will ever be able to separate us from the love of God which is ours through Christ Jesus our Lord.

ROMANS 8:38-39 GNT

There's something special about returning to the town you grew up in. As you drive around town, you realize that even though some new stores have opened and a few of the landmark buildings have been tore down, there is much that stays the same. That similarity often gives us a sense of comfort and joy as we think back on the good as well as the challenging times we shared in our school years.

Today's verse points to the consistency of God. No matter where we live, what job we have, or whatever changes could come our way, God's love remains. God's love for us is not conditional; it doesn't come with strings attached. Wherever your life has brought you, come back to God. His love for you remains.

God, thank you for your consistency in my life.

How have you seen God's consistency of his love in your life?

God Is Greater

Even the foolishness of God is wiser than human wisdom, and the weakness of God is stronger than human strength.

1 CORINTHIANS 1:25 NCV

We have a tendency to want to do things ourselves. We know what we need and how it needs to be done. Asking for help seem like admitting defeat or at least weakness. Maybe it is because we've been let down too many times, or because we don't trust others as much as we trust ourselves. Whatever the reason, it doesn't seem easy to ask for help.

But this verse reminds us that we do have someone we can trust and count on. One who is stronger and wiser than anyone we can imagine. We can take comfort in knowing that when we ask God for help, we are getting help that is greater and stronger. Today, look for ways you can trust God and rely on his strength and his wisdom. Not only in God able, he is also willing.

Heavenly Father, thank you for your greatness. Help me to find comfort today in knowing that you are in control. Help me to ask for your strength and wisdom.

*This foolish plan of God is wiser than the wisest of human plans,
and God's weakness is stronger than the greatest of human strength.*

1 CORINTHIANS 1:25 NLT

Have you ever found it difficult to explain God to someone?
Where it seems like any word you use just don't quit accurately
describe him? Where even the best analogy falls short of who
he is? It can be frustrating trying to understand God. This
frustration can either turn us away from God, because we
don't fully understand him, or it can cause us to worship him.

The greatest example of his perfect plan and strength is in
Jesus. History is filled with attempts to deal with the problem
of sin in our lives. But nothing has been successful. We are not
good enough, smart enough, or strong enough to sufficiently
deal with sin on our own. But through God's perfect plan, he
sent Jesus to overcome sin on our behalf. Tonight, pause and
thank God for his wisdom. Thank God that no matter what
comes your way, that he is stronger. Worship him. Thank Him.
Tonight, rest in knowing that he is on your side.

*Heavenly Father, thank you for your perfect and infinite
wisdom and strength. May I not try to live my life in my own
understanding and strength, but in yours.*

What are you trying to accomplish in your own strength that
you can trust God with?

Victory in Jesus

O death, where is your victory?
O death, where is your sting?"
For sin is the sting that results in death, and the law gives sin
its power. But thank God! He gives us victory over sin and death
through our Lord Jesus Christ.

1 CORINTHIANS 15:55-57 NLT

Don't skip past those words you just read. Go back and read them again, this time out loud. We have been given victory in Jesus. Victory over sin and death. And this victory comes only through the work of Jesus Christ on the cross. Without Jesus, we are hopeless and subject to the power and consequence of sin in our life. However, through Jesus, we can walk in victory!

So read those words again, nice and loud this time. This is your victory chant. This is you declaring a win over the sin in your life. Not based on your own ability or on your own skill, but on the battle that was won at Calvary on your behalf. May these words ring in your heart as you face your day.

Heavenly Father, thank you for the victory that is mine through Jesus! Help me to remember these words throughout today.

Where, O death, is your victory?
Where, O death, is your sting?"
The sting of death is sin, and the power of sin is the law.
But thanks be to God, who gives us the victory through
our Lord Jesus Christ.

1 CORINTHIANS 15:55-57 NRSV

How do we appropriately thank God for the victory that we have through Jesus Christ? We know that victory is ours, and we have seen God working in our life, especially strengthening us against the temptation of sin, but we haven't fully felt the impact of our triumph yet. We've experienced it in part, but not yet in whole.

But one day we will. One day we will stand in the presence of God and in victory over death. And on that day we will worship God. We will repeat these words giving thanks to him. Let's not wait till we get to heaven to worship God in thankfulness. We may not fully understand all that God has done for us, but let's thank him for the victory that we know is ours!

God, thank you! Thank you that we can know that we have victory over death because of Jesus. May my life reflect my thankful heart.

Take some time tonight to think through all that God has saved you from. Then thank him for it.

You Are His

Now it is God who makes both us and you stand firm in Christ. He anointed us, set his seal of ownership on us, and put his Spirit in our hearts as a deposit, guaranteeing what is to come.

2 CORINTHIANS 1:21-22 NIV

It's easy to be filled with self-doubt. We aren't good enough, we don't feel we live up to others' standards, or we compare ourselves to other followers of Jesus and feel like we just don't measure up. It's an easy trap to fall into and it often causes us to doubt.

This morning, as you read these verses, be reminded that you are anointed and chosen by God. Know that he has placed his seal of ownership on your life. He wants everyone to know that you belong to him. To top it all off, he's given us the gift of the Holy Spirit in our life to empower us to live the life that he has called us to. The Holy Spirit is also a promise of what is yet to come. You are chosen. You are loved. You are his.

Heavenly Father, thank you that you have chosen me. Help me to live today in the confidence in knowing I am yours.

It is God who enables us, along with you, to stand firm for Christ. He has commissioned us, and he has identified us as his own by placing the Holy Spirit in our hearts as the first installment that guarantees everything he has promised us.

2 CORINTHIANS 1:21-22 NLT

Have you ever walked on ice? Once you start to slip, it seems like your whole body is grasping at the air, trying to catch your feet. You look for anything that you can grab onto to stabilize yourself. It can seem like forever before you either finally fall down, or you somehow regain your footing. It's a helpless, painful, and sometimes embarrassing feeling.

Sometimes life feels like that, doesn't it? You just don't have solid footing. When you find yourself slipping in the uncertainty of life, know that God is enabling you to stand firm. He is leading you and has given you the Holy Spirit to empower you. Our trust is not placed in our own ability to stand, but in the assurance that God is with us and we are his.

God, thank you for the certainty that comes in your promises. Help me to stand firm for you.

What confidence does knowing that you have God's seal of ownership on your life bring you?

God Is Enough

"Fear not, for I am with you;
Be not dismayed, for I am your God.
I will strengthen you,
Yes, I will help you,
I will uphold you with My righteous right hand."

ISAIAH 41:10 NKJV

Sometimes it feels daunting to think that God, the creator of the universe, would ask for us to step out in faith. Jacob felt that way as he stepped into leadership of the Israelites. But God wanted to assure him that he was with him. God begins by reminding Jacob of all that he had done for the Israelites up to this point; he had proved, protected and led them, and assured them that he will continue to be with them.

God doesn't call us to do something that he isn't going to also help us accomplish. We don't need to be in fear of how we could do what God is calling us to. Just as he promised Jacob, he also promises us that he will strengthen us and help us. We can count on his presence and his help.

Heavenly Father, thank you for strengthening and helping me.

"Don't be afraid, for I am with you.
Don't be discouraged, for I am your God.
I will strengthen you and help you.
I will hold you up with my victorious right hand."

ISAIAH 41:10 NLT

How do you respond when you feel God asking you to step out of your comfort zone? Are you filled with fear of the unknown? Do you use excuses of how you are not skilled or equipped? Do you follow where he is leading, or do you stay where you are? Today's verse is another reminder that God is always leading us to new places, but he also leads with great promises.

God's promises are not just empty words that are given to convince us to follow him, but instead are words that are intended to give us the confidence that we need. He knows that we cannot do many of these things under our own ability or strength, so he has promised to give us the strength we need. Where you are lacking, God is not. Our confidence can come from his ability to accomplish what he's called us to.

God, help me to know where you are leading me and the
confidence to go where you send me.

Look for at least one way you can step out in faith this week to serve God.

Into My Heart

If anyone is in Christ, he is a new creation. The old has passed away; behold, the new has come.

2 CORINTHIANS 5:17 ESV

This verse is very black and white. There is a stark contrast between our old self that has passed away, and the new creation that we are now. It's as if there has been a line drawn on the timeline of our life. When we say yes to Jesus and begin a relationship with him, our lives are forever changed. The old hymn, "Since Jesus Came into My Heart" says:

What a wonderful change in my life has been wrought
since Jesus came into my heart!
I have light in my soul for which long I have sought,
since Jesus came into my heart!

As you look back on who you were before you met Jesus, can you see the change that has occurred? How have you been changed? How have your priorities been changed? How have your passions been changed? How has Christ brought you satisfaction and contentment that you didn't have before? How have you been changed since Jesus came into your heart?

Jesus, I am no longer who I once was. Thank you that my old self has passed away! Thank you that you have made me new.

Anyone who is joined to Christ is a new being; the old is gone, the new has come.

2 CORINTHIANS 5:17 GNT

We started this morning with the first verse of the song "Since Jesus Came into My Heart" reminding us to look back at who we once were. This evening, we are going to look at verse three:

There's a light in the valley of death now for me,
since Jesus came into my heart!
And the gates of the city beyond I can see,
Since Jesus came into my heart!

As you look forward in Christ, what do you see? Where have you seen Christ help you find victory in your life? Thank him for it! As you look forward to eternity, how has your perspective changed? May your soul sing, as the writer of this hymn penned in the chorus:

Since Jesus came into my heart,
since Jesus came into my heart,
floods of joy o'er my soul like the sea billows roll,
since Jesus came into my heart.

God, thank you for the hope that comes in knowing that I am new in you.

If you were to write a verse of this hymn, how would you describe your life since Jesus came into your heart?

Mercy and Grace

God's mercy is great, and he loved us very much. Though we were spiritually dead because of the things we did against God, he gave us new life with Christ. You have been saved by God's grace.

EPHESIANS 2:4-5 NCV

You just got pulled over for speeding. You didn't see the sign indicating the change in speeds. As you sit in your car, awaiting the officer to approach your vehicle, you know you're busted. There's no denying it; you were breaking the law, and you got caught. The only question left in your mind is, "How much is this going to cost?"

The officer asks for your license and registration, and runs your information. To your surprise, as the officer hands your cards back to you, he informs you that he isn't going to give you a ticket. The officer showed you mercy today.

This is much like the mercy that God has shown us. The consequence of our sin is death. And while we were dead in our sin, God showed us mercy by not giving us what we deserve. Today, worship him for the mercy that he has shown you.

God, I don't deserve you, but because of your mercy, you have saved me from my sin. Thank you.

Because of his great love for us, God, who is rich in mercy, made us alive with Christ even when we were dead in transgressions—it is by grace you have been saved.

EPHESIANS 2:4-5 NIV

When we think about God's saving grace, we often look back at our past and see what we have been saved from, and we look forward to heaven, where we know that we will spend eternity because of God's mercy and grace. But tonight, as you meditate on these verses, remind yourself of Christ's work in your life now.

God's love isn't just something that was shown to us two thousand years ago on the cross, and something that we will once again experience when our time on earth expires. His love is for us now, tonight. We are not just in a holding pattern awaiting that glorious day we will be reunited with him. He is with us now and he has given us life. He has made us alive through Christ.

So Christian, live alive! Live your life in the mercy and grace that has been given to you through Jesus. God loves you.

God, thank you for reminding me that you are with me now. Help me to live with the life that comes through Jesus.

What is God doing in your life today?

No Longer Far Away

In Christ Jesus you who once were far off have been brought near by the blood of Christ.

EPHESIANS 2:13 ESV

There's something special about being near to the people that we care about most. When we are afraid, being near to people that we trust brings a sense of comfort. When we are lonely, we long to be near to our loved ones. There is safety and comfort in being near. Because of Jesus' work on the cross, we have been brought near to God. We were once far off and separated from him, but after deciding to follow Jesus, we have been brought near to him.

Today, as you go throughout your day, remember that God is there with you. He's with you at work, in your class, in your meeting, sitting with you at lunch, and walking with you wherever you go. No matter what today brings your way, remember that you are not alone. God is with you.

Jesus, thank you that I am not alone. Thank you that though I was once far off, you have brought me near to God.

In Christ Jesus you who formerly were far off have been brought near by the blood of Christ.

EPHESIANS 2:13 NASB

You've been brought near to God. That's reason to celebrate! You, who were once far off and separated from God because of your sin have now been brought near to him. You've been adopted as his own son or daughter. You've been forgiven of your sins and have access to God. What an amazing position to be in.

Remember though, that it is not because of who you are, or because of what you've done, that you have this privilege. It is only because of the blood of Jesus that you have been brought near to God. It is because God sent Jesus to do what you could not that you have been forgiven of yours sins. Praise God that he knew that you couldn't do it on your own. He sent Jesus to make a way for all who would believe!

Thank you, Jesus, for what you accomplished on the cross. It is through your blood that I am brought near to God.

Take some time tonight to think through all the benefits of being near to God.

Welcome Home

You are no longer foreigners and strangers, but fellow citizens with the saints, and members of God's household.

EPHESIANS 2:19 HCSB

Welcome home! These are the words that greet American citizens as they make their way back into the country. Once the Homeland Security officers looks through your passport and verify your identity and citizenship, they will stamp your passport and say "Welcome home." You have returned. In the country you were visiting, you were just that: a visitor. Now, you are home.

As followers of Jesus, we will one day hear the words "Welcome home." These words will not be offered to us from a uniformed officer, but by our heavenly father. He will welcome us home, into eternity, where our citizenship is verified, not by a passport or birth certificate, but by the blood of Jesus. Through Jesus we are welcomed into Heaven and brought into the family of God.

Jesus, I look forward to the day that I will hear "welcome home." Until that day comes, help me to live with anticipation and hope.

You are no longer strangers to God and foreigners to heaven, but you are members of God's very own family, citizens of God's country, and you belong in God's household with every other Christian.

EPHESIANS 2:19 TLB

There are so many things to be thankful for in tonight's verse. Take some time to slowly reread it. It's filled with the truth that, when we begin to understand its implications, can completely change our identity. So often, we define ourselves by our last name, our group of friends, or our home country. But there's so much more.

This verse reminds us that we are not strangers to God. We are citizens of heaven and members of God's family. We are reminded that these privileges are not ours because of the country that we were born in, the family that we are a part of, the amount of money in our bank accounts, or how many good things we have done. These privileges are available to anyone who follows Jesus. Praise God!

Thank you, God, that I am known by you. Thank you that I am a citizen of heaven and a member of your family! Thank you for making this possible to me and all who would believe.

What if our identity was formed more out of our citizenship in heaven than the citizenship listed on our passport?

No Longer

For you were once darkness, but now you are light in the Lord.
Walk as children of light.

EPHESIANS 5:8 HCSB

Have you ever heard someone share a testimony of how their life was dramatically transformed when they met Jesus? They may have shared about how before they met Jesus they struggled with addictions that controlled their lives. They may have shared about how they had run-ins with the law. These testimonies are powerful examples of a life that has been brought from darkness to light.

But what if your story is much different? What if your story is that you put your trust in Christ at an early age? Is your testimony any less powerful than the man who struggled with addiction? No! Before Christ, we were all living in sin, separated from God. It is only through Christ that we are forgiven and transformed. No matter what your "darkness" story is, if you have placed your faith in Jesus, you have been transformed and made new. Jesus has brought light to your darkness. Thank him today as you live for him.

Jesus, you have transformed my life from darkness to light!
Thank you!

In the past you were full of darkness, but now you are full of light in the Lord. So live like children who belong to the light.

EPHESIANS 5:8 NCV

If you were to write a thank you note to Jesus for his work in your life, what would it include? What would you thank him for? What examples would you give of how your life has changed? How would you describe your thankfulness to him? You have much to be thankful for. It would be worth your time to write him a thank you note.

Even more so, how are you living your new life as a thank you note to him? How are your actions, decisions, and attitude displaying your thankfulness to him? Our verse today tells us that our life has been changed from darkness to light, "so live like children who belong to the light." The way we live is our opportunity to show not only the change that has happened within us, but also our gratitude to him.

Jesus, you have changed my life and made it new! You have brought hope to my hopelessness. May my life reflect the change that you have made!

How can you show your thankfulness to Christ tomorrow?

Worthy of the Gospel

Just one thing: Live your life in a manner worthy of the gospel of Christ. Then, whether I come and see you or am absent, I will hear about you that you are standing firm in one spirit, with one mind, working side by side for the faith that comes from the gospel.

PHILIPPIANS 1:27 HCSB

If you are a fan of college or professional sports, you've probably heard of a player being suspended from the team for "conduct detrimental to the team" or something similar. The athlete did something, on the field or off the field, that didn't align with the values, rules, or expectations of the organization. Sports teams take seriously the brand of their team. Coaches are notorious for reminding their players that they represent the name that is written on the front of their jersey.

As followers of Jesus, we have a similar responsibility. Paul reminds us that the way that we live our life represents not only ourselves, but Jesus Christ as well. He tells us to live our lives worthy of the Gospel. We do this, not out of obligation to our organization, but out of thankfulness for what Christ has already done for us.

Jesus, you have done so much for me. Help my life to always be lived worthy of your Gospel.

Above all else, you must live in a way that brings honor to the good news about Christ. Then, whether I visit you or not, I will hear that all of you think alike. I will know that you are working together and that you are struggling side by side to get others to believe the good news.

PHILIPPIANS 1:27 CEV

As you read through this verse, what do you learn about Jesus and the gospel message?

Paul is saying that Jesus' message is life changing. He says that it's so important that our whole life should bring honor to it. He continues by showing the unifying power of the gospel. He says that the gospel unifies us even when we are not together, and that it brings believers together to work in unity for one cause. Finally, he also says that the good news is worth sharing, encouraging us to come together as the body of believers to continue to tell the story of Jesus so that others would believe. Take some time tonight to think about how the good news is impacting your life.

Jesus, thank you for the reminder of the power of the good news in my life. Help me to live accordingly.

What message does your life share with others?

God's Work

The saying is trustworthy and deserving of full acceptance, that Christ Jesus came into the world to save sinners, of whom I am the foremost. But I received mercy for this reason, that in me, as the foremost, Jesus Christ might display his perfect patience as an example to those who were to believe in him for eternal life.

1 TIMOTHY 1:15-16 ESV

Paul understands the full extent of what God has done in his life. He was well aware of his past and how, if anyone is undeserving of forgiveness, it was him. Paul used to spend his time doing whatever he could to stop the message of Christ from spreading. Paul vehemently opposed the gospel message of Jesus, and even went so far as to persecute those who did believe it. It's easy to see why he would feel like he was undeserving.

When Paul met Jesus, his life was radically transformed. He went from persecutor to persecuted. God's forgiveness and grace is for anyone who will receive it. If God's grace was extended even to Paul, then it is extended to each of us as well. Sometimes we forget to personalize Christ's work on the cross. All of us are in need of a Savior.

Jesus, thank you that your death on the cross was for even me. Thank you that I am forgiven.

How true it is, and how I long that everyone should know it, that Christ Jesus came into the world to save sinners—and I was the greatest of them all. But God had mercy on me so that Christ Jesus could use me as an example to show everyone how patient he is with even the worst sinners, so that others will realize that they, too, can have everlasting life.

1 TIMOTHY 1:15-16 TLB

Have you ever thought about how your story could be used to help others know about Jesus? Sometimes we are embarrassed of our past, so we are hesitant to share it with others. Other times, we don't feel like our story is compelling or powerful since we don't have a dramatic plot twist of transformation. But the reality is, each of our stories are unique, powerful, and useful in sharing the story of Christ's work in our lives to others.

In Paul's life, the themes of Christ's work were his powerful transformation, complete forgiveness, and his patience with Paul. What are the themes of the Lord's work in your life? Someone else needs to hear your story. As you share our story with others, you introduce them to the everlasting life that the Lord is calling them to.

Jesus, may you be glorified as I share my story with others.

Who can you share your faith story with this week?

Our Anchor

We have this as a sure and steadfast anchor of the soul, a hope that enters into the inner place behind the curtain, where Jesus has gone as a forerunner on our behalf, having become a high priest forever after the order of Melchizedek.

HEBREWS 6:19-20 ESV

Cancer, war, sickness, abuse, divorce, death. Even reading those words stirs a sense of uneasiness within us, doesn't it? Many of us know what it's like to have these words introduced into our lives in a very personal way. They rock us. They blindside us. They have the ability to bring our lives to a standstill and send us into a spiraling tailspin all at the same time.

This morning's verses remind us that, in the storms of life, we have an anchor who will hold us steady and who will keep us from drifting away in the current. Jesus is our anchor. Jesus is our hope. He steadies our life with his unfailing promises and anchors us in God, our protector. Jesus reminds us of the hope of eternity. In the storms of life, look to Jesus.

Jesus, today I am thankful that you are my sure and steadfast anchor.

This hope is a strong and trustworthy anchor for our souls.
It leads us through the curtain into God's inner sanctuary.
Jesus has already gone in there for us. He has become our
eternal High Priest in the order of Melchizedek.

HEBREWS 6:19-20 NLT

Picture this: You're out fishing with your buddy when out of nowhere, a storm moves in. Before you know it, the boat is rocking and you're being blown further out into the lake. Your friend grabs the anchor and tosses it into the water to help stabilize the boat. You ask, "Do you think the anchor will hold us?" He responds, "I sure hope so."

Not exactly reassuring, is it? So what is the difference between hoping the anchor holds, and the hope that we have in Jesus? The hope we have in Jesus is backed by the weight of God's promises, and we know that God is faithful. The hope that we have in Jesus is not wishful thinking. Our hope in Jesus is our assurance of our eternity with him.

Jesus, my life is filled with hope in you. Thank you for your faithfulness and strength.

How has your hope in Jesus anchored your soul?

Run!

We are surrounded by a great cloud of people whose lives tell us what faith means. So let us run the race that is before us and never give up. We should remove from our lives anything that would get in the way and the sin that so easily holds us back.

HEBREWS 12:1 NCV

Running isn't easy. If you stand at the finish line of any race, be it a 10K or an ultramarathon, you will see exhausted runners cross the finish line. Running takes effort and mental strength to press through, and in many instances, the ability to keep going even when you want to quit. Running isn't easy, and neither is the race of life.

We all need running partners. People who encourage us to keep going. People who we look to as an example of faithfulness. God has surrounded us with pacesetters. People who encourage and challenge us in our faith with him. Take some time this morning to think about your heroes of the faith that encourage you. Then thank God for them.

Heavenly Father, thank you that I do not run this race of life alone. Please surround me with running partners that challenge and encourage me.

Since we are surrounded by such a great cloud of witnesses, let us throw off everything that hinders and the sin that so easily entangles. And let us run with perseverance the race marked out for us.

HEBREWS 12:1 NIV

This verse brings a lot of encouragement, but it can also be quite challenging as well. We know all too well the weight of responsibility and the challenges of the world. We know how easily we are hindered by these pressures and more. And oh, how we understand being entangled in sin.

Take courage God is not unaware of our situation and limitations. He's not asking us to do this alone. In fact, he knows that we can't. It is Jesus who first marked out our path. He knows the way, and he will lead us. It is through Jesus that we will find the strength to throw off those thing that trip us up and it is only through Jesus that we will find forgiveness and freedom from the sin that entangles us. Look to Jesus, trust in Jesus, and run to him.

Jesus, thank you that where I am unable, you are completely able! Help me to trust you as I follow.

Are you running the race of life with purpose?

Jesus Never Changes!

Jesus Christ never changes! He is the same yesterday, today, and forever.

HEBREWS 13:8 CEV

In a world that is rapidly changing, it is so refreshing to know that Jesus is not. Our world is filled with change and uncertainty, but as Hebrews 13:8 says, Jesus Christ never changes! He is the same yesterday, today, and forever. As we read through the gospels, we are not just reading about who Jesus was, but we are also learning to understand who Jesus is.

In studying the gospels, we see how Jesus interacted with others. We see the compassion that he showed towards the needy and downcast. We see joy that he had in seeing people come to know him. We see the power that he had as he performed miracle after miracle. We see his heart of service as he served all those who were around him. Jesus is still all of these things to us today. He is unchanging.

As you go through your day today, thank Jesus for his unchanging presence in your life.

Jesus, thank you that you never change. You are perfect yesterday, today and forever.

Jesus Christ is the same yesterday, today, and forever.
HEBREWS 13:8 NLT

It seems odd to think about someone's inability to change as a benefit. We live in the world of "new and improved" products. Commercials are constantly telling us about the changes that have been made to make our favorite products even better. Somehow, purchasing version 2.0 seems like we are getting something better, more powerful, and cutting edge. Change is synonymous with better and improved.

The unchanging nature of Jesus points directly to his perfection. There has never been a need for Jesus to change, because he is perfect. His love is perfect. His joy is perfect. His power is perfect. His forgiveness is perfect. His plan is perfect. Are you catching on to the pattern?

We, on the other hand, are imperfect. The more we grow in our understanding of Jesus, the more our need to change becomes evident. Thankfully our unchanging Jesus is in the business of changing his followers to become more like himself. Are you willing to allow Jesus to change you?

Jesus, thank you that I can change. Help me to become more and more like you.

Is your resistance to change holding you back from becoming who Jesus wants you to be?

Hope Is Alive

Praise be to the God and Father of our Lord Jesus Christ. In God's great mercy he has caused us to be born again into a living hope, because Jesus Christ rose from the dead. Now we hope for the blessings God has for his children. These blessings, which cannot be destroyed or be spoiled or lose their beauty, are kept in heaven for you.

1 PETER 1:3-4 NCV

We put our hope in a lot of things: bank accounts, businesses, people, etc. Unfortunately, these things let us down, wear out, or die. And with that, our hope dies as well. This can leave us in a very hopeless situation. What once was so sure, is now gone. But when Jesus is our hope, our hope will never let us down, never wear out, and never die. As long as Jesus is alive, so is our hope. As his followers, he has given us new life and new hope. This hope was confirmed as Jesus rose from the dead.

As you face trials and difficulties today, know that you are not alone. When we invite Jesus into the difficulties and trials of our life, we are bringing hope to our situations.

Jesus, thank you that you are my living hope. Help me to put my trust in you alone.

Praise the God and Father of our Lord Jesus Christ. According to His great mercy, He has given us a new birth into a living hope through the resurrection of Jesus Christ from the dead and into an inheritance that is imperishable, uncorrupted, and unfading, kept in heaven for you.

1 PETER 1:3-4 HCSB

The hope that we have in Jesus brings us hope for today. Jesus is alive and working in our life, just has he has promised. But the hope that we have in Jesus is also hope for eternity. Much of Jesus' earthly ministry was him claiming that it was through him that we could be reconciled to God and be granted access to eternal life with him. These claims were verified as Christ rose from the dead.

As a follower of Jesus, we will one day stand face to face with our creator in heaven. We will finally experience the fullness of the relationship that we were created to have with him. We will spend all of eternity worshiping him and experiencing the glory of his presence. This is the living hope that we have in Jesus. Hope for today, and for all of eternity.

Lord God, thank you for the promise of heaven. Help my hope of eternity bring perspective for today.

How does the promise of eternity bring you hope for today?

This Is Love

This is how we know what love is: Jesus Christ laid down his life for us. And we ought to lay down our lives for our brothers and sisters.

1 JOHN 3:16 NIV

Why is love so difficult for many to find? Could it be because of how our human nature has corrupted the true definition of the word? When we think of love, we think about things that make us feel good or happy, and people who we like to spend time with. We love the things that fulfil us and the people who add value to our lives. Love has a tendency to become laser-focused on its relation to us.

The example we see in today's verse shows a different kind of love. John tells us that Jesus is our example of perfect love. This love is not based on himself or his needs or feelings, but instead based on the needs of those around him. Jesus' selfless love for us brought him to the cross where he laid down his life for our sins. He knew that there was no other way, so he willingly took our place, and he'd do it all over again. He loves you!

Jesus, thank you for the perfect example of selfless love that you have shown me. Help me to love you with that same selfless love.

By this we know love, because He laid down His life for us. And we also ought to lay down our lives for the brethren.

1 JOHN 3:16 NKJV

When we think of Jesus' sacrificial love for us, we automatically think of him giving his life on the cross. Rightfully so. However, when we look at the rest of his teaching, it is no surprise that he would lay down his life. Jesus was constantly putting others' needs before his own. He was not concerned with building a reputation with the rulers and leaders. He reached out and touched the untouchable. Jesus was far more concerned with the needs of those who he was with than his own.

We can follow this example. Few of us will actually come to a time where we are in a position to give our life for someone else, but that doesn't mean that we can't follow Jesus' example. Look to the needs of others more than to yourself. Jesus has set the standard for us to follow.

Jesus, thank you for your perfect, selfless love. Help me to love like you do.

Is your love defined by what's best for you, or is it focused on others?

Partners in Creation

Then God said, "Let us make mankind in our image, in our likeness, so that they may rule over the fish in the sea and the birds in the sky, over the livestock and all the wild animals, and over all the creatures that move along the ground."

GENESIS 1:26 NIV

The Bible frequently mentions this idea that all creation is included in the joy of participating in worship. The author of creation narrative feels it necessary to mention by name each creature and its function and environment. One key distinction, however, is God's unique relationship to humanity.

Out of all the creatures, mankind is the one that bears greatest resemblance to God. The character and personhood that exists in God exudes beauty and creativity and rule. How do you use that responsibility?

God, give me a vision for what it looks to be creative as I live into my function. Help me to understand what is unique about me and how I contribute to this world.

Then God said, "Let us make human beings in our image, to be like us. They will reign over the fish in the sea, the birds in the sky, the livestock, all the wild animals on the earth, and the small animals that scurry along the ground."

GENESIS 1:26 NLT

The idea of reigning isn't normal in vocabulary. Perhaps what is most fascinating is that God invites humanity to cherish the world that has been created, but also to care for it and be responsible for it just as God is responsible for us.

As you consider your function in this world, reflect on the idea that you are a co-creator and partner with God.

God, thank you for bringing about new life in me today.

How do you bring about new life and purpose and function in a world that is often filled with chaos and disorder?

Goodness in Creation

God looked over all he had made, and he saw that it was very good!
And evening passed and morning came, marking the sixth day.

GENESIS 1:31 NLT

There's something very fulfilling when completing a task.
When you can complete multiple tasks, and feel good about
what you have completed, it's even better. Even more, when
you can see the work that you have done and be filled with joy,
it's a whole new level. It is important to recognize that at the
very beginning God felt something about the created order—
it was very good!

At times, we can become distracted or confused by views
of God that God is angry or disgruntled or frustrated. But,
it is crucial to remember that God is a God of goodness.
Remember God's goodness in your life up to this point.

God, renew my view of you so that I can see your goodness. Help
me to take delight in your creation as I draw closer to you.

God saw all that He had made, and behold, it was very good. And there was evening and there was morning, the sixth day.

<small>GENESIS 1:31 NASB</small>

God took delight in creating, in finishing, and in resting while feeling complete joy. Do you know that God takes that same delight in us? It's one thing to know that God sees us. It another thing to recognize that God sees goodness in us that can be drawn out of us as we become more and more like Jesus.

If our understanding of God's goodness in creation can continue to grow, we will truly become the creation we were always meant to be.

God, thank you that you recognize good in me even when I don't see it myself.

What good did God see in you today?

No Shame

The man and his wife were both naked and were not ashamed.

GENESIS 2:25 NASB

There can be this idea that in the midst of God's presence, we recognize our worth and how very lacking it is in comparison to the worth of God. We feel guilt and shame and tend to hide. But, the original intent in creation is that nakedness—full exposure to God—was a matter of complete joy; not just in a physical anatomical sense, but our entire being.

Because of what Christ has done, we are forgiven from sin and receive freedom from shame so that we can begin to experience complete joy.

God, remind me of your original intention for my life to experience true joy and freedom from shame. No matter what I've done or who I think I am, you consider me your child. Thank you.

The man and his wife were both naked, and were not ashamed.

GENESIS 2:25 RSV

We can be in God's presence completely unashamed, knowing that God's grace through Jesus fills us with the power of the Holy Spirit who is forming us more into his likeness.

As you reflect on your day, did you allow yourself to feel the joy of God's presence without any amount of shame because of Jesus? What did that feel like?

God, thank you for removing shame in my life.

Where did you feel the most free to be yourself today?

Awareness of God

Then Jacob awoke from his sleep and said, "Surely the Lord is in this place; and I did not know it." And he was afraid, and said, "How awesome is this place! This is none other than the house of God, and this is the gate of heaven."

GENESIS 28:16-17 RSV

There is a strange story about a man named Jacob who basically steals a blessing that is rightfully his brother's. Jacob does this by tricking his father into thinking that Jacob is actually his brother. Things don't go well between Jacob and his brother, and at one point Jacob runs away.

In his escape as well as his quest to find a wife, he stops on his journey and encounters God in a dream. As he wakes up realizes the awesome (literally, full of awe) presence of God, he is keenly aware of it. Look for God today. Will you find him in unexpected places?

God, open up my eyes to be more aware of presence; especially in ways and in places I'm not even expecting.

When Jacob awoke from his sleep, he thought, "Surely the Lord is in this place, and I was not aware of it." He was afraid and said, "How awesome is this place! This is none other than the house of God; this is the gate of heaven."

GENESIS 28:16-17 NIV

Awareness of God can sometimes happen in the strangest of circumstances. We expect it to happen in a church or in some other sacred space, but when it happens when we're on the run or in the midst of our brokenness, it can have a profound effect on us.

We become awestruck by God's majesty as well as his compassion. We are rightly transformed in those moments. We can try to run from God or run from our greatest fears, but God is giving up on us.

God, thank you for revealing your presence to me today.

Where did you see God move today? How did that affect you?

Faithful in Suffering

Joseph's master took him and put him in prison, the place where the king's prisoners were confined. But while Joseph was there in the prison, the Lord was with him; he showed him kindness and granted him favor in the eyes of the prison warden.

GENESIS 39:20-21 NIV

It can be hard as Westerners to imagine faith in the face of imprisonment or suffering through persecution. But it doesn't mean we are immune to trials in our lives. We face all kinds of hardships—relational, emotional, and physical challenges. No matter the hardship, our faith can waver and confusion increases.

Allowing our soul to sing in the midst of such circumstances seems like the last thing we desire, and yet we recognize all throughout scripture—particularly with the story of Joseph— that it is less about our faithfulness and more about God's.

God, even though I am hurting, help me to see your kindness in this. I confess that it's hard to have faith, but I trust that you are still faithful.

He took Joseph and threw him into the prison where the king's prisoners were held, and there he remained. But the Lord was with Joseph in the prison and showed him his faithful love. And the Lord made Joseph a favorite with the prison warden.

GENESIS 39:20-21 NLT

What is crucial to see in this passage is that somehow recognition of God's kindness and presence was palpable. That kindness comes through another person that Joseph would least expect—the prison warden.

Are you going through something hard? Did something not go as planned today? Don't worry about getting it all together, but do look for God's kindness and faithfulness in the middle of it.

God, thank you for your faithfulness today even if I don't always feel it.

How has God consistently been faithful in your life?

God's Presence

"I will be with you. And this is your sign that I am the one who has sent you: When you have brought the people out of Egypt, you will worship God at this very mountain."

EXODUS 3:12 NLT

God sets a rhythm for people in the beginning stages of defining his people. As he sets parameters for what life should look like in terms of devotion to him and relationship with others, there is a clear sense of a call to worship.

In the case of the Israelites' exodus from Egypt, it seems natural for there to be recognition of God's grace and goodness as he acts through Moses to liberate the Hebrew people from slavery. That recognition comes in the form of worship. It's a response to God's character and action in the world—and certainly in their world. How will you consider God's character and action in your world today?

God, I stop in this moment to worship and praise you for your liberating action in my life as well as for who you are!

"Certainly I will be with you, and this shall be the sign to you that it is I who have sent you: when you have brought the people out of Egypt, you shall worship God at this mountain."

EXODUS 3:12 NASB

As you considered God's character and action in your life, did it compel you to stop and worship? What was that experience like?

Whether you sing, paint, dance, or simply sit quietly, it's important to develop a rhythm of worship because it is a way in which we connect to the very heart of God. We remember God's presence with us as he brings us out of brokenness and pain and into wholeness.

God, thank you for giving us a way that allows us to connect with you.

When you worship, how do you imagine God's presence?

God's Providence

When the layer of dew evaporated, behold, on the surface of the wilderness there was a fine flake-like thing, fine as the frost on the ground. When the sons of Israel saw it, they said to one another, "What is it?" For they did not know what it was. And Moses said to them, "It is the bread which the Lord has given you to eat.

EXODUS 16:14-15 NASB

Sometimes when God moves in our lives in mysterious ways or provides in ways that we weren't expecting, we can often respond with a surprised, "What?!" or "What was that?!" The story of the Israelites' exodus from Egypt is a grand adventure of ups and downs for the people of God and sets a tone for them throughout all of the Old Testament.

Then Jesus comes on the scene and changes the narrative by saying, "I am the bread of life; take and eat me." Many are left saying to themselves, "What?!" Many walk away, while only a few decide to stay and partake of the mystery of God's providence. Where do you need God to provide today?

God, thank you for providing me my daily bread. Help me to trust that you will always be watching out for my needs.

When the dew had gone up, there was on the face of the wilderness a fine, flake-like thing, fine as hoarfrost on the ground. When the people of Israel saw it, they said to one another,
"What is it?" For they did not know what it was. And Moses said to them, "It is the bread which the Lord has given you to eat.

EXODUS 16:14-15 RSV

When Jesus invites his disciples to partake of him later on in the New Testament, it is not meant to be a mystery as much as it is meant to be evidence of God's providence in our lives. He refers to himself as the bread or manna from Heaven—another sign that God is still providing, but in a whole new way.

Were you able to reflect on the mystery of Christ who is the better and more sustainable manna—or bread—that the Lord has given you to eat?

God, thank you for revealing a more sustainable bread of life in Christ; make me full.

What has God recently provided for you?

God Looks at the Heart

The Lord said to Samuel, "Do not look on his appearance or on the height of his stature, because I have rejected him; for the Lord sees not as man sees; man looks on the outward appearance, but the Lord looks on the heart."

1 SAMUEL 16:7 RSV

In Western culture, appearances are everything. We have televised singing competitions that are not just about singing but also the performers' style and overall look. If the singer is talented enough as a singer to advance in the competition, the producers of the shows will have stylists work with the performers as well. The viewers call in to cast their vote on their favorite singer judging both singing and style.

But, every once in a while, a story comes about where someone very plain-looking or lacking style auditions, and everyone is expecting it to fall flat. It's the opposite. The crowd and the judges are overwhelmed by the person's voice, and yet they can't believe their eyes. What they see doesn't match what they hear. God reminds Samuel that when he looks for a leader, it will defy the world's expectations. Samuel has to look for something he can't see. Only God can truly see the heart. As you prepare to take the day, you'll most likely groom your external appearance, but will you also consider "grooming" your heart?

God, help me to have a heart that is tuned to yours today.

The Lord said to Samuel, "Do not consider his appearance or his height, for I have rejected him. The Lord does not look at the things people look at. People look at the outward appearance, but the Lord looks at the heart."

1 SAMUEL 16:7 NIV

Perhaps people considered only your outward appearance today, and it bogged you down. But, all the while, God was transforming your inward self, maybe without you realizing it.

It's easy to consume yourself with ideas that you're too fat, too skinny, balding, have bad hair, wear ugly clothes, and on and on. But rest in the fact that those things simply do not matter to God. God is continuing to form your heart even as you sleep.

God, allow my heart to be conformed to yours.

How are you looking at other' hearts instead of their appearance?

Delight

Take delight in the Lord, and he will give you the desires of your heart.

PSALM 37:4 NIV

Delight isn't a word we typically use anymore. If it is used, it's often in the context of a dessert or a possession we may own, and maybe, on some rare occasions, it refers to a person—a loved one. In our world, it's easy to desire "things"—material goods and possessions. Our economy is based on consumption. The more we desire it or take delight in it, the more our economy grows and truly gives us what we want.

We might agree at some point, however, that the "things" never truly satisfy a deeper longing in our hearts. Something unique happens when we make a shift to delighting in the Eternal. It's not a "what"; it's a "who."

God, I desire you today. Help me to understand what true delight looks like.

Take delight in the Lord, and he will give you your heart's desires.
PSALM 37:4 NLT

The psalmist understands the profound truth that if you begin to enjoy God simply for who God is, it will actually adjust the desires that we hold deep within, which is actually just more of God. That's a good thing, because God never runs out; there is an eternal supply of God and access to God and all his riches and grace and love.

Reflect on what you truly desire today. Is it something that can run out? Is it a person that will eventually let you down? Or is it the eternal God who will always be there?

God, thank you giving me what I needed today within my heart.

What are some of your true desires that come from delight in God?

Unexpected

"My thoughts are nothing like your thoughts," says the Lord. "And my ways are far beyond anything you could imagine. For just as the heavens are higher than the earth, so my ways are higher than your ways and my thoughts higher than your thoughts."

ISAIAH 55:8-9 NLT

Have you ever stopped to wonder about the mind of God or the actions of God and just thought, "Huh?" If you're a parent, it's easy to say to a child after they've taken a marker to piece of furniture or drawn all over the wall and ask, "What were you thinking?" Do you ever find yourself saying that to God?

You're in good company because the people to whom Isaiah was writing were deeply confused about God's behavior while they were in exile. They wanted to know, "God, why is this happening to us? Have you forgotten about us?" Isaiah reminds them to think higher and outside of how they might normally think. Where do you need to think outside your limits today?

God, help me to trust you even when your ways don't make sense. Make my heart like that of a child.

"My thoughts are not your thoughts,
Nor are your ways My ways," declares the Lord.
"For as the heavens are higher than the earth,
So are My ways higher than your ways
And My thoughts than your thoughts."

ISAIAH 55:8-9 NASB

God is patient and allows us the freedom and grace to wrestle with these questions. Even when Jesus arrives in yet another unexpected way, the people are confused. And so, not surprisingly, he asks us to think like a child in order to understand the ways of God's Kingdom.

Logic and reason—the things adults use—are not necessarily needed. But utter trust and wonder are surely welcome.

God, thank you for thinking and acting in ways that are sometimes outside of my comprehension.

How were you able to put your trust in the unexpected ways of God today?

Joy of All Creation

*"You will go out with joy
And be led forth with peace;
The mountains and the hills will break forth into shouts of joy
before you,
And all the trees of the field will clap their hands."*

ISAIAH 55:12 NASB

Be led forth with peace. Hopefully you're reading this at the beginning of your day and you can imagine that God is leading you into every situation—at work, at school, in your home—with peace. Often times, before we begin our day, we imagine the chaos we might step into, and yet Isaiah provides a vision of joy and peace. But then, the statement turns a bit mystical.

The whole of creation gets involved in the ceremonies. Mountains and hills are "speaking and shouting" and trees are "clapping!" How might you take joy in what God is doing today?

God, thank you for the beauty of what I see in the world. Help me to have a heart of joy and peace.

"You shall go out in joy,
and be led forth in peace;
the mountains and the hills before you
shall break forth into singing,
and all the trees of the field shall clap their hands."

ISAIAH 55:12 RSV

We might wonder why this is important. Have you ever considered observing creation and getting frustrated with rocks, trees, mountains, or oceans? Or do they tend to have a calming effect—an ability to help us recognize we are surrounded by beauty.

Isaiah means to tell us that God involves even nature in the joy of what it means to be alive. Reflect on the creation that saw today with joy. Did it spur you on into peace?

God, thank you for your creation and being the source of my joy.

What comes to mind when you think of all creation praising God?

Fasting

"Is not this the fast that I choose:
to loose the bonds of wickedness,
to undo the thongs of the yoke,
to let the oppressed go free,
and to break every yoke?"

ISAIAH 58:6 RSV

When reflecting on the awe that God brings and the thought of our soul singing out, we don't often think of something like fasting. Fasting involves sacrifice and laying aside something that has perhaps become burdensome. It denotes a certain sobering activity. Even in Isaiah's view, fasting is not just an individual act of sacrifice, but a communal activism on behalf of the oppressed.

Have you ever considered how much more closely connected to the heart of God we might be if we were to live into a lifestyle of sacrifice for the sake of others? Might our souls begin to truly sing out when we have removed the clutter from our minds and hearts so that we begin to elevate our faith and trust in the God who calls us to a wholesome solidarity with those in unjust situations? Consider today what clutter you might remove today, this week, or this year.

God, reveal to me what true sacrifice could look like in my life.

"Is not this the kind of fasting I have chosen:
to loose the chains of injustice
and untie the cords of the yoke,
to set the oppressed free
and break every yoke?"

ISAIAH 58:6 NIV

One slight difference that we see in the NIV translation of this verse, versus the NLT translation, is the word chosen—instead of the word choose. It's as though God communicates that this is already decided.

Extinguishing injustice is simply what he has done, is doing, and will continue to do. You may have removed some clutter from your life today, but how might you participate in the mission of justice as a lifestyle? Reflect on what God might be calling you to.

God, give me a heart for those experiencing injustice so that I participate in your activity in the world.

Have you ever fasted? Would you consider it in the near future? What could you offer as a fast? How could fasting reveal what your heart clings to?

In Awe

Lord, I have heard of your fame; I stand in awe of your deeds, Lord. Repeat them in our day, in our time make them known; in wrath remember mercy.

HABAKKUK 3:2 NIV

We tend to be obsessed with fame—whether it's the fame of others or our own fifteen seconds of fame that we hope for. To think of the Lord as famous requires a different mindset. We must remove our projections of celebrity or illegitimate power and riches, fashion and beauty.

Even the people had hoped for something that they didn't end up getting. They wanted a warrior to unseat the oppressor; instead they ended with a peasant refugee who washed peoples' feet. These are the deeds that Habakkuk might not have imagined as he stands in awe of God, and yet he connects said deeds to the mercy of God. Stand in awe of God's mercy in Christ today.

God, thank you for your mercy. I stand in awe of you!

I have heard all about you, Lord. I am filled with awe by your amazing works. In this time of our deep need, help us again as you did in years gone by. And in your anger, remember your mercy.

HABAKKUK 3:2 NLT

The deeds of God are something Habakkuk longs for to see and experience. What deeds did you see God do in the world today? Is God famous for his mercy in your life? Is it something that causes you to stand or maybe lay prostrate in awe of who God is and what he has done in our world in years gone by?

Reflect on God's mercy that took place in your day today. Stand in awe and in silence before you rest.

God, thank you for showing your good deeds to me and to others today.

What about God causes you to stand in awe of him?

Rejoice in Singing

For the Lord your God is living among you. He is a mighty savior.
He will take delight in you with gladness. With his love, he will
calm all your fears. He will rejoice over you with joyful songs."

ZEPHANIAH 3:17 NLT

How do you picture the Lord? How do you imagine God in
your presence right now in this moment? Pause for a moment
and let your mind reflect. Often times, young people will
picture something of an authority figure—a cop, a world
leader, a parent; others might imagine a close friend or
companion. Zephaniah gives a unique image of a soloist with
a giant smile.

He doesn't seem to be singing for his own pleasure, but
that delight is directed in you as his child—his creation. It
is important to remember that in the book of Genesis, the
creation narrative paints a picture of God as pleased with his
creation, and now he is singing.

God, thank you for your song that you sing over me and for
calming all of my fears.

"The Lord your God is in your midst,
A victorious warrior.
He will exult over you with joy,
He will be quiet in His love,
He will rejoice over you with shouts of joy."

ZEPHANIAH 3:17 NASB

God is not an angry bearded man in the sky, holding thunderbolts and ready to pounce at any given moment. He is powerful, no doubt. But the form his power takes is counter to the world's image of power.

God is one who sings with gladness in his heart over you. Imagine that version of God as you rest tonight. What song might he be singing?

God, sing me to sleep and allow me to experience your love while I rest.

How do you picture God? Does your picture cause you to rejoice?

Christ's Work

The Spirit of the Lord is upon me,
because he has anointed me to preach good news to the poor.
He has sent me to proclaim release to the captives
and recovering of sight to the blind,
to set at liberty those who are oppressed,
to proclaim the acceptable year of the Lord.

LUKE 4:18-19 RSV

At the end of World War II, many of the Allied forces returned to their home countries. There are videos and images of people in the streets in places like the U.S., Great Britain, France, and Russia dancing and singing. They are overjoyed at what has just taken place. Victory for sure, but also liberation and an end to the violence—at least for a time.

If anything causes the entire globe to sing and dance, it would be good news of freedom and hope and liberation. That kind of good news transcends culture and time. Jesus is preaching the same message out of the book of Isaiah. This is his work. How will you participate in that work today?

God, I pray that your good news of freedom and hope in you would impact me in a whole new way today.

The Spirit of the Lord is on me,
because he has anointed me
to proclaim good news to the poor.
He has sent me to proclaim freedom for the prisoners
and recovery of sight for the blind,
to set the oppressed free,
to proclaim the year of the Lord's favor.

LUKE 4:18-19 NIV

The sermon that Jesus preaches out of Isaiah is a call to action. He is promising that God has come to do liberating work. The response of the people isn't exactly singing and dancing, however. They didn't expect to hear those words from Jesus necessarily.

If there was any action to be taken, it was to work to overthrow the Roman Empire, but Jesus had something else in mind that was much larger.

God, I pray on behalf of the poor, prisoners, blind and oppressed in the world today. Please move in power to bring them good news.

When Jesus brings good news to you, how do you respond?

No Condemnation

"God did not send his Son into the world to condemn the world, but to save the world through him."

JOHN 3:17 NIV

There are times where being part of a church service and singing in worship can feel lethargic and untimely. Perhaps we face something challenging or our view of God is skewed. Maybe we feel as though God is distant or even angry with us. Along the way an image of God was presented to us that actually perpetuated more fear and worry than hope and trust. We might even feel at times that God is just waiting for us to fail so that he can condemn us.

That's not all that far off from how the ancient world viewed gods and the supernatural realm. The gods were viewed as angry, and individuals or whole societies would have to work to somehow gain their approval. The God of the Israelites, however, was quite different. He was a God of mercy and justice. Jesus embodies God. If you are connected to Jesus, you are no longer living in fear and condemnation.

God, thank you for your mercy and for coming into world—not staying distant or apathetic.

"God sent his Son into the world not to judge the world, but to save the world through him."

JOHN 3:17 NLT

When Jesus shows up as the Son of God, the image of God comes to full expression in him. The kind of ministry Jesus does looks nothing like rules and regulations. He doesn't seem angry except at religious leaders.

Instead, he goes to the ones on the fringes and grants them new life and freedom. How did that change your perspective of God today? Let the image of God in Christ be an encouragement that you are no longer condemned; but you have been saved through him.

God, thank you for saving me from sin and brokenness and setting me free.

In what ways do you still live with condemnation? What would it be like to be free of that?

True Worship

"The time is coming—indeed it's here now—when true worshipers will worship the Father in spirit and in truth. The Father is looking for those who will worship him that way. For God is Spirit, so those who worship him must worship in spirit and in truth."

John 4:23–24 NLT

These passages come out of a story where Jesus and a Samaritan woman are discussing where the appropriate location is for worship—the temple mount in Jerusalem or a mountain in Samaria. Jesus gives her quite a different response than she is expecting. He's not concerned with a geographical location as much as a spiritual location—as in a condition of one's heart.

Often we relegate worship to an hour per week in a building where other believers are assembled. Yes! Regular corporate worship is absolutely good and healthy for the body of Christ, but true worship flows from a healthy condition of one's heart and the location matters not.

God, I worship you in this moment, right here and right now! I love you; thank you for who you are.

"An hour is coming, and now is, when the true worshipers will worship the Father in spirit and truth; for such people the Father seeks to be His worshipers, God is spirit, and those who worship Him must worship in spirit and truth."

JOHN 4:23-24 NASB

You may have found yourself stuck in traffic or alone in your bedroom and because the Spirit of God is within you, your activity in that moment could be an act of worship. Later on, in the New Testament, the apostle Paul speaks about your whole life being an act of worship.

Don't wait for the "right" moment to worship God. If your heart is mindful of the presence of God, simply respond in worship. It could be a verbal praise or a lyric of a song or simply a smile. As you rest, set your mind and your heart on God.

God, I am yours, and I surrender to your will for me. Make me a lifestyle worshipper.

When have you felt most connected to God's worship?

The Spirit's Work

"The Helper, the Holy Spirit, whom the Father will send in My name, He will teach you all things, and bring to your remembrance all that I said to you."

JOHN 14:26 NASB

As we consider what it means to be taught, we often connect that with knowledge for our brains. We might not necessarily associate teaching with our soul. More often than not, however, Jewish thinking sees the mind, heart, soul, and strength all wrapped together as one cohesive unit. They are not separate elements operating independently of one another.

When Jesus tells his disciples that he's sending the Holy Spirit to teach them all things, they are not just cognitive lessons, but also a teaching for the soul. The Spirit works to train our soul to be in devotion with God. Allow the Spirit to work within you today.

God, have your Holy Spirit move within me—my whole being—so that I learn the things of you.

"When the Father sends the Advocate as my representative—that is, the Holy Spirit—he will teach you everything and will remind you of everything I have told you."

JOHN 14:26 NLT

We have experiences deep within us that are often unexplainable—it is work that only the Spirit can do. The NLT names the Holy Spirit "the Advocate" which carries with it another meaning. We have one who represents God and advocates for our needs as the Spirit teaches us.

Having an advocate for you is a reminder that you're not alone and you aren't left to your own devices to figure everything out in isolation. You have help with the Holy Spirit.

God, thank you for sending your Holy Spirit to teach me new things about you.

What new teaching did you allow yourself to learn from the Holy Spirit today? As the Holy Spirit connects to your heart, mind, and strength, how have you let him begin to permeate your soul?

Remain in Jesus

"Yes, I am the vine; you are the branches. Those who remain in me, and I in them, will produce much fruit. For apart from me you can do nothing."

JOHN 15:5 NLT

The word remain sometimes feels like the words wait or stay. It can have a sort of passive feel to it. But in this passage, there is a bit more energy and motion as Jesus uses an agricultural illustration of a vineyard. Yes, a vineyard has some static elements to it, but over time, there is growth and movement that happens organically.

The vineyard goes through seasons and changes, but all the while the branches remain connected to the vine. Are you connected to Jesus? Do you find that you are helpless without that connection?

God, thank you for being the vine that holds me in place and for the freedom to move within my boundaries.

"I am the vine; you are the branches. If you remain in me and I in you, you will bear much fruit; apart from me you can do nothing."
JOHN 15:5 NIV

While Jesus often gives agricultural illustrations, another image that might help is an anchor. A boat can be anchored in a body of water, but it doesn't mean the boat can't move; it stays within a perimeter. Humanity is often moving, shifting, and growing. That will never change, but as we go through change, we are called by God to remain anchored or connected to Jesus.

Our soul's deepest need is to find rest and safety in the one who created our soul to begin with. The currents may work to pull us or break us, but if we remain, there is freedom and growth.

God, thank you for being my anchor that holds me close but allows movement and freedom.

How do you remain in Jesus?

Peace and Forgiveness

"Peace be with you! As the Father has sent me, I am sending you." And with that he breathed on them and said, "Receive the Holy Spirit. If you forgive anyone's sins, their sins are forgiven; if you do not forgive them, they are not forgiven."

JOHN 20:21-23 NIV

Sometimes, the thing that satisfies the soul the most is peace in the middle of fear. This passage comes in the context of the disciples fearing for their lives as they hide from Jewish leaders. They are under the threat of being associated with Jesus and if they are found, they may experience the same treatment as Jesus. And yet, in all of that, Jesus says, "Peace." But then he also gives them a task—one that seems counterintuitive—forgiveness. Forgive the people that just killed me, forgive the people that want to kill you. Picking up a sword won't change the world, but forgiveness will.

Sometimes, what holds us back from experiencing true peace in our souls might be unforgiveness. Is there a grudge you hold? It might be the thing stands in the way of experiencing the peace of Christ.

God, give me the strength and the courage to forgive so that I can experience true peace.

"Peace be with you. As the Father has sent me, so I am sending you." Then he breathed on them and said, "Receive the Holy Spirit. If you forgive anyone's sins, they are forgiven. If you do not forgive them, they are not forgiven."

JOHN 20:21-23 NLT

Jesus said peace twice. Why do you think that is? Did you find yourself needing peace after peace today? It almost seems in short supply as so many other things constantly distract us. The fears that easily creep in can cause us to wonder if Jesus really cares about our situation. But, he also breathes on them. He reminds them of his closeness.

Can you sense and feel the closeness of Jesus right now before you rest? Receive the Holy Spirit and know that the heart of God is to be close to you.

God, thank you for your breath in my lungs and your closeness so that I can receive peace and give peace.

Is there someone you need to forgive so that not only can they be free, but you can too?

Doubt and Belief

He said to Thomas, "Put your finger here, and look at my hands. Put your hand into the wound in my side. Don't be faithless any longer. Believe!"

JOHN 20:27 NLT

Thomas always gets the name "Doubting Thomas," but it's often associated negatively because of Jesus' rebuke to not be faithless anymore. But it should also be considered that Jesus does, in fact, allow Thomas to still touch the wounds of Jesus. Jesus doesn't completely write him off, he engages Thomas' doubt and invites him to believe.

Do you have doubts? Do you struggle with belief? Is there a way that you can experience a tangible encounter with Jesus through something sacred? Doubt is okay. It's not an enemy to faith, but it can enrich faith if it is engaged. Jesus is not afraid of your doubt, but don't walk away; Jesus might have something more for you today.

God, help me in my doubt. Thank you for not walking away from me in my doubt.

He said to Thomas, "Reach here with your finger, and see My hands; and reach here your hand and put it into My side; and do not be unbelieving, but believing."

JOHN 20:27 NASB

As you consider your day, were there moments of doubt? Were there moments where it felt like Christ engaged you in your doubt? Simply taking the time to read this devotional reveals that you still have interest in what God is doing in your life.

Earlier in the gospel narrative, a man says, "I believe, but help me in my unbelief." That's a worthy prayer to pray and it doesn't seem as though Jesus is bothered by it. Don't rest anxiously thinking your doubts are an annoyance to God. He will engage you over and over.

God, I believe, but help me in my unbelief.

What doubts do you still have? How can your doubts be related to your wonder of who God is and what God is doing?

Love in Action

*God demonstrates His own love toward us, in that while we were
yet sinners, Christ died for us.*

ROMANS 5:8 NASB

Actionable love is a whole new level of love as compared to
verbal love. Now, no doubt, there is power in words. When
you hear the words "I love you," they can have an effect on
you. But to see love in action is entirely different thing.
Even more, you know it's truly love when you were the least
deserving of it. Out of almost the entire Bible, it could seem
like this verse captures the heart of God and the heart of the
Gospel in the most simplistic and profound ways.

If you want your soul to come alive in a whole new way, reflect
on just this verse for an entire day, week, month, or even
year, and watch it change you. But, actually, for today, read
the verse at least three times, and then begin to pray the verse
into your day.

*God, thank you for demonstrating your love by dying for me when
I was still a sinner.*

God shows his love for us in that while we were yet sinners Christ died for us.

ROMANS 5:8 RSV

You probably made mistakes today. That's okay. We all did. It's important to remember that sin is bigger than just our mistakes. Individual sins, or missing the mark, are also symptoms of a greater and more systemic sin problem. It's an entanglement within which we are stuck and can't get out. It's the kind of sin that needed not just forgiveness from but victory over.

This verse shows not only the power of Christ's death on a cross, but also his heart to carry out the will of God for us. Reflect on that once more before you fall asleep.

God, thank you for the victory over the whole of sin and brokenness in the world.

When have you felt most loved because of someone's actions?

Fruit of the Spirit

The fruit of the Spirit is love, joy, peace, patience, kindness, goodness, faithfulness, gentleness, self-control; against such there is no law.

GALATIANS 5:22-23 RSV

There's something special about going to a restaurant, but then it's another experience to go to an all-you-can-eat buffet. You pay one fee to get access to everything. You might pay a little more depending on the restaurant or the buffet, but if the food options are really good, it's totally worth it. To have the Holy Spirit is like having access to an all-you-can-eat buffet. If you get the Holy Spirit, you get it all—all of the fruit.

Some may be experienced more than others throughout different seasons of your life, but when you tap into the presence of the Holy Spirit, no matter what, you become full like never before—fuller than any buffet could ever accomplish. What's more is that others with whom you interact also have access to the spread. When you are filled with love, joy, and peace, others get to experience and participate in that fruit as well. Today, be filled with the Holy Spirit and allow the fruit to be demonstrated in your life.

God, fill me to the full measure of your Spirit so that others can know you more as well.

*The fruit of the Spirit is love, joy, peace, forbearance, kindness,
goodness, faithfulness, gentleness and self-control. Against such
things there is no law.*

GALATIANS 5:22-23 NIV

Did you experience the buffet today? Most likely you needed
forbearance as well. We don't use that word often, but the
idea of bearing with one another doesn't necessarily have a
positive feel to it. It's more of a "have-to" kind of thing.

Sometimes we develop this image in our minds that living
out the Christian faith is supposed to be easy, neat and clean;
but the Spirit helps us to bear with one another as well. It's
almost as if God knew we would have relationships that are
just not easy.

*God, thank you for giving the forbearance to be in relationships
even when it's hard some days.*

Did you bear with someone today? How did it go?

Jesus Is Life

The life appeared; we have seen it and testify to it, and we proclaim to you the eternal life, which was with the Father and has appeared to us.

1 JOHN 1:2 NIV

John tries to convey that Jesus is the embodiment of true life. The Jewish person in the ancient world is often consumed and even mystified with the concept of eternal life or abundant life. It's a life not just experienced in the afterlife, but a life that begins today. With Jesus' presence, God—Immanuel—is fully revealed and present and because we have Jesus, we have life.

As you go throughout your day, reflect on the fact that Jesus gives life because Jesus is life. How might that direct your thoughts and feelings for the day? Can you bring life into others?

God, since life appeared in your son Jesus, will you also appear in me. Give me abundant life today.

This one who is life itself was revealed to us, and we have seen him. And now we testify and proclaim to you that he is the one who is eternal life. He was with the Father, and then he was revealed to us.

1 JOHN 1:2 NLT

Testify and proclaim seem like big tasks. We might get images of shouting on a street corner, or bursting into a room and yet we never really see Jesus doing this. He is often trying to get away from crowds and yet crowds are drawn to him. He waits to speak until they push to get him to say something. It's only then that he begins to testify and proclaim who God is.

Did you feel pressure to have to say something specific today and be a certain way? Or can you take comfort in the possibility that you lived humbly and showed compassion on others? If so, you were—in a sense—testifying and proclaiming the eternal nature of God as well. Eventually you might use words as well. Allow God to prepare you heart for those moments.

God, thank you for revealing yourself to me today.

How has your life in Christ been a proclamation before?

God Is Light

This is the message we heard from Jesus and now declare to you: God is light, and there is no darkness in him at all.

1 JOHN 1:5 NLT

Have you ever tried walking across a room in total darkness? Did you stub your toe or bump into anything? It's a painful realization especially when you think, "I probably could've just turned on the light." The people of God find themselves in the dark, in a sense, as they try to keep following a resurrected Christ is no longer among them in the physical sense. They have to rely on the Holy Spirit. But God is still light, and Jesus made that light known. Before that point, it did seem like stumbling around because God hadn't been revealed to them in that way yet.

What areas of your life seem to have darkness? Would you allow God to show up and bring light there?

God, shine your light in the dark areas of my life today so that I can see and live.

This is the message we have heard from Him and announce to you, that God is Light, and in Him there is no darkness at all.

1 JOHN 1:5 NASB

Light has the ability to expose things that were hidden in darkness. You could be searching around for your keys in the darkness and all the while they might be right in front of you, but because there's no light, it takes that much longer. Sometimes we struggle in life but don't really know why. Maybe the issue is right in front of us, but we aren't exposing to the light of God in Christ and so it remains hidden.

If you found yourself struggling or walking in darkness today, would you take this moment to confess to God that you need his light to shine within you. Ask God to reveal some of those more hidden things that you're not even aware of.

God, help me to see what's right in front of me so I can be filled with your light.

What things in your life are still in the dark, hidden from the light?

True Living

The one who says he abides in Him ought himself to walk in the same manner as He walked.

1 JOHN 2:6 NASB

Abiding in Christ is not simply a safety net that we fall back on when we are down or lonely or tired. It also means we take an active part in the world just as Jesus did. We copy his mannerisms, his behaviors, and his ministry. John is writing to a group of people to do likewise. He says, in a sense, if you want to truly live, live like Jesus. Do what he did and say what he said.

As you go throughout your day, reflect on the life and ministry of Jesus. What did he do and say, and how might you copy those same things?

God, help me to live like Jesus today and take an active role in the world.

He who says he abides in him ought to walk in the same way in which he walked.

1 John 2:6 RSV

Jesus walked everywhere. Unless you go to Israel, you can't get a real idea of what that might have been like to travel for days from the Galilee area to Jerusalem. It took days to walk! It's quite challenging to consider what that might be like for us in a modern world. In the ancient Jewish world, young boys would follow their rabbis everywhere as well and copy everything their rabbi did.

When it comes to the call to walk as Jesus did, don't feel like you have to walk for days. But consider following in the footsteps like his disciples—the behaviors, the attitudes, the activity.

God, teach me to walk as Jesus walked in my heart, mind, soul, and strength.

Were you able to be like Jesus in some ways today?
How did it go?

Fatherly Love

See what love the Father has given us, that we should be called children of God; and so we are.

1 JOHN 3:1 RSV

Being called someone's child is a privilege. Maybe you had a good father or maybe you did not. Either way, it can be easy to project the image of our fathers onto the image of God. We may even start to compare the two or think that one is the exact replica of the other. So, if we had a terrible dad or absent father, we might assume God is that way, but he is better. Or if we had a good dad, he is even better than that.

Regardless, God calls us his children. John reiterates this point by saying, "and so we are." It's almost as if he is adding an exclamation, "So there, then!" In other words, live into the reality that you have a father who loves you deeply with a love that no earthly father's love comes close to. You are his child, so go into the day with that in mind.

God, thank you for your fatherly love and making me your child.

See what great love the Father has lavished on us, that we should be called children of God! And that is what we are!

1 JOHN 3:1 NIV

Lavish isn't a word we often use, but it gives us a picture of something being poured out and drenching—even soaking—the thing below it. It's not a simple trickle or even light rain, it is an outright saturation. This is the picture John gives us of the father's love in our lives.

As you think back on the day, did you experience this kind of love? Were you saturated in it even in the midst of challenges or hardships? To know that you have a loving father to come home to no matter how old you are can make all the difference. Rest knowing that your loving heavenly father has a place for you to rest and be safe.

God, keep lavishing your love on me to the point where I'm suffocated by it. I don't want to experience anything other than that.

At what points throughout the day did you feel the most like a child of God?

Holiness of Jesus

Each of the four living creatures had six wings and was covered with eyes all around, even under its wings. Day and night they never stop saying: "'Holy, holy, holy is the Lord God Almighty,' who was, and is, and is to come." Whenever the living creatures give glory, honor and thanks to him who sits on the throne and who lives for ever and ever.

REVELATION 4:8-9 NIV

Reading apocalyptic literature can certainly help us to imagine a world outside of our own and what's right in front of us. John paints an interesting and rather bizarre picture for us of creatures who sing over and over, "Holy, holy, holy!" It's not like they are robots who are forced into this hymn; they simply can't but shout this over and over because God is unlike anything or anyone else in the entire universe. We get an image of a God who is over and in and through the entire cosmos, and his glory fills it to overflowing.

As you reflect on the God you serve, love believe in today, does the glory and power of God overwhelm you? Sing and shout, "He is holy!"

God, thank you for your holiness and that there is none like you!

Each of these living beings had six wings, and their wings were covered all over with eyes, inside and out. Day after day and night after night they keep on saying, "Holy, holy, holy is the Lord God, the Almighty—the one who always was, who is, and who is still to come." Whenever the living beings give glory and honor and thanks to the one sitting on the throne (the one who lives forever and ever).

Revelation 4:8-9 NLT

God is the beginning and end to all things. His presence transcends time and space. John conveys that by saying, "the one who always was, who is, and who is still to come." There is no end to his eternal love and grace and gives the audience of this letter hope in the midst of their suffering and persecution. It shows us that no matter what we face there's another realm that God is about to usher in to this world.

Heaven will come crashing into the earth, and it'll be unlike anything any of us have ever seen, because Jesus is still coming back. Did that give you hope for the day? Does it put some of the challenges you may have faced into perspective?

God, I trust you will come back. Until you do, give me hope to face each day.

What about Jesus causes you to see him as holy and set apart?

Jesus Is the Lamb

One of the twenty-four elders said to me, "Stop weeping! Look, the Lion of the tribe of Judah, the heir to David's throne, has won the victory. He is worthy to open the scroll and its seven seals." Then I saw a Lamb that looked as if it had been slaughtered.

REVELATION 5:5-6 NLT

Early on in the book of Revelation, John gives us the image of the Lion of Judah. It signifies how he viewed David and his kingdom. David was a powerful warrior and overcame the enemy with military might. He was an absolute hero to the people of God. But then John says he sees a lamb. Immediately we see two very different animals that are images of Christ. What's even more is that the words "Lion of Judah" don't show up in the rest of the book of Revelation, but lamb does.

It's as if to say that we all thought he would be a lion like King David, but it turns out the king is more like a lamb who is slain. He is more meek and mild, but in that humility is power—power unlike the world's power. As you go throughout your day, show others the power of Christ, not through force and might, but through humility.

God, thank you for the image of a lamb who is humble and gentle.

One of the elders said to me, "Stop weeping; behold, the Lion that is from the tribe of Judah, the Root of David, has overcome so as to open the [a]book and its seven seals." And I saw between the throne (with the four living creatures) and the elders a Lamb standing, as if slain.

REVELATION 5:5-6 NIV

One of the most confusing books in the Bible is Revelation. We are often not sure what to do with it. Should it be used as means of predicting the end of the world; is it John writing prophetically against the Roman Empire; or is it something completely different? One thing we can agree on, however, is that it consistently shows Jesus at the center of all things and that should give us hope.

Whether the people of God faced a giant oppressor in the Romans, or we face trials and tribulations today, we can find Jesus on the throne. As you considered your day today, were you able to see Jesus at the center?

God, thank you for putting Jesus at the center of all things in my life.

Did the humility and gentleness of Jesus guide your behavior and attitude today?

God's Home

*I heard a loud voice from the throne, saying, "Behold, the
tabernacle of God is among men, and He will dwell among them,
and they shall be His people, and God Himself will be among
them."*

REVELATION 21:3 NASB

The word among shows up three times in just this one verse.
John can't express enough how important it is for the people to
know that God's home will now be among them—in their midst.

God's home will no longer be this mystical or separate entity,
but actually the very ground they walk on—the ground we walk
on. We will eventually be in a place where we are no longer
wondering, "Where is God?" because he will be right here
among us in the most tangible way.

*God, keep revealing your home among us. May your kingdom come
on earth as it is in heaven.*

I heard a loud voice from the throne saying, "Behold, the dwelling of God is with men. He will dwell with them, and they shall be his people, and God himself will be with them."

REVELATION 21:3 RSV

How did your day go today knowing that God's dwelling place is here on earth and will be even more when Christ returns? Did it change how you interact with the earth and with others?

Imagine what it might be like to have a perfect leader, father-figure, presence in our midst at all times. Everything is free and everywhere is love. This is the image John presents us with—a God who makes his home a place where everything is taken care of. Dwell on that as you sleep tonight.

God, thank you for making your home in my heart. Transform me to be prepared for an even fuller expression of your home among us.

What things remind you of home?

No Sorrow

He will wipe away every tear from their eyes, and death shall be no more, neither shall there be mourning nor crying nor pain any more, for the former things have passed away.

REVELATION 21:4 RSV

The idea of no more pain and sorrow can seem like unfathomable concepts. How do we even begin to think in such a way? Considering the pain and turmoil and persecution the people of God faced all throughout scripture it almost seems like an impossibility and yet John is insistent in his determination to create an image of a day where sorrow no longer exists. It's not even a thing in God's space in eternity.

When heaven meets earth, this will be our new reality. But until then, we begin to embody this mindset. How do we bring this joy into our world?

God, help me to envision the future and bring it in to the every-day.

He will wipe every tear from their eyes. There will be no more death' or mourning or crying or pain, for the old order of things has passed away.

REVELATION 21:4 NIV

Some days are just filled with hardship. Maybe you got in a fight or you really did lose a loved one recently. It's evidence that death still has a grip on our lives; and yet, we know that life wins out. Death is not the end of our story. It's what we put our hope and trust in because of Jesus' death and resurrection.

The resurrection is the reason we cling to hope. Can you envision God wiping away your tears? Sorrow and death is old news. It has passed away and new life is beginning. This is the way of God. Take joy in this new reality as you rest tonight.

God, thank you for making a new path so that death and pain no longer win.

In what areas of your life have you felt the most joy after sorrow?

Newness

*He who was seated on the throne said, "I am making everything
new!" Then he said, "Write this down, for these words are
trustworthy and true."*

REVELATION 21:5 NIV

How do you feel when get something brand new? Depending
on what it is, it can really fill us with happiness, but eventually
that new thing wares out over time, as does the happiness. The
work of Christ is not concerned with happiness as much as it
is joy—a joy that is sustained by newness.

Some of the final words of Jesus are not really final at all, but
instead a new beginning. He is making all things new. It's a
present and future tense. Newness just continues to happen
over and over in the new world that God is creating in Christ.
But, that newness can start today as well. How is Christ
making you new today?

*God, thank you for doing new things in the world. I look forward
to the day when everything is made new.*

The one sitting on the throne said, "Look, I am making everything new!" And then he said to me, "Write this down, for what I tell you is trustworthy and true."

REVELATION 21:5 NLT

If you were to go to the beginning of the Biblical narrative in Genesis, you might see that the whole of creation is subjected to a curse and ultimately to death and decay. The apostle Paul describes similarly in the letter to the Romans in chapter 8. But, both he and John have an image of a release from that death and decay, and newness that enters into all of creation.

Relationships, governments, business, culture, art, the earth—it's all restored to full health and purpose. Dwell on this idea as you rest tonight, knowing that God's purpose is to restore all things and make them new.

God, thank you for restoration and renewal. You make all creation new.

What new things has God done in your life?

Always on Duty

"Do not be afraid of the terrors of the night,
nor the arrow that flies in the day"

PSALM 91:5 NLT

God is a protector—night and day he is always "on duty."
When the lights go out and we seek the peace of rest, God
is not at rest. During the day when the arrows fly, the
expectations of our employer press on us. The demands
of family require us to drive across town and back, then
someone pulls out in front of us when we are already running
behind, and we fear the loss of control that comes in this
moment, know that he is there with you.

God is ever-present, knowing and seeing all things. He
desires that we would live in this reality, showing that we
trust him fully and show others what it means to live in that
trust.

God, I'm thankful that you are with me at all times, and I'm
especially grateful that you are more than present. You are
watchful of me, and watchful over me. Amen

You will not fear the terror of the night,
nor the arrow that flies by day,

PSALM 91:5 ESV

God was with you all day. He saw everything that happened to you. He saw everything that you did. He heard all that you said. When you were sad, he grieved with you. When you were angry at an injustice, he was too. He was there.

Rest easy as you reflect on the reality of that. You'll be tempted to languish on mistakes- harsh words, curt responses, or too quick actions. Make right what you can, and then trust in the God who sees all things. Don't be devoured by things prowling for you; instead, trust in his goodness.

Father, thank you for this day. Help me to not be fearful of might have been said or done differently, but to rest in your presence. Amen

What does trusting God around the clock look like for me today?

Proclaim

It is good to give thanks to the Lord,
to sing praises to your name, O Most High;
to declare your steadfast love in the morning,
and your faithfulness by night.

PSALM 92:1-2 NRSV

Begin today with thanksgiving by making a list of five things that you are thankful to God for. Don't think about your day—the tasks ahead, the appointment you've scheduled, or the places you'll go. And when you do transition to those things, thank God for them too. There is nothing that's ahead of you that our God doesn't know about.

Throughout the rest of your day, be on the lookout for ways to thank him—for the people you meet and the conversations that happen, for the moments you were on time, and for the times you weren't.

God, grant in me today a spirit of thanksgiving, joyfully dining your praises and remembering that all things are gifts from you.

It is good to give thanks to the Lord,
to sing praise of the most high.
It is good to proclaim your unfailing love in the morning,
your faithfulness in the evening.

PSALM 92:1-2 NLT

Our God is faithful. He was with you throughout the day. He heard your thanksgiving, even when you weren't intentionally praying. He was paying attention to the way you demonstrated grace to others. He saw the way you expressed trust, even when that one thing didn't go your way.

Each day and night, we have opportunity to talk about him, to sing to him, to pray to him, and to point others to him and the hope he offers. In all of our circumstances, he worthy of our praise and thanksgiving. Proclaim it!

You were with me all day, and my heart with filled with
thanksgivings and praise for you because of it. I am thankful for
you, for calling me to constant praise and remembrance of you.
Praise you!

How can I live in this mindset of praise and thanksgiving each day?

Share

Sing to the Lord; praise his name.
Each day proclaim the good news that he saves.
Publish his glorious deeds among the nations.
Tell everyone about the amazing things he does.

PSALM 96:2–3 NLT

Each day we are given an opportunity: we can speak of the good news that he has saved us, or we can be silent. We can point out his deeds to all that we meet, or we can take the credit. We can be amazed and in that amazement, we can demonstrate him, or we can remain unimpressed.

Often, we look for his guidance in big choices and large decisions because that's when we think it matters most. But praise also comes in "small packages," in tiny moments and brief conversations. Choose to look for those today!

God, please help me to be on the lookout today for the opportunity to share your works in the smallest of ways—a "please" or "thank you," a wave to allow someone to turn in front of me, or even a "Praise God!" when it counts.

Sing to the Lord, bless his name;
proclaim good tidings of his salvation from day to day.
Tell of his glory among the nations,
his wonderful deeds among all the peoples.

PSALM 96:2-3 NASB

There is still time to proclaim those "good tidings." That's the "great news" of the phrase "from day to day." It's never too early, or too late to pass this news along. People that you know are able to hear about it, even if they are on the other side of the world, maybe from you, and maybe, just maybe, from someone else.

If there is someone that you ought to reach out to as the day winds down, take a moment and do that now. Even a brief text of encouragement will make a huge difference in the life of someone who needs it.

God, right now, there are people who I know that need to be aware of your good news, your glory and deeds. I pray for them that they'd meet someone soon, even tonight, who will pass on your news to them.

How can I be the answer to someone's prayer in this same way?

Help Me

I look up to the mountains—
Does my help come from there?
My help comes from the Lord,
who made heaven and earth.

PSALM 121:1-2 NLT

It's an old movie cliché: there's a group of people surrounded by an enemy, or maybe a small town in need of supplies— food or medicine. With the passing of each day, the situation becomes more and more dire, the need to be rescued greater. The people look upward and outward. They know their rescuer can only come over the pass through the mountain range.

The good news is that our rescuer knows the way. Not because he found an old map or because he is being led by a faithful guide. Our help knows the way because he made the way. And he made the mountains. Our help is the Lord.

God, I'm looking for you to rescue me, and I'm wondering when you will arrive! Cause me to remember that you are on the way. And because you are the way, and even made the way, your arrival is right on time.

I lift up my eyes to the mountains;
Whence will my help come?
My help is from Yahweh,
maker of heaven and earth.

PSALM 121:1-2 LEB

Help has arrived. Yahweh sent Jesus. Elsewhere in Scripture, we learn that all things were made through Jesus. We can look and look for him, but he has come. He already helped. He gave not only of himself to be that help; he gave himself as the help. He is both here through the Spirit and returning as the Son.

We can access this help right now by reaching out to the Holy Spirit within us, and seeking guidance. We can ask him for strength. We can ask him for peace and comfort. We can ask him for the right words and proper actions. This is the same Spirit who made all things and his desire is for you to be rescued. Reach out to him now!

Father, thank you for helping me. Thank you for rescuing me. Thank you for the Spirit, the proof of this help. I trust and hope in you.

What kind of help are you looking for? And, from where?

Listen

Just as the Holy Spirit says,
"Today if you hear his voice,
do not harden your hearts as
[your fathers did] in the rebellion
[of Israel at Meribah],
on the day of testing in the wilderness."

HEBREWS 3:7-8 AMP

Be still. Listen. Close your eyes and breathe, in through your nose and out through your mouth. Listen. Ask God to speak to you. Just listen. Do this same exercise throughout the day. On break. Between classes. As you wait for your children to end practice.

Listen also as you interact with people. Adopt a posture of listening. He may speak through your family, your spouse, or children. He may speak through a co-worker. He may speak through a song or television program. And, if he does, do not harden your heart to him. Listen.

Father, I'm here. I'm listening. I want a soft heart that will receive your words like soil receives seeds. I want to hear you.

That is why the Holy Spirit says,
"Today when you hear his voice,
don't harden your hearts
as Israel did when they rebelled,
when they tested me in the wilderness."

HEBREWS 3:7-8 NLT

"Today when you hear…" What did he say? How did you respond? How was your heart? God speaks, we hear and then we must decide. Our rebellion against him tests him—his mercy, his grace, his patience.

Thanks fully, these things that he offers to us are a part of his nature, and as such, they are limitless, they drive us towards repentance. And when we repent, he forgives and he speaks again, every word attacking our hearts so that we might hear him ever clearer.

Lord, that you for speaking to me constantly, for loving me enough to talk with me and to me about your love and desire for me to be open to you. I'm here, listening.

What did God say to you today and who did he say it through?

Provider

The Lord is my shepherd:
I have all that I need.

PSALM 23:1 NLT

What would it be like to have "all that you need"? Would the food be unlimited? When you removed something from the refrigerator, would it immediately be replaced? How about your clothes? Would you have closets and closets full? What might your bank account look like? Billions? Trillions?

Or, would there be just enough for that moment? Would you have food only for the next meal? Would there be one pair of socks left for today? Money for just one more cup of coffee? Just what, exactly, do you need?

Father, you are my shepherd and you provide all that I need,
because you know just what I do need. Help me to see that today.

The Lord is my Shepherd [to feed,
to guide and to shield me],
I shall not want.

PSALM 23:1 AMP

What did you need today? Probably food, clothing,
transportation, perhaps the company of others. Oxygen,
probably.

Was it enough? Is your stomach full? Praise the Shepherd.
We're you warm (or cool) enough, praise the Shepherd. Did
you enjoy meaningful conversation, did you get where you
needed to go and back? This is all the work of your Shepherd
who provided what was needed, when it was needed.

Lord, thank you for being my provider. You did and do more than
just give, you give according to what I need because you are what
I need. You are my shepherd, and I lack nothing.

How can you become more aware of your own needs, then see
how God meets them?

Worthy

He lets me lie down in fields of green grass.
He leads me beside quiet waters.
He gives me new strength.
He guides me in the right paths
for the honor of his name.

PSALM 23:2-3 NIRV

God's actions show that he is worthy, that his name is to be honored. By treating us kindly, not only is he worthy, but when we talk about the way he cares for us, his flock, it increases the value of his name. His integrity increases and he becomes known as the God who loves according to our needs.

When we follow him in his leading, we show that we trust him and that he is trustworthy. Then, because his reputation is "on the line," every next move he makes shows that he is indeed worthy.

Lord, your name is worthy to be lifted up and worshiped because you consistently show that you are looking out for us, you show who you are through your actions of love and by being true to your Word and nature. Today, help me to honor your name.

He lets me rest in green meadows;
He leads me besides peaceful streams.
He renews my strength.
He guides me along right paths,
bringing honor to his name.

PSALM 23:2-3 NLT

We show honor to those who deserve it. Sometimes, that honor is based on a rank or a role. God receives honor because of his love—the way he treats those who specifically are unworthy of the honor bestowed on them.

We don't deserve green meadows or peaceful streams or renewed strength or guidance along right paths. But, we are his and he is bound to care for us as an example of who he is. And he is love.

God, I am yours to love and to care for. I am thankful that your good name matters, which is why you care for it and protect it as you do me.

How does your obedience bring honor to God's name?

Comforter

Even if I walk through a very dark valley,
I will not be afraid,
because you are with me.
Your rod and your shepherd's staff comfort me.

PSALM 23:4 NCV

It's our desire to find comfort. We call it "comfort food"
for a reason. It's not a blanket; it's a "comforter." It's not
"shopping"; it's "retail therapy." A life of peace, ease, and rest
is the good life. When life gets difficult, it is to these (and a
great many other) things that we run to because they offer a
temporary respite.

God calls us to something more than temporary rest and
immediate comfort. God calls us to trust in him. He has a big
stick, and it is there to fight off and drive away the things that
threaten us. Enter the valley, and do not fear. He is with you.

Lord, I praise you because you are with me. You're not empty-
handed; your rod and staff convince me that you are ready to
defend me. Help me to talk in that today.

Even when I walk through the darkest valley,
I will not be afraid, for you are close to me.
Your rod and your staff protect and comfort me.

PSALM 23:4 NLT

God's rod and staff is both a defender against and a guide for us. He uses this tool to direct us where we need to go; he taps ups, pokes us, and prods us through the valley to safety. The tool itself indicates closeness because it is merely an extension of his arm.

There is protection in the tool because when we feel it, we know that he is near.

God, teach me to accept your guidance as coming from a loving father. Sometimes, I just need your words, other times, it's the rod and staff that motivates me. Either way, I need you.

How has God's protection offer you felt like punishment?

Cook

You prepare a feast for me
in the presence of my enemies.

PSALM 23:5 NLT

When you prepare something, you gather the ingredients, weighing and measuring carefully. A feast is not a fast food, drive-through meal on the go. There is lots of food, and there a several courses; if anyone leaves the meal hungry, it won't be due to a lack of food.

When you prepare something for someone specifically (me, as the psalmist indicates), you've made what you know they need and enjoy. And if it's all done in the presence of enemies, it is eaten not in some far away, hidden place or even in full view of our enemies. It is eaten in their midst, in their very presence.

Good Shepherd, you have shown your intentionality in preparing for me a meal of epic proportions today. Help me to be hungry for everything that you offer me, that I may be in anticipation of good things.

You prepare a feast for me
right in front of my enemies.

PSALM 23:5 NIRV

I began my day in prayer that prepared me for the meal ahead. With the passing of every hour, I spent more and more time with you. I ate and ate. When my enemies approached, I remained at your table because the meal with you was so good.

At day's end, I push away from the table, not because the food is gone, but because I've had my fill. And your left-overs are the best.

Lord, the food you made for me was the best, a real feast. Your provision just kept coming, each course more glorious than the last, and each bite more filling because I was with you. Thank you for filling me up.

How can you get ready for tomorrow's meal?

The One Who Blesses

You honor me by anointing my head with oil.
My cup overflows with blessings.

PSALM 23:5 NLT

No one likes to be chosen last. As a child, many of us were
chosen last on the playground at least once. As an adult,
perhaps you've received a "mercy invite" to a party or event.
God never sends these kinds of invitations; he is personal
and purposeful. And most of all, he honors us by caring for us
personally. The pouring on of oil is personal because, while
he anoints all of his sheep, he knows just how much we as
individuals require because we are different.

Begin your day today feeling honored by him.

Lord, you honor me today by caring for me personally. You've made
me yours and shown this by covering me with your blessing and
honor.

You honor me as your guest,
and you fill my cup until it overflows.

PSALM 23:5 CEV

Have you ever been the guest of honor? Maybe you received an award, or it was at your wedding. When you arrive, you're announced, and all of those gathered will rise to their feet, perhaps they will clap and cheer, raising their glasses to you in honor.

God is worthy to be praised and he calls us into his presence. We feel honored to be there with him. And then, in some counterintuitive way, he fills our cup, he makes us feel special, he shows us honor. He does this because he loves us and cares deeply for us. What a joy to be his!

Father, you've invited me to your party and then you've made me feel special for coming. You have blessed me beyond measure, and I praise you for it.

Why might God give us undeserved blessings and honor?

Pursuer

Surely your goodness and unfailing love
will pursue me all the days of my life.

PSALM 23:6 NLT

"You're it!" And off you run. Sometimes you're chasing someone else, and when you tag them, you shout, "You're it!" Now everyone else knows who to run away from. Other times, it's you who is being pursued; you run around trees, hide in bushes, even running near other people in the hopes that your pursuer will give up chasing you.

God never gives up. His goodness and unfailing love is always "after" you because he is always "after" you. You can run. You can attempt to dodge him. But why? Today, allow him to catch you. Be captured by him. Rest in his goodness and love.

God, catch me!

Surely goodness and love will follow me
all the days of my life.

PSALM 23:6 NIV

Your goodness and love has followed me everywhere today. I saw it when someone opened a door for me. I saw it when someone waved at me to let me go first at a stop sign. I heard it in the kind words of a coworker. I saw it when the sun shone through the clouds, even for a brief moment. I tasted it in my afternoon cup of coffee.

No matter where I went, you were there following me. I saw that, and I saw you. I see you even now at the end of my day through my memory. And I'll sleep well knowing that you are still chasing me down.

Father, thank you for always being around me. I can't go anywhere without seeing your goodness and love. I praise you for this.

How can I pursue others with the goodness and love of God?

Homeowner

I will dwell in the house of the Lord
Forever.

PSALM 23:6 NIV

If you've ever lived with someone else, you'll agree with Benjamin Franklin's comment about guests, like fish, they begin to stink after three days. This is because "who we are" (and "who they are") comes out eventually. Idiosyncrasies show and the "real us" comes out, and life begins to be uncomfortable. Friendships and marriages are put to the test.

God is telling us that there will come a time when we will live with him forever. Not just for a few days or weeks, but forever. Throughout Psalm 23, God is revealing himself as one who cares for his people. This care is not just revealed through providing rest, meals or guidance; it culminates by us living with him forever.

Father, thank you for allowing me to live in your house. For loving and accepting me in spite of who I am and for showing me that there is a better home with you.

I will live forever
in your house, Lord.

PSALM 23:6 CEV

Whether you live in an apartment, condo, house or you're rocking the "van life," people want to live in a place that they can call their own. God's kingdom is different in that while we are an integral part of it, it still belongs to him. As adopted sons and daughters, we live in his home. And along with that living space, we also live according to his rules, we must submit to him and his ways.

We find comfort, peace and rest in his home. And it's perfectly set up by him to accommodate us perfectly, and forever.

God, you've invited me to be in your kingdom and I get to live there forever. Thank you for preparing a place for me that I may thrive in. Amen

What might it look like for you to "live" in God's house?

Set Free

There is no condemnation
for those who belong to Christ.
And because you belong to him, the power
of the life-giving Spirit has freed you
from the power of sin that leads to death.

ROMANS 8:1-2 NLT

This is some of the best news that we could ever read. Because we belong to Jesus, we will not face judgment by him. But this news is more than an "escape plan" for the future; this means life for us today! We no longer "must" sin because the same Spirit that brought Jesus back to life frees us from our own sinful ways.

Today, be set free. Live in ways that shows new life. Speak to others in the same way that Jesus has spoken to you. Allow your words to bring freedom and life.

God, these verses relieve so much pressure on me. You love me and care for me and you have set me free. Let me seek our ways to live in that same freedom today. Amen

Those who belong to Christ Jesus
are no longer under God's sentence.
I am now controlled by the law of the Holy Spirit.
That law gives me life because of what Christ Jesus has done.
It has set me free from the law of sin that brings death.

ROMANS 8:1-2 NIRV

Today was about living in the freedom that Christ brings,
living outside the law that brought death. Today was about
living life guided by the Spirit; you were free to speak life into
people. You were free to be graceful and loving and merciful
to everyone you came into contact with. You were free to
repay evil with good.

Tomorrow, and every day for the rest of your life, you can walk
and live in that same freedom because you are free. Rest well,
and be ready for another day of freedom.

*Father, thank you for the freedom that you have given me, for the
delivery from punishment for my sin, and for the freedom to share
the word about this freedom to others. I am free because of who
you are and what Jesus has done.*

How can you be ready to tell others about the freedom that
Christ offers to them?

For Our Own Good

We know the God causes everything
to work together for the good of those
who love God and are a called according
to his purpose for them. •

ROMANS 8:28 NLT

God is in charge. Allow that, for a moment, to sink in. He knew what time you were going to wake up this morning. He knew how you'd spend your first hour awake. He knows what your thoughts will be as you read these very words (written several months before you'll actually read them). He knows how fast you'll drive to work today. If you have a doctor appointment scheduled this afternoon, he knows the outcome of that, too.

And, if you love him, if you are one of those that Paul is referring to in theses verses, each and everything mentioned above is working together for your own good. Each of the above things, as well as the literal hundreds or thousands of other things that will take place around you, are all taking place for that same good. What an amazing God we serve!

God, to know that you are constantly at work in and around me is awe-inspiring, it's humbling, it's amazing. Only you can bring all of these things together in ways that grow me and glorify you. Praise you!

We know that for those who love God
All things work together for good,
for those who are called according to his purpose."

Romans 8:28 esv

"This is for your own good." You probably heard that growing up on more than one occasion. Usually it was in the context of what you were not allowed to do—maybe you wanted to have a second helping of dessert or stay up an hour later than usual. Mostly, your parents said that because they knew something that you didn't know.

This is the same way with God. He knows all and sees all. He has the ultimate view, and he sees everything at once—past, present and future. He Know all the possible outcomes of our actions. And despite our freedom to make poor decisions, he still manages to grow us and receive glory. This is for our own good.

Father, I'm thankful that you love me so much that you allow all things—the things I deem "good" and even the ones I deem "bad— to somehow make you more known in my life. Give me more opportunities to see you at work in all things.

What is something that happened today that caused growth in you and God to be glorified?

Rest

God, show us your favor. Bless us.
May you smile on us with your favor.

PSALM 67:1 NIRV

While its exact meaning is unknown, some interpret the word Selah to mean "rest." If this is the case, we ought to consider why we might "rest" after reading from God's word. In this part of Psalm 67, we are asking for God to give us something, his favor and his blessing. We are asking for God to look on us and joyfully give us a measure of approval, an acknowledgement that he is pleased with us.

And then, we pause for reflection on who God his, his character and nature. We see, when we stop to see, that he has shown us this favor, we see that we are indeed surrounded by his gifts and attitude of approval.

God, I want to pause right now, I want to stop and just see you at work.

May God be merciful and bless us.
May his face smile with favor on us.

If you've ever made someone happy, and all of us have, a
smile from them is an excellent and obvious reward. God is
no different. God does not show us mercy or shower us with
blessings merely because he has to, God does these things
because he takes great joy in them. It pleases him to love us,
to give us what we need AND what we ask for.

God loves us. Think on that for a moment. There are 7
billion people on the planet, and he loves us. Each one of
us. Personally. He knows what mercy looks like for you right
now. He knows exactly what blessing you will require twenty-
five minutes from now. And this gives him so much joy and
pleasure! That is worth reflecting on.

Lord, help me to stop and think about your amazing, incredible
and immeasurable love, mercy and blessings on my life. I'm so
thankful that you take joy in that.

What might it look like for you to take joy in being merciful
and blessing others?

Peace

Then your ways will be known on earth.
All nations will see that you have the power to save.
God, may the nations praise you.
May all of the people on earth praise you.
May the nations be glad and sing with joy.
You rule the people of the earth fairly.
You guide the nations of the earth.

PSALM 67:2-4 NIRV

Even a cursory read through the news reveals a world
in turmoil. Division reigns and there is little peace and
understanding even among neighbors, much less nations.
This psalm began by asking for God's blessing, because
without it, we have no real peace.

After this huge ask of God, we rest in the hopes that he will
act, that he will bring peace. We rest because in giving this
request to him, it becomes his to do with as he wishes.

Lord, you truly have the ability to act and bring peace that the
world is in need of. Instead of being filled with angst over a broken
world, I ask that "all the nations will see that you have the power
to save."

May your ways be known throughout the earth,
your saving power among people everywhere.
May the nations praise you, O God.
Yes, may all the nations praise you.
Let the whole world sing for joy,
Because you govern the nations with justice,
and guide the people of the whole world.

PSALM 67:2-4 NLT

It seems like the nations and the "powers that be" have free reign. For those aware that you are both beyond and above their power, their response is to praise you. We ask that the nations may recognize this, while at the same time, we are able to find peace because of the justice that you will bring to them.

God's justice is perfect because it saves, it renews, and redeems. He governs with full regard of everyone and takes into account each person- not because of their economic status or capacity to contribute, but because of their need for him. He governs and he guides. And we sing for joy.

God, I pray that you'd be known throughout the earth, that all would experience your saving power. Help us to praise you and sing over your justice for us.

What are some ways that I can demonstrate justice to those who need it?

Praise

God, may the nations praise you.
May all of the people on earth praise you.
Then the land will produce its crops.
God, our God, will bless us.
God will bless us.
People from one end of the earth to the other
will have respect for him.

PSALM 67:5-7 NIRV

Note the order of this portion of Psalm 67. We proclaim that all nations would praise God, and after they've done so, the blessing comes. We act, we ask, and he responds and we know it's him. Our praise comes before the blessing because we praise in hope. We praise in faith.

Because we do so, we can claim that he will act. The land will produce crops. The blessings will come. And our praise will rise.

God, give me the courage to praise you in this way, before and in anticipation of the blessing. I don't know what today's "crop" looks like, but I will praise you still.

May the nations praise you, O God.
Yes, may all the nations praise you.
then the earth will yield its harvests,
and God, our God, will richly bless us.
Yes, God will bless us,
And people all over the world will fear him.

PSALM 67:5-7 NLT

The earth can only yield what is planted. When little seed is sown, the crop will be small. The manner in which we praise God and the fruit we see from the praise is the same way. When all the nations gather in praise, the harvest is rich.

At the end of our day, we can look at the harvest around us, our thoughts and emotions, the results of our conversations and interactions and we can take stock of how we planted the seeds of all of that fruit. Were we generous and kind on our sowing, or did we hold back? Did we sow hurriedly, or carefully and patiently? Look at the harvest!

Lord, help me to honestly evaluate the crop I harvested today. Was it as lush and fruitful as it could have been? As the yield is revealed tomorrow, grant me the presence of mind to take stock of my sowing.

Why is the Bible filled with references to crops, fields, and harvests?

I Am the Way

Jesus told him, "I am the way,
the truth, and the life.
No one can come to the Father
except through me."

JOHN 14:6 NLT

Most of us wake up in a dark room, so our first few steps are usually a bit tentative. We walk carefully, unsure of where we left our shoes or what our pets placed on the floor in the night. As we waken, the way comes back to us, our confidence grows as we walk to the light switch or to the closet or to the washroom.

Jesus, however, is the way. He is the way to the Father. When we are with the way, we find the Father. In the same way, as we walk with him, we become more confident that the Father is just ahead, waiting for us to arrive. Walk confidently into the day because you know the way; his name is Jesus.

Lord, I know the way and he is bringing me to you. Help me today
to stay with him as he brings me to you.

Jesus answered, "I am the way
and the truth and the life.
No one comes to the Father
except through me."

JOHN 14:6 NIV

Before GPS, it used to be really easy for us to "lose our way"
when driving. All it took was one wrong look at the map, or
missed sign, or the wrong direction at a crucial turn, and you
could find yourself miles out of the way. Now, when we turn
the wrong way, we hear a pesky voice "recalculating"; this
helps us get back on track.

As you walked with Jesus today, did you hear him
"recalculating" and did you stay by his side? When he told
you to be kind, were you? When he led you down a path that
surely "seemed wrong," did you stick it out and trust him, or
did you veer off because your way was better? Jesus is the way,
and he's taking you to the Father.

Jesus, thank you for being the way. Thank you for always knowing
where I need to go and for boldly leading me to the Father.

How did Jesus lead you to the Father today?

I Am the Truth

Jesus told him, "I am the way,
the truth, and the life.
No one can come to the Father
except through me."

JOHN 14:6 NLT

Let's go back to those initial steps in the morning. We left our shoes in the closet, and we have no pets to drop things in our way. We even walked across the dark room last night from the light switch to the bed. But what if there is something on the floor? Again, we walk carefully because doubt creeps in. And doubt creeps in because we've forgotten the truth.

As you begin your day today, as you interact with people and situations arise, you'll be tempted to doubt what you know to be true about yourself and about others. You are fearfully and wonderfully made, regardless of what others may say to you. Because of that, your value does not come from what you produce, but from God. These thoughts, because they come from Jesus himself, are true, and they take you to the Father.

Jesus, today please tell me the truth about every situation that I find myself in.

Jesus answered, "I am the way
and the truth and the life.
No one comes to the Father
except through me."

JOHN 14:6 NIV

The end of the day can be an exhausting time. Not just
because the work day went long or because of the unexpected
flat tire or the surprise homework assignment. The end of
the day can be exhausting because of the finality of it. There's
no "do-overs" or "take backs" on things done or said. What
you had hoped for the day is overtaken by the reality of it, the
truth of it.

The good news is that Jesus is truth. The good news is that
his truth is real truth, and regardless of what you said or did,
he offers salvation and forgiveness to you. And once they are
offered by him and accepted by you, the truth is that you're
back before the Father in right relationship with him.

God, I am so thankful for the truth that Jesus is and how this truth
reveals you to me.

How can you trust in the truth that Jesus gives you new life?

I Am the Life

Jesus told him, "I am the way,
the truth, and the life.
No one can come to the Father
except through me."

JOHN 14:6 NLT

Have you ever met "the life of the party"? She's the gal (or he's the guy) who goes around talking to everyone else, asking questions, jumping up and down, and is frequently the most excited (exciting?) person there. They seem to exist to make sure that everyone is having fun.

Jesus is the life. Jesus does more than heal us, he gives life. Jesus does more than forgive us, he removes the weight of our sins from our shoulders. As you begin your day, remember that you're alive, and this life comes from Jesus!

God, I'm taking breaths and my eyes are open. I'm alive! Help me to truly live today!

*Jesus answered, "I am the way
and the truth and the life.
No one comes to the Father
except through me."*

JOHN 14:6 NIV

As the day winds down, things seem to get quiet. The birds disappear, traffic slows, and it gets dark. Normal daytime activity slows and it appears that not much is going on. But, as the sun sinks, "new" life reveals itself. Crickets chirp and nocturnal animals begin to appear. The street lights come on and those on "the night shift" head to work.

Then, a most amazing thing happens as that same sun sets. Stars, always present, begin to reveal themselves. Millions of them. This "life," previously unseen, becomes obvious to us. Life in Jesus that leads us to the Father works in the same way- we know what life really looks like because Jesus- his words and deeds, his mercy, love and grace, is real life.

Jesus, you are not just life, you are my life! Thank you for revealing who I really am.

What might it look like for you to live a revealed life?

Our Champion

We must keep our eyes on Jesus,
who leads us and makes our faith complete.
He endured the shame of being nailed to a cross,
because he knew later on he would be glad he did.
Now he is seated at the right side of God's throne!

HEBREWS 12:2 CEB

If you've ever been hiking with others (and you're not "on point"), you know how important it is to keep your eyes on the person in front of you. You watch their feet as they step around obstacles. You watch their head as they duck low hanging branches. You even learn from their little slips and slides about where not to step.

With Jesus, this is a bit different. He knows exactly where he is going and he leads strong. As we watch him, our faith grows stronger. No hill is too hard, no river is too wide because he endured the ultimate shame by paying the penalty for our sins. He did this all for the great reward of being seated next to God in heaven. Walk as he walked, and your reward will be great, too.

Jesus, help me to keep my eyes on you today. As you lead, I, and my faith, will follow.

We do this by keeping our eyes on Jesus,
the champion who initiates and perfects our faith.
Because of the joy awaiting him, he endured the cross,
disregarding its shame. Now he is seated in the
place of honor beside God's throne.

HEBREWS 12:2 NLT

A "champion" is a sight to behold. Regardless of which sport it is, the "champion" is the epitome of focus, drive, excellence, and toughness. They seemingly endure all things, stopping at nothing to succeed.

Jesus is our champion. He is the initiator of our faith; he is there at the beginning, and he starts us off to ensure that we begin strong. He is there with us; he is perfecting us, staying with us as we go and ensuring that we remain with him. And because he is perfecting us, he is also present at the end. He is there, with God himself, watching as his completed work is perfected by his own work on the cross.

Jesus, thank you for not just sending me off on my own. You are
with me every step of my day, from beginning to end, perfecting me
and making me yours.

In what ways have you felt Jesus with you?

Be Disciplined

"No discipline seems pleasant at the time,
but painful.
Later on, however, it produces a harvest
of righteousness and peace for those
who have been trained by it."

HEBREWS 12:11 NIV

How do you spend the first few minutes of your day? It's likely that what you do in those early moments will set the tone for your entire day. Things like prayer and scripture reading are spiritual disciplines, and I suggest you spend those crucial first few minutes with God.

You can even start this time while still in bed! Once you're really awake, you might simply pray through the Lord's Prayer. Then, go to your Bible and read a portion. An easy way to begin this would be at Psalm 1. You might paraphrase what you read or journal thoughts. As you struggle initially with this "first 15," remember Hebrews 12:11.

Lord, I want the fruit of our relationship to be lush and beneficial.
This requires training on my part. Grant me the desire to be
disciplined.

No discipline is enjoyable while it is happening—
it's painful!
But afterward there will be a peaceful harvest
of right living for those who are trained
in this way.

HEBREWS 12:11 NLT

How do you spend the last few minutes of your day? Like those first waking moments, this time also requires a little discipline because it's so easy to hop online "just one more time" isn't it? What might God desire of us in this time?

Similar to the few minutes, I suggest something for the "final 15." You might re-read the psalm from earlier in the day or look at your journal entry. Perhaps, you'll spend this time thanking God for his work in you, or asking him to search your heart in the hopes that he'd reveal any unresolved issues that remain. As time goes by, the disciplines of the "first 15" and "final 15" will begin to sprout into, "a peaceful harvest of right living."

Father, as I end my day, I want to spend these final moments with you. Grant me peace as I prepare for tomorrow.

What will be the most difficult part in implementing these disciplines?

Celebrate

Nehemiah continued,
*"Go and celebrate with a feast of rich foods and sweet drinks,
and share gifts of food with people who have nothing prepared.
This is a sacred day before our Lord.
Don't be dejected and sad,
For the joy of the Lord is your strength!"*

NEHEMIAH 8:10 NLT

It's shortly after the people return to Israel after the Babylonian Captivity, and God's people have just had the law read to them. They hadn't heard it in years and they are cut to the heart as the weight of their sin and disobedience wears on them, they cry and mourn. This is frequently our response to God's conviction on us.

Nehemiah call the people beyond this. He tells than that this is a time to rejoice because God has delivered them form their sin. The time for mourning has passed, the people are home and they have an incredible opportunity to start over in obedience. Today, as you reflect on your past, rejoice because God has saved you.

Lord, give me the strength today to walk in celebration because of the salvation you've given me.

Nehemiah told the people,
"Enjoy your good food and wine and
share some with those who don't have anything to bring.
Don't be sad!
This is a special day for the Lord,
And he will make you happy and strong."

NEHEMIAH 8:10 CEB

When people return to God, it is something worth celebrating. But notice what the verse says, "This is a special day for the Lord." His people have returned and while they eat and drink, God also rejoices.

God rejoices in and with his people because these moment demonstrate his truth and faithfulness, they reveal that he does not leave his people without hope. Like the prodigal son, his people are back and he receives the praise.

Father, I'm thankful that you rejoice with us. You're with us and your presence makes us happy and strong.

How can you see God rejoicing with you?

Love Like Jesus

Live a life filled with love,
following the example of Christ.
He loved us and offered himself as a sacrifice for us,
A pleasing aroma to God.

EPHESIANS 5:2 NLT

Jesus tells us that the world will know who his true followers
are by our love. And, all too often, it's easy to reduce loving
others to kind words or friendly actions. That's a good start,
but there is more to it.

Paul writes that love really looks like Jesus. True love offers
itself up and sacrifices for others. True love allows others to
have their say and their way. What Jesus offered up to us was
not merely an example in his death, it was and is an example
for us in the way that we live. We follow in his footsteps when
our lives are demonstrations of him.

God, today, help me to be a demonstration of the sacrifice of Jesus.
I want to be sacrificial in my words and deeds today.

Walk in love
as Christ has also loved us and given himself for us,
an offering and a sacrifice to God
for a sweet-smelling aroma.

Imagine if this verse began with the phrase, "Walk in the forest," we'd likely have a word picture of someone on a path surrounded by lush plants and trees, an immersive experience. Or, "Walk in the city," we'd likely see someone on a crowded sidewalk, with tall buildings racing skyward and cars at stop lights.

To walk in something means that we are to be surrounded by it and be immersed by it. We see trees or buildings and we are awed by them. To walk in love means for us to allow it to affect us, to give out a response. To walk in love means that all we do is love, we give of self and give up self. To walk in love means to not be able to help it because we are caught up in it. This is what smells sweet to God.

Lord, I thank you for the ability to walk in love, to be immersed and surrounded by the love of Christ, and to help others to be immersed in it as well.

How can the way I love others be an aroma that points them to God?

Servers Win

He sat down, called the twelve disciples over to him,
and said, "Whoever wants to be first must take last place and
be the servant of everyone else."

MARK 9:35 NLT

We live in a world where most of us strive to be noticed. The easiest way to do this is to be first. And, the easiest way to be first is to talk about oneself over others, to ensure that everyone else sees your accomplishments above and beyond what others may do, to make sure that your contributions are noticed, even at the expense of others.

Jesus calls his followers to live differently. There is nothing wrong with "being first"; the problem arises when we consider how we get to that point. For disciples, the proper way is to assume the role of servant. Practically, we can highlight the efforts of others over our own and we can talk about others more and ourselves less. We can just serve.

God, today, give me the attitude and posture of a servant. Help me
to look for ways to serve others and build them up.

He sat down and called the twelve.
And he said to them, "If anyone would be first,
he must be last of all and servant of all."

MARK 9:35 ESV

When I was in student ministry, I, along with others, would serve at various summer camp weeks. One of my close friends and I were often responsible for creating the camp booklet for the students– part devotional, part informational, it listed the names of all of the adult leaders and helped the kids navigate their week of camp.

One of the most humbling things that my friend always did was to include her own name at the end of the list, and in a much smaller font than anyone else's. While we might be tempted to chalk this up to false humility, with her, it was nothing of the sort. She was most interested in seeing to it that others received the credit because serving was just something she did, it was a part of who she was. We knew her role at camp, and not because her name was on a list. We knew her role at camp because of how she served.

God, I don't just want to serve others, I want the attitude of a servant and the humility of a servant.

What might it look like for you to "be small"?

Keep Growing

I pray that your love will overflow more and more,
and that you will keep on growing in knowledge and
understanding.

PHILIPPIANS 1:9 NLT

We tend to think about growth in terms of a trip; we start
at "point a" and end at "point b." We hope to arrive at our
destination early so that we might have more time with
friends and family, or be able to get a few hours of extra rest.
We also want to get there as cheaply as possible; if we are
flying we'll scour the internet looking for the best price.

But that is not how discipleship works. It is not how growing
in our relationship with Jesus works. All we can do is grow in
his direction; we will not arrive until we die and are joined
with him in eternity. But that is also the good news for those
in Christ. All we can do is move towards him because of
the work of the Spirit within us, and with each step in his
direction, we move further from who we were apart from him.

Jesus, I want to move towards you today. I'm grateful that you are
always my destination and when I look, I see you clearly.

I pray that your love will grow more and more.
And let it be based on knowledge and understanding.

PHILIPPIANS 1:9 NIRV

For Christians, the more we learn about God, the more we love him. We spend time in his Word and learn about who we are- we are sinners who are separated from God. Time in his Word also reveals who God is- he is a pursuer of sinners and desires to show them love, mercy and grace.

This is just one reason why studying the Bible is not an empty ritual or a task to be checked off. We read scripture for knowledge and understanding, and grow in those things, so that our love would grow. Not merely our love for and of God, but that our love for others would also grow. And that this love would be manifested in actions, thoughts and words.

Father, I want to grow in my love- not just from an emotional standpoint, but a love that is grounded in who I am as a sinner and who you are as a redeemer. Help me to seek that truth out in your Word.

What are some ways that you can pursue God and grow in your love?

Think Well

Finally, brothers, whatever is true,
whatever is noble, whatever is right,
whatever is pure, whatever is lovely,
whatever is admirable—
if anything is excellent of praiseworthy—
think about such things.

PHILIPPIANS 4:8 NIV

It's easy to allow our minds to wander, especially in the morning. We think about rushing our kids to school or to our first appointment of the day. We might wonder how we will get it all accomplished. For some, we're already thinking about when we will be able to get back to bed!

But what if we stopped and asked ourselves in the midst of all of that craziness the following: What is true? What is noble? What is right? What is pure? What is lovely? What is admirable and praiseworthy? And how can we go through the entire day thinking about those things? How might the day be different? Perhaps more importantly, how might our actions and words be different?

God, today let me pause and reflect on Philippians 4:8 as I go through my day.

Finally, brethren, whatever things are true,
whatever things are noble, whatever things are just,
whatever things are pure, whatever things are lovely,
whatever things are of good report,
if there is anything praiseworthy—
meditate on these things.

PHILIPPIANS 4:8 NKJV

Well, how was the day? One of the most powerful and
worthwhile things a person can do at the end of the day is
take a moment to meditate on how you spent your day. And,
your day was more than words and actions. Those words and
actions were borne of something, they came from somewhere.

By spending time in, and studying, God's Word faithfully,
we find our ourselves spending time and studying whatever
is true, whatever is noble, whatever is just, and all the way
through Philippians 4:8. We find ourselves being obedient to
the instruction. And, we find ourselves being changed by him.

Lord, I want to be surrounded by the things that bring you glory
and I see that I'll find those things in your Word. Give me the
conviction I need to read and learn from it.

What are some ways that I can train myself to "think well"

Be Like Me

"Whatever you learned or received or heard from me,
Or seen in me—put it into practices.
And the God of peace will be with you."

On the surface, Paul's statement here sound very bold, even uncomfortably so. As Christians, we tend to shy away even from hints of making more of ourselves than we ought, and with God reason. It is Christ who receives the glory in our lives, Jesus has done the saving work for us.

At the same time, once we've been redeemed by Jesus, our lives are changed. Everything about us ought to be demonstrably different. Our thought life is different; we can read Philippians 4:8 to see what we ought to be focusing on. Our activities are also different and Paul is pointing to himself, as one made new by Jesus, as an example of that.

Lord, thank you that I have a tangible example of a new and redeemed life in Paul, one that brings peace.

The things which you learned and received and heard and saw in me, these do, and the God of peace will be with you.

PHILIPPIANS 4:9 NKJV

Paul's instructions are simple- do what he says and live how he lived, and we will have God's peace on us. As simple as that is for us, we often want the peace without the obedience. While God's mercy and grace is indeed offered to all freely, we must respond in acceptance.

Obedience brings peace because we have nothing to fear from a God whom we obey. Obedience brings peace because we are at rest in the fact that we are doing what God asks us to do. Obedience brings peace because the Holy Spirit dwells within us, assuring us that our actions are honorable and true. It's not just the peace of God that receive, God gives us himself. Because of this, obedience brings peace because we have God.

Father, help me to walk in the obedience that brings me to your peace, but to you.

Are you walking in obedience that brings the God of peace?

A Cheerful Heart

A cheerful heart is good medicine,
But a broken spirit saps a person's strength.

PROVERBS 17:22 NLT

We all face challenges in life, and often our response can make all the difference. This can be a conscious choice for us. When things don't go our way, our first step ought to be prayer asking God to help us with our thoughts and feelings. We are not acting in denial of reality but are asking God to help us remember the hope that he gives us that can transcend our immediate circumstance.

Maybe you work at a job that you dislike; perhaps a school assignment is due and you are behind. Take a moment and ask God for a right heart and renewed spirit and go into your day looking for opportunities to show others what that matters.

God, I want to be of right attitude today; you know what the day holds and I don't. Help me to trust in you, and that begins with my heart.

A cheerful heart is a good medicine,
but a downcast spirit dries up the bones.

PROVERBS 17:22 NRSV

With the day coming to a close, it's easy to let your attitude slip as you consider the day- what you didn't get done, how conversations could've or should've gone differently, or perhaps you really struggled with sin and lost.

What God desires from us in these times is to go to him and talk with him. His call for us to cast our burdens on him, regardless of their weight, is real. God's desire for us is that we'd walk in new life with him; Jesus doesn't just change our actions, he changes our hearts. Give yours to him fully and be healthy.

Father, I'm thankful that even my attitude can be shaped by you. Please give me a spirit of joy and cheer so that I might be changed from within.

What is the most difficult part of giving your heart and attitude over to God?

Revealing

Your Word is a lamp to guide my feet
And a light for my path.

PSALM 119:105 NLT

The psalmist compares God's Word to a lamp; it provides just enough light to see the few steps ahead of us. There may be a huge precipice just 10 feet to our left or right, but those next few steps? We can take them comfortably because we can see exactly where to put our feet. It's also a light for the path. We often see lights on a path, spaced just enough apart, so we can walk confidently ahead, seeing the larger picture.

God's Word is a lamp in that it reveals just enough of what we need to know for where we are right now. We read it and take a few steps. It's also a light because it tells us the bigger picture of God's story; there may be some dark spaces, but if we move to, and with, the light, we will be fine. Why? Because he set those lights there, he's already been where we are heading. Be faithful with his Word today and utilize it as it is meant to be used.

God, help me to be in your Word and be comforted by the light you provide. Amen

Your words are a flashlight to light the path ahead of me and keep me from stumbling.

PSALM 119:105 TLB

God's Word reveals much to us. It tells us the truth about him. In it, we learn that God is a creator, the maker of all things. He desires good things for his people and that we'd simply recognize him and praise him for this; he wants us to acknowledge him in worship. God's Word also reveals truth about us. Rather than acknowledge him, we would rather live as though we are him.

When we live this way, what is revealed to us is the darkness ahead. We here we are going, absent God's influence, is to death and destruction. We go deeper and farther onto a dark path away from him, and his words, the light, reveals the depth of that darkness. What he calls us to is to the light. In the midst of our sin and lost ness, he is there with us, revealing to us not only the possibility of our own destruction, but also showing us the way out.

Lord, your Word reveals to me the truth about myself. Thank you for being honest with me and showing me the truth about my situation without you.

What are some things that God has shown you about himself in his word?

This Way

Study this Book of Instructions continually.
Meditate on it day and night so you will
Be sure to obey everything written in it.
Only then will you prosper and succeed
In all you do.

JOSHUA 1:8 NLT

God's Word is a like a meal with never-ending courses. It is designed to continually be read, studied and reflected on. Throughout the Old Testament, we see that Gos's people were experts at one thing: forgetting. No matter how many times God acted to deliver them, they consistently forgot who he was and what he did.

While they did follow the letter of the law in regard to rites and rituals, it was inner obedience that was lacking. This is why we see soften instructions like this, to help the people know and understand why they were to do what God was calling them to. Continual study and meditation brings about an inner life change that leads to true obedience, which in turn leads to prosperity and success in the Lord's eyes.

God, give me the courage to read and study your Word faithfully
that I may be transformed by it.

This Book of the Law shall not depart from your mouth, but you shall meditate on it day and night, so that you may be careful to do according to all that is written in it. For then you will make your way prosperous, and then you will have good success.

JOSHUA 1:8 ESV

If you've ever moved to a new town, you know that it takes a while to get the lay of the land. When going to the grocery store, you likely go the same way for the first few times, maybe even using your GPS, until you are comfortable enough to go on your own.

This text seems to depict God's Word as a type of roadmap that we study confidently and consistently until we know the way. And at the same time, we don't put this map aside because with God's moral instructions and life change expectations, its far too easy for us to get off track. While there are many ways to the local grocery store, there is only one way to God, and this is clearly laid out for us in his word.

Lord, I'm thankful that you've given me the path to follow that gets me to you. Help me to know that I don't need blaze my own way, but to trust in what you've provided to me.

What are some ways you've tried to go your own way to get to God?

Dead to Self

I have been crucified with Christ.
I don't live any longer. Christ lives in me.
My faith in the Son of God helps me to live my life in my body.
He loved me. He gave himself for me.

GALATIANS 2:20 NIRV

We are dead.

That's a really strange concept for us to wrap our minds around. In Ephesians 2, Paul writes that for those who do not have Christ, they are dead. What they need is the life that Christ offers. Now, Paul writes that we are also dead, this time because it is Christ living this new life in us.

What is needed from us is for our sinful selves to die because without that, Christ won't live in us. The Spirit that God gives us brings us this new life brings us real life.

God, help me to die to my sinful self, help me to experience what it means for me to crucify my sin so that I might have the new life that Jesus provides.

My old self has been crucified with Christ.
It is no longer I who live, but Christ lives in me.
So I live in this earthly body by trusting in the Son of God,
Who loved me and gave himself for me.

GALATIANS 2:20 NLT

Christians live in a bizarre space of "now/not yet." God has given us live in Christ, yet we live in the midst of a broken and sinful world. It's not just the sin of others that we deal with, though. We still have our own brokenness that is being drawn out of us. How do we, as sinful people, live out this new life?

We trust in God. We trust in the sacrifice of Jesus. We trust in his death that it was indeed enough. We demonstrate this trust by the way that we live for him. We go forward in life acting like we are new because we are new. And, he gives us this ability by living vicariously through us. We do these things because he loved us and died so that we might live this new life.

Father, thank you for the live offered me by Jesus. Thank you for the way I get to live "newly" each and every day because of what he did.

What are some of the things that still need to die in your life?

Death to Life

*"I tell you the truth, those who listen to my
Message and believe in God who sent me
will have eternal life. They will never be
condemned for their sins,
but they have passed from death into life."*

JOHN 5:24 NLT

Jesus is calling people to listen and believe. We listen to his
message; we read through the Gospels and seen not just
what he has to say, but we see how he lived his life. He loved
and served. He healed. He brought hope. He revealed the
wickedness that lies within our heart. He showed us a new way.

He also pointed to God. All that he did was in light of this
relationship to God, his father. He only did what his father told
him. He believed in God and wants us to have the eternal life
that God offers. God freely gave his son, and Jesus freely gives
us the message he was sent to deliver. Let's live in belief of it!

*God, I listen and believe in your message. You not only told us
what to do, you showed us what an obedient life is like. Thank you
for your perfect example.*

*"What I'm about to tell you is true.
Anyone who hears my Word and believes
Him who sent me has eternal life.
He will not be found guilty.
He has crossed over from death to life."*

JOHN 5:24 NIRV

It's reality. Even after we enter into relationship with God, we still sin. We don't want to. We're even empowered not to by the Holy Spirit within us. But we do it anyway. And this is why the gospel of Jesus is really good news.

Our salvation is in him. At the end of time, we'll be put on trial, our sins available for all to see. It will be clear just how much we actually needed and need Jesus. And then? We won't be found guilty. Because of Jesus, because of his Word and actions proclaimed to us and in light of our flawed response, he will allow us to enter in free and clear because of what he did. Take comfort tonight in the salvation offered for you. You're not guilty because of what he did.

God, thank you for the offer of salvation that comes through Christ. You make all things new through him, and that includes me. I cannot wait to cross into real living with you.

How can you begging to live this new life today?

The God Who Sees Me

She gave this name to the Lord who spoke to her: "You are the God who sees me," for she said, "I have now seen the One who sees me."

GENESIS 16:13 NIV

Hagar was having the worst kind of day! She was an Egyptian slave thrown into the precarious situation of being "given" to Abram by Sarai for the purpose of bearing children. When Hagar did become pregnant, she was mistreated by Sarai and likely ignored by Abram. One day, Hagar decides to flee to the desert. There, the Lord sees her and delivers words that must have added confusion to her life of chaos: to submit to Sarai; that she would have increased descendants; and that her son will be a "wild donkey of a man." By most standards, this was a horrible day.

But through this encounter, Hagar experienced El Roi (literally, the God who sees me)! What a gift that must have been in the ugly chaos of her life! In the midst of her hardship, she was known and seen by the one who matters most! She was no longer feeling alone or ignored. You, too, are loved by El Roi. As you go about your day today, remember El Roi (God sees you)!

Loving God, I praise you because you see me in the midst of my chaos. You do not turn your eyes away from me because you are El Roi. Help me remember this today.

Then she called the name of the Lord who spoke to her, You-Are-the-God-Who-Sees; for she said, "Have I also here seen Him who sees me?"

GENESIS 16:13 NKJV

What kind of day did you have today? Were you bored by the mundane? Was there a chaotic mess or a wonderful surprise? Know that no matter what your day held, El Roi! God saw you. Folded five loads of laundry? El Roi. Graded papers or paid bills? El Roi. Argued with your children or spouse? El Roi. Frustrated by a co-worker? El Roi. Enjoyed a fabulous date night? El Roi. Found the house of your dreams? El Roi. God saw it all! His eyes and his heart were never off of you. Nothing was too boring or too extravagant for the Lord to attend to.

Now, knowing that God saw you, look back on your day and see him. Where was he in the mundane, chaotic messes or wonderful surprises? Find him there and thank him.

El Roi, thank you for seeing me today. Help me to look back and see you. And, as I sleep, let me rest without care knowing you see me, even as I slumber.

What good things did God see you in today?

Revel with a Cause

*Rejoice in the Lord always; again I will say, rejoice! Let your
gentle spirit be known to all men. The Lord is near.*

PHILIPPIANS 4:4–5 NASB

Doesn't the Message translation of this verse in Philippians
get you excited? It sort of paints Paul as a colorful, free
spirited, yet purposeful, people loving Jesus follower who
is oozing with joy as he prepares a party for God's arrival.
Paul makes a point that as you rejoice and celebrate God, you
should be well aware of others. Let others see that you are for
them and with them. That you are available to meet them and
walk with them. Why? What difference would that make? It
will help point them to Jesus. So they can receive him, just as
you have.

As a Jesus follower, we are to reflect his image to others.
When we revel in God, we will overflow with his love toward
others and treat them as Jesus would. That kind of love is
desperately needed and welcome to any party.

*Dear God, help me to celebrate you all day today. Give me an
overflowing, celebration-ready attitude toward you and those I meet
along the way. Help me reflect your love and point people to you.*

Rejoice in the Lord always. I will say it again: Rejoice! Let your gentleness be evident to all. The Lord is near.

PHILIPPIANS 4:4-5 NIV

Your day is nearly done. Were you able to celebrate God all day today? Did you burn extra spiritual calories trying to keep up with Paul? If so, you might be ready for the more subdued, but still focused and purposeful, NIV translation. Rejoice! Do it always. And then do it again. And, in your rejoicing be mindful of those around you. Gentleness will flow from this rejoicing, again pointing others to God as he draws near and as his kingdom comes. No need to be over the top. Be authentic and be gentle. Our world needs this gentleness! And you, by God's grace and because of your joy in him, can give it where it is most needed.

As you get ready to sleep, rejoice in the Lord. And, as you rejoice, let his gentleness wash over you and allow you true rest.

Dear Lord, thank you for the day that you have provided. I may not have reveled or rejoiced in you as much as I wanted to. Allow me to rejoice in you now and let your gentleness be evident in me and through me. Give me true rest that comes from you alone.

In what ways did you revel or rejoice in the Lord today?

Strong & Courageous

"This is my command—be strong and courageous! Do not be afraid or discouraged. For the Lord your God is with you wherever you go."

JOSHUA 1:9 NIV

Do you ever start your day feeling weak and scared, unsure or weary? Of course, you do. Everyone has "one of those days." But God, in his boldness, commands you to be strong and courageous! It's not a suggestion, it is a command. God loves you and walks with you wherever you go, whenever you go, and in whatever your circumstances you face. Because of this, you can approach your day in strength and courage!

What are you facing today that makes you feel afraid or discouraged? Talk to Jesus about those things that are weighing on your heart today. And then, listen to his voice saying, "Be strong and courageous! Do not be afraid or discouraged! I am with you today in everything you have going on! You can have my strength and courage today!" Now go forth and be free from fear and discouragement today!

Dear Lord, thank you for being with me always! Nothing that comes my way is a surprise to you. I can stand in strength and courage because you are with me.

"Have I not commanded you? Be strong and courageous. Do not be frightened, and do not be dismayed, for the Lord your God is with you wherever you go."

JOSHUA 1:9 ESV

You made it through the day! The Lord walked with you through it all! One step in front of the other with God beside you, even carrying you. It may not have been a perfect day, but the fact remains that God was in the midst of it, sharing his strength with you. Praise God that his truths stand even when your emotions may fail you.

Reflect back on your day and praise the Lord for moments when you overcame fear. Give him glory for a situation where you were braver than you thought you could be. Ask him to show you where he was in each high and low. Finally, rest in his strength and courage as you drift off to sleep.

Thank you, Father, for instructing me to move toward brave courage! Thank you for being with me wherever I went today! Let me rest now in your strength and your courage.

Where did God give you courage today?

No Busy Signals

On the day I called to you, you answered me.
You made me strong and brave.

PSALM 138:3 NCV

Can you remember back to the days of the busy signal?
That dreaded "Beep! Beep! Beep!" on the other end of the
telephone line? Today, your call might go to voice mail. It
often happens when you really need the other person on the
other end to pick up and respond to your call.

God never has a busy signal. He is always available to listen
and hear you! He never misses your call. Uttering even a word
to Jesus can provide you with relief and thanksgiving and
strength. Before you pick up a phone today to call a friend
seeking advice or to share a celebration, call on Jesus first.
Listen and sense his encouragement and strength shared
back to you. If you don't hear him right away, do not take the
quiet as a busy signal. Rather know without a doubt that he
has heard you, that he loves you, and that He is giving you
strength!

Jesus, Thank you that you hear me when I call. As soon as I pray,
you listen and you answer. You give me strength to encourage me.
You are never too busy for me.

In the day when I cried out, You answered me, and made me bold with strength in my soul.

PSALM 138:3 NKJV

It is wonderful to have a friend to reach out to or call upon. God is a friend that is always there for you. He heard you today as you called out in celebration or despair. He was never out of earshot. He never put you on hold for something more important. Believe that!

Do you know it pleases him when you cry out to him? If you have not done so yet today, cry out to God now. Let him know what is on your heart and your mind. Share with him, your joys and your frustrations. Know that he will hear you and that he cares deeply about you. And, expect that he will answer by giving you boldness, strength and encouragement.

God, you want me to call out to you! You really do. Hear me now and know what I need from you. Give me strength in my soul for all that lies on my heart and mind today.

How did God encourage you or give you boldness today?

The Best Home

How lovely is Your tabernacle,
O Lord of hosts!
My soul longs, yes, even faints
For the courts of the Lord;
My heart and my flesh cry out for the living God.

PSALM 84:1-2 NKJV

The author of the Psalms talks about the God's home as a beautiful place that he always longed to be. Picture the home that you always wanted to live in. What would it look like? How would it be decorated? Remember it is a place to live in so make sure you are picturing a dwelling that is welcome and cozy, not some lavish but unlivable or pretentious palace. When you are in this place, you can't help but sing praises. How does God welcome you in?

As you go through your day today, keep this picture of God's home in your heart and mind. Ask God to reveal it to you as you go.

God, I long to dwell in a place as lovely as yours! I long to stay even a day in your house, yet prefer to have it be my constant place of rest. Will you show me your home more clearly as I go throughout my day.

How lovely is your dwelling place, Lord Almighty!
My soul yearns, even faints, for the courts of the Lord;
my heart and my flesh cry out for the living God.

PSALM 84:1-2 NIV

While the dwelling place of the Lord is an actual physical place, it is also the place of submission to God. When you meet with God through prayer, reading the Bible, praising him, and being with other believers, you are in his presence. When you choose God's will and make decisions that honor him, you are in the dwelling place of the Lord. And, the more your heart will become a welcome home for Jesus. The more your heart will look like the home you pictured earlier today.

May you find your dwelling place more consistently within the will of the Lord. And, in return, may your heart and soul be transformed more and more into a welcome dwelling place for the Lord.

Lord Almighty, you want me to live in your dwelling place. You want me to walk in your will and make decisions that honor you. Help me to stay in your will. Allow my heart to be shaped more like yours each and every day.

How did you picture the house of the Lord?

Better

For a day in your courts is better
than a thousand elsewhere.
I would rather be a doorkeeper in the house of my God
than dwell in the tents of wickedness.

PSALM 84:10 ESV

Remember that amazing home you pictured yesterday when you thought about the house of the Lord? Now imagine that this home is so fantastic that you would be more content to stay here for one day than to vacation for a thousand days on the beautiful Greek Isles.

Are you catching this? God's house—the place the Lord resides—is that amazing. In fact, the author knows that even being a servant in this house is more precious than being an honored guest in a palace of sin (in a place apart from God). One day in his house is greater than all your days numbered elsewhere. But, as a follower of Jesus, you can be confident that you will have days upon days in his eternal home. How awesome is that!?!

God, may my heart long today for even one day spent in your dwelling place. And may I trust in Jesus so that all my days will be spent with You.

Better is one day in your courts than a thousand elsewhere;
I would rather be a doorkeeper in the house of my God
than dwell in the tents of the wicked.

PSALM 84:10 NIV

Isn't it awesome to know that even though eternity may seem far away, you can be in the dwelling place of the Lord today? Choosing God's plan allows you to be in his presence now. Stepping out of your comfort zone and into the place Jesus calls you, even for a day, is better than anything. Serving God and others—even as a doorkeeper or a floor scrubber—is far more valuable than being served or dwelling outside of God's purpose.

As you end your day, reflect on the decisions you can make that put your feet on the path God has called you to. Allow him to show you his plan so that you can be in his presence now. Rejoice in the role you play in God's house today.

Lord, thank you that I can be in your presence today. I ask that
you would show me how to serve and which steps to take so that
I can be in your courts, even for this day.

How will you choose to be in God's presence today?

Beautiful Timing

God made everything beautiful for its own time.
He has planted eternity in the human heart,
but even so, people cannot see the whole scope of God's work
from beginning to end.

ECCLESIASTES 3:11 NLT

Sometimes it feels like we wait forever for things to be just the way we want them. We wait for winter to turn to spring, for our hair to grow to just the right length, and for our children to outgrow their terrible twos. And some things, more important things, seem to take even longer to reach a place of beauty.

But guess what? God has got all the important stuff figured out. In fact, He made everything to be beautiful in just the right time. He is the best keeper of the clock and the best creator of all things lovely. You can trust that his timing is perfect and that beauty can rise from all circumstances. Let that truth give you confidence and peace today!

God, help me to trust your timing today. Forgive me for worrying when I am impatient in my waiting. Allow me to see beauty unfolding in your perfect plan.

God has given them a desire to know the future.
He does everything just right and on time,
but people can never completely understand what he is doing.

ECCLESIASTES 3:11 NCV

Praise God that he takes care of things from beginning to end! Praise him even more that he does not expect us to know or understand all that he has done and all that he is doing. That is a relief! God is continually working out the details to make all things beautiful at just the right time. We don't need to understand it. It just is!

As you look back on your day, can you see glimpses of God at work? Do you see his beauty cropping up when you didn't expect it? What perfect timing was unfolding? Thank God for each of those observations! Ask him to make you more aware of how he is working eternity out each day.

Father God, I saw you working your perfect timing today. I don't understand it all, but I can trust that your plan is unfolding. Thank you for making beauty come at just the right time!

What did God make beautiful for you today?

Praise Him

Accept our praise, O Lord, for all Your glorious power.
We will write songs to celebrate your mighty acts!

PSALM 21:13 TLB

This morning, start off your day right away by praising the
Lord for all he has done. Acknowledge who he is and how
much he means to you. He is mighty and strong. He is without
fault. He is the creator of heaven and earth. By his hands all
things were made.

There is nothing God cannot handle. There is nothing that
surprises him! Speak truths about God out loud, praising him
for his power. Celebrate him through song and invite him
into your day.

O Lord, you are amazing and full of power! You are holy and just!
You bring praises to my lips! I welcome you into my day today.

Be exalted, O Lord, in your strength!
We will sing and praise your power.

PSALM 21:13 ESV

It is hard to imagine that anyone can miss the power of God! He was before all things and through all things. As the Creator, he said, "Let there be light." And there was. He parted the Red Sea through a man named Moses. He defeated giants through a shepherd boy named David. As Jesus, God turned water into wine, healed the blind, walked on water, fed the multitude, and calmed raging seas. He cast out demons and made the lame to walk.

Today, God, through his Spirit, continues to heal and comfort and bring peace into places of chaos. God's strength is right in front of us. Shout it out! Sing it out!

God, you are great! Show your strength to people who too easily miss what is right in front of them. Help me to reveal your strength to others! How great Thou art!

In what ways did you see God's strength revealed today?

Keep on Moving

Let us stop going over the basic teachings about Christ again and again. Let us go on instead and become mature in our understanding. And so, God willing, we will move forward to further understanding.

HEBREWS 6:1, 3 NLT

Ever been stuck in a rut? Maybe you are bored with the same dinner recipes week after week or stalled out on an exercise plan (or lack thereof). We can also get stuck when it comes to understanding God's Word and his teachings. The author of Hebrews gives warning about getting stalled in the "basic teachings about Christ." Not that the basics—repentance from sin, faith in Jesus, baptism, resurrection—aren't important. Fundamentals are necessary aspects of trusting Jesus. But, going deeper into God's Word will bring about growth and change. It will solidify the bedrock that you cling to when your faith is tested. It will bring you greater breadth and depth to understanding just how wide and how deep God's love is for you.

So, as you enter the day, ask God to keep you moving forward in maturity with Christ and in understanding of his Word.

God, you want me to move forward in my understanding of you today. Open my eyes to see you more clearly. Impress your words upon my heart so that I may know you more.

Leaving the elementary teaching about the Christ, let us press on to maturity. And this we will do, if God permits.

How did you do today? Did you dig deeper into God's Word? Was your time with God more meaningful? Don't be discouraged if you didn't do as well as you hoped. Growth takes time! It is reassuring that God has lots of time for you. While he wants you to press on to maturity, he will not leave you stranded while you work this out with him.

As you end your day, why not tell God exactly what you need to move forward in faith? Be bold in your requests and actively look for his response. Your list may look like this:

God, I need more time with you, a mentor, a Bible translation that I understand, focused attention, a dynamic worship service, a quiet space to meet you, a study guide...

Dear Lord, please equip me so I can grow in my understanding of you. Thank you that you will never leave me, even when I am slow to grow.

What do you need most to move forward in faith?

Joy in the Morning

Sing to the Lord, all you godly ones! Praise his holy name. For his anger lasts only a moment, but his favor lasts a lifetime! Weeping may last through the night, but joy comes with the morning.

PSALM 30:4-5 NLT

Good morning to you, beloved one seeking God! It is a new day. There is much to be thankful for! You may have had a rough night. You may be in a hard season. You might be feeling afraid or out of God's view. There is more ahead and God is with you. He has not left you. He has not forsaken you. He is with you in the midst of all. His love and favor for you are real and present now. They will never fade.

So praise him this morning! Celebrate joy! If you don't see the joy just yet, anticipate that joy is coming. He has promised it.

Good morning, Lord. I praise you today! I praise you for things you have already done and for things yet to come! I have seen my share of weeping and now I am ready to embrace your joy.

Sing praises to the Lord, O you his faithful ones,
and give thanks to his holy name.
For his anger is but for a moment;
his favor is for a lifetime.
Weeping may linger for the night,
but joy comes with the morning.

PSALM 30:4-5 NRSV

Good evening, child of God! The Lord is with you as this day
ends. Was today a day of laughter and joy for you? Hopefully,
you can look back and say, "YES! This is a day that God made
just for me!" If so, praise him now and thank him to his face.

And yet, it may have been a day with too many tears or bumps
and bruises. If that was your kind of day, be assured that God's
love and his favor are still upon you. Tell him how you feel and
then thank him for what he is doing behind the scenes. Look
for moments of joy that may not have been obvious. Expect joy
and laughter to come in time. He says it will.

Good evening, God. You know how my day went and loved me
through all of it. I praise you for how you are working through my
sorrows and my joys.

Where did you see joy in your day today?

For Such a Time

If you keep quiet at a time like this, deliverance and relief for the Jews will arise from some other place, but you and your relatives will die. Who knows if perhaps you were made queen for just such a time as this?

ESTHER 4:14, NLT

What a lot of pressure Esther must have felt when she begged for mercy on behalf of her people. At the same time, she must have felt extremely empowered. Esther was a key player in the history of Christian faith.

Guess what? God is empowering you, through his Holy Spirit, to be a key player in his story too! God has designed and gifted you to make a difference in this time and place. Look around you and see where your gifts and talents are needed. Ask God to reveal what it is that he wants you to do as part of his story. By the way, do you notice that "his story" when given just a nudge becomes "history"? Yes, by acting out your role in his story, you become a part of history.

It is so cool, God, that you use people to fulfill your plan. Empower me to make a difference in this world. Show me my place in your story.

"If you keep quiet at this time, someone else will help and save the Jewish people, but you and your father's family will all die. And who knows, you may have been chosen queen for just such a time as this."

ESTHER 4:14 NCV

You, likely, do not live in a palace. Chances are, you are not considered royalty by most people. Yet, as a child of God, you are a son or daughter of the King and an heir to his kingdom. You are part of his story! You have been brought to this specific time and place to play your role in God's redemptive plan.

Do you know what that looks like for you? Where do you have influence? Where will your voice carry the Gospel the clearest? What steps can you take to show Jesus to those around you? Be bold, be brave, be ready to do your part—for such a time as this.

Thank you, Lord, that you made me royalty. Help me use my status as your child to impact the world around me. Give me bold vision to see my part in history.

What is the impact that God wants you to make in such a time as this?

Common Sense Living

He has told you, O mortal, what is good;
and what does the Lord require of you
but to do justice, and to love kindness,
and to walk humbly with your God?

MICAH 6:8 NRSV

Too often people try to complicate God. They muddy the
waters of "religion" and create obstacles to life with God.
God's Word, specifically His plan for how we are to live
well, is not that complicated. Micah the prophet spells it
out in the verse above. Read it again and soak up the words.
Jesus made it even more simple when he said the greatest
commandments are to love God and love others!

Hopefully, this gives you a sense of freedom. Living a life well
does not have to be tied up in rules and regulations but in the
common sense that comes when you humbly consider what
is fair, just, and compassionate toward others. Love well and
live well today!

Thank you, God, for not expecting complicated living from me.
And, help me to take seriously the way that I love you and love
others today.

He has shown you, O man, what is good;
And what does the Lord require of you
But to do justly,
To love mercy,
And to walk humbly with your God?

Micah 6:8 NKJV

God's recipe for a good life is not a big mystery. There are no secret ingredients or hidden tricks. In fact, God has laid it all out for us through his own actions and, more clearly, through the actions of Christ. Do justly. Love mercy. Walk humbly with God. No shocking surprises there!

Although the recipe is uncomplicated, it is not necessarily easy. It does require sacrifice and love. It definitely requires humility. Therefore, ask God tonight to show you how to follow this three-part plan for living well. Study Jesus's examples of justice and mercy. Praise Him that his way is not full of obstacles, but it is full of love.

Heavenly Father, forgive me when I try to complicate the way to good living. Show me how to live life well by studying Jesus's life, doing justly, loving mercy, and walking humbly with you.

What is one thing you can do to "do justly" this week?

A Promise Sent

"Now I will send the Holy Spirit, just as my Father promised. But stay here in the city until the Holy Spirit comes and fills you with power from heaven."

LUKE 24:49 NLT

God is pretty amazing! The disciples were no doubt confused and concerned about Jesus's death and resurrection. They were likely scared about what had happened and what was ahead. So Jesus reveals to them that, though he is leaving, they will not be alone or apart from God. The Holy Spirit would come and fill them with power so that they could do incredible things in Jesus's name!

Realize that if you trust in Jesus, God is telling you the same thing today. He has sent you the Holy Spirit. He has filled you with his power! That means, you can go out and do fantastic things in the name of Jesus today. How great is that?

Holy Spirit, I love that you do not leave me alone. You are a promise sent. Thank you for coming and filling me with your power. Work in and through me to do amazing things on your behalf today.

"Listen carefully: I am sending the Promise of My Father [the Holy Spirit] upon you; but you are to remain in the city [of Jerusalem] until you are clothed (fully equipped) with power from on high."

LUKE 24:49 AMP

God knows that you were never meant to be alone. His plan from the start included relationship with people. From walking in the garden with Adam and Eve to hanging out with sinners and tax collectors, God values personal connection with those want to know him. So, when Jesus left earth, it made perfect sense that he would send the Spirit to fill his people.

Doesn't this show you how much you mean to God? God longs to be in a close relationship with you. Not only that, but he gives you access to his power through the Holy Spirit. How extravagant! Allow these truths to settle into your heart and mind as you end your day. God loves you and promises never to part from you. His Spirit is evidence of that!

Father, thank you that you desire relationship with me! You love me so much that you fill me with your Holy Spirit. Thank you for sending me this promise!

How does it feel knowing that God wants to be close to you?

Love One Another

Dear friends, let us practice loving each other, for love comes from God and those who are loving and kind show that they are the children of God, and that they are getting to know him better.

1 John 4:7 TLB

Good morning, dear friend! Do you know how much you are loved? God loved you so much that he sent his son Jesus into the world so that you could have eternal life! That is a sacrificial and extravagant love that you will never fully be able to replicate or attempt to repay. Because of this love fully given, God calls us to love one another in return. He wants us to make a point of practicing loving kindness each day.

As you start your day, make a conscious effort to practice love today. Ask God to show you who he wants you to love. Listen to him as he guides you and tells you how to love others well.

Loving Father, you poured out your generous love in ways that I cannot repay. Thank you! Show me who needs your love today. Help me love others sacrificially so that they see you in me.

Dear friends, let us love one another, for love comes from God.
Everyone who loves has been born of God and knows God.

1 JOHN 4:7 NIV

Good evening, friend! How did your love challenge go today?
Did you find yourself thinking of ways you could share God's
love? If you did love well today, way to go! Praise God for
your commitment to sharing his loving kindness. If things
didn't go as planned, do not be dismayed. There are plenty of
opportunities to practice God's love in days to come!

As you end your day, thank God for those to whom you were
able to show love. Praise him for love that you felt from
others. Then ask him to show you those who still need to see
him more clearly through the love others give. Pray for each
of these people by name.

Dear God, thank you for love that comes from you. Thank you for
those who showed me loving kindness today. Help me to love others
more and point them to you.

Who is someone that could use God's love this week?

The Greatest Gift

The wages of sin is death, but the gift of God is eternal life in Christ Jesus our Lord.

ROMANS 6:23 NIV

What is the best gift you have ever received? Do you remember when you got it and from whom? Some "best" kid gifts over the decades include:

From the 70s - Mood Rings, Mattel Electronics Football, anything Peanuts, and a Bee Gees' LP
From the 80s - Light Bright, Teddy Ruxpin, Cabbage Patch Dolls, and Big Wheel
From the 90s - Gameboy, American Girl Dolls, Boom Boxes, and Polly Pockets
From the 2000s - Tamaguchi, Webkinz, Guitar Hero, and Heely Shoes

It is fun to reminisce on gifts from our youth. But the greatest gift we could ever receive is eternal life through Jesus. Trends come and go, batteries run out, and eventually "things" fall apart. Redemptive love and everlasting life are gifts that never grow old or out of style. If you have accepted this gift, thank God today! If not, ask him to unwrap this gift for you so you can see just how sweet it is.

Heavenly Father, I am thankful for all the fun earthly gifts I have been given in my lifetime. None of them compares to the gift of life you offer me. Thank you!

The wages of sin is death, but the free gift of God is eternal life in Christ Jesus our Lord.

ROMANS 6:23 NRSV

For many, gift giving is such a joy filled opportunity. Yes, it is wonderful to receive a great gift, but the rush that can come with finding "just the right thing" for one you love can be even better!

Imagine how God must feel every time someone opens his gift of salvation. Imagine the look on his face when one of his children says, "YES! I love this gift. I accept this gift of eternal life. I believe what Jesus has done for me. Thank you! Thank you!" God surely rejoices with his angels just as Jesus describes in parables of the lost coin, the lost sheep, and lost son. Let that image sit with you and rejoice along with him.

Dear God, you must be so thrilled when someone opens your gift of salvation. Thank you for your generosity! Help me to point others to you and your gift of life.

Do you prefer receiving or giving gifts? Why?

Child of God

Everyone who believes that Jesus is the Christ has become a child of God. And everyone who loves the Father loves his children, too.

1 JOHN 5:1 NLT

What is the best part about being a child? Maybe it is the fact that you don't have to worry about a job or paying bills. Perhaps it is that someone else does a lot of the chores while you can play. Most likely, it also has something to do with the love that comes to you just by virtue of being a child and a part of a family.

When you become a follower of Jesus, you become a child of God. Amazing! Soak in that for a moment. Allow the meaning of that to fill you up today. Don't let it hang there as cliché. As God's child, you are an heir to his kingdom (heaven), his power (through the Holy Spirit), and his love. Not only God's love, but the love of the greater family of God becomes yours as well.

Dear God, let me really understand what it means to be your child today. Allow me to receive the love you and your family have for me.

Everyone who believes that Jesus is the Christ has been born of God, and everyone who loves the parent loves the child.

1 JOHN 5:1 NRSV

There is nothing sweeter than being in a family filled with love. Children do best when they have families securely rooted in love for one another. They are better able to handle the hard things that come and more likely to give love to others in mutual and meaningful ways.

Hopefully, the thought of God's love for you as his child never left you today. Hopefully, the thought of being a part of the greater family of God revisited your thoughts as you went about your business today. As you look back on the day, consider what you would have done differently if you had felt convicted in God's love. Or, if you were able to remember your place in God's family today, imagine how different your day would have been if you did not sense God's great love for you. Lean into his love, dear child!

Father, I praise you for the sweet gift of family. Let me rest tonight in your loving care. Help me to love others well tomorrow.

What does it mean to be a child of God?

Right-ness vs Righteousness

The fruit of righteousness will be peace;
the effect of righteousness will be quietness
and confidence forever.

ISAIAH 32:17 NIV

As a believer in Christ, do you strive to be right or be righteous? It feels good to be right, doesn't it? But being right is a moment by moment experience. There are many opportunities in which your right-ness can be tested and for you to pass or fail. Being right is often about proving oneself ("See, I was right.") or besting someone else ("I knew that, but they did not.").

Righteousness, however, is more about a rhythm and pursuit in life. It is about living in line with morality or justice. As a follower of Jesus, righteousness is walking in such a way as to reflect Jesus, to share his love and justice with those who need it. It is not about proving yourself over others. Today, seek righteousness over being right. Ask God to show you how.

Jesus, today I want to strive for righteousness over being right.
Will you show me how? And then, reveal the peace that comes
as a result.

Out of justice, peace.
Quietness and confidence will reign forever more.

ISAIAH 32:17 NKJV

Have you ever been on the receiving end of comments from a Miss Smarty Pants or a Mr. Know-It-All? You know what that feels like. Even if Miss Pants or Mr. All is right, it is their air of "I know better than you" that makes you roll your eyes or, worse yet, feel like you are the lowest man on a very tall totem pole. Mr. All does not seem to care if his words wound you and Miss Pants seems more concerned about herself than the betterment of all. This looks nothing like quiet confidence.

Contrast this to someone that you know who may be right often, but is more interested in righteousness, in working toward justice and concern for others. They have no interest in besting you, but in the best for you. So even if they are right, you can rest in their right-ness, rather than bemoan it. Seek out this kind of living, one of righteousness over right-ness.

Dear God, let me be a person of quiet confidence and peace.
I would rather sleep easy with righteousness than worry about
always being right.

Is it "easier" to be right or righteous?

An Unexpected Reunion

"He got up and came to his father. But while he was still a long way off, his father saw him and felt compassion for him, and ran and embraced him and kissed him."

LUKE 15:20 NASB

Have you ever people-watched at baggage claim in an airport? If so, the image of a long-awaited embrace of two people who have been apart for too long is likely familiar. A happily weeping mom rushing to squeeze her young son returning in his military camouflage, a husband running up with roses and a loving kiss for his wife returning from travels to her parents, grandchildren jumping up and down to get closer to their grandparents coming for a visit. These images can be superimposed onto the story of the father running to his son in Luke 15.

The difference in this story, however, is that the son left home on bad terms. He wanted out from under his dad's roof. He only came back when he hit rock bottom and had nothing left. Yet, his dad rushed to him as if there was nothing but love between them. This unexpected reunion is the stuff of Jesus. Know that this is the kind of love he has for you!

Father God, you are the heart behind unexpected reunions and extraordinary love! Thank you for the image of a father rushing to his son when he least deserves it. Let me rest in that love today.

*"He returned home to his father. And while he was still a long
distance away, his father saw him coming, and was filled with
loving pity and ran and embraced him and kissed him."*

LUKE 15:20 TLB

If you have ever been a part of a long-awaited reunion, you
know how sweet it can be. Whether you reunited with a
parent, a friend, a spouse, or even your loyal pup, you know
the overwhelming feelings that can come with it. Your mutual
love made this reuniting a joyful affair.

Now imagine returning to someone you left in hurt and
pain, as if they meant nothing to you, but to whom you are
now sorry. Imagine if they ran to you the way the father did
in Luke. Once you got past the confusion of this unexpected
reunion, wouldn't your heart beat in a way it never had
before? Wouldn't you be stunned by this gracious love and
mercy? This is the way Jesus loves you. When you push him
away and then return, his merciful love welcomes you home.
Accept his homecoming today!

*Dear Father, thank you for running to me and welcoming me
home whenever I stray from you. Help me to run straight to you
without fear.*

Do you need to have an unexpected reunion with anyone?

Clean Slate

Who is a God like you, pardoning iniquity
and passing over transgression
for the remnant of his inheritance?
He does not retain his anger forever,
because he delights in steadfast love.

MICAH 7:18 ESV

God loves you, Precious One! He does not hold grudges
against you. There really is no one who wipes the slate of
sin (wrong-doings) clean better than God. God is more
concerned about forgiveness and relationship with his people
than he is with sitting in a state of begrudging anger. Does
he experience anger toward sin and desire just living from
his people? Of course he does! But he also knows we are not
perfect. He forgives us and removes our sin "as far as the east
is from the west" (Psalm 103:12)

Start your day by thanking God for his merciful love. Confess
your wrong-doings and allow his forgiveness to wash over you.

God, there is no one like you! Thank you for your merciful love.
Forgive me for all that I have done against you and others.

Where is another God like you, who pardons the sins of the survivors among his people? You cannot stay angry with your people, for you love to be merciful.

MICAH 7:18 TLB

How precious are these words about God: "You cannot stay angry with your people, for you love to be merciful"? Doesn't that just give you warm-fuzzies? The God of the universe, who has every reason to be annoyed and angry with those of us sin again and again within his universe, does not stay angry. He loves showing mercy and forgiveness toward his people.

No doubt, Dear One, you were not perfect today. You may have been really close, but it is unlikely you were entirely without sin today. What a relief knowing that God will not hold that against you as you lay your head on your pillow tonight. Ask him for forgiveness. Praise him for his mercy. Rest well in the warm fuzziness of his grace.

Father, I am so thankful that I can rest in your mercy tonight. You know my weaknesses and love me anyway. I praise you for the way you love me!

How does God's mercy give you peace?

Sunk Sin

He will again have compassion on us;
he will tread our iniquities underfoot.
You will cast all our sins
into the depths of the sea.

MICAH 7:19 ESV

Have you ever stood at the end of a dock or pier and thrown a rock out as far as you could? There is a degree of satisfaction in the size of the splash or in the "kerplunk" sound when the rock hits the water. There is a soothing sense that comes from ripples dissipating into stillness. There is an odd feeling of completion in the sinking of the rock.

God is a master of sinking our sin to the bottom of the sea. He wants the sin to be gone, so that there is no trace left to haunt or shame us. The ripples of sin will no doubt appear, but God desires that they dissipate into freedom and restoration. Picture God hurling your sin into the depths of the ocean today. Start your day in his freedom!

Lord, thank you for your great compassion. Take my sin and sink it. Free me from shame and guilt so that I can live in your freedom.

Once again you will have compassion on us. You will tread our sins beneath your feet; you will throw them into the depths of the ocean!

MICAH 7:19 TLB

The day is nearly done. The sun has or will be setting soon. Are you still carrying around the weight of sin from days gone by? Did you pick up any new sin "stones" during your day's journey? Remember that God does not sink your sin once and then move on assuming you will sin no more. He "once again" has compassion on you. He "once again" is willing send your sin to the depths. Trust him with this task of sinking sin!

If you live near a body of water, maybe you need to go rock throwing this week. Write your sins on rocks and hurl them as far as you can into the water. If you don't have the luxury of water, write your sin on some Charmin and flush it down the toilet. Talk to Jesus as you do. Let him know what sin you need sunk.

God, I admit that I am not good at letting go of sin. I need you to sink my sin and show me your grace. Help me confess and then accept your compassion.

What sin do you want God to sink for you?

Promises Kept

You will give truth to Jacob
And unchanging love to Abraham,
Which You swore to our forefathers
From the days of old.

MICAH 7:20 NASB

Our heavenly father is a keeper of promises! He is true to his Word. Micah referenced God's faithful compassion showed to Abraham nearly 1400 – 1500 years earlier. He saw God's faithfulness revealed time and time again through the history of the Old Testament. He trusted that God would continue to pour out forgiveness and blessings on his people.

If you ever feel like the Bible is an ancient relic of historical significance but no personal application, think again. If you doubt that God's Word could be written for you in this day and age, check your thoughts. God's love and compassion today is just as great as it was in the time of Jesus, in the days of Micah, and the long ago of Abraham. If you aren't sure of that, talk to God. Ask his Holy Spirit to bring his Word to life for you today.

Holy Spirit, breathe on me today. Make your Word come alive.
Show me that you are true to your promises of days long ago.

You will bless us as you promised Jacob long ago. You will set your love upon us, as you promised our father Abraham!

MICAH 7:20 TLB

You made it through another day. Hooray! That is actually a big deal. Some days can be tough and here you are—a survivor of the day. Hopefully, the Holy Spirit was at work today, reminding you that the Word of God is as true today as it was when it was written. Hopefully, you saw glimpses of God's compassion and love being set upon you, just as it was promised to Abraham.

Isn't that a cool image, by the way? The image of God "setting his love upon you"? It is almost as if he has a blanket of love and compassion that he gently sets upon your shoulders and wraps around you. As you fall into your bed tonight, let that image comfort you. And, may the peace and compassion of God fill you.

God, there is nothing better than your love. Thank you for setting it upon me. Thank you for being faithful to all the generations.

How does it feel when promises are kept?

Fearless Living

For the Lord will remove his hand of judgment and will disperse the armies of your enemy. And the Lord himself, the King of Israel, will live among you! At last your troubles will be over, and you will never again fear disaster.

ZEPHANIAH 3:15 NLT

Zephaniah is one of the very last books of the Old Testament. Zephaniah was a prophet speaking to the people of Israel. His relatively short book gives warnings to the Israelites to wake up and change their selfish ways. He sees all the goofy things they are doing and how they are walking away from God. His words warn of God's future judgement.

Yet, Zephaniah ends with hope and reassurance as a response to Israel's repentance. It is a reminder that God longs for relationship. He wants to live among his people. In his mercy, he will rescue his people and bring peace again, ultimately through Jesus. With this promise, fear can fade! The same promise of salvation and freedom from fear is meant for you today.

Father, it is easy to walk away from you sometimes. Help me always turn back to you. Thank you that you want to walk with me and drive away fear.

The Lord has stopped punishing you;
he has sent your enemies away.
The King of Israel, the Lord, is with you;
you will never again be afraid of being harmed.

ZEPHANIAH 3:15 NCV

What would it mean to live a life without fear? What would look different in the way you take on the challenges of the day? What risks would you take to love others more?

According to Zephaniah's prophecy, God's plan for his people includes removing all fear. He tells them to listen up, repent, stop doing the goofy things you are doing and then watch and see how the Lord responds. Doesn't that sound like a good idea? You know that God ultimately wants the best for you. You know his plan is good. His idea of loving God and loving others makes perfect sense. So trust that and get to it. And, when you do, get ready to live a fear-free life!

Dear God, can I really live a fear-free life? Show me how to love you, love others and stay on the path you planned for me. I want to know you are with me so I can live fear-free.

What would you do if you lived fear-free?

Thanks for the Love

Give thanks to the Lord, for He is good;
His love endures forever.

PSALM 118:29 NIV

Welcome to another day, Loved One! Yes, you are a loved one, beloved in God's eyes. The love he has for you is never ending. It goes on and on to the end of time. It endures all things that have been and all things that will be. Wake up and breathe in his love today!!

God's love for you comes from his ultimate goodness and his Creator-Father heart. Take the next few minutes to thank him for just how good he is. Thank him for what he has done in creation. Thank him for the ways he has gifted you. Thank him for the people in your life that mean the most to you. Thank him for sending Jesus to die on the cross for you. Thank him for walking with you today and always. Thank him for all that comes to mind.

Lord, you are good! You love me always, even when I don't deserve it. Thank you for all that you do in my life and for all the good gifts you have given me.

O give thanks to the Lord, for he is good,
for his steadfast love endures forever.

PSALM 118:29 NRSV

The day is nearly done. It is just about time to call it quits:
quit working, quit doing chores, quit paying bills, quit
watching TV, quit reading, and quit overthinking your day. It
is almost time to rest, sleep and renew.

God's love never stops to rest. It never quits. God's love is
always active and moving in your life. It is interesting that
God built rest into his rhythm when he created everything.
"On the seventh day God had finished his work of creation,
so he rested from all his work" (Gen. 2:2), but that his love
never rests. Love must not feel like work to God. That's how
much he loves you! Thank God for how good he is. Then, quit
and rest in his great love for you!

Wonderful God, you are so good! Thanks for your love. Even as I go
to sleep tonight, your loving eyes are upon me. You do not give up
on me. I praise you for your love!

How do you know God loves you?

Prized Creation

"If God so clothes the grass of the field, which today is, and tomorrow is thrown into the oven, will He not much more clothe you, O you of little faith?"

MATTHEW 6:30 NKJV

Have you ever been to a botanical garden or conservatory? What about an aquarium? Both of these places shout out God's creativity and attention to detail. The variety of flowers on earth and the fish in the sea is astounding. The colorful and vivid designs can inspire awe and wonder in young and old alike. Knowing that God put so much detail into a flower in the forest or a fish in the sea that may never be seen is mind blowing. God must surely love his creation!

Do you know that you are God's most prized creation? When God created people, he said it was very good, not only good. Dwell in this knowledge today. Believe that you are a beloved work of art and one that God takes pride in.

Creator God, you make things beautiful! You care about your creation. Thank you that I am one of your very best works of art. Help me to live in that knowledge today!

"If God cares so wonderfully for flowers that are here today and gone tomorrow, won't he more surely care for you, O men of little faith?"

MATTHEW 6:30 TLB

God cares for you! You do know that, don't you? Think back to those flowers and fish from this morning. Do you ever picture them worried or concerned, wondering if the creator has forgotten about them? It is kind of a funny picture: a fish wringing his fins while he looks for a new place to swim or a flower straining to look for the next drop of rain to come its way. Obviously, fish and flowers can't reason the way we do and, therefore, are immune to such worry. But the point still stands. God tends to them, gives them their beauty, and supplies their need for their appointed time.

God cares for you! He cares more for his people than all of his other creations. Tonight, trust that care. Ask for and rest in his provision. Give your concerns to God rather than worrying and wringing your hands.

Loving God, sometimes I am prone to worry. Give me confidence in your care for me. Remind me that I am more valuable to you than all the flowers in the world.

How does it feel knowing you are God's prized creation?

Pay Attention

My children, listen to what your father teaches you.
Pay attention, and you will have understanding.
What I am teaching you is good, so remember it all.

PROVERBS 4:1–2 GNT

It is hard to take advice from others sometimes. We want
to have it all figured out on our own. And, at certain stages
in life, advice from a well-meaning parent feels the least
welcome of all. Yet God knows the value of wisdom that
comes from age, experience, and a place of love. The writer
of this Proverb (likely Solomon) understood that he loved his
children and had good things to share with them. He wanted
his wisdom to benefit them.

Ultimately, this verse points to God's instructions for you,
through the Bible. He wants you to lean into his word,
understand it and live it. God's Word for you is good. It is life
giving. Wake up and pay attention to it today.

God, you have given me your Word because it is good! Help me
to understand your Word and how it applies to my life. Let me
remember your wisdom today.

Listen, children, to a father's instruction, and be attentive,
that you may gain insight;
for I give you good precepts:
do not forsake my teaching.

PROVERBS 4:1-2 NRSV

Have you ever found yourself nodding and saying, "Uh huh, yep" when you listened to a story or advice from someone, but then realized that you don't know what they said. You went through the motions of listening, without actually paying attention. Afterwards, you hope you didn't miss anything important or offend the person you were talking with. You are not alone!

That can also happen with reading God's Word and even this devotional! You can go through the motions of reading without actually letting the words sink in for understanding or revelation from God. Wake up and pay attention! Listen to what God is saying to you through his Word. Gain insight on how to live and follow through. You can do it!

Father God, I do not always do a good job paying attention. I get distracted and lost in my thoughts. Focus my heart and mind to hear you and your words today.

When do you have a hard time paying attention?

Shine

The way of the righteous is like the first gleam of dawn,
which shines ever brighter until the full light of day.

PROVERBS 4:18 NLT

Picture in your mind, the sweet image of dawn breaking over the horizon. It starts without announcement in quiet anticipation. Color then streams across the skyline before the sun itself even makes an appearance. The top of the sun begins to push above the earth, bringing increasing brightness until finally, the full sun has blazed its way above the horizon. Dawn breaks from stillness to brilliance in matters of minutes. And the earth goes from darkness to light.

God's Word says the way of the righteous is like this. The longer you walk with Jesus and sit in his radiance, the brighter you will become. From stillness to brilliance you will shine. And, you will shine light to the world around you, bringing darkness into light. Let the dawn break for you, in you and through you today.

Father, the dawn brings light to this world. You are the light of the world. Shine bright for everyone to see and let your light shine brightly through me.

If the path of the just is like the shining sun,
That shines ever brighter unto the perfect day.

PROVERBS 4:18 NKJV

You are glowing! Maybe you are glowing with just a little spark or a little ember. Maybe you are full on mid-day sun, shining with brilliance. The fact that you are seeking out God by way of this devotional means that you are starting on, or well onto, the path of right-living with Jesus. Soak up that "Sonshine" for a moment and allow yourself to glow.

The cool thing is, the more you walk the way with Jesus, the brighter you will shine. You have a lot of glowing to do! Even as time begins to fade in the dusk of your days, as a Jesus follower you will continue to shine. Praise God that he keeps you in his light so that you can reflect it to a world that needs you! Shine on!

Son of God, you shine with brilliance! Thank you for shining your face on me. I want to share your light with others. Help me to grow and glow in your way today!

Where does God want you to shine?

Blessed

"The Lord bless you and keep you;
The Lord make his face shine upon you,
And be gracious to you;
The Lord lift up His countenance upon you,
And give you peace."

NUMBERS 6:24-26 NKJV

As you wake this morning, do not doubt for a minute that the Lord wants to bless you! Allow this ancient blessing, passed from Lord to Moses, to speak to you in a new way today. Read through it again, but this time, be sure to pause after each line and reflect on the meaning. Questions or statements are provided after each line to prompt your reflection:

"The Lord bless you and keep you;
(How has God blessed you or cared for you recently?)
The Lord make his face shine upon you,
(Stop and sense God smiling on you. Feel the warmth of his love.)
And be gracious to you;
(How has God been gracious to you? Accept his grace.)
The Lord lift up His countenance upon you,
(Know that God looks on you and supports you.)
And give you peace."
(Accept and rest in his peace.)

Lord, thank you for blessing me. Let me accept your love, grace, support, and peace.

"The Lord bless you, and keep you [protect you, sustain you, and guard you];
The Lord make His face shine upon you [with favor],
And be gracious to you [surrounding you with lovingkindness];
The Lord lift up His countenance (face) upon you [with divine approval],
And give you peace [a tranquil heart and life]."

NUMBERS 6:24-26 AMP

There is something to be said about tradition. If you grew up in the church, this ancient blessing—in one version or the other—is likely something you know. Tradition has kept this blessing alive and well and for good reason. God's people need to be reminded that he is for them. You need to be reminded that God loves you and wants the best for you. This blessing is a great tradition!

At the same time, familiar words can be taken for granted and rushed over. Hopefully, this morning, you took time to slow down and reflect on these words. As you end your day, read this blessing once more soaking in the Amplified Bible's added meaning. Rest in God's benediction over you.

Dear God, your words stand the test of time. Thank you that you still encourage your children today through this blessing. I am blessed.

What is your favorite part of this blessing?

I Am

God said to Moses, "I Am Who I Am. This is what you are to say to the Israelites: 'I Am has sent me to you.'"

EXODUS 3:14 NIV

How many names do you have? Likely you have, at minimum, a first, middle, and last name. How about nicknames or pet names given by friends or loved ones? What do each of these names mean to you?

God has lots of different names for himself in the Bible. Some examples are Elohim, Adonai, El Roi, and Yahweh. Perhaps God's strongest name—a name filled with confidence and truth about who he is—is one he calls himself in Exodus 3:14: I Am. I Am Who I Am. This name sets God apart as THE ONE. The one who was and is to come. The one who really needs no introduction. What an awesome name!

Today, may I Am bring you peace. May I Am hold you close. May I Am remind you that you are loved. And may I Am send you into your day with strength and power.

Dear Great I Am, your name is powerful. It is filled with strength. It leaves no doubt about who you are.

God said to Moses, "I Am Who I Am"; and He said, "You shall say this to the Israelites, 'I Am has sent me to you.'"

EXODUS 3:14 AMP

The Amplified Bible is a version of the Bible that sometimes uses explanations or clarifying words within the text or verses to amplify the meaning so that the reader understands what the verse is really saying. Notice in the Amplified version above, there is no additional amplification of the name God calls himself. God's name I Am who I Am does not require anything added to it. It stands alone. Unlike Popeye saying "I yam what I yam, and that's all that I yam" that leaves you wondering what is missing, God's name is I Am who I Am. He doesn't need to anything to it. His name alone is everything.

Hopefully, this name I Am gives you great confidence in the one to whom you belong. Trust I Am is all that you need. He alone is everything.

Dear God, you are everything. Give me confidence to trust in you alone. I praise you for who you are!

What name do you have that means the most to you?

Forgiveness

Love prospers when a fault is forgiven
but dwelling on it separates close friends.

PROVERBS 17:9 NLT

Doesn't it stink when a fault or even an honest mistake interrupts a relationship? Friendships can be shaken off course when one or the other causes hurt or frustration. A spouse may hurt the other without even realizing it, creating all sorts of chaos. But guess what? When a fault or hurt is forgiven, love can grow! Something that was dark can be returned to light. Joy in relationship can be wholly restored.

This is what Jesus is all about. He died on the cross to forgive all the mistakes that we have made. He does not dwell on our sins. He casts them aside and says come to me, friend. Is there something you need God to forgive you for? Do you need to seek forgiveness from a friend? Is there a friend who need your forgiveness? Ask God to guide you in restoring relationships today. Let love prosper as a result!

Thank you, Jesus, that you are all about forgiveness. I know I have hurt you and others. Forgive me. Help me to forgive those who have hurt me. Let love prosper in my relationships.

One who forgives an affront fosters friendship,
but one who dwells on disputes will alienate a friend.

PROVERBS 17:9 NRSV

Another day is nearly done. Phew! It would not be surprising if somewhere along the line, someone offended you today. What are you going to do about it? You can sit here and dwell on it, trying to figure out how to get back at them. That doesn't sound good, does it? Or you could take a step in the direction of forgiveness. You can do it!

As you seek to forgive someone, ask God to show you why you were hurt and what you can do about it. Decide if you need to talk to the person or not. Maybe being hurt was more about you than them. Trust that God's Word is true and that forgiveness is a good step to take. Pray for the person who hurt you and pray for yourself. Praise God that he has forgiven you in all of your mistakes. Ask him to help you move forward in forgiveness.

I need you, Lord, to help me forgive. Give me understanding and wisdom. Open my eyes and my heart to forgiveness.

Who do you need to forgive today?

Together

Then those who gladly received his word were baptized; and that day about three thousand souls were added to them. And they continued steadfastly in the apostles' doctrine and fellowship, in the breaking of bread, and in prayers.

ACTS 2:41-42 NKJV

God loves it when we do life with one another as many in the early church did. The early church grew like wildfire as Jesus's immediate followers went out and shared his message with others. After one of Peter's sermons, three thousand people accepted the truth about Jesus and committed to following him. Wow! Can you imagine that?

This movement of three thousand may have been the birthplace of church potluck dinners as we know it today! This unity and commitment to one another could have been part of the reason people came to believe in Christ. Life lived together is a beautiful thing. When it is done in Jesus's name, with prayers backing it up, it becomes even more precious! Praise God that his plan includes his people doing life together.

God, thank you that you want us to do life well with other believers. Help me to connect to the local church body more. I want to live in unity with others!

Those who believed what Peter said were baptized and added to the church that day—about 3,000 in all. All the believers devoted themselves to the apostles' teaching, and to fellowship, and to sharing in meals (including the Lord's Supper), and to prayer.

ACTS 2:41-42 NLT

What would it be like today to hear a message so Spirit filled that 3,000 people would decide to follow Jesus all in one day? Isn't that amazing? Equally amazing was the commitment of these new believers. It says all of the believers devoted themselves to teaching, fellowship, sharing meals, and to prayer. Imagine what our churches would be like if church members were "all in" like this!

God's plan from the start of time was unity with and between his people. Throughout his story, God continually connected himself with those who loved him. And, he encouraged relationship between those who loved him. As you end your day, ask God to show you what steps you can take to be more united with him and with his people.

Lord, show me how to devote myself to you and to caring for other believers. I know that together is better. Help me get closer to a place of unity.

How does unity help the church?

Shield of Love

You bless the godly, O Lord;
you surround them with your shield of love.

PSALM 5:12 NLT

What is your favorite all time superhero weapon or tool?
Wonder Woman's invisible plane is pretty cool, though
slightly confusing. Superman's heat vision would definitely
come in handy when camping. And, Spiderman's webs are
undeniably awesome!

The images of superheroes may come to mind when thinking
on Psalm 5:12. The Lord has a super cool tool in his "shield of
love." Putting on your best Sunday School imagination, how
would this shield look? When and how would it be used? How
would God know you need it? It is fun to imagine. In reality,
God's shield of love is an everyday part of his protection
plan for us. When we walk with the Lord, his love is always
available to us. As you go on your way today, imagine that you
have a physical shield of love around you. What difference
might it make?

Lord, you are better than any superhero I could imagine. Thank
you for the shield of love that you surround me with. Help me to
use your love well today.

You, O Lord, will bless the righteous;
With favor You will surround him as with a shield.

PSALM 5:12 NKJV

What was it like walking around with your shield of love today? Did you remember that you were surrounded by God's love? Tell God any thoughts that you have about it.

God's love is really good, isn't it? He loved the world so much that he sent Jesus to the cross. That in itself is unimaginable love. Yet this verse in Psalms suggests that his love for godly and righteous is unique. He will bless the righteous and surround them with love and favor. Like a good father, he wants to protect and bless those that belong to him. Tell God how much you love him today. Ask him to show you how to love him more and walk a path of righteousness. Then, rest confidently in his favor and love, knowing that he blesses you.

O Lord, your love is so good. You loved the world so much that you sent Jesus into it for all humanity. Thank you for this love. Help me to walk more in line with the godly way and protect me with your favor and love.

What does God's shield of love look like to you?

You Can Do It

I can do all things through him who strengthens me.

PHILIPPIANS 4:13 ESV

Paul, the writer of Philippians, never pretended that life was perfect. He talked about the thorn in his flesh, being hungry, being beaten, and being shipwrecked. And yet, he found a way to be content and find joy in all circumstances. He knew he could get through anything that he needed to face. The secret to success was Jesus.

What are you facing today? Is there anything that you are nervous about or discouraged by? None of it will surprise Jesus. Tell him what you are facing and how you are feeling. He will listen and walk through it with you. The challenges may not be taken away from you, but you will not be alone to face them. You can make it through anything! Believe this fact today.

Jesus, you know that my life is not perfect. There are challenges that I am facing today. I believe that I can make it through anything with you on my side. Please walk with me and make yourself known.

I can do all things through Christ, because he gives me strength.
PHILIPPIANS 4:13 NCV

You did it! You made it through the day and are still breathing. God did not leave you alone for one minute of it. There may have been obstacles, but you made your way around them. Rejoice in that this evening!

As you begin to rest for the evening, realize that God can give you strength and power in all of your circumstances. No doubt there have been times when you pulled through something and wondered how you made it. Could that have been strength or power from Jesus? Grow in your confidence of his strength. Trust that you really can do all things through Jesus. As you end your day, let God know where you still need his power. He is there for you!

Jesus, I am ready to rest in you. You saw me through another day and I am thankful for that! Help me to understand more how your strength and power are available to me. All I need to do is ask.

Where do you need God's power to show up this week?

What a Name

Unto us a child is born,
unto us a son is given,
and the government shall be upon his shoulder.
And his name shall be called
Wonderful Counselor, Mighty God,
Eternal Father, Prince of Peace.

ISAIAH 9:6 MEV

Naming a baby is a big deal! Some parents wait to name a child until they can see what characteristics the newborn displays. Some parents pick out names far in advance of the child's arrival. Names can be chosen based on how they sound, what they mean, or a combination thereof. Some parents even choose a name in hopes of what their child will become.

Isaiah prophesied long before Jesus came about the name he would have. There was no waiting around for the character of Jesus to be revealed. Though, in reality, Isaiah already knew the characteristics of Jesus because of how God showed up in the Old Testament. Isaiah predicted the qualities of Jesus in expectation of what he would be to the world: a wonderful counselor, a mighty God, an eternal father, and a prince of peace. What a name was given to Jesus! Reflect on his name as you start your day.

Jesus, you have the best names ever! They fit you perfectly. Thank you for being my counselor, God, father, and prince of peace!

A child is born to us!
A son is given to us!
And he will be our ruler.
He will be called, "Wonderful Counselor,"
"Mighty God," "Eternal Father,"
"Prince of Peace."

ISAIAH 9:6 GNT

The book of Isaiah is full of prophesies about the coming king Jesus. This verse in particular is a call to remember who the Christ child would become. Read through verse 9 again and focus on the names prophesied for Jesus. What do each of those names mean to you?

Wonderful Counselor: How does Jesus listen to you and counsel you day to day?
Mighty God: Do you see Jesus as strong and powerful? Do you recognize him as God?
Eternal Father: What fatherly qualities does Jesus have? Do you trust him as a daddy?
Prince of Peace: Does Jesus rule in your life as a bringer of peace?

As you close your day, remember that Isaiah's words about Jesus were true. Let these truths rest in your heart and mind tonight.

Jesus, thank you for coming into a world that needed you. I love you!

Which of these names for Jesus are most meaningful to you?

Stand and See

"Don't be afraid. Stand firm and see the Lord's salvation that he will accomplish for you today. The Lord will fight for you, and you must be quiet."

EXODUS 14:13-14 CSB

Fear gripped peoples' hearts. Pharaoh's vast army of Egypt was chasing them. Had they made a big mistake in leaving? They saw no answers to their problems. They cried out to God, but their cries were more like complaints than prayers of faith.

Moses' words were more than a pep talk or motivational speech. The danger threatening them was real, but the deliverance they were about to see was also real. God was about to do something soon that would be visible and would solve their problem. All they had to do was trust and not fear.

Fears subside when we gain a new vision of God and what he is doing in the world. We need to pay attention and see God's actions around us. Watch today for the activity of God in your life. He is here, and he is here for you.

Almighty God, you are my deliverer. I know you are powerful and can do great things in my life. I ask that you would show me your salvation in a fresh way

"Fear not, stand firm, and see the salvation of the Lord, which he will work for you today. The Lord will fight for you, and you have only to be silent."

EXODUS 14:13-14 ESV

Two times in these verses, we read the phrase "for you." The clear witness of God is that he is for his people. Think of what it would be like to have almighty God there for you? Sometimes we feel like we are all alone in our struggles. But here we read of a God who is there and who actively intervenes, even fights for his people!

What did the people have to do to gain God's deliverance? The action required by the people was minimal and doable. They had only to stand and be silent. First, they needed to stand firm and not run away. Next, they needed to be silent and not complain or worry. Those two actions can be harder than they seem, but demonstrate we trust the Lord and have given him control over our problems.

How has God been there for you in the past? Praise erupts, unhindered, when we see God work in our lives.

Father, you have been there for me in the past and I can trust you to be there for me now. I give to you my concerns tonight. Help me to stand firm and quietly wait for the answers you will bring.

What could happen in my life this year if I stand and watch the Lord fight for me?

Strength in Victory

"The Lord is my strength and my song;
He has become my salvation.
This is my God, and I will praise Him,
my father's God, and I will exalt Him."

EXODUS 15:2 HCSB

A victory after a long struggle leaves a sweet taste. Soon we forget the struggle and exult in the victory. This verse is part of a song Moses and the children of Israel sang. The struggle behind this song was Israel's deliverance from Egypt, after a long struggle of being slaves to now being delivered, from being chased to being free, from facing certain death to being fully alive. God had miraculously opened a sea for them to walk through, then closed the sea, drowning Pharaoh's ferocious army behind them. They were free!

But this was a new feeling. They had felt weakness and fear. All their lives they had been suppressed, held down. But now everything changed. They went from being powerless, to victorious. Now the Lord was their strength and confidence.

Today you have the same Lord. If he is your strength, he will also be your salvation and victory.

Father, I admit that sometimes my life feels like a long struggle. But today my confidence is in you. You are my God and I will praise you.

"The Lord is my strength and song,
And He has become my salvation;
He is my God, and I will praise Him;
My father's God, and I will exalt Him."

EXODUS 15:2 NKJV

What would it be like to have God as your strength? Sure, we have our own sources of strength. But at some point, our own sources of strength can become exhausted. They may not always be there for us.

The children of Israel watched God do something incredible that they would never forget. When they came to the end of their own resources, they stepped into God's resources as their strength. God's resources never run out. He has than enough strength for any struggle we face.

How do we know the Lord as our strength? Like Israel, we need to admit our weakness before him. We need to ask him to apply his answers to our point of need. Then we need to step out— like Israel did in crossing the sea—and trust him. The God who does not change is there to offer his strength for you today. And when he is our strength, our heart will want to sing.

Father, be my strength tonight. You know my point of need. I admit there are times when my own strength runs out. I will trust you.

What would it look like to have God as my strength?

In His Presence

"My Presence will go with you, and I will give you rest.."

EXODUS 33:14, NIV

Moses was given a job that seemed overwhelming. Leading as many as two million people through an unforgiving wilderness, nomad land was filled with problems. How would there be enough food and water? What about medical support? How would he protect them if enemies attacked? How would he settle conflicts when people didn't get along with one another?

Ever since sin and conflict entered the world, people everywhere have sought for peace. There is something within that longs for a better life. We notice it when we find ourselves saying, "My life will be good when…" or "If I can just get through this difficulty, or reach this goal, or achieve this milestone then my life will be good." Our natural goals are good but can leave us in a constant state of restlessness.

God doesn't offer a life without stress or problems. However, God does offer to go through life with you and give you rest. Your Creator knows just what you need. And he promises to go with you today.

God, at times my life feels overwhelming. Today I claim by faith your presence with me. I need your rest. Thanks for being a loving Father who gives me just what I need.

"My presence will go with you, and I will give you rest."

EXODUS 33:14, NRSV

Moses understood what was important. He did not want to move through life unless God went with him. At that time, the Lord used to speak to Moses face to face, just like a person speaks with a friend (Ex. 33:11). Once he knew the presence of the Lord, he was spoiled for life on his own.

You were made for rest. Sabbath rest was designed by God as the weekly reward for six days of work. But rest is more than absence from work. If rest and recreation becomes our goal, life becomes unsatisfying. Too long of a summer vacation leaves a child (and parents) restless. People who retire without new things to do can become restless and their health may decline. But true rest—the kind you were designed for—is the culmination of knowing God's presence is with you. God's presence—even during a busy time in life—refreshes and restores.

As you finish this day, seek his presence. There you are promised perfect rest.

Father, thank you for the peace and rest you give me. But most of all, Lord, draw me into your presence. Restore my soul as I rest in you.

Am I experiencing the peace of God in my life?

Before You and for You

*"The Lord your God who goes before you will fight for you Himself,
just as He did for you in Egypt before your [very] eyes."*

DEUTERONOMY 1:30 AMP

Few of us would pick a fight, fights are largely to be avoided.
As we grow older we learn to use words not fists, and to give
more space for others to disagree. But some fights come to
us. They are unavoidable. Fights may come in the form of an
unexpected medical diagnosis, the loss of a job, the dashing
of a dream. The fight may not be with another person, but the
struggle is just as real.

Moses was preparing the people of Israel to prepare to enter
the Promised Land. Fights loomed ahead for them. The
people they would face would be bigger and taller, and their
cities would be large and fortified, as the critics complained.
But no foe they would face would be a match for the living
God.

God still fights for his own today. How does he do this? He
goes before us. God is eternal so he knows the future. He
knows what tomorrow will bring. He is present in the future
to work for our good.

*Father, you know the fights in my life today. You know the
struggles I'm facing. I thank you that you go before me into this
day and that I do not go alone.*

"The Lord your God who goes before you will himself fight on your behalf, just as he did for you in Egypt before your eyes."

DEUTERONOMY 1:30 NASB

God does real things in a real world for real people today. How can we be sure of this?

The promises of God are not locked into time, dated in history and not to be repeated again. The promises of God are rooted in his character and nature which do not change, so God still acts the same way for his people today. God still goes before his people and fights for us today.

Moses' reminded the people, "just as he did for you in Egypt before your eyes." Moses knew that God's deliverance must be seen and remembered. God's deliverance must be observed, because too many miss what he is doing. God's deliverance must be remembered, because too often we forget what he has done for us in the past. But the stories are there. We have a past with God in that we've known him to go before us and be for us. And if your God is with you, you can be assured there are more victories in your future.

God, I thank you tonight that you have already gone before me into tomorrow. Where would I be without your protection and guidance? I rest in your love tonight.

What victories does God have ahead for you this year?

Seeking Him

From there, you will search for the Lord your God, and you will
find Him when you seek Him with all your heart and all your soul.

DEUTERONOMY 4:29 HCSB

Sin is real, and sin's most profound effect is to put distance
between us and the One who created us. That distance causes
us to feel loneliness, fear, shame, confusion, uncertainty and
even a sense of being unloved.

When Adam and Eve were first created, the Bible tells us that
they enjoyed daily walks in the garden where they were able
to speak without distance. Their communication was out of
love without a hint of shame or fear. But after their sin, there
was distance. God's first question to them was, "Where are
you?" God knew their location, but wanted them to be aware
they were now lost and separated from him.

God wants to be found again. But many of the habits and voices
in our life can prevent us from seeking him. He wants us to
seek him with all of our being. What does that look like for you
today? What can you do to seek and enjoy your God today?

Father, I thank you that you are not a God who is hidden, but one
who wants to be found. Draw me to yourself today. May I seek you
with a freshness and with all of my being.

From there you will seek the Lord your God, and you will find Him if you search for Him with all your heart and all your soul.

DEUTERONOMY 4:29 NASB

As Moses prepared the people of Israel to enter the Promised Land, he warned them of the dangers ahead. The biggest dangers were not in the foes they would face, but in their own disobedient heart. Israel was warned against pursuing false gods, objects made by men to substitute for the real God. But as long as they obeyed the Lord, they would find he was more than enough for any battle ahead.

We serve a God who is present and able to do all that we need. The Lord doesn't hide from us, but our sins and wrong ideas can prevent us from seeing him. What Moses observed is true today. God can be found and God wants to be active in our lives. But we must seek him with all of our desire, all of ourselves. We will not know intimacy with God through half-hearted devotion. But the God who wants to be found is waiting again. And finding him brings deep satisfaction.

Father God, you are the highest pursuit of my life! I thank you that my life is not an endless searching without finding. I thank you that you are there to be found. And knowing you is my greatest joy.

As you seek after God right now, what does he want you to find?

He Never Fails

The Lord your God is a compassionate God; He will not fail you nor destroy you nor forget the covenant with your fathers which He swore to them.

DEUTERONOMY 4:31 NASB

As the people of Israel prepared to enter into the Promised Land and the good life God promised, they were reminded of the God who was leading them.

First, any movement into our future must begin with remembering God and his nature. He is compassionate. He always displays a loving nature that comes alongside us and understands our needs.

Second, beyond his nature we must remember God's actions. There are three important actions God is known for. He will not fail you. He is utterly reliable and can always be counted upon. Next, he will not destroy you. He is unlike the capricious gods conjured up by false religions. God works for our good, not our harm. Finally, this God of ours does not forget us. He doesn't forget you or his promises to you, just like he did not forget those who followed him before you.

Almighty God, where would I be without your compassion to me? What would I do without your gracious actions on my behalf? I rejoice and remember that you are the God who never fails.

The Lord your God is a merciful God. He will not leave you or destroy you or forget the covenant with your fathers that he swore to them.

DEUTERONOMY 4:31 ESV

Our God is a compassionate and merciful God. Out of his love he never leaves us, he doesn't harm us and he never forgets us. The key that unlocks this truth is that he is personal and he is known. This God is the Lord your God. And nothing can diminish that personal allegiance between you and him.

The people of Israel found this to be true. God did so many things in their past. The fact that they were alive and free demonstrated that their merciful God was active among them. But there were more victories in their future. The one who had not left them, nor harmed them, nor forgotten them would continue to do so.

This personal, compassionate, active God has promised many things to you in his word. The promises are born out of his nature, so they never change. Think of three ways God has shown his mercy to you this year. You can be sure he will never fail you in the year ahead.

Heavenly Father, you are faithful to me. I commit myself anew to you as I sleep tonight, knowing your mercies will continue for me tomorrow.

What promise are you trusting God for tonight?

Firmly Planted

He shall be like a tree
Planted by the rivers of water,
That brings forth its fruit in its season,
Whose leaf also shall not wither;
And whatever he does shall prosper.

PSALM 1:3 NKJV

Life can become messy. Things happen that can turn our lives upside down. The world can feel like a dangerous place.

The writer of this Psalm wrote of the difference that following God makes. Each of four descriptive phrases shows what God does for us during the troubles of life. First, he plants us firmly by streams of water. We are purposely placed with full access to people and resources that give us life and sustain us. Second, we are made fruitful to bless others. The touch of God on our life is evident and is an opportunity to reach out to others in need. Third, our leaf does not wither. Dry times in life do not discourage or destroy us. Finally, he prospers us. This is not limited to financial prosperity, but is deeper — truly restoring us, and wider — extending out into all aspects of our lives. When the storms of life threaten, the foundation and blessing of God is most clearly seen.

Father, I thank you for planting me firmly by that which gives me life. Thank you for the people and resources you've blessed me with. Thank you for being my living water that daily restores my soul.

That person is like a tree planted by streams of water,
which yields its fruit in season
and whose leaf does not wither—
whatever they do prospers.

PSALM 1:3 NIV

Water is essential to life. The land where the Psalmist wrote could be dry, water was scarce. Of all the major cities in the world today, Jerusalem is rare in that it is not near any natural river or ocean. It was not until King Hezekiah's day, that reservoirs were built to store water so there was plenty. When God sent rains, even the desert would blossom and produce bountiful flowers, fruit and other produce.

The difference is the water. Water brought life and meant life. When we delight in the Lord and his word, we are given the life-giving water we need to flourish. Jesus would later reveal to the Samaritan woman at the well (John 4:10) that he has living water to give to any who will ask him.

Father, I thank you for the life you have given me. Remind me again of what you've done for me. You've planted me, you've made me fruitful, you've restored me, and you bring your blessing to my life in rich ways. Thank you for your firm foundation.

Have I found my delight in the Lord and his Word today?

Help, Lord

But you, Lord, tell them, "I will do something!
The poor are mistreated and helpless people moan.
I'll rescue all who suffer."

PSALM 12:5 CEV

As you see the news in the world this week, does it seem like evil people and wrong ideas dominate? This was exactly David's experience as he wrote this Psalm. How then do we respond when each day we are reminded that much evil exists and many bad things are happening?

First, we are to be aware of the problems in the world around us. Christians are not to turn away from them, or live in blissful ignorance. Second, we can be released from the burden of fixing the world on our own. Truly Christians should train and be involved in influencing society for good, but the God who made the world is the God who can fix the world, not we ourselves. Third, we go to God with our sadness (as David did), and leave it with him to revenge the evil.

Those of us who have grieved deeply over the evil of this world will rejoice most greatly when we see our Lord's deliverance. And it will come!

As I hear the news today, Lord, I'm reminded of the evil in human hearts around me. Remind me again of your lovingkindness, and that a time is coming when you will arise and rescue those who suffer.

"Because of the devastation of the afflicted,
because of the groaning of the needy,
now I will arise," says the Lord;
"I will set him in the safety for which he longs."

PSALM 12:5 NASB

As David begins this Psalm, his first words are, "Help,
Lord." David felt the injustice that was around him. Before
he was king, he was a young, humble shepherd boy that his
older brothers didn't appreciate. As a young man, he had
a powerful king on the hunt for his life. As a king, he later
had a unique vantage point to see the suffering of those in
his nation, but also to do something about it. Ultimately, he
knew the real hope was to be found in the God who is both
compassionate and mighty to save.

We must be careful not to become calloused to the suffering
of people around us. We have a God who cares and gets
involved in the sufferings of the afflicted. He promises to
provide the safety we long for. We must regularly cry out to
God in prayer for the needs of those around us.

We follow our God's example and reach out to the afflicted in
his power and in his name.

I thank you, God, that you care about the world I live in. You care
about the afflicted and the needy, about the mistreated and the
helpless. Help me to care as well.

God Answers

*I sought the Lord, and He answered me
and delivered me from all my fears.*

PSALM 34:4 HCSB

People are designed with a built-in sense of curiosity. As a small child, you began to ask "why?" When you encountered a problem, you wanted to solve it. As we grow older, we learn to seek out what we need and want. We find a friend, a job, a place to live.

Sometimes we continue to seek, but come away unsatisfied. As a child, we longed to be older and bigger. Maybe we couldn't wait to drive or finish high school, or the next educational level. Maybe we thought life would be fulfilled when we got married, or had a baby, or when the kids grew older, or when the mortgage is paid off, or when we retire. There is within us a seeking mode. But often we keep pushing back the finish line to our goals. We come to realize that accumulating things and accomplishing goals do not always satisfy our seeking heart.

How different it is to those who seek the Lord. When we seek him rather than things, we gain answers. When he is our life-long pursuit, we are delivered.

Father, it is you alone that I seek today. I know that I am satisfied in you and you are worth seeking. Help me to remember that throughout this day.

*I sought the Lord, and he answered me
and rescued me from all my fears.*

PSALM 34:4 CSB

Fear is one of the great motivators in life. Sometimes our fears have little basis. Fear can drive people to make decisions that may not be wise. Sometimes our fears are very real, signaling real danger. Fear can wake us up to a situation we realize must be addressed.

David knew fear. This psalm was written after he fled for his life from King Saul. But his fear drove him to another enemy, Abimelech. David knew he was trapped, so he acted like a madman in front of Abimelech. Abimelech considered him harmless, and a nuisance so he left David alone. David was filled with continuous praise as he realized that God had delivered him from two different enemies who would have killed him.

Fear is natural. But all of our fears need to be taken before God. When we seek him with our fears, we are promised he will answer and rescue us from them. Even fear cowers before Almighty God.

Powerful God, you alone are the answer to my fears. I lay them at your feet. Give me rest in your presence and in your deliverance.

What fears do I need God to rescue me from?

God's Goodness

Oh, taste and see that the Lord is good!
Blessed is the man who takes refuge in him!

PSALM 34:8 ESV

Finding help from our troubles can spark our praise and thanksgiving to God.

David wrote this Psalm after being delivered from his enemies. The title reminds us of the story told in I Samuel 21 where David was under attack from King Saul who wanted to kill David. Saul's son, Jonathan, was David's dear friend and hadn't believed his father would kill David. But when he discovered it was true, he signaled David to flee for his life. As Saul pursued David, David fled into the hands of another enemy, Abimelech, King of Gath. To avoid trouble, David acted like he was insane. The king of Gath was disgusted and left David alone. David's life was spared and he knew it was a direct answer from God who delivered him.

There are times when we stop and reflect on all God has done for us. He is good and has done good things for us. He has clearly been our refuge, our secure place. What are you thankful for today?

Father, I thank you for your goodness in my life. Remind me of the many ways you have shown your love around me. I take comfort in knowing you are a good God.

O taste and see that the Lord is good;
How blessed is the man who takes refuge in Him!

PSALM 34:8 NASB

We remember how good God is as we "open our mouths and taste" and when we "open our eyes and see." Our faith becomes stale when we fail to pay attention to all God is doing. Beyond observing what God has done, the Psalmist here tugs at our sleeves and calls us to get involved in what he is doing. Taste for yourselves!

Once, there was someone on a cruise who had a particular dessert he couldn't get enough of. In fact, he ordered it seven nights in a row! But, five years later, that fleeting dessert has no real value. He may have a distant memory of its taste, but he no longer has satisfaction from it.

Faith can be like that. We may have tasted God in the past, we may have memories of what he did at one point in our lives. But fulfilling satisfaction in God comes by tasting of his goodness every day.

Lord, I want to do more than remember your goodness in my life in the past. That's a good start, and I'm grateful for past answers to prayer. But now I need to taste again. Allow me to experience your goodness in a fresh way today.

Are you ready to run to him again?

Satisfaction

O fear the Lord, you His saints;
For to those who fear Him there is no want.
The young lions do lack and suffer hunger;
But they who seek the Lord shall not be in want of any good thing.

PSALM 34:9-10 NASB

What brings you satisfaction? For David who wrote this Psalm, finding the Lord God is the chief goal that brought the highest level of satisfaction to the human heart. In these verses, David reveals two actions we must take to be truly satisfied.

First, we must fear God. This isn't the paralyzing terror David was delivered from in Psalm 34:4. This is a reverence fueled by awe, as we recognize God's greatness and holiness. Once we are aware of him, all else pales in comparison.

Second, we must seek him. Seeking God is no half-hearted task that we can put at the end of our to-do lists. Jesus reminds us that we have to love the Lord God with all heart, soul, mind and strength (Mark 12:30). This has been called the Great Commandment, because it is primary in following Jesus.

Father, I thank you for the satisfaction I have in following you.
You fill the deepest desires of my heart.

Fear the Lord, you his holy people,
for those who fear him lack nothing.
The lions may grow weak and hungry,
but those who seek the Lord lack no good thing.

PSALM 34:9-10 NIV

As David wrote these words, he expressed a deep satisfaction for the action of God in his life. David feared the Lord, reverencing God above everything else. David also sought the Lord. In Scripture, we are reminded that seeking the Lord must be with all that we have: all of our heart, our soul, out mind, and our strength. Seeking the Lord is a life-long pursuit that becomes our primary focus.

There are great rewards for those who find their satisfaction in the Lord. The strongest of the animal kingdom will eventually lose what they are known for: strong running and victorious hunting. But those who seek the Lord will not weaken or grow hungry. They will continually be replenished with good things.

What's in your heart today? Are you satisfied in him?

Father God, replenish my supply tonight. I often grow tired and
weak. I need your strength. I need your filling in my life. I am
satisfied in you and what you give me.

What do you need from God tonight? Find your satisfaction in him.

Present Help

God is our protection and our strength.
He always helps in times of trouble.

PSALM 46:1 NCV

The direction of our focus makes all the difference when trouble comes. We can focus on our problems, for which there are many. If we do this, we'll always have much to think about, since our problems never run out. But our joy will surely be diminished. Or we can set our thoughts on God who can fight for us and deliver us from our problems. This is what the Psalmists recommend.

What do we know about God in this verse? We see that he is an unchanging refuge. He never changes who he is. He always is loving, merciful, powerful, just and holy. God is never fickle; he never changes his heart about us. As you are faced with troubles today, remember the God who is present and ready to help.

Father, thank you for the many times you have protected me and been strong when I felt weak. Help me to remember today your help that is available to me. In Jesus' name.

God is our mighty fortress,
always ready to help
in times of trouble.

PSALM 46:1 CEV

Trouble comes to everyone in life. The direction of our focus makes a difference when trouble comes. If we focus on God we realize he is the fortress to protect us against the storms of life. This fortress or refuge is always there for us and does not change.

As you finish the day, are there troubles on your mind? Are you burdened for someone you love, someone you spoke with today, or something you witnessed? The troubles the Psalmist writes of literally refer to the tight spots, the jams we find ourselves in. If we run to anyone or anything else, we may be disappointed. But the Almighty God wants to be you refuge. He is stronger than any problem you have and always present when you find yourself in the tight places of life. Go to God as your mighty fortress.

Father God, I thank you that you are my mighty fortress, my refuge in times of storm. I thank you that you are there for me right now, and that no matter what tight place I find myself in, I can run to you for help.

In what ways has God been my mighty fortress this year?

Our Resource

God is in the midst of her; she shall not be moved;
God will help her when morning dawns.
The Lord of hosts is with us;
The God of Jacob is our stronghold. Selah

PSALM 46:5,7 NASB

You have a story that's worth remembering and worth telling to others. As a follower of God, you have a history of times when God has been there for you. Israel was unique from all the ancient peoples in the ways they recorded their history. Their stories were important because God was present in them.

The follower of God always has an advantage when trouble comes. First, God is in the midst of us. The writers of the Psalms knew that God was present among them and showed up whenever trouble came.

Second, God's help comes just at the right time. The writers tell of God's help coming "when morning dawns" or at the break of day.

God is writing your story today. And God's help comes at just the right time. Watch for his work in your life today.

Dear Father, I thank you that you are my rich resource. Thank you for the work of Jesus in my life. You provide for me each day just what I need and just at the right time. Show me your works today again, Lord.

God is within her; she will not be toppled.
God will help her when the morning dawns.
The Lord of Hosts is with us;
the God of Jacob is our stronghold. Selah

PSALM 46:5,7 HCSB

Our life's story takes on rich significance when we observe God's actions on our behalf. God's love shows up throughout our life. Do you remember when he answered your prayers? Do you recall the times when he has provided for your needs? Do you recognize times he has protected you and those you love? Have you counted on him for guidance and watched him direct your paths? God is in our midst, so we won't be toppled.

When our powerful God raises his voice, the earth melts. Whatever the trouble, whatever the need that we have, God speaks and the troubles are over.

As you consider God's actions in your life, be encouraged. The eternal God who designed you to bear his image, desires to walk with you and meet all your needs. You have a story to tell.

Eternal Father, thank you for being my rich resource. Everything I need you have provided. What I have needed most—your presence— is my true treasure.

What stories does God have planned for your life in the year ahead?

Stillness

"Be still, and know that I am God.
I will be exalted among the nations,
I will be exalted in the earth!"

PSALM 46:10 ESV

Do you ever long for peace and quiet? What would that look like? Maybe you picture sitting in a boat on a still lake, or feeling the breeze after climbing a tall mountain. Maybe it's that magical moment when the children are in bed and you have a little time to yourself. Maybe it is sitting by a fire with a good book or cup of coffee. Our world can get pretty noisy and there are times we'd like to turn down the volume of our everyday lives.

The Lord says "Quiet!" to the evil forces that cause chaos, doubts and confusion. The Creator of the universe speaks. He alone reigns. The battle is over. The verse will be fulfilled at the end of time and speaks not just to our hopes, but of God's glory when all the earth must be silent before him.

We live in a noisy, restless world that doesn't want to acknowledge God. But the Savior speaks today for quiet. And if we stop and listen, we will know that he is God, that he alone reigns, and that no force is greater than our God.

Father God, you speak and the nations are silent. Jesus, your words immediately calmed the sea. As I think of your greatness, I am silent before you. You alone are God.

*"Be still, and know that I am God;
I will be exalted among the nations,
I will be exalted in the earth."*

PSALM 46:10 NIV

Our deepest longing is realized when we are still before
him and know our God. In Philippians 3:8, the Apostle Paul
announced that the only thing which mattered to him in life
was to know Christ. As we are still in God's presence, we first
recognize that he is exalted among the nations. There is no
power greater than his power.

When we sing in worship, we aren't just singing music
to satisfy our own tastes. Instead, we are proclaiming
prophetically the reign of our God over the circumstances of
a noisy, restless world. When we hear in the news of more
trouble, we remember who alone reigns over the world.
When our own lives become stormy, we are comforted that
our God is over all of the earth.

The faith that saved you takes on deeper meaning as you are
quiet in his presence and press on to know the living God.

*Father God, I want to know you more. I want to experience you
in all of the times of my life. You are the answer this noisy world
needs. Give me greater understanding into your heart, I pray.*

What have I learned about God recently?

Awesome Glory

Come and see what God has done,
his awesome deeds for mankind!

PSALM 66:5 NIV

The writer of this Psalm calls each of us to recognize the awesome glory of God. This is necessary because we forget. The other problem is that we become distracted with other things and fail to reflect on what God has done.

Early Americans spoke often about God's providence, his watch care over the affairs and direction of our nation. We named cities Providence, to remember God's supervision over their young nation. Although we don't see the physical hand of God, we know he is ultimately in control of the seasons, the nations and their boundaries, the rulers, and in general the affairs of the world. This is not to overlook the suffering and evil that occurs each day. But for the child of this awesome God, we recognize that no evil by man or nature supersedes his governance, and when evil comes he promises to be present with us.

What has this awesome, glorious God done in your life? What have you seen?

Almighty God, you are glorious. Your actions toward people are beyond comprehension. I am thankful to know such an awesome, glorious God.

Come and see the works of God,
He is awesome in His deeds toward the children of men.

Psalm 66:5 amp

God is not an abstract concept to philosophize about. He is
not some unknown deity unobservable to human awareness.
The God who is unseen invites us to come and see his works.
Each of us has seen things that God has done in our lives. He
saves, he delivers and he restores. God heals, answers and
provides. God brings peace and purpose. And behind the
scenes, this awesome, glorious God rules and keeps watch.

What have you seen? As you've thought about this awesome
God today, you are invited to join in, making his praises
glorious. Rest tonight in the knowledge that he cares, and he
watches over us all. His deeds are awesome and he reaches
out to the children of men.

O God, let me behold your glory. You invite me to come along
with you in my life. You invite me to see the things you are doing.
Remind me of your works, that I may join in with the choir of the
ages telling of your awesome glory.

What have I seen of God's glory recently?

Joy

Come and listen, all who fear God,
and I will tell what He has done for me.

PSALM 66:16 HCSB

The God who is beyond our senses invites us not only to come and see, but also to come and hear.

There have been times when people have reported hearing an audible voice of God. Three times God first appeared to Moses by fire in a burning bush (Exodus 3). In Exodus 34:6, Moses hid in a cave as the Lord passed by, calling out his name and that he is compassionate, gracious, slow to anger, and abounding in lovingkindness and truth. When God appeared to Elijah (I Kings 19), it was not in the strong wind, nor was it in the earthquake or fire, but in a gentle blowing wind.

We are revived by hearing from the Lord. We hear him primarily by reading his written word, the Bible, and also hearing others tell of God and his works in their lives. Sometimes his Spirit speaks to us within, and his gentle nudges align with his written Word in our life. Listening to God brings deep joy. Pay attention to him today, and what he has to show you.

Lord Jesus, I long to hear your voice. Speak to me in your Word,
in my heart, and throughout my day.

Come and listen, all who fear God,
and I will tell what he has done for me.

PSALM 66:16 CSB

Once we listen to God, we want to tell others. We can only tell of what we've heard and what we've experienced from God. Each of us has unique things to say of what he has taught us, what he has done for us and what he has done for those we know and love.

No one can deny what God has done for you. And your story with God needs to be told. When we tell "what he has done for me," several things happen. First, it enriches our faith. We need to tell it. Second, we give God credit for he is worthy and our soul is full and designed to pass along what he has done for us. Third, those around us need to hear it. People in our circle of influence need to know the reason for the hope within us. Telling them will sustain and energize their faith in God as well.

Father God, my hope is in you tonight. You have done wonderful
things in my life. Give me opportunities to tell those around me
of all you have done for me.

Who have you told about God's goodness lately? What is it that needs to be told?

Be My Rock

Be to me a rock of habitation to which I may continually come;
You have given commandment to save me,
For You are my rock and my fortress.

PSALM 71:3 NASB

Whether we admit it or not, there are times in our lives when each of us becomes discouraged. Sometimes little things can discourage us. An unkind comment can brush against us. We may even feel the sting of a mean-spirited attack from a coworker, neighbor, or even close friend. Maybe our old confidence and courage have slipped away as we've grown older. This was the experience of the one who wrote this psalm.

The writer had followed God for many years and been through many struggles. At times, he faced shame and attacks from evil, cruel people. But more than that, he faced fears of aging, being set aside and forgotten as he grew old. The end result was that he knew depression, overwhelmed by many troubles and distresses.

But above all of this, he still had a deep hope within him. God was his rock, and now he wanted a fresh dose of hope. To enter into a life with God, is to enter a life of hope.

Father God, through the years you have been my rock and I have
frequently come to you with my prayers. You know my heart.
Revive my strength, Lord. In you I trust.

Be my place of safety
where I can always come.
Give the command to save me,
because you are my rock and my strong, walled city.

PSALM 71:3 NCV

Maybe as you review this verse, you could use a fresh dose of hope. In Isaiah 40:31 we're told that the people who wait and hope in the Lord renew their strength and rise up with wings just like the way eagles soar. Our hope is based on the God we serve. This God is strong. The fears we face are no match for God's ways. As a refuge, God is always our safe haven. As a rescuer, he is a savior who always comes through for us. As a rock, he is someone strong on whom we can build our lives.

Are you facing any troubles? As you have moved through this day, has discouragement set in? The troubles we face can at times appear overwhelming. But God is always there to be called on. And he is always stronger than our fears and the troubles we face.

Father in heaven, you have been my hope and strong rock for many years. Every time I've come to you, I know you have been there for me. As I rest, may I rest in you.

How has God been my rock in the past? Am I certain he will be there for me in the future?

Nearness of God

O God, do not be far from me;
O my God, hasten to my help!

PSALM 71:12 NASB

The writer of this psalm knew the God who was near from our beginning. The words here picture God as a loving parent who bears us in his arms and carries his children.

Holding a new born baby in your arms is a sweet, bonding experience. Remember how they look? Babies are so helpless, even their cries are sweet. They are comforted as you hold them close. Maybe you even examine every little detail— their tiny fingers and toes. Just being there from the beginning creates a special bond.

Do you know that God was there for you like that? Not only was God near from the beginning, he has been near in times of trouble. If you can recall a time when God has lifted, carried, and sustained you in the past you will have a stronger ability to receive the hope God wants you to have today. Since he has been there in the past, you can know he will be near in the future.

God, I thank you that you are near. You knew me from before I was born, and you've never left me during times of trouble. Your love encourages me today. I know that you will be with me no matter what happens this day.

God, don't be far away from me.
My God, come quickly and help me.

PSALM 71:12 NIRV

The nearness of God is not always felt, but it is always true. Prayers in the Bible, such as this, are inspired by God. The God who authored the prayer will always answer that prayer. And the prayer for God to be near and quickly come to our help is what God wants to do for your life.

As you look back in your life, can you see his intervention? Maybe he steered you away from bad influences? Maybe there was an accident you were protected from? Maybe you felt all alone, or felt like giving up, but you knew he had not abandoned you. God is near to help!

Hope is only as good as the object in which we place our faith. If our hope is only in ourselves, this will not get us through the times of trouble. But if our hope is in God, we know that we are in good hands. Because God is near.

God, I thank you that you are always near to me.

Does God seem near to you today? Are you aware of his help in your life?

Always Hope

Even when I am old and gray,
O God, do not forsake me,
until I declare thy strength to this generation,
thy power to all who are to come.

PSALM 71:18 NASB

Here we have the testimony of someone advanced in years.
There is something about a strong word about your God
which increases hope. Hope and praise go hand-in-hand.
Hope builds as we declare his strength.

In Psalm 71, the writer expressed his excitement toward his
God for his righteousness; his deeds, which are mighty and
wonderful; and his power and might. The writer reflected on
the times God had restored his life, always been faithful, and
redeemed him. His life had been changed because he had
encountered a powerful Lord.

As you reflect on your years of following God, what has he
done for you? Have you observed his power in your own life?

Father God, you are the God of the ages. Fill my heart with hope
today as I give you praise and pass along what you've done for me
to the next generation.

Even to old age and gray hairs,
O God, do not forsake me,
until I proclaim your might to another generation,
your power to all those to come.

PSALM 71:18 ESV

You have a faith that is durable, one that can survive your years. Children are drawn to the Lord Jesus, but even in our elder years, ours is a faith worth following. This is because we have a Savior who never changes. We are reminded that Jesus is the same yesterday and today and forever (Hebrews 13:8).

The key element for establishing hope in our life is a personal encounter with the Lord, and utter reliance upon him. Do you know this amazing God who fills lives with hope? Do you agree that our God is a strong God who is near and is worthy of our praise?

If so, then you have a story to tell. The next generation needs to hear how God has shown strength to you. God has planned hope for your future that you can know today, this week. Call upon the Lord who is strong. He will renew your hope again.

Father God, you have been faithful to me throughout my years.
Remind me of when my faith was new. Renew me with your hope so
I can pass along what you've done in my life to the next generation.

What has God done for me that I need to share with those younger than me?

Passing through the Waters

"Fear not, for I have redeemed you;
I have called you by name, you are mine.
When you pass through the waters, I will be with you;
and through the rivers, they shall not overwhelm you."

ISAIAH 43:1-2 ESV

Few people can live long without confronting some form
of fear. We naturally fear danger that is outside of us such
as a physical threat, not having enough money or a secure
job, even a looming illness. There are also fears within that
can cause anxiety, sleeplessness, even a sense of feeling
trapped with no way out. These are like waters that we all pass
through. Whatever our fears, the Lord's Word to us today is
strong: Do not fear! Those words may be easy to say, but can
be very hard to practice.

We are helped by understanding the reasons not to be afraid.
First, we should not fear because we have been redeemed.
The cross of Christ dispels fear.

Furthermore, we should not fear because we are personally
known by God, we belong to God. The promises of God dispel
the fears of man. God is greater than our fears.

Thank you for your promises to me today, Lord. May I listen more
to your promises than my fears today. I trust in you.

"Do not fear, for I have redeemed you;
I have called you by your name; you are Mine.
I will be with you
when you pass through the waters,
and when you pass through the rivers,
they will not overwhelm you."

ISAIAH 43:1-2 HCSB

God reminds us of four important reasons to not fear. First, we have been redeemed.

Second, we should not fear because we are personally known by God. He has called us by name. He knows you personally.

The third reason is that you belong to God. You are his personal, beloved possession. And God will always take care of that which he prizes as his own. The fourth reason naturally follows. No matter what trouble comes he promises to be with you.

My Father in heaven, I am amazed at you. Who am I that I should be so favored in your sight? Thank you for walking through the waters of life with me.

Do I realize that I am the Lord's and that he watches over me?

Precious and Honored

"Since you are precious in My sight,
Since you are honored and I love you,
I will give other men in your place and other peoples in exchange
for your life.
Do not fear, for I am with you."

ISAIAH 43:4-5 NASB

Do you see yourself as God sees you? Many people don't. We often listen to what others say around us, rather than what God has to say. Your Creator knows you best, and has some important things to say about you.

You are precious as he looks at you. The God of the universe not only knows you are there, but he looks at you as prized. He has appraised your worth and considers you precious, costly. You have been singled out by God and made his own child.

As you go throughout this day, rejoice in what the Lord God has to say about you.

My Lord and my God, I praise you that you look at me in this way.
You are aware of me and you have made me your child. Lift my
heart today as I align my thoughts with yours.

"Since you are precious and honored in my sight,
and because I love you,
I will give people in exchange for you,
nations in exchange for your life.
Do not be afraid, for I am with you."

ISAIAH 43:4-5 NIV

This morning we reflected on what it means to be precious in God's sight. Beyond being considered precious, you are honored. Because of your high worth, you are valued by him. We are honored by the choice of God. And his assessment is the one that truly matters.

But most importantly, you are loved. You are in his heart. You are loved by the one who knows you best, and has infinite, perfect love to give.

Because of this, our life takes on a richer meaning. We don't have to fear because he is with us.

Father God, I confess that sometimes it is difficult to think of myself like this. By faith I take you at your word, and thank you that I am precious and honored in your sight.

What difference does it make to me that God thinks of me this way?

Forgiven and Forgotten

I, I am he who blots out your transgressions for my own sake,
and I will not remember your sins.

ISAIAH 43:25 ESV

Remembering mistakes in the past are of little value. They are done and cannot be undone. But hope still remains. The Lord wants to deal with the sins of our past. The sins of our past can be wiped out and erased.

The enemy of your soul will remind you of past wrongs, but the lover of your soul will show you his cleansing so you can move on with his plans for your future.

At the core of our dilemma is usually what we focus on. Our sins can carry a great weight and occupy our deepest thoughts. The Lord God invites us to have a different focus: "I, even I am the one" he says. This is a triple reference to God himself directing our attention to God alone. If we focus on our sins, they will loom as an enemy difficult to conquer. But if we focus on our powerful, forgiving God, the sins lose their power and their appeal.

Father God, I thank you for the forgiveness you provide through Jesus Christ my Lord. I thank you that you don't remember my sins, but you cleanse and blot them out.

I, even I, am He who blots out your transgressions for My own sake, and will not remember your sins.

ISAIAH 43:25 MEV

The power behind God's forgiveness is both his ability to forgive and his motivation for forgiving. God says he forgives "for his own sake." What does this mean?

He can forgive because ultimately all sin is against him. Not only does he have the power to forgive, His character compels him to forgive. God is compassionate and merciful. Forgiveness is in the very nature of God. The act of God's forgiveness is complete, because he will blot them out, remembering them no more.

Forgiveness is so essential to our well-being. Forgiveness restores our relationship with God, and he wants us to extend that to others. Jesus connected the idea of forgiveness with his teaching on prayer (Matthew 6:14,15). Because God is a forgiving God, he expects and empowers his children to forgive others as well.

Father God, I thank you for forgiving me when I did not deserve it. Give me the grace to extend your forgiveness to others in my life.

Who do I know who needs my forgiveness?

For the Thirsty

I will pour out water on the thirsty land and streams on the dry ground; I will pour out my Spirit on your offspring and my blessing on your descendants.

ISAIAH 44:3 NASB

Dryness is a condition we try to avoid. Writers who go through a dry period have few creative thoughts to write about. A business going through a dry period may be losing customers and money and at risk of going under. Dryness usually means that what was alive is now shrinking, wilting, and in danger of staying alive.

Israel knew dryness physically and spiritually. Living in a desert, a lack of physical water meant their crops would not produce, their livestock would suffer, and their lives faced a fragile existence. In these verses, Isaiah gives the people hope from God. Israel is God's servant and the recipient of his love. And when God loves someone, his blessing follows. The dry, thirsty ground can look like a field of cracked pieces of pottery. But as water would be poured onto the thirsty land, first the ground would cover, then the streams would swell and new life would dominate.

Are you thirsty today? Ask God for his renewal.

God, my life seems dry at times. Wash over me with your Spirit, refreshing my family and those around me. Your love for me is refreshing like streams of water in a dry land.

I will pour water on the thirsty land
and streams on the dry ground;
I will pour out My Spirit on your descendants
and My blessing on your offspring.

ISAIAH 44:3 HCSB

Water was used throughout Scripture as a symbol of God's life
and blessing. Israel had much desert land, and Jerusalem was
a major city without a river or water source. King Hezekiah
had to build large cisterns to hold water, otherwise there was
no natural source. When Jesus visited with the Samaritan
woman at the well in John 4, he promised living water. God's
blessing never will run out, we will not exhaust his supply.

God still pours out his water on the thirsty today. Many trudge
through life, unaware of how thirsty they really are. Many
even try to live the Christian life without reliance on the
Spirit of God each day. But for those who realize their thirst,
God has refreshing waters to pour out.

God, pour out your Spirit on me and my family. I stand with open
hands to receive your blessing in my life.

What in my life needs God's water and blessing to be poured
over?

A Wall of Fire

"For I," saith the Lord, "will be unto her a wall of fire round about, and will be the glory in the midst of her."

ZECHARIAH 2:5 KJV

In 587 BC, Nebuchadnezzar conquered Jerusalem, and destroyed the walls around the city. This left the city without defense, open to anyone to pillage and plunder whatever was left behind. Seven decades passed, and groups returned to rebuild the city walls and temple. Zechariah came from a priestly family so he was involved in rebuilding the temple that had been destroyed earlier. Zechariah was given visions that God would be a protector for his people. Specifically, God was to be a wall of fire around the city, so Jerusalem would be safe from her enemies. God would be the glory in the middle of the city.

God revealed himself by fire and glory earlier. In the wilderness, God led the people by a pillar of fire by night and cloud by day. When the tabernacle was completed, the glory of the Lord filled the place. Ezekiel saw a similar vision after the exile of God's glory returning and filling the house. Fire speaks of God's protection, and glory reveals that God is present.

This is the God we serve. He protects and he is present. And God is present, there is no need to fear.

Almighty God, be a wall of fire around my life and those I love today. I thank you for your protection.

The declaration of the Lord: "I will be a wall of fire around it, and I will be the glory within it."

ZECHARIAH 2:5 HCB

Our Scripture reading today was a prophecy from Zechariah, who looked ahead to a day when the fallen city of Jerusalem could be inhabited without man-made walls for protection. How could they survive invading armies if they didn't build walls to protect them? The answer was this: The Lord would be their wall. His protection would be like a wall of fire circling them, too fearsome to ever try to run through. Any man-made form of protection can fail. But when God is our protector, we are always secure.

There are areas where we need his fire of protection as a wall around us. We need his protection over what our heart loves and what we think about with our minds. We need God's wall of fire around those we love to protect and guide. While we do our best to protect ourselves from those who would harm us, we can go to our God to encircle us with his wall of fire.

Thank you, God, for your protection. Thank you for wanting me and those I love to be safe. Guard my heart and my mind as well. I rest in your wall of fire tonight.

In what areas of my life do I need his protection?

Apple of His Eye

"For he who touches you touches the apple of his eye."

ZECHARIAH 2:8 ESV

God's people had been defeated and exiled to a far-away land. Many thought God had abandoned them in sending them into exile. Many lost hope and gave up on the dream of being a called-out people for God. Were they back to square one, as when they were slaves in Egypt?

But God did not forget them. After 70 years, he put in the minds of godless kings to send them back to the Promised Land and even pay for their return and supplies to rebuild Jerusalem. The promises of God to Abraham had not ended. As the people would return from exile and reestablish life in Jerusalem, they needed hope and encouragement.

God viewed his people as deserving full protection. Why? Because they were precious to him.

Do you need his protection today? Are you aware of the special place you hold in God's heart? Are you aware of his desire to protect you?

Father God, you are a good Father. Thank you for the place I have in your heart. By faith I claim your protection for me today.

"For whoever touches you touches the apple of his eye."

ZECHARIAH 2:8 NIV

The figure of speech, "apple of his eye" is common in our own language. Literally, this means the pupil of his eye, that which is precious and especially worthy of protection. David prayed that the Lord would keep him as the pupil or apple of his eye (Psalm 17:8). The wisdom writer wrote that we should keep the teaching as the apple of your eye (Proverbs 7:2). So this phrase refers to something very precious, very dear to us. We protect most that which is most dear to us. Literally, we would protect our eyes, because they are precious to us.

Here is an insight into the ways of God. Almighty God viewed his people as precious and deserving of full protection. To touch you, would be like poking God in his eye! God rises up to protect that which he loves.

Do you realize how loved you are by God? Rejoice in his love tonight and be confident of his protection.

Thank you, Father, that you see me in this way. Such thoughts are beyond my understanding! I rejoice in your love and in the protection you provide for your own.

How does my life become richer as I realize God thinks of me this way?

Sing for Joy

"Sing for joy and be glad, O daughter of Zion; for behold I am coming and I will dwell in your midst," declares the Lord.

ZECHARIAH 2:10 NASB

Have you ever gone through the day with a song stuck in your mind? You find yourself humming it on the way to work, and it pops up throughout the day. Glad singing reflects the joy of your heart. People who carry a joyful tune are often lighthearted as they go through their day.

In this verse, Zechariah gives two commands to sing and be glad (or rejoice) because God is about to do something very significant. Joy would come to the people of the world because the Lord God was coming and would dwell among them.

The Hebrew word for "dwell" is derived from the same word for "shekinah." When the presence of God came into the tabernacle in the wilderness, the shekinah glory was present. God was now enthroned among them. God was on his throne, his kingdom had come, and he would rule the people.

Will you experience his joy today? Remember the Lord has come!

Thank you, Lord, for coming and living among us. Thank you for your presence in my life today.

"Daughter Zion, shout for joy and be glad, for I am coming to dwell among you"—this is the Lord's declaration.

ZECHARIAH 2:10 CSB

In this verse, a clear formula is presented to us. The Lord's coming and dwelling among us = joy.

Jesus, in the prayer he taught his disciples, told us to pray for God's kingdom to come and for his will to be done. These naturally follow, because when God comes and sits on his throne, only what He wants is done on earth.

Is your heart glad today? The Lord has come and is present with you. God doesn't come to the outer edges of our lives, he comes to the center to sit on his throne. When God is on the throne, his will is done.

Father, I pray that your will be done in my life today. Give me joy as I remember that you are here with me today.

When I remain in Jesus, I enter into his joy. How can I abide in him today?

One Good Thing

The Lord answered and said to her, "Martha, Martha, you are worried and bothered about so many things; but only one thing is necessary, for Mary has chosen the good part, which shall not be taken away from her."

LUKE 10:41-42 NASB

Mary and Martha were two sisters who ministered to Jesus. But they responded to Jesus in two very different ways. These two ways are also common to how many live their lives today.

Martha was distracted with all her preparations and to-do lists. She was so focused on getting her tasks done that Jesus described her as "worried and bothered."

Jesus pointed to a better way. Jesus didn't mean for us to do less work and be lazy. Instead it's to do the most important work, as Mary was doing. Throughout Scripture we are reminded to love the Lord with all of our heart, soul and strength. And when we love the Lord this way, as Mary did, joy and energy flows into our lives, even if we carry out the most mundane tasks.

As you go throughout this day, consider how you might keep in mind, the one good thing that Jesus spoke about.

Lord God, I thank you that you don't call me to a life that filled with worry and burdens. Instead, you fill me with joy as I put you first. Remind me of this throughout my day.

The Lord answered her, "Martha, my dear, you are worried and bothered about providing so many things. Only a few things are really needed, perhaps only one. Mary has chosen the best part and you must not tear it away from her!"

LUKE 10:41-42 JBP

Martha's focus was on how she was doing and how much she still had to do. Because she was preoccupied with her own work, she looked at her sister and concluded that Mary must not care. When we focus only on our job to be done, life becomes all about us and we can become critical of others.

Jesus used this daily episode to teach a lesson we need to practice today. Yes, there is much to do in life, but we must keep the one good thing first and foremost. Loving Jesus with all of our being, as Mary did, places us in his presence where we can draw from his love and joy. Loving Jesus also accomplishes the most for eternity. A life well-lived is one that puts Jesus first.

Lord God, forgive me for times I work so hard without thinking of you and drawing from your life. Release me from worrying and being burdened about my life. Renew me as I put you first.

How might my life be different today if I focused on one good thing?

What God Cares About

He said to them, "Whenever you pray, say:
'Father, Your name be honored as holy.
Your kingdom come.
Give us each day our daily bread.
And forgive us our sins,
for we ourselves also forgive everyone in debt to us.
And do not bring us into temptation.'"

LUKE 11:2-4, HCSB

What does God care about? What's important to God? Some may conclude that God is so busy with the big affairs of the universe that our daily issues of no concern to him.

Jesus didn't just teach how to pray in giving a prescribed formula to memorize and repeat. Instead, Jesus spoke to the core issues of prayer. Pray God's heart. Pray what is important to God.

The core of Jesus' prayer was that God's kingdom would come: that life here would be like life in heaven.

God's thoughts about us our great, but they meet us where we live.

Father in heaven, your will be done today in my life. Thank you for providing for me and delivering me from evil today.

He said to them, "When you pray, say:
'Father, hallowed be Your name.
Your kingdom come.
'Give us each day our daily bread.
'And forgive us our sins,
For we ourselves also forgive everyone who is indebted to us.
And lead us not into temptation.'"

LUKE 11:2-4, NASB

The question the disciple asked, "Lord, teach us to pray" was one of prime importance to Jesus. He did not live a moment without prayer, his intimate and dynamic communion with his Father. He was saddened, even upset as he witnessed people around him praying hypocritically.

When an honest heart asked Jesus how to pray, he was quick to answer. Pray what is on God's heart. Pray for his kingdom to come, for our daily needs to be met, for our forgiveness and reconciliation, and that we be steered away from temptation. This is what God wants you to pray for. This is what God cares about.

Father in heaven, I am grateful that you are concerned about the everyday details of my life. Thank you for providing for me in every way.

As I come before God in prayer, what do I need most from him?

Generous Father

*"If you sinful people know how to give good gifts to your children,
how much more will your heavenly Father give the Holy Spirit to
those who ask him."*

LUKE 11:13 NLT

What is God like? Through a lifetime of obedience and
experiences we begin to understand. But people who do not
spend a life seeking God often come to wrong conclusions. If
someone didn't know God, when problems come, they might
think God likes to inflict suffering. Or maybe they would
include God simply doesn't care. Maybe they would surmise
that God is not powerful enough to stop the problem. Or
worse, they may conclude there is no God at all.

Jesus gives a picture of God that is unlike any understanding
from man-made religions on earth. The heavenly father,
Jesus said, is generous. Do you think human fathers get joy
out of giving good gifts to their children and watching their
smiles as they receive them? "How much more," Jesus said,
does your heavenly father?

*Thank you, Father, that you are generous to me. You have blessed
me in many ways. But most of all, I thank you for your Holy Spirit,
and the life in Christ you have given me to live.*

"If you then, who are evil, know how to give good gifts to your children, how much more will the heavenly Father give the Holy Spirit to those who ask him!"

LUKE 11:13 ESV

Not only is God a generous Father, he gives the best gifts. Here, Jesus said, God will enjoy giving the Holy Spirit to any who asks him. The Holy Spirit is the presence of God himself in our lives. The gift of the Holy Spirit is the entrance into the abundant life Jesus promised.

This generous Father you have offers the greatest gift you could have ever have. The wealthiest person could spend a lifetime gathering trinkets, but still miss the most important thing. But even the poorest person can have the most priceless gift, simply by asking a generous God to give his Holy Spirit.

Father, I thank you for the gifts you give. I thank you for your Son who came to die for my sin. I thank you for your Holy Spirit, whom you sent so you could remain with us and in us. You are a generous Father!

What gifts does your generous Father have in store for you this year?

Two Kinds of Sorrow

When God makes you feel sorry enough to turn to him and be saved, you don't have anything to feel bad about. But when this world makes you feel sorry, it can cause your death.

2 CORINTHIANS 7:10 CEV

Everyone faces sorrow at some point. We encounter sadness, even guilt over mistakes made, opportunities lost, as well as the troubles we encounter in our lives. As we grow older, we can look back with regrets over mistakes made in the past.

Conviction from God does not linger. Its only purpose is for us to ask forgiveness, gain God's cleansing and be immediately restored to fellowship with God and other Christians. Once we are forgiven, godly sorrow is removed.

If you are carrying around guilt, God has an answer for you. He's waiting to forgive you and release you from the burden you've carried for too long.

Father, I confess each sin you make me aware of today. Remove sorrow from my life and restore me to your joy.

The sorrow that is according to the will of God produces a repentance without regret leading to salvation; but the sorrow of the world produces death.

2 CORINTHIANS 7:10 NASB

When we are reconciled and restored, we are no longer separated from God, and our joy returns. Sorrow from God does not linger after this. There is no more reason for the pain.

The enemy of our souls uses guilt, to control us and keep us in a state of misery. If forgiveness from God does not remove the sorrow, then the source of the sorrow is being used by our enemy.

The two ways we react to sorrow also are very different. God's way produces repentance and salvation. God's way leaves no regrets and we are able to live life in his joy.

God has a better way! If you've known sorrow, bring it immediately to God. Accept his restoration and cleansing. Know the joy of your salvation today.

Father God, I thank you for your cleansing in my life. Remove the effects of sorrow I may have carried around for too long. Allow me to know the joy of your salvation today.

Do I know the joy of his forgiveness in my life today?

Increase the Harvest

He who supplies seed to the sower and bread for food will supply and multiply your seed for sowing and increase the harvest of your righteousness.

2 CORINTHIANS 9:10 ESV

What does it take to have a life that makes a difference in this world? For the Christian, we might say that the un-surrendered life is not worth living. For when a follower of Christ surrenders their life to God, much can happen.

Our example is the seed. First, God gives the seed. No one can make a seed out of nothing. That seed is small and does not look like much at first. A single seed could grow into a large apple tree that produces bushels of apples each year bearing multiple seeds each.

For the seed to have an impact, it needs to be scattered, or sowed. Seeds stored safely in a jar bear no fruit. But to scatter the seed, it means giving up control. We put the seed in the ground where we can no longer see it.

God's timing is everything. The impact of a life comes when we give what we've been given, we release and sow our gifts, and we wait for God to give the increase.

Father in heaven, I thank you that you supply, multiply and increase what I need and the effect of my life. You are a good Father. My trust is in you.

*He who supplies seed to the sower and bread for food will also
supply and increase your store of seed and will enlarge the harvest
of your righteousness.*

2 CORINTHIANS 9:10 NIV

As we reflect on the seed, we realize that we serve a generous
Father who has given us so much in life. We think about
family, friends, work associates, neighbors, and the many
who serve us in my communities. God has also provided for
us and protected us. God has given us abilities and resources
where we can help others.

These verses remind us that God has richly supplied. God has
also multiplied and increased. Single acts of love we share
can be multiplied thousands of times. We may not see the
effect of these seeds, or know when they will bear fruit in
harvest. We leave all of this in God's hands. The impact of our
lives will be measured in his terms.

*Father, may my thoughts, desires and actions be pleasing to you.
Use my life to influence many in this world. Let them see your love
and grace through me.*

Am I trusting God for the impact my life will make on others?

Inner Strength

I pray that out of his glorious riches he may strengthen you with power through his Spirit in your inner being, so that Christ may dwell in your hearts through faith.

EPHESIANS 3:16-17 NIV

This is a prayer for each of us and those times when doubts and discouragements trouble us. These, the Bible says, are felt in the "inner man", the deep places where we need to be strengthened.

There are many things that weaken our inner self, weaken our faith and our resistance to the lies and discouragements around us.

Beyond aging, life itself batters us every day. We become ill, we face a financial reversal, a disappointment at work, a friend who wasn't there for us. These are all outer circumstances that can wear on us. But the inner man can be renewed.

The inner self—that will last for eternity, where Christ dwells—can be strengthened. How strong can we get? As strong as God's grace, "out of his glorious riches." And out of the riches of God, he wants to strengthen you today.

Father God, by faith I claim your inner strength today. Strengthen me with your power in my inner being.

I pray that he may grant you, according to the riches of his glory, to be strengthened with power in your inner being through his Spirit, and that Christ may dwell in your hearts through faith.

EPHESIANS 3:16-17 CSB

Did you know God wants your inner self strengthened? Strength, confidence and tireless energy are characteristics of the strength of youth. But the inner strength God promises here is not limited to the young. When we allow Christ to indwell us by faith, we gain stronger "faith muscles" to believe, a bolder confidence to tell of God's goodness, and tireless prayer to persist for those requests we must not give up on.

As we grow older and our bodies decline, our inner self can grow stronger. And this is what God prays for you today. God desires for your inner self to be strengthened with his power. Agree with him, and allow him to strengthen your inner self.

Father, I ask tonight that you would strengthen me in my inner being. Grant me greater faith to believe you, bolder confidence to reveal you to others, and a tireless persistence to pray and never give up.

What could a stronger "inner you" accomplish this year for God?

Love in Four Dimensions

I pray that you, being rooted and firmly established in love, may be able to comprehend with all the saints what is the length and width, height and depth of God's love, and to know the Messiah's love that surpasses knowledge, so you may be filled with all the fullness of God.

EPHESIANS 3:17-19 HCSB

One thing different about following Christ is that our Savior does not fill a grave somewhere. Other leaders have their teachings and inspiration, but have no life to give. Because Jesus is alive and conquered death, he now has life to give. And that life is filled with love.

Christ's love is described here in 4 dimensions. Love's breadth reminds how big is God's heart to love everyone, including people not like us. His love is long stretching throughout time. His love is deep beyond what we could ever understand. His love reaches its height as we consider God's eternal purpose.

Christ has life and love to give you today. And his love is inexhaustible in its supply.

Father, I thank you for your love. Your love goes beyond what I could ever ask for or think about. Make me strong in your love today.

I pray that you, being rooted and firmly established in love, may be able to comprehend with all the saints what is the length and width, height and depth of God's love, and to know Christ's love that surpasses knowledge, so that you may be filled with all the fullness of God.

EPHESIANS 3:17–19 CSB

God's love has length. God's love began before eternity and has no interruptions. There is no broken line in the length of God's love.

God's love has depth. How deeply does God love? As we look to Jesus, we see one who gave up the privileges of heaven, humbled himself to take on a human body and suffer insults and beatings before proceeding to death.

The height of God's love reflects his ultimate purpose for us. This love surpasses our knowledge because we won't grasp it with our intellect alone. God reveals his love as we experience being loved by him.

Father, thank you for your love. May I be rooted in your love so my life is drawn from it. May I be established in your love so I will never waver.

Are you so bold as to enter in to God's prayer for you?

God Is Not Surprised

He has not left himself without testimony: He has shown kindness by giving you rain from heaven and crops in their seasons; he provides you with plenty of food and fills your hearts with joy.

ACTS 14:17 NIV

It's easy to feel shocked when seasons suddenly switch. One morning you may wake to green grass and promising skies. The next, the wind may drive snow across the yard, covering everything in its path.

One thing is certain. We might be surprised when things change in our lives, but God is not. His gentle kindness provides what we need when we need it. Since the birth of creation, life on earth has been in a state of beautiful flux. It was not made to stay static, stuck in one season or time. Neither are we, his children, created to be the same for our entire lives.

Father, you know me. You know how my heart sometimes resists change. Remind me of how carefully you orchestrate the seasons, and how nothing that happens to me in this life comes as surprise to you.

He did not leave himself without witness, for he did good by giving you rains from heaven and fruitful seasons, satisfying your hearts with food and gladness.

ACTS 14:17 ESV

Some days, when life catches us off guard, the whole day feels like constant adjustment. It's like wearing pants that are just a little too tight; the dig of the fabric reminds us to reposition.

God brings change as a reminder that we might need to reposition ourselves, our understanding, or our actions. Yet his testimony given to us in his Word remains, steady as the oak tree with its deep tangle of strong roots. He will provide for both the needs of our bodies and our hearts, understanding that both are important. Food on the table, joy in our hearts - two of the very basic things we need to thrive.

Father, thank you for your kindness. Let us see the places you are providing for us, even when we're knocked off center by change. Help us to trust your heart, and search out where we may need to reposition our responses to the circumstances in our lives.

What is an area of pending change in my life that I am resistant to?

Land-Marking Faithfulness

Then Samuel took a stone and set it up between Mizpah and Shen.
He named it Ebenezer, saying, "Thus far the Lord has helped us."

1 SAMUEL 7:12 NIV

When you go hiking at high elevation for the first time, you're likely to notice cairns, which are piles of rocks strategically marking what may or may not look like a trail. Cairns make it easier to see where you're going, and where you've been, which is especially helpful when the trail goes missing and you're not quite sure which way is the best way to get to your destination.

The great thing about cairns is that anyone can build them. All you have to do is find a few stackable rocks, pile them somewhere visible, and trust that whoever comes behind you will be encouraged by knowing someone else has been here before, marking the way.

Samuel's Ebenezer stone was just that, a landmark of God's faithfulness. If you had your own Ebenezer to lay today, where would you put it? What aspect of God's help in your life would it show?

Lord, help me look for places in my life where I can build spiritual cairns, so that every time I look back on them, I'm reminded of your faithful help.

Then Samuel took a stone and set it between Mizpah and Shen, and named it Ebenezer, saying, "Thus far the Lord has helped us."

1 SAMUEL 7:12 NASB

What is it about rocks piled up on one another? Most people, it seems, are drawn to them. We climb them, run over them, paddle by them, drive past them, vacation to them, build our houses with windows that overlook them.

Whatever the reason may be, it's easy to see how rocks are good vehicles for meaning. They are strong. Steady. Unshakable. For Samuel, placing and naming a rock in commemoration of God's help mirrored his strong, steady, unshakable faith.

Thus far, the Lord has helped us. May we seek out our own sturdy stones of remembrance, naming them, placing them, guiding others with their stories.

Lord, thank you for those times in my life when your help was so evident that I could do nothing but point to you, hands raised, overwhelmed. You are good, and your love endures forever.

Where can I mark an Ebenezer in my life today?

New Every Morning

The steadfast love of the Lord never ceases;
his mercies never come to an end;
they are new every morning;
great is your faithfulness.
"The Lord is my portion," says my soul,
"therefore I will hope in him."

LAMENTATIONS 3:22–24, ESV

Some mornings, it's all we can do to roll ourselves over and get out of bed. As much as we want to rely on a good night's sleep, it doesn't always come. Restless thoughts, fitful dreams, and noises from across the hall seem to all be louder in the middle of the night, and some mornings, we find ourselves standing, palms down on the bathroom counter, staring at our reflection, trying to rally for the day.

How important these verses become on those mornings! No matter the magnitude of what happened in the night, God's loyal love absolutely could not have run out. He is standing next to us, holding out his mercies which are new every morning.

Father, how great your faithfulness. I want to think it, say it, revel in it over and over today. Your store of mercies cannot, will not ever run out. Fill me with gratitude for this truth.

Because of the Lord's great love we are not consumed, for his compassions never fail. They are new every morning; great is your faithfulness. I say to myself, "The Lord is my portion; therefore I will wait for him."

LAMENTATIONS 3:22-24, NIV

There's a children's book called Alexander and the Terrible, Horrible, No Good, Very Bad Day. It starts out with Alexander, a young boy, detailing how terribly his morning started, and consequently, how everything else that happened to him the rest of the day just wasn't fair.

Poor Alexander. Nothing that day went his way, and at the end of the book, his mother had to tell him the honest truth; some days are just like that.

Truth-tellers often have the difficult job of teaching us the hard things. Even when days go the opposite direction we want them to, every tomorrow comes wrapped in fresh love and mercies from our heavenly father.

Lord, even if it's been a day, help me to close my eyes and picture you standing next to me tomorrow morning, holding out exactly what I need to step into the day. Let me rest in this knowledge tonight.

Thank Jesus for his mercies that fall fresh every morning.

How to Live

Finally, all of you, be like-minded, be sympathetic, love one another, be compassionate and humble. Do not repay evil with evil or insult with insult. On the contrary, repay evil with blessing, because to this you were called so that you may inherit a blessing.

1 PETER 3:8, 9 NIV

A group of women met to pray for their children, and for one another. The gathering called together mothers from all walks of life, from any age, and in any stage. The connective tissue that brought them together was simple: they were all like-minded, wanting to focus on one thing—prayer.

Being a part of a like-minded group is one of life's biggest satisfactions. There's so much to learn, so much to celebrate, and so much to enjoy about finding another person, or group of people, who value the characteristics Peter talked about: sympathy, love, compassion, humility.

Father, if it's been too long since I've rallied a group of like-minded people together, forgive me. Open my schedule, my house, my fridge; anything it takes to bring me together with other believers so I can be encouraged by their presence.

Finally, all of you should be of one mind. Sympathize with each other. Love each other as brothers and sisters. Be tenderhearted, and keep a humble attitude. Don't repay evil for evil. Don't retaliate with insults when people insult you. Instead, pay them back with a blessing. That is what God has called you to do, and he will grant you his blessing.

1 Peter 3:8, 9 NLT

Do you ever consider it your job to bless others? When your think about what you have to do at work, does it include blessing those around you? It seems strange, talking about blessing this way. We ask God to bless us, but do we look for ways that we can do the same for others?

Peter's message here is simple; there are no exceptions. As believers, we have a special responsibility in our communities to live, love, and conduct ourselves in a way that honors God and blesses those around us.

Father, help us to live up to what you ask of us. Fill us with the Spirit so that it's easy for us to act in the ways you want us to. May we be agreeable, sympathetic, loving, compassionate, and humble. Make it our job to bless, and, in turn, receive blessing back.

Am I a part of like-minded group of believers? If not, how can I try to connect with one?

View of Mercy

Answer me, Lord, out of the goodness of your love; in your great
mercy turn to me.

PSALM 69:16 NIV

If you had to draw a picture associated with the word mercy,
what would you draw? A pair of tender arms, reaching out
from a white robe? Loving hands touching the head of a child?

Mercy can be these things, certainly.

But don't forget that mercy can also be a shovel cutting into
the dirt. Mercy can bury a wrong, and then cover it over with
freshly turned earth. God's mercy can be blunt as it is gentle,
and fierce as it is tender.

Lord, turn to me. Let me see your eyes ablaze with mercy, mercy
that went into the depths with the ugliness of my sin, mercy that
left it there, mercy that came roaring back to life. Your heavy-
handed mercy rolls away stones and shocks those in mourning.
It releases captives and sets prisoners free. Thank you that your
mercy is as strong as it is soft.

Answer me, O Lord, for Your lovingkindness is good;
According to the greatness of Your compassion, turn to me.

PSALM 69:16 NASB

Very few of us understand how physical and emotional stress wind themselves up in our bodies. It's not until they manifest in some sort of bodily outcry that we understand the weight of what we've been carrying.

Sometimes we do not remember that God's mercy has the power to lift that weight away from us if we just call out to him. The psalmist's cry is a beautiful example. "Answer me, because you love me. Let me see your great mercy full-face."

We ache for full-face mercy, the kind that sees us with both eyes, straight on, with nothing peripheral to cloud or distort its vision. We deeply want to be seen, understood, and ultimately, forgiven. When we come face to face with that kind of mercy, we experience a tingling sense of release. Of lightness. Of renewed hope.

Father, see me. Hear me. Know me. Your full-faced attention and mercy are so powerful, and I want nothing more than to remain fixed in your sight.

If you had to draw a picture of what mercy looks like, what would you draw?

Always Beloved

"You are a people holy to the Lord your God. The Lord your God has chosen you out of all the peoples on the face of the earth to be his people, his treasured possession."

DEUTERONOMY 7:6 NIV

It is not easy to accept our bodies the way there are on any given day. We are always ready to point out this flaw, that imperfection. Some parts work, other parts don't. Some parts are lovely, others are less so.

But the truth about treasure is this: a treasure's worth is measured in the eye of its beholder. Our grandfather's wool overcoat might be a treasure to us, not because of its inherent value, but because its smell and texture remind us of being held tight in our grandfather's arms.

Moses, while he was writing Deuteronomy, saw fit to remind us three times, in chapter seven, 14, and 26, that God calls his people a treasured possession. Not because we are perfect; we know we are anything but. No. Because he chose us.

Father, sometimes we struggle being called treasures. Show us our worth in you. Show us your son, reflected in our actions, and your glory, reflected in our lives.

> *"You are a people holy to the Lord your God. The Lord your God has chosen you to be a people for his treasured possession, out of all the peoples who are on the face of the earth."*
>
> DEUTERONOMY 7:6 ESV

When you roast a chicken, the product that you want to see coming out of the oven, the grill, or the smoker is a burnished bronze bird with crispy skin and tender, juice-filled meat. However, cooking isn't always like that. Skin can get soggy and meat can go dry. The project you spent hours preparing, cooking, roasting, and basting can go from perfect to overdone in a matter of minutes. Here's what doesn't change. The chicken is still a chicken.

Beloved, you are always beloved. Not because of how you turn out. Not because of how you look. You are beloved because God chose you, named you, called you so, and that is what you are. Believe it. Rest in it. Rejoice in it.

Father, thank you for your calling. Thank you for telling us, again and again, that we are your treasure. Help us to see those around us with the same eyes, so that they too can know the secure hope of being called yours.

What is one area I can stop beating myself up over and accept how God views me instead?

Of Context and Choice

Do not merely listen to the word, and so deceive yourselves. Do what it says. Anyone who listens to the word but does not do what it says is like someone who looks at his face in a mirror and, after looking at himself, goes away and immediately forgets what he looks like.

JAMES 1:22-24, NIV

Animals have no understanding of reflection. When a cat sees himself in a mirror, his frame of reference does not say, "Hey, that's me!" Instead, it says, "That's another cat!" They are creatures with no context.

In the same way, James warns us against listening without doing, as creatures with no understanding or context would behave. It's not enough just to listen to the Word of God. We, as humans created in the image of God, must take the next step. We have to act on the things we hear. We don't need to keep looking in the mirror over and over. We need to turn around and move forward.

Lord God, we want to understand our context, not just stare at ourselves over and over without comprehending what we should actually be doing in this world. Share your words, and wake us to action.

Be doers of the word, and not hearers only, deceiving yourselves. For if anyone is a hearer of the word and not a doer, he is like a man observing his natural face in a mirror; for he observes himself, goes away, and immediately forgets what kind of man he was.

JAMES 1:22-24 NKJV

We all have people in our lives who like to tell us how to act. It's human nature. If we care for others, it's inevitable that we will notice something they could do differently in order to be better. In most cases, that's just how our brains work. We problem solve. We share some piece of wisdom that's made a difference for us.

Now let's put ourselves on the other side of the fence. Someone has shared something that clearly is smart, true, and worth acting on. We now have a choice: to take the advice and better ourselves, or to hear the advice but not let it spark any change in us.

Where are you today? What in God's Word have you heard but resisted or simply forgot to do?

Lord God, give us a sensitivity towards actually living the way you've called us to live, instead of simply hearing, watching, or reading about it.

What godly advice has someone given me that I need to act upon?

Two Are Always Better

Two are better than one because they have a good return for their labor. For if either of them falls, the one will lift up his companion. But woe to the one who falls when there is not another to lift him up.

ECCLESIASTES 4:9-10 NASB

Most of the time we hear these verses in the context of marriage, but that's not the only type of relationship they apply to. Friends who offer their time, effort, and encouragement have the power to uplift their close companions in ways they may never understand the depth of.

Let's face it. No matter what season of life we're in, difficulty finds a way of creeping in. This is when friendships matter, and matter most. But woe to the one who falls alone, with no one to help him dust his hands off and grunt back into standing.

What kind of friend are you? Who have you given a good return to recently? If we are not meant to live this life alone under a rock, in what ways are you connecting with those around you?

Father, help us bump up against someone who needs us today. Give us eyes to see them, and a willingness to help.

Two are better than one, because they have a good reward for their toil. For if they fall, one will lift up the other; but woe to one who is alone and falls and does not have another to help.

ECCLESIASTES 4:9-10 NRSV

Anyone in charge of multiple children knows that at big events, you don't go it alone. Unfortunately, sometimes, that means you either have to skip something, or ask for help if your partner is busy.

Asking for help is a humbling thing, not matter how many times you do it. There's no easy way to look someone in the eye and say, "I can't do this alone. Will you help?" Uttering these words is a strange combination of failure and relief, and the sooner we get over the former, the better we'll all be for it.

Solitude is wonderful, to a point. Community is wonderful, to a point. The intersection of those two things is a beautiful meeting that benefits both sides. When we share in the work that all of us have to do, we share in the wealth that comes from laboring side by side.

Father, search out those places we want to hide from the world and tend to ourselves. Remind us how much better they could be if we just asked for help.

Who can I talk to about God's greatness to me tomorrow?

Magnificent Praise

Great is the Lord and most worthy of praise; his greatness no one can fathom. One generation commends your works to another; they tell of your mighty acts.

PSALM 145:3-4 NIV

When we spend any amount of time in a National Park, we start to understand the allure it must have held on someone in a previous generation in order to preserve the space. Wild places capture us in a way no other created thing can, begging us to take notice of their wide vistas and explore their narrow trails.

National Parks became designated as such because someone saw fit to recommend those wilderness spaces to others. In the same way, we should find our God's greatness so rich and deep that we cannot help but telling others about it.

It's easy to read those words and agree. Our God is great. But what are we doing as today's generation to tell others about the things our Father has done, both in the past and in the present?

Father, don't let it be enough for us to read about the things you've done and then close our Bibles and move on with the everyday. Spring up a well of praise inside of us that begs to be shared.

The Lord is great and worthy of our praise;
no one can understand how great he is.
Parents will tell their children what you have done.
They will retell your mighty acts,

PSALM 145:3-4 NCV

Deer hunters have a unique perspective on the natural world.
They sit outside for hours on end, waiting patiently for just
the right animal to walk by. They watch as wind rustles the
chestnut-brown oak leaves that still cling to the trees in
November, and listen as squirrels and birds chatter and scold.

It's rare to hear a hunter disparage the process of hunting.
More often than not they speak reverently about the
experience, and of the things they saw as they waited.

What if we could talk about God's magnificent hand in our
lives the same way we talk about the world's activities that we
love and take interest in?

Father, there are no boundaries to your greatness, no words loud
enough to match the volume your praise deserves. Let us share your
goodness with others with the same fervor and readiness that we
share our interests.

Who can I talk to about God's greatness to me tomorrow?

The Truth about Everything

His divine power has given us everything we need for a godly life through our knowledge of him who called us by his own glory and goodness.

2 PETER 1:3 NIV

In the early 90's, a Christian singing group named "Acapella" recorded a simple rendition of 2 Peter 1:3. The entire song consisted of that one verse, which kept building until all four voices united in the strength of their parts.

If you have problems with songs getting stuck in your head, do yourself a favor. Listen to this one. Listen to it a few times, and let Peter's firm reminder play on a loop in your brain. As believers, we have everything we need to live a godly life, simply by knowing our Christ. But remember, having "everything" isn't a promise of certain bank account balances, perfectly working vehicles, or a well-stocked pantry.

Peter's "everything" statement reminds us to look past what we think we need into the truth.

Father, forgive me for the times I become too focused on something that isn't essential to living a godly life. What I need most is you.

His divine power has granted to us all things that pertain to life and godliness, through the knowledge of him who called us to his own glory and excellence.

2 PETER 1:3 ESV

In Spanish, there are two words for the English verb "to know": saber, which means to know a place, a person, a thing, and conocer, which means to understand something deeply in the heart.

What kind of knowledge of Jesus did you live out today? Was it a saber sort of day, where you went through the motions, knowing what to do without really putting much thought into? Or was it a conocer day, a day where you understood Christ's message of love and provision so deeply that you knew, without a doubt, that all your needs were cared for?

Father, I want dive past the surface of knowing who you are and allow myself to sink deeper in understanding your heart. Fill me with that sort of knowledge about yourself, God. Let the words of your scriptures reveal who you are, and let me trust that that knowledge is everything I need.

How can I get to know Jesus better?

Unwavering Habit

Never be lazy, but work hard and serve the Lord enthusiastically. Rejoice in our confident hope. Be patient in trouble, and keep on praying.

ROMANS 12:11-12 NLT

It's easy to create a well-worn groove of routine in our lives. We wake up at a certain time, or always drink from our favorite blue mug. Habits help us order our days, but rarely do we associate them with zeal or joy. Those big emotions seem much easier to find in new situations, not in the everyday ordering of the clock.

However, verse 12 goes on with the imperative statements. Be patient in affliction, faithful in prayer. It cannot be an accident that Paul listed these four things: zeal, joy, patience, and faithfulness next to one another in Romans 12, a chapter on how believers are to live.

Paul understood the difference between living, and living well. Zeal and joy must be followed by patience and faithfulness. No life can be lived solely on the mountain top. The journeying up and down between mountains must be fortified.

Father, meet me where I am today, be it in the glory of the mountain top, or the struggle of somewhere in between. Give me all four: zeal, joy, patience, and faithfulness, so that I'm ready for whatever comes next.

Never be lacking in zeal, but keep your spiritual fervor, serving the Lord. Be joyful in hope, patient in affliction, faithful in prayer.

ROMANS 12:11-12 NIV

In this fallen world, every blue-sky day is paired with the darkness of night. We cannot have one without the other. So, when Paul tells believers not to burn out, but to stay fueled and aflame, expectant, without quitting, we see the importance of living every day with an unwavering light.

People flock to light when it's dark outside. It's a place we can see, and be seen. When circumstances swell with sadness, it becomes imperative for us keep ourselves fueled and aflame, as verse 11 implores us, so that the world can be pointed to the ultimate source of light and life, Jesus Christ.

Father, darkness is undeniable, but if we live the way Paul tells us to, so also is light. Shine through us. Breathe into our weak flickering, and build us into dancing orange flames as we seek to live the call you've given us.

What is one way I can be a light to those around me in times of confusion?

Everyday Offerings

I appeal to you therefore, brothers, by the mercies of God, to present your bodies as a living sacrifice, holy and acceptable to God, which is your spiritual worship. Do not be conformed to this world, but be transformed by the renewal of your mind, that by testing you may discern what is the will of God, what is good and acceptable and perfect.

ROMANS 12:1–2 ESV

When you think about giving an offering to God, do you think of the plate being passed at church? What would happen if, instead of you pulling out your checkbook, you threw in your driver's license?

God wants more than our money. He wants our identity; so much so that he asks us to give him our normal, ordinary, nothing-new life. Why? Because out of the overflow of our lives comes praise. When we live our lives in full acknowledgement and joy in Christ, we give him the best thing we have to give: ourselves.

Father, my ordinary life doesn't seem like much. Take my living sacrifice, my flawed body, my tired mind, and give me the strength to embrace what you've done for me.

I urge you, brethren, by the mercies of God, to present your bodies a living and holy sacrifice, acceptable to God, which is your spiritual service of worship. And do not be conformed to this world, but be transformed by the renewing of your mind, so that you may prove what the will of God is, that which is good and acceptable and perfect.

ROMANS 12:1–2 NASB

Abraham and Isaac provide a poignant picture of living sacrifice. Abraham, who had longed for a son, stood on the mountain with a knife in his hand, shaking, but willing to listen to God who had proved so faithful to him. In turn, God honored Abraham's true heart and spared his son.

Thankfully, Christ's sacrifice for us made the old ways of worship obsolete. Instead, we can come to him directly, without the need to shed any blood, offering instead ourselves: our loves, desires, abilities, ideas, and thoughts.

Father, transform us. We lay down our bodies, our wants, and our needs as worship. Hear our hearts.

In what areas do I need to untangle from the world and renew my way of thinking?

Giver of Life and Breath

The God who made the world and everything in it is the Lord of heaven and earth and does not live in temples built by human hands. And he is not served by human hands, as if he needed anything. Rather, he himself gives everyone life and breath and everything else.

ACTS 17:24-25 NIV

When you look for God, where do we go? The answer in the past may have been church, but today, churches are closing at an alarming rate. And while this might concern us, we have to look to look hard at what the Scriptures say.

God does not live in a physical church. Instead, he pours life and breath into our bodies and wakes us, blinking and stretching, into every day that he's given us. Imagine if we, his people, lived as the church was meant to operate - beckoning those around us to find God in us: in our actions, in our words, in our love?

Be encouraged, dear soul. The Lord of heaven doesn't need a temple. Instead, he wants you, his personal emissary of life and breath, to go into the world and share his love. Are you willing?

Father, breathe into me. Build me up as your living, active church.

He made the world and everything in it, and since he is Lord of heaven and earth, he doesn't live in man-made temples; and human hands can't minister to his needs—for he has no needs! He himself gives life and breath to everything, and satisfies every need there is.

ACTS 17:24-25 TLB

We all have daily moments of need. Think back on your day today. Was there anything that caused you to call out to God and ask for his help? Did you ask in a spirit of trust, knowing that the one you petitioned was no less than the maker of the world and everything in it?

It's easy to cry out in frustration ("A little help here, God!"), annoyance ("Sure could use a hand right now, Lord!"), or even doubt ("If you're listening, please fix this!"). Remember: God is big enough to hold our feelings and emotions. He isn't flustered by our real speak.

But he also wants us to remember who he is: the Creator of all; the Lord of heaven; and the Lord of the earth. He has no needs, but wants to meet ours.

We praise you, Father. Thank you for giving us needs, and a means to satisfy them.

What does asking in a spirit of trust look like for me going forward?

Today and Always

The Lord appeared to us in the past, saying: "I have loved you with an everlasting love; I have drawn you with loving-kindness."

JEREMIAH 31:3 NIV

In the movies, when a character draws another into his or her arms, we get a beautiful glimpse of the joint appreciation that action brings for both the lover and beloved.

Now imagine the look on God's face as he pulls you, his child, in close. Picture the way he closes his eyes, squeezing you tightly. Feel his chin on your head, his strength pulling you closer to him.

Sometimes it's difficult to picture our heavenly father being tender toward us, but in those times, we need to trust the truth of the pictures he draws for us in his word. Take him at his word, believer. You are pulled in, held close—today, and always.

Father, remind my heart today that from the very beginning, I was drawn, just as I am today, by your kind and loving hand. Thank you.

The Lord appeared to him from afar, saying,
"I have loved you with an everlasting love;
Therefore I have drawn you with lovingkindness."

JEREMIAH 31:3 NASB

It's easy, far too easy, to focus on all the unlovable things about ourselves. We couldn't do this, didn't do that. We are too much of this, not enough of that. These feelings threaten us, over and over, shaking the shoulders of our wellbeing with their unfairly tight grip.

When Jeremiah recorded these words for all the people of God, he gave us the power to knock the bully away. Yes, maybe we forgot this, broke that, lost this, failed at that. So did the Israelites. They forgot God's promises, broke his law, lost their faith, failed to remember their place in God's family. Still he told them, "I've never quite loving you and never will."

Soul, you are wanted, and you are loved. Throw off the weight of your imperfections, and allow yourself to be drawn into your father's chest.

Hold me, Father. Fight off my accusers, cut loose my burdens. Thank you for seeing me as I am, and loving me continually.

What failures can I put down today and pick up God's love for me instead?

Importance of Kindness

Anxiety weighs down the heart, but a kind word cheers it up.

PROVERBS 12:25 NIV

It happens to all of us. We make a bad decision. We're late to drop someone off. We forget to plan for an important meeting. As we're rushing around, trying to pick up the pieces of whatever it is we've dropped, our minds can't seem to stop looping the same messages of failure and disapproval.

Anxiety is the ice you can't see on the road; it's only after your wheels are spinning that you realize it's there. Thankfully, all it takes is grit to gain traction and start to move forward.

Kind words, whether they be in the form of an apology, a reassurance, or a glowing compliment have an amazing power. They break into our anxious, and our circuitous thought patterns, and throw gravel on the slickness of our worries. Upon hearing them, we find our shoulders lowering, our breath slowing, our mind suddenly freed to think about something else.

Kindness is daring and important. We never know who, or how it might make an impact.

Lord God, fill my mouth with kind words today. Let me encourage those around me battling anxiety, and may the words I speak reflect your love.

Heaviness in the heart of man maketh it stoop:
but a good word maketh it glad.

PROVERBS 12:25 KJV

Have you ever looked at the ceiling and imagined it to be the floor? That's what anxiety looks like—a broad, empty space where everything around you is upside down. Your priorities. Your faith. Your ability to apply truth.

Heaviness of heart is a picturesque description of today's panic, fear, anxiety, or depression. But kindness? Kindness is a universal balm. It transcends time and culture. And though it may not fix our problems, it has the ability to bolster our gratitude, faith, and hope in the midst of our struggles.

Father, when we are wrapped up and tangled in the cares of our world, bring us your kindness. Give us eyes to recognize your hand and your heart in the simple ways others are blessing us.

Who is one person I can be tangibly kind to in the coming days?

Pain and Pleasure

Return to your rest, my soul, for the Lord has been good to you. For you, Lord, have delivered me from death, my eyes from tears, my feet from stumbling, that I may walk before the Lord in the land of the living.

PSALM 116:7-9 NIV

Sometimes perspective is everything. Today might feel thick, heavy, or overwhelming. But in a few hours, all of that could change. You might look back at it tomorrow and breathe a silent prayer of celebration that God's deliverance once again came through for you.

It may take a day, a week, a month, a year to see how things have moved in your life. Or perhaps what you are battling against hasn't changed yet, and will not change in the foreseeable future. Even so, try taking on the perspective of the psalmist, trusting that what you've gone through (or are continuing to go through) has the capacity to bring you yet closer to Jesus.

Lord God, when I can't see the forest for the trees, remind me of the importance of perspective, and of remembering your faithfulness.

Return to your rest, O my soul,
For the Lord has dealt bountifully with you.
For You have rescued my soul from death,
My eyes from tears,
My feet from stumbling.
I shall walk before the Lord
In the land of the living.

PSALM 116:7-9 NASB

When was the last time you felt at rest in your soul? Was it during a time when everything in your life was in harmony, and sounded lovely all together? Or was it directly after a difficult period in your life, when you knew what true rest meant because you had just been living through the nightmare of experiencing otherwise?

The trick is this: God wants us in both. He wants us to know we can trust him in blessing and stumbling alike.

Lord, give us eyes that see pain and pleasure as equal partners in this life, both able to produce in us things that wouldn't otherwise have grown.

What difficulty can you look at in perspective now that it's passed?

Ebenezer

Then Samuel took a stone and set it up between Mizpah and Shen.
He named it Ebenezer, saying, "Thus far the Lord has helped us."

I SAMUEL 7:12 NIV

Do you ever look back at your life and think about how far
you've come? Do you think about the ways God has blessed
you and provided for you? Do you remember the answers to
prayer and miraculous works he has done in your life over the
years? It is important for us to be able to remember the help
that God has given to throughout our life, because that gives
us strength to continue to trust him for what is to come.

Life is hard, but God is faithful. Saying to ourselves, "Thus far
the Lord has helped us," allows us to remember that this God
who has done so much in our lives to bring us to this point,
will continue to be with us as we move forward into the great
unknown that lies ahead.

Heavenly Father, thank you for all that you have done for me.
Please help me to remember your work in my life and to continue
to follow you.

After this happened Samuel took a stone. He set it up between Mizpah and Shen. He named the stone Ebenezer. Samuel said, "The Lord has helped us to this point."

I SAMUEL 7:12 ICB

How often have we sung the following words from the hymn, "Come Thou Fount of Every Blessing," by Robert Robinson, and never understood what he was talking about:

> *Here I raise my Ebenezer,*
> *Hither by Thy help I've come;*
> *And I hope, by Thy good pleasure,*
> *Safely to arrive at home.*

What he is talking about is this verse from 1 Samuel is when Samuel took a stone and set it up as a memorial for what God had done for them. As we continue on our journey of following God, we need to be able to look back and see the ways that God has provided for us.

Heavenly Father, thank you for all the ways that you have helped me in the past and for all that you are doing for me moving forward.

If you were to erect an Ebenezer kind of rock like we see in this verse, what might you specifically be remembering about how God has helped you thus far?

Warm Arms of Grace

Let him have all your worries and cares, for he is always thinking about you and watching everything that concerns you.

1 PETER 5:7 TLB

Have you ever wondered why wounded animals hide? A few years ago, our family cat went missing. We found him huddled in the corner of a little-used outbuilding, attempting to self-nurse a broken leg. After a number of veterinarian calls and potential treatment plans that would have wiped out our savings, we opted to side with the vet whose opinion was to crate the cat, keep him warm and in good company, and let him heal naturally.

Our family was thrilled to welcome Clifford our cat into the fireplace room of our home. Never was a hurting creature so coddled, loved, and spoiled with three young nurses catering to his every need. In the end, he healed, and walks perfectly to this day.

God knows our needs. He also knows that bringing our hurts into the warm arms of grace, both from our heavenly father and the people we trust, will heal us faster than keeping ourselves separate, licking our wounds on our own.

Father, give me the ability to hand over my worries and cares. Thank you for thinking about me, and watching everything that concerns me.

Casting all your anxiety on Him, because He cares for you.
1 PETER 5:7 NASB

Ask any fisherman, and they'll tell you about the hope that accompanies each cast of the line into the water. Sometimes the hope might be bigger, depending on the circumstances (new line, new lure, new lake). Other times, it's as normal and steady as their old rod and favorite lure. Either way, hope is present.

The other thing a fisherman will tell you is that sometimes it takes repeated casting in order to produce a fish. Why? We don't always catch a fish on the first try, and worries have a way of coming back to us.

It's as though Peter understood the returning nature of anxiety, and wanted to exhort us to keep casting all our cares on Jesus. Our minds have a way of circling back into the depths of what if, instead of staying with what is.

Father, wrap me in your care. Show me how to be continuous in my casting and hopeful in the practice.

Where do I tend to hide my hurt instead of reaching out for healing?

To Wait and Trust

Now we see in a mirror dimly, but then face to face; now I know in part, but then I will know fully just as I also have been fully known.

1 CORINTHIANS 13:12 NASB

Antique mirrors are curious things. They bloom with strangely patterned spots and cloud with age. Even so, people snatch them up at flea markets and repurposed shops and hang them in their homes, as is. There is a certain allure in the reality of imperfection.

Stylish or on trend as antique mirrors may be, few of us would buy them for everyday use. Why? Because seeing something dimly is no match for seeing it directly.

This life is full of moments when our understanding is clouded by our humanity and our position on earth. Earlier, in verses 9 and 10, Paul writes, "For we know in part and we prophesy in part; but when the perfect comes, the partial will be done away." It may not be until Jesus comes, or we arrive in heaven, that our questions will be answered.

Father, give us grace to sit with our unanswered questions in our laps. It is not easy to only see part of the picture, but you promise to bring light to our understanding when you return. Let that be enough.

Now we see in a mirror dimly, but then face to face. Now I know in part; then I shall know fully, even as I have been fully known.

1 Corinthians 13:12 ESV

It's frustrating at times not to what God is up to, isn't it? We are told to wait and trust and praise our way through difficulty, but the very human side of us begs to know the answer to the question why?

Imagine what it will be like to look at Jesus in the face, and hear him answer all of our questions. Understanding will bloom as wide as a sunflower in August, and we will finally see why the things in our lives that were difficult had to happen when and as they did.

Father, what a day indeed, to look into your face and understand fully what you were doing in our lives here on earth.

Think of what you'd like to ask Jesus when you sit down with him someday.

Real-Time Trust

Surely God is my salvation; I will trust and not be afraid. The Lord, the Lord himself, is my strength and my defense; he has become my salvation.

ISAIAH 12:2 NIV

As believers, we most likely think of salvation in terms of Jesus' sacrifice on the cross in order to save us from our sins. But the word salvation is even more all-encompassing than that. In the old testament, the word salvation would have brought up shaking memories of deliverance that were very close to the surface.

Imagine being saved from Pharaoh's army and walking through a supernatural path on the floor of the Red Sea. Think of the battles that were not in the Israelite's favor, but that they won anyway. In context of the old testament, the deliverance aspects of salvation were shakingly, quakingly real.

We may not have those direct experiences, but it would be impossible to look back at our lives and not see the places God has delivered us from: our sin, our poor decisions, our family struggles, our physical ailments, our difficulties at work. Though they may not have been Rea Sea stories, they are no less important. God's salvation is continually at work in our lives.

Father, show me my Red Sea moments. Let me see your delivering hand of salvation, and renew my reasons to trust in you.

See, God has come to save me! I will trust and not be afraid, for the Lord is my strength and song; he is my salvation.

ISAIAH 12:2 TLB

We all need a rescuer. When a child finds himself in a difficult place, his first response is to cry out. Parents or caregivers immediately appear, saving him from the situation and soothing his pain. As a result, that child trusts those who rescue him, and looks to them first when another issue comes up.

Isaiah also experienced his heavenly father's saving hand, and had the temerity to put it down into words we could all connect with. See, God has come to save me! I will trust and not be afraid! Even as a grown man, he understood the value of affirming his trust and his salvation in God.

Whether you are young or old today, take time to call out, praising your father for his saving arms. He is altogether worthy of being called your strength, your song, and your salvation.

Father God, thank you for everything salvation means to us as your children. Fill our mouths with praise as we acknowledge your all-encompassing love.

Where has God parted the Red Seas in your life?

The Weight of Untruth

"Out of all nations you will be my treasured possession. Although the whole earth is mine, you will be for me a kingdom of priests and a holy nation."

EXODUS 19:5 NIV

Sometimes we need to be reminded that we are God's treasure, his chosen people. It's easy to feel alone, trapped in our own minds and our own duties and concerns. We do not feel treasured. We feel lonely, tired, bone-weary of carrying the weight of the world that we think belongs to us.

Funny, because we weren't meant to. The weight of our worlds should be reserved for shoulders that are able and capable, shoulders made of divine strength and boundless love. Our inability to hold it all should not frustrate us—we were not created to be so independent.

Unfortunately, it's hard to let ourselves put that burden down, isn't it? It's difficult to let ourselves be loved, treasured, cared for. Oftentimes, we simply don't know how to do it. We have been independently working and slogging through for so long, that unbuckling the weight and putting it down seems like a foreign idea, or sadly, one that we don't even entertain because it will seem all the heavier when we pick it back up again.

Father, grab us by the shoulders and speak your truth firmly in our lives. We are beloved.

"If you will indeed obey My voice and keep My covenant, then you shall be a special treasure to Me above all people; for all the earth is Mine."

EXODUS 19:5 NKJV

Have you ever struggled to receive a compliment? Sometimes, it's the hardest thing in the world to acknowledge someone's appreciation of us. It might be because we struggle with pride, or it might be because we hear compliments so little that we don't know how to believe the other person. Or worse, perhaps we think we know ourselves too well, and what someone else is praising about us simply can't be true.

Whatever our hang-up is about receiving compliments, we would do well to listen carefully to our heavenly father when he affirms who we are to him: his special treasure, a kingdom of priests, a holy nation. God cannot lie, and our worth is not, and has never been in question to him. May we have the grace and humility to accept that truth, internalize it, and live as such.

Father God, if we believe your Word to be true, then we must believe you when you speak our worth over us as well. Help us not to listen to the untruths we harbor about ourselves, and instead, replace them with the healing power of your truth.

What affirmations do we need to do a better job believing about ourselves?

Get after It

Prepare your minds for service and have self-control. All your hope should be for the gift of grace that will be yours when Jesus Christ is shown to you.

1 PETER 1:13 NCV

It is increasingly easy, in our world of ever-present screens and notifications, to be distracted from what we're doing. We find ourselves coming to a halt every time we sneak a quick peek at whatever article, update, or post came zinging through a moment ago.

It's hard to believe that this can do us much good. Information is useful to a point, but the real-life work that we accomplish by digging in, getting messy, creating, learning, building, growing, and doing is what awakens us to how God's Word connects with our everyday lives.

We don't just work to work, however. We roll up our sleeves, and kick it into gear in order to be ready to receive what God has in store for us when he sends Jesus back. That readiness might look different to all of us, but no matter what it may be, let's focus on our Father's goals and live for his coming kingdom today.

Jesus, it's not enough to say we look forward to your return. We ache for it, long for it. Spur us into rolled-up sleeves and undistracted minds as we go about our day today.

Gird up the loins of your mind, be sober, and rest your hope fully upon the grace that is to be brought to you at the revelation of Jesus Christ.

1 PETER 1:13 NKJV

If the phrase gird up the loins of your mind makes you scratch your head a little, you're in good company. The context for this phrase doesn't really exist anymore, especially in today's world of specialized clothing for every activity you can think of.

Historically, girding up your loins meant tucking up the loose ends of your robe into your belt. That way they wouldn't get caught between your legs as you ran, or be able to trip you up. As comical a picture as this might seem, girding the loins was the best way for a man to remove any distraction from his clothing and get something done if he needed to move quickly.

What did you need to get done today? Did you find yourself able to narrow your sights and focus, or were there loose ends that kept wrapping themselves around you as you tried to move forward?

Jesus, save me from anything that wants to tangle, trip, or distract me. Set my mind on you, and allow me to rest my hope in your coming grace.

Think of two ways to minimize distraction in your life.

Nature of Time

Blessed is the one who reads aloud the words of this prophecy, and blessed are those who hear it and take to heart what is written in it, because the time is near.

REVELATION 1:3 NIV

One of the biggest difficulties we as believers can have with the book of Revelation is the issue of time. On the one hand, here's the disciple John prophesying some amazing things and telling us to be alert and ready because the time is near.

On the other hand, we have a modern-day calendar that cannot deny that Revelation, though written with urgency, was indeed written 2000 some odd years ago. So to read "the time is near" and yet have to match the imminence of John's words with the reality of this long stretch of time that has occurred since his writing creates a dissonance of understanding in our minds.

We may not understand God's timing, which we're told is not like our own. But we can understand his blessing, which makes a direct impact on our day to day lives. Just because we have not seen a prophecy come to fruition doesn't make it any less true. Listen and take heart, Christ-follower. The time is near.

Father, build up our urgency at hearing and applying your Word to our lives. Let us not lose faith when your timing looks different than what we'd prefer.

Blessed is he that readeth, and they that hear the words of this prophecy, and keep those things which are written therein: for the time is at hand.

REVELATION 1:3 KJV

Have you ever spent time with a friend who has a different concept of time than you? Perhaps you make plans, arranging to meet at a certain time, and they show up half an hour late. Or maybe you're the one misjudging the clock, leaning on your friends' generosity of understanding. Everyone has a different concept of timeliness, which is why it's important to clarify if it's important to meet at a very certain hour.

John's word to the church may not have given a specific date or hour of his prophecy's fulfillment, but nevertheless, he made sure to denote its swift and certain coming.

Blessed are you, readers and hearers and keepers. Keep faithfully at your work, remembering that God's return is at hand.

Father, we do not claim to understand what your version of time looks like. Help us lay claim, instead, to the blessing of sharing, hearing, and keeping your words.

What areas of your life need a little more urgency in light of Christ's return?

Wind and Flame

He makes winds his messengers, flames of fire his servants.

PSALM 104:4 NIV

If you've ever worked to start a fire, you know the fickleness of flames. One moment they look like they've caught and are growing, and the next minute, you turn around and they've disappeared, smoldering instead into char.

It's not easy to coax a spark into flame. Today we have the luxury of commercial fire starters and burn-ready matches, but even so, a good fire depends on a number of variables being carefully aligned.

Thankfully, we serve a God who has no need of our man-made tricks. His greatness and power need no extra coaxing to ignite and command a legion of flames that go wherever he bids.

The next time you stare into a fire, imagine your God flicking his wrist and drawing flame from air. This is no mere magician's trick; this is the great and mighty God of the universe, powerful enough to hold fire as his servant, yet tender enough to care for our individual needs.

Father, I praise the works of your hands, which roar and crackle with heat and might.

You make the winds your messengers;
you make fire and flame your ministers.

PSALM 104:4 CEB

No matter where you live, at one time or another you've probably felt the full force of wind pushing against you. It's startling, isn't it? This unseen power halts for nothing, instead growing stronger as it moves around buildings or trees or any obstacle in its way.

Psalm 104 opens by blessing the Lord for his grandeur, and continues on praising God for his intricate involvement with his creation. Involvement that includes making even the winds which blow over the earth his messengers. No detail is missed, no creature forgotten. Our Lord, our God commands them all.

When was the last time you made a list of all the ways you see God at work in the world around you? Try it tonight.

Father, you are Lord over wind and flame, earth and sea, creature and mankind. Don't let us forget the broadness of your goodness, or the scope of your power.

Make a list of where you see God's power in your life.

Good in Sadness

The Lord is good to those whose hope is in him, to the one who seeks him; it is good to wait quietly for the salvation of the Lord.

LAMENTATIONS 3:25-26 NIV

The writer of Lamentations, traditionally thought to be Jeremiah, has a mouthful to say in chapter 3. He starts his writing by saying this: I am the man who has seen affliction by the rod of the Lord's wrath. The purpose of his writing was to lament the fall of Jerusalem, an event he'd been prophesying about for over forty years.

Lamentations is a beautiful mixture of sadness, mourning, and yet a call to hope in and return to the Lord who allowed the destruction of the city of his people. As readers, we can't help but hear the conflict in the writer's voice as he details the anguish of Israel, but still needs to remind them (and perhaps himself as well) that even so, the Lord is good to those whose hope is in him.

Do you have a Jerusalem-like sadness in your soul today? Look to Lamentations. Listen to how Jeremiah deals with the dichotomy of God's judgement, and God's goodness.

Father, I have a hard time knowing that both loving kindness and sharp discipline can come from the same hand. Give me a mind to understand both, and a heart that is secure in both hope and seeking after you.

The Lord is good to those who wait for him,
to the soul that seeks him.
It is good that one should wait quietly
for the salvation of the Lord.

LAMENTATIONS 3:25-26 NRSV

Even standing alone, these two verses sound like an exhale.
Earlier in the chapter, Jeremiah has spent a chunk of time
recounting Israel's sadness and destruction, but in verse 21,
he starts to turn his tone.

He spends the rest of the chapter reiterating why, even in
the midst of destruction, God is still worthy of our hope and
trust. The Message translation of these verses couple passion
with waiting and diligence with seeking, reminding the
Israelites, and us, of our roles in the aftermath of correction
(even though they may be the farthest from what we feel
capable of doing).

Passion. Diligence. Quiet hope. Can you muster those
things tomorrow? Can you, even in the pain of whatever
circumstance you're facing, say with Jeremiah that there's
something worth remembering here?

Father, quiet hope is incredibly difficult when we are faced with
trial. Open our hands, that we can grasp it firmly.

Where can you open your heart to passionate waiting, diligent
seeking, and quiet hope?

Increase Our Faith

The apostles said to the Lord, "Increase our faith!" He replied, "If you have faith as small as a mustard seed, you can say to this mulberry tree, 'Be uprooted and planted in the sea,' and it will obey you.

LUKE 17:5-6 NIV

There's an iconic scene in the movie Indiana Jones and the Last Crusade where Indy must take "the leap of faith" from the lion's head, which is at the edge of a cliff whose bottom is shrouded in utter darkness.

We can see Indy wrestling with his ability to make his next move. He consults his map. Crinkles it back up. Takes a deep breath. Claps his hand to his chest. Sticks out his leg. And then, Indiana Jones steps into the thin air of the unknown.

Taking that first step of faith is incredibly frightening. It might look like selling a house, changing vocations, or finally talking to someone we've known for a long time about our faith.

Where is your faith asking you to step out into today? Can you trust in the power God promises if only you believe?

Father, give us strength to trust you in the moments where a blind step of faith is required.

One day the apostles said to the Lord, "We need more faith; tell us how to get it."
"If your faith were only the size of a mustard seed," Jesus answered, "it would be large enough to uproot that mulberry tree over there and send it hurtling into the sea! Your command would bring immediate results!

LUKE 17:5-6 NLT

Did you feel God nudging you in any direction today regarding your own "leap of faith"? How did you respond? Are you still pausing, like Indiana Jones, at the edge of your cliff?

Often times, the best way to step into the unknown where God is calling you is by looking back at the places he's provided for you. This is how we as humans understand who we can trust. When people have shown up for us, or positioned themselves in our corner repeatedly, we know they are good for their word.

Make no mistake. Your all-powerful God is capable of anything, and you have his power at your disposal when you possess even a poppy seed sized speck of faith.

Father, build in us a deep sense of trust in the places you require us to have faith.

Listen to that quiet leading in your spirit. Your God is worthy of your faith.

Mighty Gathering

"If you are unfaithful, I will scatter you among the nations, but if you return to me and obey my commands, then even if your exiled people are at the farthest horizon, I will gather them from there and bring them to the place I have chosen as a dwelling for my Name."

NEHEMIAH 1:8-9 NIV

You don't have to look far to hear stories of displacement and exile. The difficulty is knowing how to respond to them. For many of us, home is a given. It's not someplace we've ever had to leave in the middle of the night, our hands lingering on a door frame we know we probably won't ever touch again.

Nehemiah mourned, fasted, and prayed after hearing the news of his people in exile. Then he called out to God, reminding him of his promise to Moses. We too can trust that promise that God has the power to gather his children in a new dwelling, a place where His name is glorified.

Father, stir our hearts for our displaced brothers and sisters around the world. Remind us that we can do more than feel sad, worried, or confused about their loss. We can give our emotions back to you, and trust the power of your mighty, gathering hands.

"If you are unfaithful, I will scatter you among the peoples, but if you return to me and keep my commandments and do them, though your outcasts are in the uttermost parts of heaven, from there I will gather them and bring them to the place that I have chosen, to make my name dwell there."

NEHEMIAH 1:8-9 ESV

Parents value their children's obedience. There's nothing quite so gratifying as asking a child to do something, and watching them obey the first time. Even so, rewards are often necessary to spark the correct behavior. Perhaps this is why God needed to remind his children that if they returned to him and obeyed his commands, he would gather them up from the far corners of the earth and put them back in the place he marked.

As we pray for the physical losses today's displaced peoples face, let's not forget to pray for their spiritual losses as well. Many find themselves questioning their beliefs for the first time, and in these moments, God moves, asking only for obedience to his call.

Father, be present to those seeking refuge, and use your church wherever you need us. Let your voice be loudest, and your promises of a new home bring hope.

What is one country marked by displaced people that I can pray for tonight?

Eyes to See

Great are the works of the Lord;
they are pondered by all who delight in them.

PSALM 111:2 NIV

When you're preparing to climb a mountain, you start by
filling your backpack with the necessities: food, raingear,
sleeping bag, compass. But there's one thing you don't need
to pack. Entertainment. The best part about reaching a
mountaintop is the moment when you find a comfortable
rock, sit down, and simply stare across the wide expanse of
landscape and sky.

In that moment, God's majesty is the only thing you can take
in. You don't tighten your hiking boots and immediately start
scrambling down the rocks. You sit. Enjoy. Take delight in
what God has made.

Lord of the heavens and the earth, help me to carve out space
today for delight. Open my eyes a little wider to the places you are
at work in the physical world.

Great are the works of the Lord,
studied by all who delight in them.

PSALM 111:2 NASB

Maybe you found God at work today. Maybe you didn't. Maybe
you stopped to notice the intricate knee bending of a ladybug
walking across a windowsill. Or maybe you sat in a space
dominated by screens and deadlines, and only noticed how
the clock seemed a little too slow.

The psalmist doesn't tell us where to look for God's works.
He simply says, "they are pondered by all who delight
in them." That means that even if we aren't in a place
surrounded by splendor, we can still find ways to think about
God's greatness in our lives. The laugh of a child can fill us
with blessing. The thoughtful gesture from a coworker can
remind of God's care and provision.

No matter where you find yourself today, let God's greatness
fill your mind. Think about it. Talk about it. Encourage
another person with it.

Father, amaze me so much by your works that I want to learn more
about them.

What's one of God's miracles that I can learn more about?

Heart of Hospitality

Show hospitality to one another without grumbling.
1 PETER 4:9 ESV

When you get ready for a big event that's happening at your home, how do you go about it? Do you scrub the toilet with a song in your heart, or do you complain under your breath about how much work it is to get ready for guests?

There's no shame in fessing up to your grumbling. It's a rare gem of a person who enjoys cleaning toilets and putting away shoes and figuring out what will make guests feel welcome and comfortable.

However, Peter exhorts you to get beyond your complaints. Why? Because true hospitality seeks to lovingly serve those who walk through the door. As you prepare to open your home to a visitor this week, make it a point to prepare in a calm, thoughtful, and loving way. Your guests will sense it, and your father will bless you for it.

Lord God, help me to go about my work in a way that glorifies you and blesses others.

Cheerfully share your home with those who need a meal or a place to stay for the night.

1 PETER 4:9 TLB

There are some people who have an amazing gift for hospitality. They always seem to have a set of clean blankets and sheets, a comfortable bed or couch, and enough food in the fridge to share. Others of us have a hard time opening our doors, worrying that what we have to offer isn't good enough.

True hospitality doesn't require a perfectly matched home, new furnishings, or a pantry stocked to the brim. True hospitality is a simple sharing of necessities without the need to impress. It can say "out of my abundance, I'm happy to share" or "out of my little, I'm happy to share" with equal heart.

What would it take for you to feel hospitable and not stressed out when someone wants to come into your home? Take steps toward those changes, so that you can cheerfully share as Peter taught.

Father, fill me with the spirit of true hospitality and give me opportunity soon to put it into practice.

What are three things I can do to make it easier to feel hospitable?

Unfailing Love

If you are suffering according to God's will, keep on doing what is right and trust yourself to the God who made you, for he will never fail you.

1 PETER 4:19 TLB

This is a hard verse to read. What does it mean to suffer according to God's will? Believer, there aren't many who have an answer. What we can take away from it today is this: if it's God's will that we go through whatever we are currently facing, that also means that he himself knows the trials that have been allowed into our lives.

It may be incredibly hard to act as Peter tells us, and "keep on doing what is right and trust yourself to the God who made you." Sometimes our hurt and confusion overtake us. But finish the verse. For he will never fail you.

This a large statement, but if anyone can make it, it's Peter, the disciple who was conflicted, who denied Christ, and who fell on his face into the water he was supposed to be walking across. Peter knew suffering. But God knew Peter.

In the same way, God knows us. He has not failed us yet, and will not fail us now.

Father, we don't like suffering, but we cling to the promise that you will never fail us.

Let those who suffer according to God's will entrust their souls to a faithful Creator while doing good.

1 PETER 4:19 ESV

Many people have a favorite hymn that comes as easily to them as scripture does. 1 Peter 4:19 is a perfect parallel to the hymn "Day by Day." If you've never heard it, take a moment to look up the full lyrics and let their profound depth comfort you as you read and think through this verse again tonight. Here's the first verse:

> Day by day, and with each passing moment,
> Strength I find to meet my trials here;
> Trusting in my Father's wise bestowment,
> I've no cause for worry or for fear.
> He, whose heart is kind beyond all measure,
> Gives unto each day what He deems best,
> Lovingly its part of pain and pleasure,
> Mingling toil with peace and rest.

Your father is wise is his bestowment. Take heart. He knows what he is doing, and he is worthy of your trust.

Father, we know your heart is kind. Give us the strength to take this life in stride, knowing you walk beside us every step of the way.

What difficulty can you hand over to God tonight and replace with trust?

Restoration and Joy

"When I bring you home again from your captivity and restore your fortunes, Jerusalem will be rebuilt upon her ruins; the palace will be reconstructed as it was before. The cities will be filled with joy and great thanksgiving, and I will multiply my people and make of them a great and honored nation."

JEREMIAH 30: 18-19 TLB

Bless the Lord, oh my soul. He sees you in your times of sadness, your struggle, your brokenness. He promises to rebuild your hope on its old foundations, and lovingly restore you the way young couples dive into the project of restoring old mansions. Your faith will be great again. You will laugh with thanksgiving, and your voice will echo joy out the open windows.

But that's not all. Jeremiah goes on to tell the Israelites that things will just get better and better, and the next verse is even more powerful. Depression days are over.

If you've ever struggled with depression and anxiety, let the truth of these words run over you like cold, clean water. You, soul, will thrive and flourish. Yes, even from where you are now. This is not an empty promise, or a vacant hope. This truth is meant for you.

Father, your words are life to me. I can't wait to see your restoration and joy pour out of me.

"I will restore the fortunes of Jacob's tents and have compassion on his dwellings; the city will be rebuilt on her ruins, and the palace will stand in its proper place. From them will come songs of thanksgiving and the sound of rejoicing. I will add to their numbers, and they will not be decreased; I will bring them honor, and they will not be disdained."

JEREMIAH 30:18-19 NKJV

It would be nearly impossible to keep silent if someone came in, rebuilt your broken, busted out home, and reestablished your place inside of it.

Some of us will never have to face this challenge, and sadly, we are lesser for it. Imagine seeing firsthand the might and glory and kindness of your heavenly father as he goes to work, restoring what once was shattered in your life.

Thanksgiving would come naturally as breathing, wouldn't it? There would be no other way to pour out your gratitude for such kindness.

Sing your songs. Shout them aloud. God is worthy to be praised. He has restored your soul.

Father, I want to praise you with everything I have. Thank you for your restoration and rebuilding.

Is God rebuilding your life? Take a closer look. Then praise him for it.

All-Encompassing Praise

Praise God, from whom all blessings flow;
Praise Him, all creatures here below;
Praise Him above, ye heav'nly host;
Praise Father, Son, and Holy Ghost.

DOXOLOGY HYMN

Praise God, from whom all blessings flow. Sometimes you're grateful for the little things: a spouse who remembers what you've forgotten, a family table fully surrounded by chairs, a twilight walk, a tired child who just wants to be close. But it doesn't take long to realize that those little things—the things that don't seem like much on their own - are actually quite the opposite.

Praise Him, all creatures here below. God loves praise from his people, young and old alike.

It doesn't matter if you're three and thanking him for a favorite treat, or you're 45 and are breathing a quick thank you that you have enough money for the obligations at the end of the month. Your heavenly father loves it when you appreciate his gifts in all the walks of your life. Let your mind awaken by thinking about what he's blessed you with today.

Father, you are the great giver, and I am overwhelmed with the blessing of being your child.

Praise God, from whom all blessings flow;
Praise Him, all creatures here below;
Praise Him above, ye heav'nly host;
Praise Father, Son, and Holy Ghost.

DOXOLOGY HYMN

"Praise Him above, ye heav'nly host." Imagine, as you're settling your spirit before bed tonight, how amazing the singers of heaven's choir must sound. Think of the best concert you've ever attended, and how broadly the music overtook whatever space you were in. Now multiply that tenfold, and feel the magnitude of praise God loves receiving from his heavenly host. Someday you will have the joy of joining with those voices.

"Praise Father, Son, and Holy Ghost." Now picture, as you're standing among the throng of worship, seeing the Father, seeing Jesus, and seeing the Holy Spirit all together at one time. It's beautiful to picture them together, yet separate, glowing in glory.

Father, Son, and Spirit, I praise you for your active, moving presence in my life today.

Identify the ways your life was directed, blessed, or moved by each member of the Trinity today.

Watchtower Waiting

I wait for the Lord, my whole being waits, and in his word I put my hope. I wait for the Lord more than watchmen wait for the morning, more than watchmen wait for the morning. Israel, put your hope in the Lord, for with the Lord is unfailing love and with him is full redemption.

PSALM 130:5-7 NIV

Everyone loves sleep. There's not a single one of us who would deny the need for a solid stretch of it every night. We wake up recharged, somehow ready for another day in the action. But if you were a night watchman in old testament times, you put aside the natural rhythm of sleep in order to do you work protecting the city.

Watchmen waited eagerly for morning because it meant relief from the next guard. It also meant that they were awake during the darkest, most uncertain times of night. Attackers could be hiding, or siege could be massing. Watchmen were tasked with warning, preparing, and protecting their post at all costs.

It's that kind of waiting on the Lord that the psalmist exhorts us too, not once, but twice. Even in the darkness we can't see through, we must sharpen all our senses, listening, feeling, testing for what God is telling us.

Father, keep us alert in our waiting upon you, un-dulled by darkness or inactivity. Your Word is our hope, your message full redemption.

*That is why I wait expectantly, trusting God to help, for he has
promised. I long for him more than sentinels long for the dawn.
O Israel, hope in the Lord; for he is loving and kind and comes
to us with armloads of salvation.*

PSALM 130:5-7 TLB

Have you ever waited for something that simply didn't come?
Realizing that someone on the other side didn't hold up
their end of the bargain is ultimately frustrating. However,
we never have to worry that God won't come through on
his promise to help us in our times of need. Over and over,
scripture points to his faithfulness, his kindness, his love.

That help might arrive in a different form than we were
expecting, or it might take longer to arrive than we would have
wanted. Do not be discouraged. If you are waiting on God's help
and rescue today, soak yourself in these verses from Psalms
130. God hears your longing, and promises to come through—
not just with a token salve but with armloads of salvation.

*Father, help me to wait expectantly for your salvation. Reignite my
trust with the fire of your love and kindness and the reality of your
imminent grace.*

Realign your waiting heart to a posture of expectancy and
hope today.

Jesus Stops

When Bartimaeus heard that Jesus of Nazareth was nearby, he began to shout, "Jesus, Son of David, have mercy on me!" When Jesus heard him, he stopped and said, "Tell him to come here." So they called the blind man. "Cheer up," they said. "Come on, he's calling you!"

MARK 10:47, 49 NLT

A pastor once asked the question, "What does Christ do for us?" People in the audience shouted out about how Jesus heals, redeems and forgives, but it was a young man in the back who offered one of the more profound statements. He simply said, "He stops." Jesus was constantly surrounded by people who needed him and called out to him. It must have been tiring and overwhelming, but over and over again Jesus stopped. He took the time to be with people, to care for them and to minister to their needs. Why did he stop? He stopped because he loved them. And that is still true today.

This same Jesus who stopped for people like Bartimaeus, will stop for us as well. He is not in too much of a hurry. He is not too busy. He hears us when we call on him and he stops.

Heavenly Father, thank you that you love me enough to stop and care for my needs when I call out to you.

When he heard that it was Jesus of Nazareth, he began to cry out and say, "Jesus, Son of David, have mercy on me!"
And Jesus stopped and said, "Call him." And they called the blind man, saying to him, "Take heart. Get up; he is calling you."

MARK 10:47, 49 ESV

When you cry out to Jesus do you stop and take the time to listen for a response? Many times, when we pray for a need, we don't really take the time to stop and see God's response. We go on with our lives without any real expectation that God is going to respond at all. Wat happened when Bartimaeus cried out to Jesus? Jesus stopped and then he called Bartimaeus to himself. What if Bartimaeus had moved on and missed that call?

Throughout the Gospels we see that Jesus stops when people cry out to him. And he has never stopped stopping. Maybe it is time for us to stop too. What if after calling out for Jesus to intervene in some area of our lives, we actually stopped and listened and expected him to respond?

Lord, I am crying out to you today in expectation. I am quieting my soul to listen for your response. Hell me to hear you today.

When you call out to God do you stop and wait for an answer?

Rescued and Reborn

He saved us, not because of works done by us in righteousness,
but according to his own mercy, by the washing of regeneration
and renewal of the Holy Spirit, whom he poured out on us richly
through Jesus Christ our Savior.

TITUS 3:5-6 ESV

Have you ever thought about what it means to be saved? A
good alternate word would be the word, "rescue." We were
stuck in our sin and headed to eternal separation from God
in Hell when he reached out and rescued us. God didn't save
us because we were worthy of being saved. He didn't save us
because we were good. He didn't even save us because of our
potential for good. He saved us because he loved us and we
needed saving.

It is not easy for us to admit our need to be rescued. It makes
us feel helpless. But that is what we are. Without the saving
grace of our Father in Heaven, made available through Jesus
Christ, we would have been lost. He rescued us.

Heavenly Father, without you I would have been lost, thank you
for rescuing me.

He came to save us. Not because of any virtuous deed that we have done but only because of his extravagant mercy. He saved us, resurrecting us through the washing of rebirth. We are made completely new by the Holy Spirit, whom he splashed over us richly by Jesus, the Messiah, our Life Giver.

TITUS 3:5-6 TPT

Not only have we been rescued, we also have been reborn. There is a spiritual regeneration process that the Holy Spirit does in our lives. Who we were does not need to define us anymore. No matter what we have done in the past, we have been given new life in Christ. And notice also that in these verses Paul gives us the image of the Holy Spirit being poured out on us richly and he uses the phrase "extravagant mercy." He is not being stingy. He is not holding back.

No matter how messy our lives were, he pours out on us generously all that is needed to wash us clean and give us new life. He is not worried about running out as if there might not be enough grace to go around. His work of salvation is complete in our lives. We are rescued and reborn.

Father, thank you for giving me new life in you. Thank you for pouring out your Holy Spirit on my generously and showing me grace.

Are you still letting your old life define you even though you have been reborn?

Faithful

If we are faithless, he remains faithful,
for he cannot disown himself.

2 TIMOTHY 2:13 NIV

What does it mean to be faithless? It doesn't mean to not have faith. It means to be unworthy of faith. Someone who is faithful can be counted on to do what they say they will do. Someone who is faithless cannot be counted on in the same way. We are faithless people when it comes to our relationship with God. We mess up, we go our own way, we do our own thing, and we faithlessly fail to live out what we say we believe.

But notice what this verse reveals to us about God. Even when we are faithless he remains faithful. That means he will always keep his side of the covenant. He will always show us grace, mercy. love and forgiveness even though we continually mess up. That is not an excuse for us to mess up more, but a good reminder of how we can count on him to be faithful even when we are not.

Heavenly Father, thank you that you are faithful even when I am faithless.

If we are not faithful, he remains faithful,
because he cannot be false to himself.

2 TIMOTHY 2:13 GNT

Notice that Paul says that God remains faithful because he
cannot be false to himself. Nothing is impossible for God, but
one thing he can't (or won't) do is something that is contrary
to his nature. Who God is, is who God is. He will always act in
a way that is true to his nature. He will not deny himself. That
means that we can count on him to continually act according to
what he has revealed to us about who he is. He won't change.

Our circumstances may change. Our thoughts and feelings
may change. Our understanding of who he is may change. Our
level of faith and trust in him may change. But God remains
the same. There are enough other things constantly changing
in our lives isn't it great to know that God remains the same?
We can always count on him.

God, thank you that in a constantly changing world, you will
always remain constant. Thank you that I can trust in you to be
faithful.

In what ways might you be living a faithless life?

Sin Costs

Indeed, under the law almost everything is purified with blood, and without the shedding of blood there is no forgiveness of sins.

HEBREWS 9:22 ESV

Blood represents life. We need our blood to survive. But this verse points out that blood was also needed for the forgiveness of sins. In the Old Testament, the people would take an animal they had raised or purchased and sacrifice it to atone for their sin. It wasn't literally the blood of the animal that saved them or washed them, but it symbolized their desire for cleansing from God. It pointed ahead to the salvation that would come through Christ's sacrifice on the cross.

The blood of the bulls and goats symbolized how Christ's blood would eventually be spilt to atone for the sins of mankind. It might seem cruel today to think about that Old Testament system of animal sacrifice, but at least the people under that system understood the cost of sin. It is important for us to recognize that our sins are atoned for because of Christ's sacrifice. We need to recognize that dealing with sin costs something.

Dear Jesus, thank you for the tremendous cost you paid for my sin.

Actually, nearly everything under the law was purified with blood, since forgiveness only comes through an outpouring of blood.

HEBREWS 9:22 TPT

It is easy for us to take sin lightly and thereby to take grace lightly. We forget how great a price was paid for our sin. When we ask for forgiveness for our sins it is not like God says, "It's okay, don't worry about it, it's no big deal." That is not how he treats sin.

When we ask for forgiveness, God says, "It is a big deal. It separates me from you. But I sent my Son as a sacrifice for your sin, because I love you. I don't treat you as your sins deserve. I choose to show you grace and mercy. Because of the sacrifice of my son, you are forgiven." Sin costs something, but Jesus paid that cost.

Heavenly Father, thank you for sending your son to shed his blood for me. Thank you for the cost that was paid for my forgiveness.

How does recognizing the precious cost that was paid for your forgiveness make you feel about how valuable you are in God's sight?

Paradise

*He said, "Jesus, remember me when you come into your kingdom."
And he said to him, "Truly, I say to you, today you will be with me
in paradise."*

LUKE 23:42-43 ESV

What in the world did the thief on the cross see in this
beaten, mocked, spit upon, crucified Jesus that caused him
to seek him as his Savior and Lord? You would think that this
was probably the moment when Jesus looked least like the
Messiah that people were expecting than at any point in his
life. Yet it is at this moment that the thief on the cross next to
Jesus recognizes his need to connect himself to this man who
was about to die. Why? Was it the way Jesus was silent before
those who mocked and beat him? Was it the way he asked the
Father to forgive them for what they were doing? Or was it
simply because at this moment the Holy Spirit opened up his
heart and let him see Jesus for who he really was?

The thief's question made no sense from a worldly
perspective, but Jesus really was about to inherit his kingdom
and the thief was welcomed to join him.

*Dear Jesus, thank you for opening my eyes and letting me see who
you really are and what you came to do for me.*

*He said to Jesus, "Remember me, Jesus, when you come as King!"
Jesus said to him, "I promise you that today you will be in
Paradise with me."*

LUKE 23:42-43 GNT

Are you looking forward to paradise? What do you think it will
be like? Scripture is a little bit vague about what exactly paradise
or Heaven will be like. We get glimpses, but not a very clear
picture. But the one thing Scripture is not vague on is actually
the most important thing we need to know about Heaven.

That most important thing is that in Heaven we will be, for
all eternity, in the presence of Christ. Jesus tells the thief on
the cross, "Today you will be with me in paradise." It doesn't
really matter where Heaven is or even exactly what it will be
like. It is the presence of Christ that makes it paradise.

*Dear Jesus, I look forward to being with you for all eternity. Thank
you for dying on the cross to make that possible.*

What do you think your response will be when you get to see
Jesus face to face for the first time in paradise?

Thanksgiving

Oh give thanks to the Lord, for he is good,
for his steadfast love endures forever!

PSALM 107:1 ESV

This Psalm begins with the instruction to give thanks to
the Lord because he is good. But what about when life does
not feel so good? Right now there are people all over the
world who are facing persecution, famine, hardship, war,
sickness, depression, anxiety, poverty, broken relationships
and so many other terrible things. Sometimes when our
circumstances are not good it is easy for us to doubt God's
goodness. This verse reminds us that God's goodness doesn't
change simply because our circumstances change.

We live in a sin-cursed world, and that means that we are
going to face tough times. Goodness is a characteristic of
who God is regardless of what our circumstances might be.
We need to begin with that foundational truth about God and
then try and understand our circumstances in light of the
truth about who he is.

Heavenly Father, I thank you that you are good. Help me to rely
upon and trust that truth about who you are even when my
circumstances might be tough.

Oh give thanks to the Lord, for He is good,
For His lovingkindness is everlasting.

        PSALM 107:1 NASB

Does your family have the tradition on Thanksgiving of going around the table and saying something you are thankful for? That is a good practice, but we need to do it more than just once a year. Giving thanks is important. Giving thanks is good because God deserves our thanks, but it is also good because it helps us build a strong foundation for whatever we might face in the future. It is kind of like storing up for ourselves memories of God's goodness for those times when we might not be feeling so thankful later on. We know that when times are tough we don't necessarily feel like giving thanks.

Having a storehouse of thankful memories of how God has provided for us in the past can help us to continue to trust him through those times in our life when the way is hard. Thanksgiving is a crucial part of our lives and if we are wise, we will take the time to do it, not just once a year, but all the time.

Heavenly Father, thank you for all you do for me. Please help me to take the time to give thanks and remember your goodness and lovingkindness toward me.

What are you thankful for?

Give Ear

"Give ear, our God, and hear; open your eyes and see the desolation of the city that bears your Name. We do not make requests of you because we are righteous, but because of your great mercy."

DANIEL 9:18 NIV

In William Shakespeare's play "Julius Caesar," Marc Antony utters the famous words, "Friends, Romans, countrymen, lend me your ears," Daniel is basically uttering the same thing to God in this prayer as he considers the desolation of Jerusalem. In both Antony's speech and Daniel's prayer we see a desire to be heard. Marc Antony wanted to be heard by the crowd, but Daniel is making a more audacious request. He wants to be heard by God.

Have you ever thought about how truly amazing it is that when we pray we are actually calling out to the almighty Creator of the universe and asking him to hear us? That is pretty incredible, but what is even more amazing is that not only does he hear us, he actually listens to us when we pray.

Heavenly Father, thank you that you not only hear me, but you actually take the time to listen to me when I call upon you.

"O my God, lean down and listen to me. Open your eyes and see our despair. See how your city—the city that bears your name—lies in ruins. We make this plea, not because we deserve help, but because of your mercy."

DANIEL 9:18 NLT

Notice that when Daniel makes this plea he is not relying upon how deserving he is of God's help, but rather relying instead upon God's character. He does not say that God should listen to him because he is worthy of being listened to, but because he knows that God is merciful. Daniel knows that God loves his people and that he chooses to deal with them with grace and compassion. Thankfully our prayers are not reliant upon how much we deserve God's help.

God helps us not because of how deserving we are, but because of his mercy. God loves us and has a covenant relationship with us. So, when we pray, let's depend upon his character rather than on our worthiness to be heard.

Heavenly Father thank you that you hear me when I call to you and that your help for me is not based upon my worthiness, but upon your mercy.

What aspect of God's character are you most dependent upon right now?

Knowing God

"My ears had heard of you but now my eyes have seen you. Therefore I despise myself and repent in dust and ashes."

JOB 42:5-6 NIV

We get to know about God when we read the Bible and listen to others talk about him, but we don't really get to know him until we experience him. It's when we take what we know about God and trust him to be who he says he is that we really get to know him. Notice that Job says these words only after a time of tremendous struggle and pain. It is in the midst of that tough time that he actually comes face to face with God and gets to know him.

Let's not be satisfied with just knowing about God. It is good for us to get to know about him, but in life when what we know about God is put to the test that's when we will really get to know him.

Heavenly Father, help me to know you.

"I have heard of You by the hearing of the ear, But now my eye sees You. Therefore I abhor myself, And repent in dust and ashes."

JOB 42:5-6 NKJV

So after Job has gone through all this tough stuff and has come face to face with God, his immediate reaction is to fall on his knees in repentance. That is not surprising. When we finally find ourselves seeing God clearly in all his greatness, it will also cause us to recognize our filthiness.

The light of his goodness exposes all of the ugly thoughts, motives, actions and desires in our lives. Our tendency then is to want to run away and hide from his light, but instead we should remain in his light, repenting of our sins, turning completely to God, falling on our knees in repentance and letting him forgive and heal us.

God, forgive me, cleanse me, shine your light on those areas of my life that you want to change. Help me to remain in you even though it is sometimes hard to have those painful things exposed in me.

Is there an area of your life where God is shining his light right now where you need to repent and turn to him?

Refuge

The Lord is good, a stronghold in the day of trouble;
he knows those who take refuge in him.

NAHUM 1:7 ESV

Did you know that deep inside a mountain on the island of Spitsbergen in Norway there is a seed vault that is meant to withstand just about any natural disaster? It was built as a place to safely keep seeds from all over the world so that they could be used to repopulate the plant life of the earth in case of an extinction level event. It is basically a seed stronghold for times of trouble.

Imagine if a disaster was approaching. Where would be the safest place for you to hide? What stronghold would you run to for safety? This verse tells us that the Lord is our safe place. He is the stronghold where we can run when trouble comes.

Heavenly Father, you are my safe place. Thank you for being my stronghold for times of trouble.

The Lord is good,
a refuge in times of trouble.
He cares for those who trust in him.

NAHUM 1:7 NIV

Have you ever been a refugee? Have you ever been through a
time of trouble like a hurricane, flood, war, or famine where
you have had to leave your home and go to a place of refuge?
Many people truly know what it means to have to run to a
place of refuge. In those situations, those places are welcome
sites for those in need.

This verse speaks of the Lord being a refuge for times of
trouble. If you go on and read the rest of Nahum 1 you will
find that it is not all good news. This verse stands in stark
contrast to the verses around it that speak of those who do
not trust in God. In this chapter, Nahum is prophesying about
the destruction of Nineveh. This refuge would stand out
greatly compared to the destruction spoken of in the rest of
the chapter. This verse points out that the Lord is a refuge for
those who trust in him.

God, thank you that you are my refuge. I trust in you.

Are there people around you who are in need of coming to
God for refuge? Can you introduce them to him?

Gentleness

"I know, Lord, that our lives are not our own.
We are not able to plan our own course.
So correct me, Lord, but please be gentle.
Do not correct me in anger, for I would die."

JEREMIAH 11:23-24 NLT

It is so good that God is gentle with us when he corrects us. He is a powerful God and very capable of wiping us off of the face of the earth. But thankfully this all-powerful God is also gracious, compassionate, merciful, loving, patient and gentle. He does want what is best for us and he will correct us, but he does so in a way that allows us to grow rather than destroying us in the process.

Jeremiah recognizes God's gentleness and that emboldens him to seek God's correction. The same should be true of us. We want to learn from our mistakes, so let's go to our loving Father for the correction we need and trust him to be gentle with us.

Heavenly Father, I thank you for your gentleness. I know that I need your correction. Please help me to follow you.

*"I know, O Lord, that a man's way is not in himself,
Nor is it in a man who walks to direct his steps.
Correct me, O Lord, but with justice;
Not with Your anger, or You will bring me to nothing."*

JEREMIAH 11:23-24 NASB

We have a tendency to want to direct our own lives. It is hard for us to give up control. We think we know best the direction for us to go. The problem is, our lives are not our own. Our lives belong to God. He alone knows what is best for us. Our view is very short-sighted.

We can only see a little bit ahead. God has a much better view than we do and is in a much better position to direct our steps. That means when we get off track or go our own way, we need his correction to bring us back to the way to go. Sometimes the biggest barrier in the way of our success is simply our unwillingness to give up control and follow God.

God, I recognize my need for your direction, correction and even discipline. Help me to let you lead me.

Is there a place in your life where you are still the one in control? Are you hesitant to let God direct or change your steps? What is holding you back?

More Than an Idol

Like a scarecrow in a cucumber field,
their idols cannot speak;
they must be carried
because they cannot walk.
Do not fear them;
they can do no harm
nor can they do any good.
No one is like you, Lord;
you are great,
and your name is mighty in power.

JEREMIAH 10:5-6 NIV

What a beautiful analogy of the difference between man-made gods and the one true God. Man-made gods are nothing more than scarecrows in a cucumber field. They have no power of their own. They can do nothing. And yet people bow down and worship them. That means that they are worshipping the things that their own hands have made.

On the flip side, there is one true God who is real and powerful. He is great and his name is mighty in power. He alone is deserving of our worship.

God, I know that I am to have no other gods before you. Forgive me for the ways that I have allowed anything else in my life to take the position that only you deserve. Please help me to worship only you.

Their gods are like
helpless scarecrows in a cucumber field!
They cannot speak,
and they need to be carried because they cannot walk.
Do not be afraid of such gods,
for they can neither harm you nor do you any good.
Lord, there is no one like you!
For you are great, and your name is full of power.

JEREMIAH 10:5-6 NLT

When we pray to God we are calling upon a great God whose name is full of power. Let's never forget that. Let's not look at God like he is a lucky rabbit's foot or a four-leaf clover that might bring us good luck.

Let's not treat God the same as throwing a penny in a wishing well. Let's recognize that God has ears to hear and the power to change our circumstances. Let's recognize that when we pray we are coming before a God who is great and whose name is full of power.

Heavenly Father, I praise you that you are more than an idol. I praise you for your infinite power. I ask you to accomplish your work in my life.

In what ways have you been treating God like nothing more than an idol?

Open Wide

For it was I, the Lord your God,
who rescued you from the land of Egypt.
Open your mouth wide, and I will fill it with good things.

PSALM 81:10 NLT

Throughout the Old Testament we see that God had a very interesting relationship with the people of Israel. He was constantly rescuing them and taking care of them, but they had a tendency to forget about him and to wander from him. In this verse we see God reminding his people of how he rescued them from Egypt. He miraculously delivered them from the hand of Pharaoh and led them out of slavery. Yet after winding up in the wilderness they began to complain about how good they had things while in Egypt. They forgot about what God had already done for them and rather than trusting in God, they chose to complain.

We do the same thing. We tend to focus on our current circumstances and forget all that God has done for us. When we do that it is easy to begin looking elsewhere for our mouths to be filled when we should be trusting in and waiting upon God.

Heavenly Father, please forgive me for the times I have forgotten about all that you have done for me. Please help me to trust in and wait upon you.

I am the Lord your God,
who brought you up out of the land of Egypt.
Open your mouth wide, and I will fill it.

PSALM 81:10 ESV

Have you ever seen a nest full of hungry baby birds? What do they do? They crane their necks back, look up at the sky, and open their mouths wide. Why? Because they know that their momma bird is going to be coming with some food, and she is going to drop that food in their mouths and they will be fed. They open their mouths wide in expectation so that she can fill it.

The same should be true of us. Our God loves us. He has already provided for us in so many ways. He wants to feed us, physically, emotionally and spiritually. We should be like those baby birds, expectantly gazing up to Heaven with our mouths open wide (metaphorically speaking), ready to receive from him all that he wants to give us.

God, please help me to be keep my mouth open wide for you. I need the food you have to offer.

What does it look like for us to open wide our mouths expectantly waiting for God to fill us?

Another Sympathy Card

*I have said these things to you, that in me you may have peace.
In the world you will have tribulation. But take heart; I have
overcome the world."*

JOHN 16:33 ESV

Have you ever received a sympathy card that offers some pithy
statement that feels like nothing more than an empty cliché
in the midst of your grief and pain? We face tough times on
this earth. Everything is not always perfect in our lives. In
those moments, we don't need someone's feeble statement
about how everything is okay when we know it's not.

This verse is powerful because Jesus doesn't deny our
suffering. He doesn't pretend that everything is okay
when it's not. In this verse, Jesus lets us know that tough
times are going to come, but we can take heart and keep
going because ultimately God is in control. He doesn't just
offer us sympathy, he offers us himself. That's much more
meaningful than anything we might find in a sympathy card!

*Heavenly Father, thank you that you don't deny my struggles. Thank
you that I can trust in you because you have overcome the world.*

"I told you these things so that you can have peace in me. In this world you will have trouble, but be brave! I have defeated the world."

JOHN 16:33 NCV

It is important for us to recognize that it is Jesus saying these words. When Jesus came to the earth, he became fully man even though he was fully God. That is a big theological concept that is hard to understand, but it is important for us to recognize that it means that Jesus understands our struggles. When he tells us that in this world we will experience difficulties, he knows what he is talking about because he has walked in our shoes.

We can take heart, because he has conquered the world. He laid down his life for us and then rose again in victory and he now sits at the right hand of God interceding on our behalf. So, when we pray, we are praying to someone who knows what we are going through and who has overcome. And he is helping us to overcome as well.

Dear Jesus, thank you that you understand what I face.
Thank you that you know my struggles. Thank you that overcame.
Please help me to overcome.

How does knowing that Jesus understands your struggle help you take heart?

Beautiful Feet

How then will they call on him in whom they have not believed?
And how are they to believe in him of whom they have never
heard? And how are they to hear without someone preaching?
And how are they to preach unless they are sent? As it is written,
"How beautiful are the feet of those who preach the good news!"

ROMANS 10:14-15 ESV

On the beaches of Normandy, June 6, 1944, over 150,000
soldiers landed on beaches that were some of the most
heavily fortified positions of World War II. They marched
up those beaches into the teeth of the German defense.
Their goal was the liberation of France. It is estimated that
there were over 4,000 casualties on those beaches on that
day alone. These soldiers, both the living and the dead, will
forever be remembered for setting foot on those beaches.

Around 2,000 years ago, Jesus Christ left heaven and set foot
on this earth. He lived a sinless life and then died on the cross
taking the sins of the world upon himself. His footprints on
this earth will always be cherished for giving his life for the
freedom of all mankind. That is the good news that this verse
refers to and it is that good news that Paul is calling us to bring
to a world that needs to hear this message of freedom.

Dear Jesus, thank you for setting foot on this earth to save me and
bring me freedom.

How, then, can they call on the one they have not believed in?
And how can they believe in the one of whom they have not heard?
And how can they hear without someone preaching to them?
And how can anyone preach unless they are sent? As it is written:
"How beautiful are the feet of those who bring good news!"

ROMANS 10:14-15 NIV

Paul gives us a very logical argument in this passage. The logic is childlike in its simplicity. This Gospel message is Good News! We are living in a world filled with people who need this message. And how can they hear unless someone takes the message to them?

What a powerful challenge for us to recognize that we have been given a message that needs to be shared. We can be that beautiful person bringing the good news to someone who has never heard it so that they too can trust in the Lord.

Heavenly Father, please open my eyes to see those around me who don't know you. Help me to be open to going and telling others who need to hear this good news.

Who are the people you know who need to hear this good news?

Crossroads

"Stand at the crossroads and look;
ask for the ancient paths,
ask where the good way is, and walk in it,
and you will find rest for your souls.
But you said, 'We will not walk in it.'

JEREMIAH 6:16 NIV

The world around us has discarded the Bible as irrelevant and instead embraced relativism. They have shunned the idea of absolute truth. What about you? Do you really believe that God's way is the best way? Is his path the right path? It's like we are standing at a crossroads and we have the opportunity to consider the way to go.

Are we going to trust God and follow his plan for our lives or are we going to choose our own way. The Lord very clearly lays out for us that his way is what is best for us. Do we trust him?

Heavenly Father, I trust you. I believe you path is the way for me to go. Help me to follow you.

"Stand at the crossroads and look.
Ask for the ancient paths
and where the best road is.
Walk in it, and you will live in peace."
But they said, "No, we will not!"

JEREMIAH 6:16 GNT

Throughout the Old Testament we see over and over again what happens when God's people choose to not follow God's plan for their lives. All of those stories stand as a warning for us. He wants us to choose to do things his way. But still today we stubbornly choose to ignore God's plan. We learn his ways. But rather than following him, we choose to follow our own counsel. Then we wonder why we don't have peace.

This plea from the Lord to choose his path is repeated throughout Scripture. It is not just in the Old Testament. We see it in Jesus' words as well. God is calling out to us as we stand at the crossroads.

God, lead me. Forgive me for the times I have gone my own way.
I recognize that I don't know the way to go. Lead me and help me
to follow you.

Where have you strayed from the path God wants you to be on?

Fire and Smoke

The satraps, the prefects, the governors, and the king's counselors gathered together and saw that the fire had not had any power over the bodies of those men. The hair of their heads was not singed, their cloaks were not harmed, and no smell of fire had come upon them.

DANIEL 3:27 ESV

This is from the amazing story of Shadrach, Meshach, and Abednego. They stood up in the face of religious persecution and were thrown into the fiery furnace, but God spared them and brought them safely out. It is an amazing story, but maybe the most amazing detail has to do with the smell. Have you ever heard the phrase, "Where there's smoke there's fire?" If we can see and smell smoke we naturally assume that there must be a fire nearby.

In this story there is an obvious fire, but after being thrown into it not only were these men not harmed, they did not even smell like smoke when God delivered them. Normally, if we even stand close to a campfire we will come away with the smell of smoke so prevalent that we will find ourselves getting a whiff of it for days. God's miraculous power is so complete that he allowed them to come through the furnace as if the fire wasn't even there. He truly is an all-powerful God.

Heavenly Father, I stand amazed at your power and the completeness of your miracles.

The satraps, the prefects, the governors and the king's high officials gathered around and saw in regard to these men that the fire had no [effect on]the bodies of these men nor was the hair of their head singed, nor were their]trousers [damaged, nor had the smell of fire even come upon them.

DANIEL 3:27 NASB

Imagine the impact this miracle had on the crowd that had gathered. Imagine how their opinion of God was changed by this event. When God intervenes in our lives in miraculous ways it brings honor and glory to him.

Throughout the Old Testament God used the people of Israel to display himself to the world. Now he uses us, his Church, to accomplish the same purposes. If we will follow him, even in the midst of opposition he can work in miraculous ways to take care of us and bring himself glory.

God, I trust you with my life. May you use me to display yourself to this world.

What might God want to do through your life to bring him glory? Are you open to ways that he might want to use you?

Traveling Salesman

"Behold, I stand at the door and knock. If anyone hears my voice and opens the door, I will come in to him and eat with him, and he with me."

REVELATION 3:20 ESV

Have you ever heard a knock upon your door and figured it was some kind of salesman wanting to sell you something? People often come by our door looking to sell us anything from cookies to carpet cleaning and everything in between. We figured that the only reason they would come by our house is that they want something from us.

Make no mistake about it, Jesus is no traveling salesman. He is not knocking on our door because he wants something from us, but because of what he wants to give us. He has come to bring us life. He is offering forgiveness of sins, reconciliation to the Father, and the hope of eternal life. And he is offering all of it as a free gift. How incredible that Jesus Christ, our Savior, comes and knocks on our door seeking to bring us life.

Dear Jesus, thank you for knocking on my door, revealing yourself to me, and bringing me life.

"Behold, I stand at the door and knock. If anyone hears My voice and opens the door, I will come in to him and dine with him, and he with Me."

REVELATION 3:20 NKJV

Jesus is not looking to sell (or give) us a bill of goods and then leave us to figure out what to do with it. Jesus is seeking a relationship with us. He wants us to invite him in, not just for a sales pitch, not even just for a meal, but for a lifetime. He wants to abide with us. He wants to set up residence in our lives. He is in this for the long haul. When we open the door, we can't just take the free gift of salvation and go on our way.

We need to invite him in and welcome him into our lives. He is not just looking to save us from hell, but to give us abundant life. When we open that door, he begins a good work in our life that he will continue until he sees us safely home.

Dear Jesus, thank you for coming into my life and having a relationship with me. Help me to know the abundant life that is available to me with you.

Where is Jesus in your life? Is he sitting at the table with you as your friend or is he still standing outside on the doorstep waiting for you to invite him in?

Embracing Our Thorns

He said to me, "My grace is sufficient for you, for my power is made perfect in weakness." Therefore I will boast all the more gladly about my weaknesses, so that Christ's power may rest on me.

2 CORINTHIANS 12:9 NIV

We don't like to feel weak. We are taught that weakness is not a good trait. But Paul seems to take delight in his weaknesses. He even claims to boast about them. Why? Because it is in his weakness that Christ's power is at work. Typically, when we feel weak we want to fix whatever is wrong so that we can feel strong.

When we are able to admit our inability to do something and confess our need for God, then his power works in us to accomplish things that we never could have done on our own. Our strength sometimes gets in the way. We need to embrace our weaknesses and let God be the one who works in us to accomplish his purposes and plans.

Heavenly Father, I thank you that your grace is sufficient for me. Help me to embrace my weaknesses, trust in you, and let you work in my life to accomplish whatever you want to do.

Each time he said, "My grace is all you need. My power works best in weakness." So now I am glad to boast about my weaknesses, so that the power of Christ can work through me.

2 CORINTHIANS 12:9 NLT

The context for this verse is that Paul is talking about a "thorn in his flesh" that he had asked God repeatedly to take away. Each time he is told that all he needs is God's grace. Paul never reveals to us specifically what is the thorn in his flesh. Maybe that is a good thing, because it allows us to picture him struggling with the same things that we struggle with. Not knowing exactly what his thorn was allows us to identify with him.

Rather than removing Paul's thorn, God reminds Paul of his grace and power in the midst of Paul's weakness. Sometimes God chooses to take away the difficult things we face. Other times he chooses to use those thorns to change us and help us grow. The thorns themselves may not be good, but God can do amazing things through the thorns in our lives. Maybe it is time we learned to embrace them and let God work.

God, I need your work in my life. You know my thorns better than I do. And you know what you want to accomplish in my life. I submit to you.

Paul had learned to live with the thorn in his flesh. Have you?

Nearsightedness

We have small troubles for a while now, but they are helping us gain an eternal glory. That glory is much greater than the troubles. So we set our eyes not on what we see but on what we cannot see. What we see will last only a short time. But what we cannot see will last forever.

2 CORINTHIANS 4:17-18 ICB

Many of Paul's letters were written while he was behind bars. Sometimes those imprisonments were also accompanied by beatings. What would you be like if you ever found yourself in similar circumstances?

As we read about Paul in the book of Acts and in his many letters, we get an image of a man who was somehow able to sit in prison praising God. It is while in those circumstances that we find him singing hymns, witnessing to others, and writing letters of encouragement to believers across the Roman world. That seems very unnatural. Most people would be either crying or complaining if they found themselves in circumstances like Paul, but he had an eternal perspective that helped him see past his sufferings and focus on God.

Heavenly Father, please help me to fix my eyes upon you. The troubles I face are hard and it is easy for me to fixate on them. Please help me keep my eyes on you.

This light momentary affliction is preparing for us an eternal weight of glory beyond all comparison, as we look not to the things that are seen but to the things that are unseen. For the things that are seen are transient, but the things that are unseen are eternal.

2 CORINTHIANS 4:17-18 ESV

Many of us are nearsighted. We can see and read things when they are close to our face, but the things that are off in the distance are not as clear. We need glasses to help us better see those things in the distance. Paul had an unnatural ability to see past the visible things in this life and see the invisible God. When Paul was in prison it was like the bars didn't even exist. It wasn't because of a special kind of corrective lenses, but a choice. It wasn't like Paul was farsighted, but rather eternally-minded.

Paul points out that when weighed against each other the momentary afflictions can't compare to the glory that lies ahead. Many of us are nearsighted in life. We get so focused on the stuff right in front of our face, that we can't clearly see God. It's time to change that.

God, it isn't so easy to see you when the afflictions around me are so prevalent. Please help me to fix my eyes upon you.

What troubles are you facing now? How are they keeping you from seeing God?

441

Marathon of Life

Even youths shall faint and be weary,
and young men shall fall exhausted;
but they who wait for the Lord shall renew their strength;
they shall mount up with wings like eagles;
they shall run and not be weary;
they shall walk and not faint.

ISAIAH 40:30-31 ESV

Life is kind of like running a marathon. We start the race and it seems relatively easy because we have our stamina and energy. The longer we go, the more we realize that the way is tough and it will take endurance.

As we go through this life sometimes the way seems easy, but other times the road gets tough and it is hard even putting one foot in front of the other. But these verses suggest that as we run through this marathon of life we can rely on God. He promises that if we wait on him he will help us to run, walk and even soar on wings like eagles.

Heavenly Father, thank you that I am not alone on this marathon of life. Please help me to wait on you.

Even those who are young grow weak;
young people can fall exhausted.
But those who trust in the Lord for help
will find their strength renewed.
They will rise on wings like eagles;
they will run and not get weary;
they will walk and not grow weak.

ISAIAH 40:30-31 GNT

These verses suggest that youthful energy and physical stamina are not enough. The key to running the marathon of life is relying upon the Lord. That does not mean that we just sit around and wait for him to pick us up and carry us to where he wants us to go. It means that we run the race marked out for us, while trusting in him to help us to keep running. These verses do not promise us that the way will be easy.

Sometimes rather than lifting us up on eagle's wings, God chooses to come alongside us and gives us strength to take one more step and then another and pretty soon we find ourselves walking better than we ever have before. And before you know it, we will be crossing that finishing line.

God, the marathon of life is not always easy. Please help me to keep on running in your strength.

What does it look like for you to wait upon the Lord in this stage of your marathon of life?

In Him

Through the Son everything was created, both in the heavenly realm and on the earth, all that is seen and all that is unseen. Every seat of power, realm of government, principality, and authority—it was all created through him and for his purpose! He existed before anything was made, and now everything finds completion in him.

COLOSSIANS 1:16-17 TPT

In this verse, Paul is speaking of the preeminence of Christ. He speaks of how Jesus Christ was involved in creation and how everything was created through him and for his purpose. When we think of Jesus we tend to focus only on what he did when he was here on earth rather than his existence before the world began. We need to recognize his preeminence.

These verses remind us that Jesus was involved in creation, watched Adam and Eve fall into sin, and saw all the things that happened in this world as time went by. He saw the evil of humanity and that mankind deserves punishment rather than grace. Yet he still chose to leave his throne in Heaven to come to earth and die for us. Jesus is a king who gave up his throne to go and live with the very people he created and then he laid down his life that we might live.

Dear Jesus, thank you for leaving your kingly throne to come to earth for me.

In him all things were created: things in heaven and on earth, visible and invisible, whether thrones or powers or rulers or authorities; all things have been created through him and for him. He is before all things, and in him all things hold together.

COLOSSIANS 1:16-17 NIV

Not only was Jesus involved in creation, but as these verses point out, he is still active. His work is not done. Paul points out here that in Christ all things hold together. He didn't just create life and leave it to sustain itself. He is still in control. That is very comforting because we live in a world where our lives often feel like they are spinning out of control.

No matter how out of control life might seem, Christ is still holding it all together. He's got us. He is always in control even when it seems like our lives are not. That means we don't have to be the ones who are in control. We can leave that to him.

Dear Jesus, thank you that I can trust in you to be in control. You know how out of control my life seems right now. Please help me to trust in you.

What out of control part of your life can you trust into Christ's hands today?

445

We are His

Know that the Lord, He is God;
It is He who has made us, and not we ourselves;
We are His people and the sheep of His pasture.

Many of the problems we have in life come because we mess up the first part of this verse. We try to be God. We try to rely on ourselves rather than relying on him. We go our own way rather than doing things Gods way. But there is only one God. He is the one who made us. He is the shepherd and we are the sheep. The more we have a right understanding of that hierarchy, the better off we will be.

When we get that relationship messed up we try to do God's job, and we begin relying upon ourselves rather than on him. Let's let him be God and stick to the role we are more suited for: his sheep.

Heavenly Father, please forgive me for all the ways I try to take on your role and don't trust in you to be God. I know that is your job, not mine. Help me to keep that straight.

Know that the Lord is God.
He made us, and we belong to him.
We are his people, the sheep he tends.

PSALM 100:3 ICB

You belong to God. Let that realization sink down deep into your soul. Let him remind you of what that means for you. You are never alone. You are never without purpose or identity. You belong to God. The image of him as our shepherd and us as his sheep is powerful. There is a sense of presence in those words as well as protection, guidance, and care.

We can rely upon him to be with us, to care for us, to lead us and to meet our needs. This is our true nature. This is where we belong. We are his.

Father, thank you that I belong to you. I want to follow you.
Help me to know your voice and to let you lead me.

Are there any areas of your life where you are trying to take on God's role rather than being his sheep?

Wow

When I consider your heavens,
the work of your fingers,
the moon and the stars,
which you have set in place,
what is mankind that you are mindful of them,
human beings that you care for them?

PSALM 8:3-4 NIV

Have you ever stood out in an open field in a desolate area at night and just looked up at the sky? It is a humbling and awesome experience. It is humbling because we recognize just how small we are in comparison to the rest of creation. It is awesome because it is beautiful and stretches beyond our comprehension.

When we recognize that our Father is big enough to have created all of this creation and picture him placing each star and planet in its place it helps us to recognize just how small we are in comparison to him and we get a right perspective on what it means that he is God.

Heavenly Father, thank you for the amazing beauty of this creation all around me. I stand in awe of you.

When I look up into the night skies and see the work of your
fingers—the moon and the stars you have made—I cannot
understand how you can bother with mere puny man, to pay any
attention to him!

PSALM 8:3-4 TLB

David not only notices how great the universe is, but also
points out another realization that comes from gazing up at
the sky. When we notice just how totally amazing God is and
just how small and insignificant we are in comparison, it
begs the question why would God care at all about anything
relating to us? That is a good point.

Considering man is so puny compared to God, why does he
pay any attention to us at all? That is a profound question.
But more important than answering that question is simply
acknowledging that for whatever reason, God does choose to
bother with us. Even though we are small and insignificant in
comparison to God we are valuable in his sight. That may be
even more amazing than the stars themselves.

God, thank you for choosing to notice me. You are so amazing and
the fact that you have any interest in me at all is mind-boggling.
Thank you that I am valuable in your sight.

In what ways have you ignored the value God obviously places
on your life?

Justified and Redeemed

All have sinned and fall short of the glory of God, being justified freely by His grace through the redemption that is in Christ Jesus,

ROMANS 3:23-24 NKJV

Romans 3:23 is a very well-known verse, but for some reason verse 24 is much less familiar. Verse 23 is the bad news, but that is not the end of the statement. Paul goes on to say that even though we are all sinners who fall short of God's glory, we also all are justified by his grace. When we quote verse 23, we leave off the best part of what Paul is saying.

Rather than treating us as our sins deserve God freely gives us what we could never earn. Through Christ we are forgiven, declared righteous, and brought back to a right relationship with God. That's amazing good news.

Heavenly Father, thank you for freely giving me grace even though I have sinned and fallen short of your glory.

All have sinned and fall short of the glory of God, and are justified by his grace as a gift, through the redemption that is in Christ Jesus,

ROMANS 3:23-24 ESV

Verse 24 contains a couple of big theological words. The word justified is a legal term that means we are declared not guilty in God's sight even though we are sinners. That declaration is based not on what we have done, but on the work of Jesus Christ in our lives. We are clothed in his righteousness and God chooses to see that rather than our sin.

The other big theological word is the word redeemed. That word refers to being bought for a price and has a connection to the idea of being bought out of slavery. That means we have been declared righteous and our freedom has been purchased for us. Those are two amazing truths about our standing with God thanks to the work of Jesus Christ. But there is also a third amazing truth in these verses and that is that all of this has been done for us as a free gift. We don't have to purchase it or earn it. We just freely receive this gift from God.

Father, thank you for declaring me righteous and purchasing my freedom. And thank you for giving this all to me for free.

You have been declared righteous by God, are you living under that declaration or do you still consider yourself guilty?

Fulfillment

"Do not think that I have come to abolish the Law or the Prophets; I have not come to abolish them but to fulfill them. For truly I tell you, until heaven and earth disappear, not the smallest letter, not the least stroke of a pen, will by any means disappear from the Law until everything is accomplished."

MATTHEW 5:17-18 NIV

Throughout history God has had a plan. His plan has always been reconciling man to himself. It is not like he had one plan and then when that didn't work he came up with a different one. As Jesus says in these verses, he didn't come to "abolish the law but to fulfill it."

People in the Old Testament, in faith, looked forward to the arrival of Jesus Christ. Today we, in faith, look back at that same moment. Jesus Christ came to bring life for all those who would, in faith, believe in him. It is all one story. It is all part of the same plan and we see it play out throughout Scripture from Genesis to Revelation.

Father, thank you that you have a plan that I can count on. Thank you for sending Jesus to fulfill your law and bring us back to you.

"Do not think that I came to destroy the Law or the Prophets. I did not come to destroy but to fulfill. For assuredly, I say to you, till heaven and earth pass away, one jot or one tittle will by no means pass from the law till all is fulfilled."

MATTHEW 5:17–18 NKJV

Jesus says these words and then goes on throughout the rest of his "Sermon on the Mount" to speak of what life is supposed to be like in the Kingdom of Heaven. He speaks of old commandments like murder and adultery and says that getting angry with our brother or sister or having lustful thoughts are just as bad. The idea of living by the standard that Jesus sets out in this sermon seems impossible.

Thankfully, Jesus did what we could never do. We are not saved by our ability to fulfill all the commandments. That would be impossible for us. But we can trust in the one who did fulfill the law. He is our Savior Jesus Christ.

Dear Jesus, thank you for doing what I could never do. Thank you for fulfilling the law and then dying for my sin, so that I could be forgiven for the ways that I fall short.

Since Christ fulfilled the law for us, what might a life of thankfulness for what he has done for us look like?

Completion

I am sure of this, that he who began a good work in you will bring it to completion at the day of Jesus Christ.

PHILIPPIANS 1:6 ESV

Have you ever started a project and failed to complete it? Most of us have done that at some point in our lives. Some of us have done it multiple times. For some it may even be a pattern. Thankfully that is not true with God.

In this verse, Paul reminds us that God finishes what he starts. He began a good work in us and he will see it through to completion. That completion is when he brings us into glory on the day of Christ Jesus. It is good for us to be reminded that he's got us in his hands and he will safely see us home.

Heavenly Father, thank you that you didn't just start a good work in me, but that you are completing your work and will see it through to completion.

I am confident of this very thing, that He who began a good work in you will perfect it until the day of Christ Jesus.

PHILIPPIANS 1:6 NASB

The time in between when God began this work in us and when he will complete it is a journey. On that journey, he is at work in our lives. He is not just waiting until we get to Heaven, he has work that he wants to do in us right here on earth. The problem is that sometimes we get in the way. There are a few places in Scripture that give us the image of God as a potter and us as the clay. That is a good illustration.

Are we willing to let God be the potter while we fill the role of clay? Are we willing to yield ourselves to the work that he wants to do in us? We can trust him. He's got us. He will complete his work eventually when we get to Heaven. But he wants to do some of that work right now. Are we willing to let him do that in us?

God, I trust you to work in my life. I want you to be accomplishing your plans in me. Please help me to be fully yielded to you.

In what ways are you not yielded to the work God wants to do in you?

My Plans

"For I know the plans I have for you,"
declares the Lord,
"plans to prosper you and not to harm you,
plans to give you hope and a future."

JEREMIAH 29:11 NIV

This is one of the most misused verses in the Bible. We tend to use this verse when we are in a tough situation and want to believe that God is going to make everything better right away. Or even worse it is used as graduation advice to let someone know that God has a good plan for their lives.

If we take the time to read this verse in context we see that this is part of a letter from the prophet Jeremiah to the exiled people of Israel telling them to settle down and get comfortable in exile because they are going to be there for several decades. That seems harsh, but it is actually in this context that the verse becomes even more powerful. This means that even if we are in a tough situation that is not going to get substantially better anytime soon, we still can trust God to have a plan for us even in the midst of what we are going through.

Heavenly Father, thank you that you know what you are doing. Thank you that even if times are tough, I can trust that you have a plan for me.

"I know the plans I have for you,"
says the Lord,
"plans for welfare and not for evil,
to give you a future and a hope."

JEREMIAH 29:11 RSV

If we read just a little further along in this passage we find that Jeremiah goes on to speak of them calling upon God and seeking him with all their heart. That is actually the good plan he has for them. God's definition of good is different than ours. Our definition of good typically revolves around things like: comfort, absence of trouble, happiness, prosperity and other things related to our current situation.

God's definition of good is based on eternity and our relationship with him. What might be best for eternity may not be the same as what would feel good right now. For instance, the people of Israel probably didn't want to stay in exile, but God had a purpose for this part of their lives. His purpose was to use this time to draw them back to himself. That is where the good is and ultimately that was more important than any temporary comfort they might have been hoping for.

Father, thank you for your plan for me. You know that the best place for me is to be with you. Help me to seek you with all my heart.

Are you seeking God with all your heart?

Unworthy

If it is by grace, it is no longer on the basis of works; otherwise grace would no longer be grace.

ROMANS 11:6 ESV

What is grace? It is unmerited favor. It is being given something that we did not earn. As Paul says in this verse, if grace was on the basis of works it would not be grace. Forgiveness and salvation are bestowed on us by God.

We need to constantly remember that we are saved by grace. When we forget that we wind up trying to earn what has already been freely given to us. We are wired to think that we don't get anything we have not worked for so we figure that grace is really about what we do and don't do. But that is not grace. We are receiving what we did not and could not ever earn. So let's stop trying to earn it and instead live a life of thankfulness for what God has done for us.

Heavenly Father, thank you for your grace. I know that I could never earn what you have done for me. Help me to be thankful for what you have done.

If God chose them by grace, then it is not for the things they have done. If they could be made God's people by what they did, then God's gift of grace would not really be a gift.

ROMANS 11:6 ICB

In the hymn "Grace Greater Than Our Sin," Julia Johnson wrote these words:

> Grace, grace, God's grace,
> grace that will pardon and cleanse within;
> grace, grace, God's grace,
> grace that is greater than all our sin.

The grace that we have been given is greater than all the sin we have ever done or could ever do. Satan wants us discouraged by our sin and by our unworthiness of salvation. But this is not about us and our sin. This is about God and his grace. We don't have to be worthy of anything. If we were worthy, then it would not be grace.

God, thank you that I don't have to be worthy of your grace. Thank you for your grace and love toward me.

Are you discouraged by your unworthiness or thankful for God's grace?

Lost

"The Son of Man came to seek out and to save the lost."

LUKE 19:10 NRSV

This verse comes as part of the story of Zacchaeus. In the story, we see Zacchaeus desiring to see Jesus so he runs ahead and climbs a tree just to catch a glimpse of him as he passes by. We sometimes refer to people as seeking God. We see what Zaccheus did and consider that seeking. In this story, we also see references to both Zaccheus seeking Jesus and Jesus seeking the lost.

Think about the difference. Zaccheus' seeking of Jesus meant that he climbed a tree. Jesus' seeking of the lost means that he came to earth and diee on a cross to bring us back to a right relationship with the Father. The initiative for salvation comes from God. He reached out to us. He calls us by name. He seeks us, not the other way around.

Heavenly Father, thank you for seeking me. Thank you for reaching out to me and calling me by name.

"The Son of Man has come to seek and to save that which was lost."
LUKE 19:10 AMP

Here in Luke 19:10 we get a glimpse into the mission of Jesus Christ. He came to "seek out and to save the lost." What does he mean by lost? He means those who have been separated from God by sin and who are headed to eternal separation from him in hell. Christ came to save us from that reality.

Through his death and resurrection, Christ made it possible for us to be reconciled to God and to spend eternity with him in Heaven. He sought out and saved us. We are living in a world full of lost people. We see in this passage that God loves them and is seeking to save them just like he saved us. The question is, if lost people matter that much to him, shouldn't they matter to us as well?

God, thank you that you seek the lost. Since they matter so much to you, please help them to matter to me too.

If the lost really matter this much to God, then what does that mean for us?

Witnesses

This Jesus God raised up, and of that we all are witnesses.

ACTS 2:32 ESV

A witness is someone who testifies to what they have seen, heard or experienced. In this passage Peter speaks to the crowd about how all of the believers are witnesses of God raising Jesus from the dead. After Jesus died on the cross he rose again and appeared to hundreds of people before heading up to Heaven. There were many eyewitnesses to this resurrection.

Some people today believe that Christianity is about taking a blind leap of faith, but in reality, our faith is based on a strong foundation of eyewitness accounts about who Jesus is. Scripture is filled with stories from people who lived with Jesus and saw him before his death, saw him die on the cross, and then saw him after he had risen. Many of those people then became martyrs for telling people what they believed. Trusting in Christ requires faith, but it is not a blind leap. It is more like a step of faith that is based on a solid foundation.

Heavenly Father, thank you for the strong eyewitness foundation to my faith. Thank you for revealing yourself to those eyewitnesses and for revealing yourself to me.

God raised Jesus from the dead, and we are all witnesses of this.
ACTS 2:32 NLT

Now that we have received the Gospel, we too have become witnesses. We may not be eyewitness to Jesus' life on earth. We may not have seen him die and then seen him come back to life. He has chosen to reveal himself to us and we can testify about our experience with him. We are called to do that in the book of Acts.

We don't have to be polished evangelists. We simply need to be willing to share with others about our experience with Christ. There are others in this world who need to hear this amazing Good News and we have a testimony that they need to hear.

God, thank you for revealing yourself to me and letting me know you. Please help me to be your witness to a world that needs to know you.

Who are some people around you that need to hear about your experience with Jesus?

300

The Lord said to Gideon, "With the three hundred men that lapped I will save you and give the Midianites into your hands. Let all the others go home."

JUDGES 7:7 NIV

Are you familiar with the story of Gideon? If not, you can read more of it in Judges 6-8, but this verse is a key component of his story. The Lord used him to lead the people of Israel out from under the oppression of the Midianites. God slowly whittled down Gideon's army from 32,000 to just 300 and then God used those 300 men to defeat the Midianite army.

God didn't need a large army. With God, the numbers don't have to add up. He is able to accomplish things that defy the greatest odds. We can trust him to be able to do those same kinds of mathematical miracles in our lives today.

God, thank you that the numbers don't always have to add up for you to accomplish things. Thank you that you can do mathematical miracles. Help me to trust in you even when the numbers don't seem to add up.

"I'll conquer the Midianites with these three hundred!" the Lord told Gideon. "Send all the others home!"

JUDGES 7:7 TLB

This strategy made no sense from a worldly perspective. Why would you go into battle with an army less than 10 percent the size that it could have been? The reason is that God was in charge and his plan was to miraculously win this battle, thereby using Gideon and Israel to display himself to the world. If Gideon and the army of Israel had won the battle because of the size of their army or because of the great strategy of Gideon then they would have received the glory rather than God. This choice to go from 32,000 men to just 300 made no sense from a worldly perspective, but it made perfect sense from God's view.

What if God is calling you to do something that makes no sense? Would you be willing to do something ridiculous like this? God has a plan to win the battles in our lives too. It may not always make sense to us, but we can trust him and follow his plan.

Heavenly Father, I know that you can do amazing things. Help me to follow you even when it seems to not make earthly sense.

Is there an area in your life right now where God is calling you to trust in you in a way that may not make sense?

World's Greatest Dad

"If you then, who are evil, know how to give good gifts to your children, how much more will your Father who is in heaven give good things to those who ask him!"

MATTHEW 7:11 ESV

Have you ever seen a guy wearing a shirt that says "World's Greatest Dad?" There are so many shirts like that out there, that they can't possibly all be true. But even if there was a dad who was truly the "World's Greatest" he would still not be as good of a Father as our Father in Heaven.

God is faithful, so he never forgets or misses any important or even unimportant events in our lives. He is good and loving so all of his actions toward us are perfect. He knows our innermost thoughts and so he understands us better than anyone ever could. He is all-knowing so he always knows what is best for us. He even so loved the world that he sent his Son Jesus to bring us back to him. He truly is the "World's Greatest Dad!"

God, thank you for being a great dad. Thank you that I can always count on you.

"If you then, evil (sinful by nature) as you are, know how to give good and advantageous gifts to your children, how much more will your Father who is in heaven [perfect as He is] give what is good and advantageous to those who keep on asking Him."

MATTHEW 7:11 AMP

Did your dad give you everything you ever asked for? Did he spoil you rotten? As a child that might seem like a good thing, but in reality, it is not good to get everything we ask for. Sometimes what we ask for is not what is best for us.

This verse points out that our Father in Heaven gives good things to those who ask, but that doesn't mean he will always give us what we ask for. He knows better than we do what is best for us. That means that our prayers should not be based on what we want, but on what he wants for us. So, let's seek him as our father, trust in him to meet our needs in the way that is best, and ask him to care for us today.

Heavenly Father, I trust you. I have some ideas about what would be best for me, but instead I ask for you to give me what you think is best for me.

Do you really trust in God to give you what is best?

Return

Therefore, say to the people, "This is what the Lord of Heaven's Armies says: Return to me, and I will return to you," says the Lord of Heaven's Armies.

ZECHARIAH 1:3 NLT

This verse is written to the people of Israel after they have forsaken him and he has had to send them into exile. He says in the verse prior to this that he was angry with their ancestors. But in this verse, he encourages them to return to him. It is not too late. He wants to welcome them back.

Throughout the Old Testament, we see this process repeated over and over again. No matter how often they stray from God, he always seeks to have them come back. It is good for them that God is a forgiving and merciful God who does not treat them as their sins deserve, but is gracious and merciful toward them. And the same is true for us.

God, thank you for your grace and that you don't treat us as our sins deserve.

Tell the people: This is what the Lord Almighty says: "Return to me," declares the Lord Almighty, "and I will return to you," says the Lord Almighty.

ZECHARIAH 1:3 NIV

While this verse was written specifically to the people of Israel, we also see God's character expressed in these words. He is still this same God. He was not just forgiving and merciful toward the people of Israel, he is also the same toward us.

In the same way, he called the people of Israel to return to him, he also calls us to do the same. Even though we stray he still longs to have us back in a right relationship with him. Have you wandered away from God? Have you strayed from his plan for your life? Listen for his voice. Hear him calling out to you, "return to me."

Heavenly Father, please forgive me for the ways that I have strayed from you. Please bring me back to a right relationship with you.

Have you strayed from God? Do you believe he will welcome you back if you return to him?

Leaning on His Chest

Of Benjamin he said,
"The beloved of the Lord dwells in safety.
The High God surrounds him all day long,
and dwells between his shoulders."

DEUTERONOMY 33:12 ESV

The safest place in the world is in your father's arms. Just ask any child at 2 a.m. when the thunder grumbles in the darkness. She runs from the terrific noise and snuggles in close where, somehow, she is confident that the troubles of the world could never reach her. The Lord God blessed the tribe of Benjamin with safety, the safety that comes from having God dwell between his shoulders. Can you picture that? God promises to be the father to the tribe when the thunder roars and the lightning strikes. God promises to be Benjamin's rest when life is in chaos.

Begin your day in the safety that comes from the good news that the God of Benjamin knows how to surround his beloved.

Almighty God, you have brought me in safety to this new day. I ask for great confidence in your ability to hold me as I seek to live with you and for you today.

Of Benjamin he said,
"May the beloved of the Lord dwell in security by Him,
Who shields him all the day,
And he dwells between His shoulders."

DEUTERONOMY 33:12 NASB

As you come to the end of your day, consider the many ways in which the Lord God has been a shield for you when you needed protection from the world, the flesh and the devil. Consider how he has dwelt between your shoulders when you were desperate for comfort in your temptations, sufferings, or betrayals.

It was on the night that he was betrayed that our Lord himself took bread and broke it with his disciples, handing it to the disciple leaning against his chest. Jesus took on flesh to dwell between our shoulders. Jesus lived the life we should have lived and died the death we should have died so that could live securely as his beloved.

Eternal Son, I lean fully on your chest, the chest that bore my sins on the cross. As I lie down to sleep, grant me secure rest, knowing that if I live, I live with you, and if I die, I die with you.

What specific anxieties will you cast upon God tonight?

Our Willing King

One day the trees went out to anoint a king for themselves.
They said to the olive tree, "Be our king."
But the olive tree answered,
"Should I give up my oil,
by which both gods and humans are honored,
to hold sway over the trees?"

Judges 8:8–9 NIV

"Everyone did what was right in his own eyes," says the book of Judges. The people of Israel wanted to make wicked Abimelech king over them, but they did not know what they were asking. When a man or woman takes on authority in the Kingdom of God, they are accepting the call to lay down their lives. Leadership is an olive tree giving up the fruit of its precious oil in order to serve the people. A good king is an olive tree, but Abimelech is a bramble, giving no shade and pricking everyone who comes near.

Today, you will exercise authority and you will submit to authority. Know that God honors the fruit of laying your life down and that he has already laid his life down for you.

Almighty God, I submit my life to your authority because you rule all things well.

The trees decided
to anoint a king over themselves.
They said to the olive tree, "Reign over us."
But the olive tree said to them,
"Should I stop giving my oil
that people use to honor both God and men,
and rule over the trees?"

JUDGES 8:8-9 CSV

They longed for a good king. They asked the olive tree, the fig tree and the grape vine, but none were willing. So, they settled for a bramble. We never have to settle because our King willingly laid his life down so that we could enjoy the fruit of his labor.

How was authority exercised over you today? Willingly submit to the hand of God who can bring good fruit for you, even when those who should be serving you are not ruling like Jesus.

Eternal Father, you rule all things well. I lay down to rest tonight, confident that you credit to my account the perfect and willing sacrifice of Jesus.

What would the rule of King Jesus look like the lives of those you love?

Shout Beautifully

Shout for joy in the Lord, O you righteous!
Praise befits the upright.'

PSALM 33:1 ESV

Shouting is the proper response to our great God with every
new day. We don't shout like the prophets of Baal who are
trying to wake up their god or to get him out of the bathroom.
God did not sleep while you did, he was watching over you.
God was not resting while you were, he was working good and
glory into the world. You have risen now to join him.

As you wake to receive the gift of this new day, "Shout for joy
to the Lord!" Shout for all that he is and all that he has done
for you. Take a moment to make a mental list of the good
things that the Lord has done for you, starting with the gift of
his Son, our Lord Jesus.

Almighty God, we once again rise to a new day and receive it as a
gift from your gracious hand. For this and all these good things, we
shout our thanks in the morning.

Rejoice in the Lord, O you righteous!
For praise from the upright is beautiful.

PSALM 33:1 NKJV

Return to your "morning list of thanksgiving," whether it was a mental list or a written one. Now, add the ways in which you have seen the goodness of your God throughout the day. Praise him for it all! Praise is the natural response of God's people and it is the right thing to do.

It is right because of who he is and what he has done. It is also right because we are "the righteous." God is righteous and gives us the gift of his righteous word. We receive his Word and obey it. The righteous Word teaches us to praise. Praise fits the people of God just right, both waist and inseam. It's like a tailored garment made just for you. As you lie down, lie down with gratitude for the gift of righteousness we have through faith in Christ and the gift of his Word for the wisdom daily righteousness.

Our Lord, you have made us righteous through the sacrifice of your only Son and you have given us your word. Thank you.

What reasons has God given you to shout for joy?

With Your Mouth Full

I will bless the Lord at all times;
His praise shall continually be in my mouth.
My soul shall make its boast in the Lord;
The humble shall hear of it and be glad.
Oh, magnify the Lord with me,
And let us exalt His name together.

PSALM 34:1-3 NKJV

"Don't talk with your mouth full!" Who wants to see all that falling out of your mouth? Unless, of course, what falls out is praise. That is the picture the Psalmist wants in your head. Let your mouth be full of God's praise so that it falls out when your lips part. Let reasons to boast in your God be like the air that expands your lungs when you breath in deeply, from the diaphragm, like you're preparing to hold out that note all day long.

God is your boast today. Let your lungs and your mouth be so filled with reasons to bless him that it leaves neither room nor need to boast in yourself.

Holy Father, set a guard over my lips when I am tempted to boast about myself, fill my lungs with your blessings as with oxygen.

I will extol the Lord at all times;
his praise will always be on my lips.
I will glory in the Lord;
let the afflicted hear and rejoice.
Glorify the Lord with me;
let us exalt his name together.

PSALM 34:1-3 NIV

Psalm 34 is attributed to David "when he fled to Gath." That is, the time in the courageous man's life when he behaved like a coward; the time in the honorable man's life when he behaved like a madman in order save himself and his followers.

We all have them. We all have situations when it seems that everything and everyone is against us. We all have times in life when we have been less than honorable. Is that you today? This Psalm is the invitation for all the afflicted to breathe deep of God. Breathe in his praise and breath out the good news of his constant care in all of your afflictions.

Eternal God, ruler of heaven and earth, I recognize tonight that all good things come from your hand. I lift up my afflictions in faith that you are good and that you will deliver me as you delivered King David, my ancestor in the faith.

What fills your mouth tonight? Is it praise? Is it grumbling? Either way, cry out to the Lord your God.

Very Great

Bless the Lord, O my soul.
O Lord my God,
thou art very great;
thou art clothed with honour and majesty.

PSALM 104:1 KJV

In the book of Revelation, the returning Christ comes
in white robe on a white horse, bringing judgment and
deliverance with him. At the mount of transfiguration in
Mathew 24, Christ is revealed in robes whiter than any
launderer could bleach them. Here, our God is clothed with
honor and with majesty. They are his royal robes because
kingly purple is not fantastic enough.

The God you worship is the great king above all kings and
the great God above all gods. He wears the sunlight because
nothing else is great enough. Let the warm sun hit your face
today and remind you that he causes the sun to shine and
the rain to fall. The whole world is a theater of his glory, the
whole earth is his divine throne room.

Almighty God, you are very great! Today, open my eyes to see your
greatness in the part of the created world where you have placed me.

Let all that I am praise the Lord.
O Lord my God, how great you are!
You are robed with honor and majesty.

PSALM 104:1 NLT

Did you forget the greatness of God since this morning?
We do that, don't we? Somehow, even with all the sun and
rain, the warmth on our faces and the oxygen to breathe
and we still forget the greatness of the God who keeps it all
happening day in and day out.

We are a little like the prodigal son, wanting the Father's
money but would be just fine if the Father wasn't around.
We put on his good gifts like a robe in the morning and find
ourselves naked by noon, eating slop with the other pigs.

As the day fades, recognize the greatness of God. Not only is
he clothed with honor and majesty, but he has stooped to find
us, wherever we are on earth, and to cloth us with his Son
Jesus Christ.

O God, our God, you are very great. I know that full well, even
though I forget it quite easily.

Where do you see the greatness of God in the place on earth
where you live?

A Glad Heart

He causes the grass to grow for the cattle,
And vegetation for the labor of man,
So that he may bring forth food from the earth,
And wine which makes man's heart glad,
So that he may make his face glisten with oil,
And food which sustains man's heart.

Psalm 104:14–15 NASB

Our God created a world in which black cows turn green grass into white milk and red meat. They turn that which we cannot eat into something which we can. He created soil that, when you dig deep and drop a seed, will feed our bodies and sustain our hearts. He brought together soil and water, weather and climate in such a way that a crushed grape will ferment into a juice that brings gladness to the heart of man.

See him in these things today. Give glory to God with the gladness of your fork today. Raise a glass to your creator God, in the name of Jesus.

Creator God, you have made me glad with the world you have given me today. Help me to drink deeply of all the gladness from the earth, wherever you have given me to touch it.

He makes grass grow for the cattle
and plants for people to take care of.
That's how they get food from the earth.
There is wine to make people glad.
There is olive oil to make their skin glow.
And there is bread to make them strong.

PSALM 104:14-15 NIRV

Food is a display of God's greatness! Your gladness in it is
a display of his greatness. In Christ, we are invited to eat
at the table of God. That is, we are welcome to the table
of communion where we ritualize the Christian family
relationship in which Jesus is the host, serving us his body to
eat and his blood to drink, unto everlasting life.

If your earthly meal was sparse today, give thanks for the
heavenly meal of the previous Sunday. And, if your own table
was set with much gladness from the earth, then give thanks
for the greatness of God in every bite. Either way, give thanks
that he made the world to produce both food for the body and
food for the soul.

Blessed are you, O Lord our God, for you have brought forth bread
from the earth.

How does the particular beauty of where you live make your
heart glad?

All God's Creatures

O Lord, how manifold are your works!
In wisdom you have made them all;
the earth is full of your creatures.

PSALM 104:24 NRSV

Solomon was the wisest man on the earth. This must have been his favorite Psalm. We are told that he wrote over 3,000 wise sayings, mostly concerning trees from the cedar that is in Lebanon to the hyssop that grows out of the wall. These were the subjects of his proverbs. The psalmist's exclamation point is our daily reminder of the countless gifts of God on the earth.

Lay down and sleep in the wonder that God made them all. He sustains them all. He displays them all for the joy you will find in his wisdom!

God almighty, thank you for the trees. In wisdom, you made them all! And I don't know the half of it. Thank you for the daily display you put before my eyes. Let me never lose the wonder of it all. Let me never stop seeing your wisdom reflected in the created world.

How countless are Your works, Lord!
In wisdom You have made them all;
the earth is full of Your creatures.

PSALM 104:24 HCSB

Did you miss it? The Lord God put on a show of his glory throughout your day in his countless works. The dust in the sunbeams through the window remind us of the short duration of our lives and how we came from dust and to dust we will return. The dog in the yard eating all those things that it should not eat, warns us of our tendency to return to the same sins again and again. The onions in the garden speak of Egypt and the sourdough starter in the kitchen of a hasty deliverance. The beta fish in the glass bowl reminds us of the dietary laws set aside by the Christ in favor of fellowship around the table at which he is the host.

Creation, this creation, every bit of it is preaching to us.

Almighty God, you are the maker of heaven and the maker of earth; yet you also made the dust in the air and the light that makes it dance. Thank you for it all!

What are some of the works of God you saw today? Would you have noticed them if you did not start the day with Psalm 104?

Good News of Great Joy

May the glory of the Lord endure forever;
may the Lord rejoice in his works,
who looks on the earth and it trembles,
who touches the mountains and they smoke!

PSALM 104:31-32 ESV

The earth makes God happy. He enjoys his creation! He enjoys the way a seed falls to the ground and dies; he especially enjoys the way it lives again, that part reminds him of something very good. He enjoys the way wine makes you happy and the way oil makes your skin shine. He enjoys the way the earth continues to fear him. The earth trembles at a glance and the mountains smoke at his touch.

The God that terrifies the earth every day is your God. Consider his power throughout the day. Consider the many ways in which his power is seen in the force of nature. Consider how that power is at work in sustaining you and saving you.

Almighty God, thank you for the revelation of your joy in the created world. We find comfort in knowing you this way as we stand in awe of your mighty power.

May the glory of the Lord endure forever;
may the Lord rejoice in his works—
he who looks at the earth, and it trembles,
who touches the mountains, and they smoke.

PSALM 104:31-32 NIV

Have you been in an earthquake? The ground is the most stable thing that we know and yet it shakes, it drops, it shifts and it rolls under our feet. The earth quakes and we are terrified. Every earthquake, every hurricane, and every tornado reminds us that we are not God. We do not rule the earth. He is far more powerful than we can ever imagine.

And yet, he does not treat us as our sins deserve. Because of his great love we are not consumed. That power is at work on your behalf. He works in the world to save us, to redeem us and to make us holy like he is holy.

Gracious Father, you have not terrified me with your mighty power, but you have been gracious to me in Christ. You have not treated me as my sins deserve and this gives me more joy than I could ever imagine.

What is the greatest display of earthly power you have ever seen? How does it encourage you to know that God's grace towards you is even more powerful?

Sing with Your Being

I will sing to the Lord as long as I live;
I will sing praise to my God while I have being.

PSALM 104:33 ESV

Take a deep breath. Hold it for a second. Now, let it out. Breathe in again, and sing something. That is why you have breath, that is why you are alive. Maybe sing a line from Amazing Grace, that's always a good place to start because it is always true. "Amazing Grace, how sweet the sound that saved a wretch like me."

You can sing about the created world, "This is my Father's world, he shines in all that's fair." The is Psalmists' response to glory of God in creation. God created you to join in the choir of creation in preparation for the choir in heaven. As you prepare for the day ahead, prepare both your heart and your mouth to sing to the Lord. Sing to the Lord with your whole being.

Creator God, you made me with the ability to sing to you and so I lift my voice this morning.

As long as I live,
I will sing and praise you,
the Lord God.

PSALM 104:33 CEV

It is good to sing praise to the Lord God. He has given you a million reasons to sing to him. If you are alive, that is one and if you just took a breath, that is another. But what truly compels us to sing is the good gift of Jesus. The creator became the created. The maker of man became a man. The giver of life became subject to death.

The Lord who dwells on high, took on flesh and made his dwelling among us. We have a million reasons to sing, but we sing even more because he is one in a million and he has given us himself in Christ Jesus. Thanks be to God for his indescribable gift. Thanks be to God, the Lord, for this song.

Lord God and everlasting Father, as I lay down to sleep, your song is on my lips.

What compels you to sing today?

That Was the Day

The Lord has done it this very day;
let us rejoice today and be glad.

PSALM 118:24, NIV

"This is the day that the Lord has made, I will rejoice and be glad in it." What a wonderful admonition to receive the gift of today as coming from the hand of God, the creator and sustainer of all things. Child of God, Rejoice! This is the day! Enjoy it!

Actually, that was the day that the Lord has made. Psalm 118 teaches us to celebrate that day in which the stone the builders rejected became the cornerstone. In other words, the day that we rejoice in is the day that God revealed Jesus as the savior of the world through his death and resurrection. The day that makes us glad was the day broke the power of sin and death and restored the way to life. Today, rejoice and be glad in that day.

Our Father, your sent your only son to live the life I should have lived and die the death I should have died. Thank you!

This is the day the Lord has made;
let us rejoice and be glad in it.

PSALM 118:24, HCSB

Because of that day, this is a good day, a day worth rejoicing
in. Because the guilt your sin has been paid for on the cross
of Christ, you can rejoice in forgiveness today. Because
your enmity with God has been reconciled on the cross of
Christ, you can rejoice in the nearness of God today. Because
the bondage of sin has been broken, you can rejoice in the
redemption and freedom that is yours in Christ.

Now, today may have had troubles in it. Today may have had
sorrows and suffering in it. These things are not at odds.
First of all, that great day brought great joy to us through the
sorrows and sufferings of our Savior Jesus. Clearly, suffering
and joy do not conflict. Even more importantly, not a one
of your troubles, not a single pain that you endure will ever
remove from you the joy that Jesus gained for you on that day.
Whatever today has held for you, rejoice and be glad in Jesus.

Our Father, let my joy in that day transform the way I receive today.

What kind of sorrows make it hard for you to rejoice?

Looking Good

Since God chose you to be the holy people he loves, you must clothe yourselves with tenderhearted mercy, kindness, humility, gentleness, and patience.

COLOSSIANS 3:12 NLT

What kind of clothes should you wear today? A spiffy suit for an important meeting? A uniform for work? Maybe a ratty t-shirt and jeans for yard work and mowing? A swimsuit for a swimming pool? Or how about just some casual Saturday clothes with the favorite team logo for the college football game?

The mixture of linen and cotton isn't nearly as important, however, as what a person wears in his heart and actions. For followers of Jesus, this is especially true because, whether they like it or not, they are strategic representatives of God. What a Christian says and what a Christian does has significant ramifications about what people "see" of Christ.

So when followers of Jesus "put on" mercy in the midst of trouble, or when they choose patience over raising their voices in frustration, or when they consistently encourage those around them, others will take notice.

If that's what God is like, they'll say, then I can trust God.

God, help me to be clothed in your qualities and characteristics today. Let me be a proper representative for you.

As those who have been chosen of God, holy and beloved, put on a heart of compassion, kindness, humility, gentleness and patience;

COLOSSIANS 3:12 NASB

How'd your ambassadorship go today? Did you look the part?

The great thing about being a representative of God is that the Creator of the Universe is full of amazing qualities! In fact, he is the source of all of the characteristics mentioned in Colossians 3:12. The very things that we are encouraged to "put on" are the very things that God distributes. He emotes a heart of compassion. He shares kindness. He loves humanity through his passionate humility. He confidently graces the world with his gentleness and he approaches chaos with patience.

God doesn't ask us to act in ways that are contrary to who he is. So rest in confidence tonight that God has everything you need at his disposal to help you represent him well.

Loving God, thank you for being compassionate, kind, humble, gentle and patient with me. Let me awake in the morning ready to embody those very characteristics for others. Amen

---

Which of these qualities comes easiest for you? Which is the most difficult for you to "wear"?

Wonderful Things

Your testimonies are wonderful;
Therefore my soul keeps them.

PSALM 119:129 NKJV

We are all keepers. Some of us are hoarders. The high school yearbooks still sit on the lower shelf in the living room. Yesterday's newspaper has joined its predecessor in a stack beside the door. There will most certainly be a use for that jar lid someday. It can go in the junk drawer for now. We keep the things that matter to us and the things that we think might matter to us one day. We store up treasures for ourselves and we set aside in case of emergency.

What do you keep? What makes those things wonderful to you? What does that say about what matters to you? As you begin your day, remember that God's Word is a wonderful treasure. He intends that it would be stored up in your heart.

God in heaven, you have made yourself known to me in your word.
You have made known to me the way that I should walk. Let these
words be a treasure to me today.

Your rules are wonderful.
That's why I keep them.

PSALM 119:129 NCV

These wonderful things are not for storing up or setting aside or locking away. That's not the kind of keeping that the psalm is talking about. God wants us to observe them. That is, meticulously keep the words that God has given to us. Do them. Why? Because they are wonderful and our souls know it.

Though we are tempted to forget it sometimes and act as if his commands are burdensome or as if he is cheap and holding back from us. The world is not a better and more gracious giver than your God! The Lord your God has given you his Word as a treasure so that you will do everything that he instructed you about everything.

God, I believe you. I believe that your Word is wonderful and that your ways are right. Will you please help me to learn it and know how it applies to the life I live every day?

Do you know what the Word has instructed about your life as a worker or a student or a parent?

We Are Glad

The Lord has done great things for us;
We are glad.

PSALM 126:3 NASB

Does today have tears for you? This Psalm knows tears. The people of God had been taken captive and exiled to a foreign land. They were victims of war, their homes were destroyed and they were hauled to another part of the world where they were now forced to begin again with nothing. Why were they glad? Because they believed that God would turn their tears into shouts of joy one day because God is a deliverer.

Tears are not all there is for you as a child of God. There is deliverance also. God delivered his people at the Exodus. He delivered the people in this Psalm. He has delivered you from sin and death through the sacrifice of Jesus Christ. Let there be tears if tears are the right response to the grief you are suffering. Sow those tears before the God who delivers you, if not today, then one day.

Almighty God, you have delivered me from sin and death. I entrust you with my tears today. Please turn them into gladness.

The Lord has done great things for us,
and we rejoiced.

PSALM 126:3 NRSV

Did today have labor for you? Was it hard work? Does the
hard work seem fruitless from every angle that you look at it?
This Psalm knows work. It tells the story of the people of God
in exile, who sowed their seed season after season, trusting
God to bring the increase. They went to work faithfully, day
after day, trusting God to do the work of delivering them from
meaninglessness.

God has already delivered you from meaninglessness. God
has already delivered you from futility. Whether or not you
can see present fruit in your daily labor, God has done all the
work necessary to deliver you from the bondage of sin and he
is working in you to make you like Jesus. The Lord has done
great things for you. Rejoice!

*Eternal Father, you are a deliverer. I bring to you the places where
I feel like I am stuck and failing. In the face of them, I rejoice in
your deliverance and I trust that you are doing the best thing in
making me like Jesus.*

The fruit that God promises to bring through your labor is the
fruit of Christ like character. Does that make you glad?

Wonderfully Whole

I praise you, for I am fearfully and wonderfully made.
Wonderful are your works;
my soul knows it very well.

PSALM 139:14 ESV

The children's catechism asks, "Who made you?" To which the children reply, "God made me." The answer is the same for every human child without qualification. It is not truer for the rich than for the poor. It is not less true for the disabled than the able bodied. You are made in the image of God and have value because of the God whose image you bear. God made you, body and soul. You know this. In fact, you know it very well.

Without turning this into a reason for personal arrogance and without ignoring the reality of sin, start today simply in celebration of the good news that you were created in the image of God and that value cannot be lost by you because it was never gained by you.

Almighty God, you have made me in your image and I am infinitely confident in the value of your image. Let me see myself properly as an image bearer today.

I praise you
because of
the wonderful way
you created me.
Everything you do is marvelous!
Of this I have no doubt.

PSALM 139:14 CEB

You are truly valuable in the image of God. Why do you not want to believe this? Is there something about your body that you do not like? See here that your value is tied to the value of God, not to your evaluation of your body or anyone else's evaluation of your body.

You are truly valuable in the image of God and you are truly sinful and guilty, deserving of punishment from a perfectly holy God. Both of these are true. The wonderful news is that God the Son, in whose image you were made, took on a body like yours in order to die for your sin so that you could be restored, recreated, renewed in the image of the Son.

Holy Father, I have sinned against you. I have not used this body as you created it to be used. Will you accept the sacrifice of Jesus as a substitute for my sin so that I live the life you want me to live?

When was the last time you found the gift of your body wonderful? What about the gift of your salvation?

497

Giving Good Thanks

O give thanks unto the Lord; for he is good:
for his mercy endureth for ever.

PSALM 136:1 KJV

How many reasons can you find to give thanks this morning? Can you give thanks for your life? Can you give thanks for someone in your life? Can you give thanks for your salvation in Christ? Can you give thanks for someone you know and love finding salvation in Christ? Give thanks to God for the good things that he has done for you. Give thanks for the mercy of God.

God does good things because he is good. When he does good, it comes naturally to him. Even more profound than that is this little truth: whatever God does is good because he is the one who does it.

Give thanks. Give good thanks. Give thanks to the God who is so good that all that he does is good.

Almighty God, you are good and all that you do is good. I receive today and all that is in it as a gift from your good hand.

Give thanks to the Lord, for He is good,
For His lovingkindness is everlasting.

PSALM 136:1 NASB

God is good and all that he does is good. Yes, even in that he is still good. This Psalm continues to celebrate the goodness of God in everything that happened to the people of Israel, even some pretty bad things. How is God good in the bad things that happened to them? It doesn't say, as much as we might want it to. No, this Psalm does not have the answer to why that one thing happened in your life or why you are thinking about it again tonight.

What we do know is that the Lord is good and all that he does is good. Even when we cannot understand the situation, we can understand our God. He is good and his love endures forever.

Give thanks for the God that you know, even while you wrestle before him with what you don't know.

Gracious God, regarding that one thing that I have never been able to reconcile with your goodness, I still may not understand, but I thank you that your love endures forever.

What do you have a hard time reconciling with the goodness of God?

Song in Your Head

The ransomed of the Lord shall return
and come to Zion with singing;
everlasting joy shall be upon their heads;
they shall obtain gladness and joy,
and sorrow and sighing shall flee away.

ISAIAH 35:10 ESV

Have you ever had a song get stuck in your head? What makes the song stick? Perhaps it is the catchy tune or the meaningful lyrics. The song stuck in the heads of the people of God is a song about ransom and it comes in a variety of musical settings.

God, your God, has ransomed you from slavery to sin. You were in debt so deep you could never pay it back. Your situation before God was absolutely hopeless. Your song was a dirge and it was never going to change. But God himself paid your debt with the precious blood of Jesus and, through repentance and faith, he has given you a song of great joy.

This is the song of the redeemed. Rehearse it today. You will be singing it for eternity.

My God, my God, you have poured joy out on me and have put a new song in my head. I sing it with thankfulness today.

Those the Lord has rescued will return.
They will enter Zion with singing;
everlasting joy will crown their heads.
Gladness and joy will overtake them,
and sorrow and sighing will flee away.

ISAIAH 35:10 NIV

What song is in your head at the end of the day? Is it the song of the redeemed or the song of the beaten down in the workplace? The song of the redeemed or the song of the self-righteous who doesn't think he needs to be ransomed from anything?

It can be a battle to sing this song when other songs compete so powerfully. Fight. Keep fighting. Even when the songs of sighing refuse to flee, sing the song of the redeemed. God, your God is fighting for you and he will make the song of gladness and joy overtake you.

God and Father, I believe in you. I love to sing your song.
Sometimes it is a battle when the weight of the world comes down
on my shoulders, but I trust in your power that has ransomed me.

What do you sing to yourself instead of the song of the redeemed?

Hymn of Divine Sorrow

Then they sang a hymn and went out to the Mount of Olives.

MATTHEW 26:30 NIRV

You came into the world singing. You emerged from the security of your watery home into an atmosphere that is made for song and so you sang, or at least you cried. They can be very similar things sometimes. Praise and pain often live right next door to each other. And we respond to each with full lungs.

The very God who knit you together in your mother's womb came forth himself from a virgin's womb. He tumbled from his warm and wet security into a cold, and perhaps wet, animal trough before his lungs filled with air, our air. The creator became the created. The one from heaven began to sing the songs of earth. God, your God, sang. If we have been listening to the Scriptures, he has always been singing. All creation has been singing. And he welcomes us to sing along.

Almighty God, you entered into the world and into my song. Teach me to sing your song in the world.

Then they sang a hymn and went out to the Mount of Olives.
MATTHEW 26:30 ESV

Jesus Christ, the Son of God who took on flesh, sang a hymn
with the people he created. He sang a familiar song and he
sang it after supper. Where did he learn this song? Did his
mother teach it to him? Was it his Sunday School teacher?
Wherever it came from, it served him well at this time.

It was after supper that they sang, after that supper. Having
just told his disciples that he will be rejected, beaten and
crucified, Jesus sang a hymn. A large percentage of the hymns
of the Old Testament, the Psalms, are laments. That is, they
are sad and sometimes angry complaints to God. They say to
him, "God I know you are good, but I don't understand this!"
Jesus cried out to his Father on the way to his sorrow in order
that you might cry out to him in yours.

Almighty God, you entered into my sorrow and into my song.
Teach me to sing to you in my sorrow that I might know your joys.

How does the song of divine sorrow change the tune of song
that you are singing today?

Now You Dismiss

"Now Lord, You are releasing Your bond-servant
to depart in peace,
According to Your word;
For my eyes have seen Your salvation,
Which You have prepared in the presence of all peoples,
A Light of revelation to the Gentiles,
And the glory of Your people Israel."

LUKE 2:29-32 NASB

"Now Lord," says the old prophet Simeon when he first sees the baby Jesus in the temple. For centuries, the church has known this little declaration as the Nunc Dimittis, the "Now You Dismiss." Now, Lord, there is peace because there is salvation from sin in the coming of Jesus.

Simeon waited years for this moment. How long have you been waiting?

No matter how long you feel like you have been waiting, you can join the church throughout the ages in the Nunc Dimittis because the good news of salvation has already been accomplished. Simeon waited for the day that the Lord prepared, but that day took place 2000 years ago. The incarnate Lord that the old man celebrated is your Lord today. This peace is yours now.

Almighty God, strengthen me today to live in light of that day
when your salvation was made known.

"Sovereign Lord, as you have promised,
you may now dismiss your servant in peace.
For my eyes have seen your salvation,
which you have prepared in the sight of all nations:
a light for revelation to the Gentiles,
and the glory of your people Israel."

LUKE 2:29-32 NIV

That day changed everything and yet we come to the end of
this day and feel like nothing has changed. As you come to
the end of your day, what was different at home or at work
because Jesus Christ came according the promises of God
in the Old Testament? Do you find yourself, like Simeon,
satisfied with life because you have seen the only thing that
your heart really desires? "Now Lord, you may now dismiss
your servant in peace."

Find some peace in this as you lay down to rest. God, your
God, is the light of all nations, not just for you. He is revealing
himself to all people, not just to you. The light has shined in
the glory of Christ.

Now Lord, let the nations see your glory in Christ and come to him
to find peace.

How are you praying with Simeon for the world to see the
glory of God in the coming of Christ?

After Midnight

But at midnight Paul and Silas were praying and singing hymns to God, and the prisoners were listening to them.

ACTS 16:25 NKJV

"But" is the most powerful word in the whole of the Bible. Paul and Silas were in jail, "but" they were praying. Paul and Silas would most likely have rather been asleep, "but" they were singing.

These things seem like they are in contrast, jail and singing, late nights and prayer. Yet, they are not really at odds in God's world. The reason that these two believing men had to sing songs to God did not change because they were in chains. The God who heard their prayers, did not stop listening because they were behind bars.

As you take up the tasks of the day, whether you are free or in chains, whether things are dark or the light is shining on you, take up the songs of God in your heart and in your mouth.

Almighty God, you have given me great reason to sing. Now, please strengthen me to continue singing, even when things go dark.

About midnight Paul and Silas were praying and singing hymns to God, and the other prisoners were listening to them.

ACTS 16:25 NIV

Whether or not it is midnight as you return to a moment of reflection, remember that God is good to you even in the times of your life when it seems to being going badly. Remember and sing a robust hymn to God.

God used these songs in the momentary darkness of Paul and Silas' lives to bring light to the life of an entire family who lived in permanent darkness. God brought salvation to the jailer and all those who lived in his house through the songs that these men sang in his jail. Sing praise to God tonight, even if you do not have the strength to sing robustly. And pray that God will use your faith in the darkness to bring light to someone around you.

God of God and light of light, open my eyes to see you in the darkness and use me to bring someone from darkness to light.

What is praiseworthy about your God that cannot be touched by pain and suffering?

Blessing of Hope

May the God of hope fill you with all joy and peace in believing,
so that you will abound in hope by the power of the Holy Spirit.

ROMANS 15:13 NASB

"I hope so," we say. "I hope today will be a good day. I hope
things will work out. I hope that the future will be a bright
one." What do you hope for from this day? What do you hope
for from this series of days that, when strung together, will
make up the year to come? Biblical hope is not just wishful
thinking, it is the confident expectation that God will fulfill
his promises because God is a God of hope. God is the origin
of hope and the object of our hope. God is hope, God has
hope, and God offers hope to all who believe him.

As today begins, set your hope on God and let God's Word
teach you what to hope in. May you abound in his hope today.

God of hope, I acknowledge this morning that you and I hope for
different things. Cause me to abound in true hope today.

The God of hope fill you with all joy and peace in believing,
that ye may abound in hope, through the power of the Holy Ghost.

ROMANS 15:13 KJV

Was anything or anyone else able to do that for you today? Where else did you seek hope today?

The hope that comes from God becomes joy and peace—which results in hope—through believing in him. That's what makes this passage a benediction or a blessing. The joy that God promises is not dependent on how well you hoped in him today. The peace that God will fill you with is not waiting for you to do something peaceful. Hope will not abound in you because you reach a certain level of confidence in God alone.

As you close your eyes at the end of the day, simply believe him and receive the benediction because God wants to bless you in Christ Jesus.

God of hope, you are both the cause of my hope and what I hope in tonight. Fill me with the joy that comes from being confident in you.

What are you hoping in tonight? It is giving you joy and peace?

Controlled by Love

The love of Christ controls us, because we know that One died for all, so all have died.

2 CORINTHIANS 5:14 NCV

No one likes to be controlled. Toddlers don't like it when mom tells them what to do. Employees don't like it when bosses demand obedience. The only thing worse than being controlled is when everything is out of control. No one likes being controlled! But we all like being in control.

Control often functions out of fear. That sweet little toddler might be afraid that mom won't be able to protect him or he might be afraid that mom won't let him do what he wants to do. Even the hardest working employee can fear the loss of a job or loss of dignity at the hands of a demeaning employer. We are all afraid that the earthquake or the hurricane will prove to everyone that we are not actually God and cannot actually run the world like we claim most of the time.

Almighty God, maker of heaven and earth. I bow before you today, leaving the control of the world in your capable hands.

Christ's love compels us, because we are convinced that one died for all, and therefore all died.

2 Corinthians 5:14 NIV

Your God has been ruling the universe quite fine without you. Your God has been overseeing the affairs of your life while you were in the loins of your ancestors, to borrow a phrase from Hebrews to describe the relationship of Levi to his great, great grandfather Abraham. He has been ruling the universe so well that he has even turned the fall of the first Adam into a glorious redemption through the second Adam. He rules so well that he turned the greatest evil of human history—the cross—into the greatest good of human history.

As you lay down to rest, leaving God to run both the universe and your life, do so in complete trust that he loves you, has your good in mind and that he will bring about the best for you. How can you be sure? Because he proved it once and for all when he died for you.

Everlasting Father, you rule all things well and I trust you.
Help me to trust when I am afraid.

What are you afraid of? How do you grasp control to try to keep it from happening?

Sealed with a Promise

In him you also, when you heard the word of truth, the gospel
of your salvation, and believed in him, were sealed with
the promised Holy Spirit, who is the guarantee of our inheritance
until we acquire possession of it, to the praise of his glory.

EPHESIANS 1:13-14 ESV

The sticky part of an envelope is pretty handy. You don't
need a sponge and water to close up a letter. You don't need
a candle and a metal insignia to ensure its security until it
reaches the hands of the intended recipient.

Something is lost in the process of simplification. Beauty
is lost for one. The aesthetics of self-adhesive flap does not
compare to a centuries old family seal, pressed in hot wax. The
other loss is certainty. That stamped initial seals a promise.

God promised that your present earthly salvation will
certainly continue into a future salvation in the new heavens
and the new earth. God seals this promise, not with wax on
paper, but with the Holy Spirit on your heart.

Almighty God, I hear your promise today and I am confident in
your ability to secure it.

In him you also, who have heard the word of truth, the gospel of your salvation, and have believed in him, were sealed with the promised Holy Spirit, which is the guarantee of our inheritance until we acquire possession of it, to the praise of his glory.

EPHESIANS 1:13–14, RSV

The seal of God, his family insignia in the form of the Holy Spirit, secures the last will and testament of a father for his children. Your God has given you an inheritance that you have not earned from a family that you were not born into. He added your name to the family tree, you will be receiving a share of the eternal inheritance. He wrote it in a will and sealed it with his Holy Spirit to guarantee that no one will be able to steal, damage or alter that will until the inheritance is yours.

As you close your eyes, as they seal out the last light of day, give praise to God for his guarantee of your future salvation.

Everlasting Father, you have given me an inheritance I do not deserve. I trust in your ability to guarantee it for me.

What kind of gratitude does this promise raise within you?

The Will of God

Give thanks in all circumstances; for this is God's will for you in Christ Jesus.

1 THESSALONIANS 5:18 NIV

Sometimes we talk of the will of God as if he is playing a cruel and sophisticated shell game with our lives. "The safest place in the world is in middle of God's will." That is, if you can find it and when you do, you will never be quite sure about it.

The will of God is not hiding from you. Sure, there are things that God has not told you. Some you would never understand and some you wouldn't agree to if he told you. Others are the kind of things that you are free to decide on your own.

No, God just comes out and tells you. The will of God for your life is that you would be thankful and that you would be thankful in all circumstances.

My God and Father, I am thankful. Please make me aware today of the moments and situations in which I find it hard to be thankful.

Give thanks no matter what happens. God wants you to thank him because you believe in Christ Jesus.

1 Thessalonians 5:18 NIRV

What is that one thing in your life that makes thanksgiving stick in your throat like a chicken bone? Were your parents cruel to you when you had every right to expect kindness? Were you betrayed by someone you had every right to trust? Sometimes it really is as bad as you think it is.

What do you do with hurts and history that is actually terrible? What is the will of God for you when that happens? Give thanks. Give thanks no matter what happens. Learn the grown-up practice of allowing grief over past hurts to sit right beside joy in your present salvation. You will find that your God has provided far more for you in the death of Jesus than was ever taken from you by abuse, tragedy and betrayal.

Everlasting Father, I do not understand how some of these things ever happened in my life. But I know that I am thankful that you sent Jesus to save me.

What is it about God that makes thanksgiving possible in each and every circumstance?

Whole Souls

Now may the God of peace Himself sanctify you entirely; and may your spirit and soul and body be preserved complete, without blame at the coming of our Lord Jesus Christ. Faithful is He who calls you, and He also will bring it to pass.

1 THESSALONIANS 5:23-24 NASB

Sin has broken us down into pieces. It has broken us from one another; it has broken our families, it has broken our nations and it has broken our hearts. Sin breaks and God makes whole. That is the blessing of this promise.

The God of peace himself will do it. The God who is peace and makes peace. The God who is the prince of peace. The God who lays down his own life to remove the true guilt that makes us his enemies. The God who knew you before the foundation of the world, chose you and called you into fellowship with himself. The God who is faithful will do it. The God who always acts consistently with who he is and who does not fail to keep his promise.

Almighty God, look into my heart today and make me whole where I am still broken.

May the God of peace himself sanctify you completely, and may your whole spirit and soul and body be kept blameless at the coming of our Lord Jesus Christ. He who calls you is faithful; he will surely do it.

1 THESSALONIANS 5:23-24 ESV

As you return your attention to God at the end of the day, where did you find wounded pieces in which you long for this benediction to be fulfilled? God blesses you with wholeness both internally and externally, both in body and in soul, both materially and immaterially.

This isn't the Lord's Day service, but reach out your hands in a receptive posture and read this blessing out loud. Receive it as God affirming his desire for the pieces of your life, which are broken by sin to be healed and made whole.

Now, may the God of peace himself sanctify you completely, and may your whole spirit and soul and body be kept blameless at the coming of our Lord Jesus Christ. He who calls you is faithful; he will surely do it.

Do you want to be whole?

Working to Work

The God of peace, who brought up from the dead the great Shepherd of the sheep through the blood of the eternal covenant, even Jesus our Lord, equip you in every good thing to do His will, working in us that which is pleasing in His sight, through Jesus Christ, to whom be the glory forever and ever.

HEBREWS 13:20-21 NASB

The day ahead will likely include a good deal of work. It should. That is what we were created to do, for the glory of God. In the garden of Eden, and after, both man and woman turned to their labor as a means of fulfilling God's purpose in their part of the world. While their "labor" was different, it was equally God given and had the potential of being equally fruitful.

Start your day with the confidence that the God who created you to work for his glory and who himself worked for the glory of the Father, will equip you in every good thing.

Almighty God, as I head off to my day of work, send me out for your glory and equip me thoroughly to the task ahead.

*May the God of peace, who brought up from the dead our Lord
Jesus—the great Shepherd of the sheep—with the blood of the
everlasting covenant, equip you with all that is good to do His will,
working in us what is pleasing in His sight, through Jesus Christ.
Glory belongs to Him forever and ever.*

HEBREWS 13:20-21 HCSB

The letter to Hebrews offers this benediction to all who desire
to do the work of God. The blessing comes to us in light of
twelve chapters describing how much better the work of Jesus
is to the work of anyone or anything else in all creation.

As you come to the end of your day, find your rest and
confidence in the good news that the work of Jesus is
completed. God the Son shed his blood, the blood of the
eternal covenant, and God the Father brought him up from
the dead. There is no more work to be done in your salvation,
Jesus has done it all.

*God, as I lay down from my day of work, I rest confidently in the
finished work of Jesus.*

What is the work that God has equipped you to do? How does
the finished work of Jesus prepare you to do it?

Soundtrack of Suffering

Is anyone among you in trouble? Let them pray. Is anyone happy?
Let them sing songs of praise.

JAMES 5:13 NIV

We all have trouble. Trouble is just another word for being alive. That is not to say that life is not magnificent, it is just to honestly admit that every life has trouble in it. Trouble is not a sign that something is necessarily wrong. Trouble is part of life, but it is still troubling to have trouble. It still causes your lower back to tense up and your mind to race on ways in which you could solve the trouble if you were the one to rule the universe.

Here, at the beginning of the day, bring your troubles to God in prayer. Bring the troubles of those you love to God in prayer. Bring the troubles of the world to God in prayer. Let prayer be louder in your ears that the clamor of the world.

Lord God Almighty, you are the creator of heaven and earth.
The earth is yours and all of its fullness. I confidently leave my
troubles with you today.

Anyone who is having troubles should pray. Anyone who is happy should sing praises.

JAMES 5:13 NCV

How did your troubles fare without you today? James does not assume that they magically disappear because you prayed about them. He does not expect that the sound of them will stop ringing in your ears now that you have returned to a quiet moment before God.

There is also reason to be cheerful, a reason to be happy, right alongside your suffering. It is not that one person is happy while another suffers. It is not even that one day you suffer and another is pretty good, all things considered. The reason you have to be happy tonight, Christian, is not and cannot be troubled by your troubles. Your God is still good. Your Savior still saves. The Lord of the Psalms is still worthy of a song.

Eternal God, you are my joy tonight. As I lay down to sleep, fill my heart with a reminder of your infinite goodness to me in Jesus Christ. Let this be the soundtrack of my life.

In what ways is the goodness of God sitting right next to your troubles? How can that retune your heart?

Test Results

That the genuineness of your faith, being much more precious than gold that perishes, though it is tested by fire, may be found to praise, honor, and glory at the revelation of Jesus Christ.

1 PETER 1:7 NKJV

When you set a fire to gold, it does not die, but becomes more valuable. When the faith of a Christian is tested, it does not die, but becomes more valuable. Now, testing is not the same as temptation. One lures towards sin, which God does not do, and the other only serves to reveal what is already inside.

Peter writes to believers that were exiled, both physically and spiritually. They didn't have any gold left and the authorities were lighting them on fire. Their trials were not out of control and neither are yours. God will use them to change us. We want the circumstances to change, God wants us to change.

Almighty God, I entrust this day to you with all that it will hold. If I will be tested, I trust that you will hold me firm and use it for me good.

That the tested genuineness of your faith—more precious than gold
that perishes though it is tested by fire—may be found to result
in praise and glory and honor at the revelation of Jesus Christ.

1 PETER 1:7 ESV

Your faith is more precious than gold. The growth of your
faith is more valuable than your shrinking bank account.
The increase of your faith in God is more valuable than
the decrease of your personal comfort. When your faith is
purified, the cost is worth paying, it is a good trade, a good
investment. Tested faith is a precious gift.

God will be the one to receive praise and honor from it
because God is the one who has done it. He has caused you to
grow up through what you thought would kill you. He caused
you to become more holy out of circumstances that you
worried would defile you. As you finish your day, as you trust
yourself into the hands God who can bring gold out of trials,
desire his glory more than your own comfort.

Father, you are more precious to me than anything that trials
could take away.

How has God brought spiritual growth in your physical trials?

What Angels Long for

Concerning this salvation, the prophets who prophesied about the grace that was to be yours searched and inquired carefully, inquiring what person or time the Spirit of Christ in them was indicating when he predicted the sufferings of Christ and the subsequent glories. It was revealed to them that they were serving not themselves but you, in the things that have now been announced to you through those who preached the good news to you by the Holy Spirit sent from heaven, things into which angels long to look.

1 PETER 1:10-12 ESV

Have you ever read through the Old Testament and, by the time that you got to the Minor Prophets you ached with longing for the New Testament? Come quickly Lord Jesus! The salvation that you enjoy today is something that others waited centuries to see come to reality.

The prophets served you by writing the good news that was preached as the Holy Spirit enabled them, the Holy Spirit sent from heaven, which is also where the fullness of your salvation is kept and guarded for you.

Almighty God, give me eyes to see the blessing that is mine in salvation.

Of this salvation the prophets have inquired and searched
carefully, who prophesied of the grace that would come to you,
searching what, or what manner of time, the Spirit of Christ
who was in them was indicating when He testified beforehand
the sufferings of Christ and the glories that would follow. To
them it was revealed that, not to themselves, but to us they were
ministering the things which now have been reported to you
through those who have preached the gospel to you by the Holy
Spirit sent from heaven—things which angels desire to look into.

1 PETER 1:10-12 HCSB

The salvation that you enjoy today is a treasure that all those
men and women of faith only dreamed about experiencing in
actual day to day life. And, angels also desire to look into it.

Angels enjoy the presence of God, daily singing, "Holy, holy,
holy is the Lord." They sing like this because they can. They
sing because they are there! They sing because it is true. And,
even with all this, they longed to look into what you enjoy
every day.

Eternal God, thank you. Thank you for my salvation.

Do you value your salvation as much as the prophets and
angels do?

All the Excellencies

You are a chosen race, a royal priesthood, a holy nation, a people for God's own possession, so that you may proclaim the excellencies of Him who has called you out of darkness into His marvelous light.

1 PETER 2:9 NASB

These people don't fit anywhere and everyone knows it. They cannot vote because their governors are ignorant. They cannot work because their bosses are unjust and some cannot make their marriages work because their spouses are disobedient. Perhaps one of these is true for you. Perhaps all of them are true. What is God doing in this moment of spiritual exile when the enemies seem to have the upper hand? Where is God when you don't know where you are?

God put you there, as a part of his chosen people, to be his priest to the ignorant, unjust and disobedient people in your life. You are the king's priests. You are the priests of the one who is himself a priestly king.

O Lord God, even though I feel distant from people who should make me feel welcome, let me know I am at home because of your priestly sacrifice.

You are a chosen generation, a royal priesthood, a holy nation, His own special people, that you may proclaim the praises of Him who called you out of darkness into His marvelous light.

1 PETER 2:9 NKJV

God the King has hand-picked you and hand planted you to be part of his priestly people right where you are. This makes more sense to us on Sunday because that is where we think that is where priests belong. Priests bring people to God. Priests or pastors are the ones who lead us to God in worship. Aren't they? Yes, and no.

The reason that God has chosen you is to join in proclaiming his praises, not just in your Sunday worship, but in your Monday work. He chose you to speak and live truthfully before the ignorant, justly when faced with injustice and obediently when you suffer the consequences of someone who is disobedient. God has called you out of darkness. You are in his marvelous light. You are his royal priest.

Blessed are you, O Lord, our God, king of the universe. You have chosen me to be your very own.

What ignorance does God want you to bring truth into? What injustice? What disobedience?

Glory at Rest

If you are insulted for the name of Christ, you are blessed, because the Spirit of glory and of God rests upon you.

1 PETER 4:14 ESV

Who are you? How would you answer that question? Most of us would start with what we do for a living or with the identity of our families, some might wander into areas of education or particular interest, like a hobby or a sport. We are, in our experience, who or what we identify with, we are our name and our reputation.

This makes Peter's words a little unsettling. Insults tear at the foundation of your reputation because at least this one person thinks poorly of you. They think you do a lousy job at work or have a ridiculous golf swing or, in this case, that you're one of those Christians. Be blessed today to name the name of Jesus Christ. Be blessed to be known as one of his. That cannot be taken away with an insult.

Father, I am honored and blessed to be called your child through faith in Jesus.

If you are reviled for the name of Christ, you are blessed, because the spirit of glory, which is the Spirit of God, is resting on you.

1 PETER 4:14, NRSV

You are a child of God because of your relationship to the only Son of God. You are an heir to the treasures of heaven because of your trust in the Son who inherits everything. The ground underneath you is firm and solid, your identity in Christ cannot be shaken.

We feel threatened when we think we might lose something valuable. We feel desperate when we think we might lose ourselves. All of these things are true of you because of who Jesus is and insults do not threaten Jesus. Death does not threaten Jesus because he has already defeated it. This is now your identity through faith. You name the name of Jesus and, sometimes, that brings insults with it from fools, but it always brings glory from the Spirit. Be at rest because the spirit of glory is resting on you.

God, my God, I entrust my identity to you and thank you for the rest you have given me through Christ.

How stable do you feel in your Christian identity?

Glory in Shame

But if anyone suffers as a "Christian," he should not be ashamed but should glorify God in having that name.

1 PETER 4:16 HCSB

We can feel shame for all sorts of reasons. We can feel true shame because we were exposed in a way we hoped we wouldn't be. We know that everyone is a sinner, but it can be shameful for others to find out what kind of sinner we really are. We can also feel shame for things that aren't really shameful.

Perhaps we don't like our bodies or maybe we feel shame because we don't sin in the way that the people around us think we should. Feeling shame about things that are not shameful is misplaced. There is no shame in doing right or refusing to do wrong, even if people around you think that there is and say that there is, even if they punish you for it.

Jesus, you left the glories of heaven to live among us. You went to a painful death on the cross, scorning its shame, for me and for my salvation. Teach me to glory in you.

If any of you suffers as a Christian, do not consider it a disgrace, but glorify God because you bear this name.

1 PETER 4:16 NRSV

When you suffer because you are a Christian and dare to behave like one, don't be ashamed. When the world laughs at the content of your belief, the purity of your life or the biblical consistency of your conduct, do not be ashamed. Never consider it a disgrace to suffer as a Christian. Jesus was not ashamed to be crucified for you. The suffering of Jesus became the gateway to glory, both for him and for you. Because he suffered for sin, you are free from it, because he died to death, you no longer have to see death.

Jesus was not ashamed to call us his brothers and, in so doing, he has opened up the way to glory. If believing him causes any kind of suffering whatsoever, that is your glory. Rejoice in the honor of sharing his name.

Jesus, through your suffering you brought many sons to glory, you were not ashamed to calls us your brothers. Tonight, I give you glory that you have entrusted me with your name.

What does it look like to glorify God because of Jesus' name?

Eternal Glory

And after you have suffered for a little while, the God of all grace, who has called you to his eternal glory in Christ, will himself restore, support, strengthen, and establish you.

1 PETER 5:10 NRSV

In those old books, or perhaps old movies, people knew how to be sick. Today, we act insulted when hit with the flu or the cold that we properly name "common." They also knew how to recover, spending weeks in bed or perhaps longer in order to return to full strength and then to the responsibilities of daily life. In the day of outpatient surgeries, we expect to be back running a marathon a day after knee surgery. Sickness and injury require much time for recovery and suffering requires much grace.

The God of all grace is with you. The God of all grace has called you to his eternal glory in Christ. As you prepare your heart for the day ahead, prepare your heart for much grace.

Almighty God, you have already given me much grace and for this I am eternally thankful. Please give me the grace needed for the day ahead.

The God of all grace, who called you to his eternal glory in Christ, after you have suffered a little while, will himself restore you and make you strong, firm and steadfast.

1 PETER 5:10 NIV

Recovering is actually a thing. It is doing something. That's enough, you can sit there and let your body heal and that is a day well spent. It is sufficient productivity. Part of the reason it's enough is because God is at work in it. God is at work healing your body while you stop doing anything worse to it.

God is also at work in the difficult times in your Christian life. When you feel like people are opposed to you for your faith, God is bringing you to eternal glory. When you are certain that the struggles have broken you down and weakened your ability to stand, God himself will restore you and make you strong.

My God, I know that you are at work within my life, please let me see it. I know that you are calling me to eternal glory, please enable me to stand strong.

Where would you like to you see God strengthen your faith?

Stumbling into Glory

To Him who is able to keep you from stumbling, and to make you stand in the presence of His glory blameless with great joy, to the only God our Savior, through Jesus Christ our Lord, be glory, majesty, dominion and authority, before all time and now and forever.

JUDE 24-25 NASB

We all stumble sometimes. Sometimes, we cause others to stumble along with us. Anyone who does not stumble is perfect and there has been only one person like that so far. The assurance of this benediction is that he is able to keep you from stumbling beyond repair. A believer may stumble, but will not fall. He or she may sin, but will repent and return to forgiveness found in our Savior Jesus Christ.

The Bible has stories of believers stumbling to the point of being removed from the church and then God uses that pain to bring them back to obedience and trust in Jesus. The bottom never drops out for the Christian because God is able to keep you.

Heavenly Father, I make no excuses for my sin. Please forgive my sin and keep me from stumbling.

*To him who is able to keep you from stumbling and to present
you before his glorious presence without fault and with great
joy— to the only God our Savior be glory, majesty, power and
authority, through Jesus Christ our Lord, before all ages, now and
forevermore!*

JUDE 24-25 NIV

Jesus is the cornerstone of the temple that is the church and
he is also the capstone on the same building. Jesus is a rock of
stumbling, he is a stone in the middle of the path that some
people trip on and then kick it, as if the stone did something
wrong. Those who believe in him will never be put to shame.
Those who believe in him will be kept in this life and brought
into the glory of his presence with great joy.

Jesus is able to keep you. Jesus is able to bring you to glory.
Jesus is before all ages and Jesus is forevermore. Believe
him, obey him, follow him and, even if you stumble, you are
stumbling into glory.

*Everlasting Father, you have already conquered sin and death and
I trust that you are able to keep me.*

Where do you need to ask God for strength tonight?

Working with Others

Later, when Moses' arms became tired, the men put a large rock under him, and he sat on it. Then Aaron and Hur held up Moses' hands—Aaron on one side and Hur on the other. They kept his hands steady until the sun went down. So Joshua defeated the Amalekites in this battle.

HEBREWS 10:25 NCV

Can you picture this? Three guys standing overlooking the battlefield. They notice that when one of their friend's arms are raised the battle is going well, but the opposite is true when his arms are down.

A man's arms can only be raised on their own for so long, so without much discussion the two friends arrange for their friend's arms to remain raised. They relieved the need without forming a committee or questioning. They just did it. There are people around us that need our help today. Perhaps in helping relieve the need there is a bigger battle that is being won.

God, help me to see the needs of those around me today. May I be someone's Aaron or Hur today. Help me to see that bigger picture of what you are doing and thank you for letting me be a part of it.

Moses' hands grew heavy, so they took a stone, put it under him,
and he sat down. Aaron and Hur held up his hands, one on each
side. So his hands were steady until the sun went down. So Joshua
overpowered the Amalekites and his army with the edge of the sword.

EXODUS 17:12-13 TLV

Moses could not have done it without those around him.
It is amazing to know that God uses our relationships to
accomplish his tasks.

With God's help Joshua could have overpowered the
Amalekites, no matter where Moses's hands were, but instead
God chose to use man's submission to his plan to accomplish
the task before them. Not only did Moses need help, he had
others around him to help!

Heavenly Father, Thanks for involving me in your plans.
Thanks for allowing me to see how you move in each area of my life.
Thank you for the friends who have helped me throughout my life.
Help me to be a friend when others are in need.

Whose arms are you lifting today? What is the battle that was
taking place that you were a part of?

Reaching under the Bed

The Lord answered Moses, "Is the Lord's arm too short? Now you will see whether or not what I say will come true for you."

NUMBERS 11:23 NIV

Have you ever tried to reach something that has fallen under the bed? No matter what angle you reach at it is just a hair out of your reach. You strain reach further but you just can reach.

God doesn't have that problem no matter the issue, God's arm is long enough to reach under the bed no matter how far back the problem goes. We can trust God to have to power to resolve our problems according to his will. Nothing is beyond his reach today, tomorrow or ever.

Heavenly Father, I am grateful that your arm is long enough to reach me, long enough to take care of my needs, long enough to hold me, long enough to keep me from harm. You are an amazing God. Thank you.

The Lord said to Moses, "Do you think I'm weak? Now you will see if I can do what I say."

Numbers 11:23 NCV

Do you love the way God uses questions to correct out way of thinking? Instead of directly contradicting Moses here, God uses a question to set Moses on a path towards thinking correctly. Then when Moses is reflecting God speaks. He could have simply said, "That's it, I'm fixing the problem." Instead he used this moment to teach Moses to change his understanding of God. God still did what he had promised, still acted in accordance to his will; he just paused a moment so Moses's thinking could catch up and see the power of God revealed.

Look back at today's frustration, in the knowledge that God is at work and powerful enough to act in every situation. Do you see God's power revealed?

Almighty God, thank you that you are powerful enough. Thank you for showing me your strength and allowing me to better understand your power and working. Thank you that you are strong enough for every situation.

How was God's power revealed to you today? Is there an area you thought "God's arm was too short" for? How did you see God's Word come true?

The Best for Others

Moses asked him, "Are you jealous on my account? If only all the Lord's people were prophets and the Lord would place His Spirit on them!"

NUMBERS 11:29 HCSB

It's nice to know someone is on our side. Sometimes we seem to be surrounded by people who are only looking out for themselves. The climb up the corporate ladder is often on the backs of others. That is why it is refreshing to hear encouraging words or to hear that someone stood up for your actions.

Moses had a unique role in leading the people of Israel, yet here Moses says I really wish all the people could do my job. What a splendid example for us to want the best for others. To desire that others could grow in their relationship with Christ and in their ability to know him.

Abba Father, thank you for the people who have encouraged me to do my best, who have spoken well of me. Thank you for allowing them to be your encouragement to me.

Moses said to him, "Are you jealous for my sake? Would that all the Lord's people were prophets, that the Lord would put His Spirit upon them!"

NUMBERS 11:29 NASB

Moses wanted God's will above his own glory. Moses had been the one that God had spoken through to the people of Israel. Here we see God speaking through others, and not only does Moses allow that, he desires that God would speak through even more people. Moses was saying, "I am not special; it is the spirit of God who speaks, and it is best to let that spirit fall on all his people."

Moses shows us a fitting example of leadership and investment in others. We have the ability to empower others and let them experience the fullness of God When we do, the power of God multiplies and we accomplish more together in the power of God.

God, help me to encourage others in their walk with you. May I put aside my desire for glory for your will. Help me to empower others to follow you.

How has God spoken through you to others? Have you encouraged others to lead in your place? What keeps you from allowing others to rise to their potential?

The Ultimate Reality

Caleb silenced the people before Moses and said, "Surely, let us go up and let us take possession of it because surely we will be able to prevail over it."

NUMBERS 13:30 LEB

They had just returned from exploring the land that God had promised to give them. It was not what they had expected. Yes, it was bountiful as God had promised, but it was occupied by violent people and giants. Instead of focusing on the promise, they focused on the land. They couldn't keep their eyes off the reality that they saw.

One person saw the ultimate reality of God's promise to lead them into and take the land. Caleb saw beyond the giants to the promise. God's promises for us are multiple. He has promised victory in the long run. He has promised that we are more than conquerors. And we can trust in him to help us see the ultimate reality.

Loving Father, help me to see the ultimate reality and not focus on the giants around me. Thank you for your promises. Help me today to be reminded of your promises even while I still see the giants.

Caleb reassured the people as they stood before Moses. "Let us go up at once and possess it," he said, "for we are well able to conquer it!"

NUMBERS 13:30 TLB

Caleb doesn't dispute what they said. He just knows there is something beyond the reality of what is seen. Caleb is trusting in the promise that God has made. Yes, there are giants, yes things are in our ways, but God has promised us victory beyond the reality we can see. Things might seem impossible but what God has promised, God can do.

Caleb stood in the minority when he said, "Let us go up at once," because Caleb wanted to stand on God's side, which is the ultimate reality. No matter what we see or others around us see, the Word of God and his promises are the ultimate reality. We can trust God in the ultimate reality.

God, help me to remember that your promises are the ultimate reality. Help me to see that even beyond what I see, your promises are stronger and better than I can understand.

What are the giants you faced today? In what way has God promised to overcome these giants?

Listen Closely

Moses raised the stick and struck the rock twice with it, and a great stream of water gushed out, and all the people and animals drank.

NUMBERS 20:11 GNT

At first glance, this looks like a tremendous story of God's provision to the people of Israel, yet this simple action kept Moses from leading the Israelites into the promised land. God had told Moses to speak to the rock and it would flow with water. Moses, in a moment of frustration, strikes the rock with the staff.

It is important to remember what God speaks to us and follow his directions. God wants to provide and will provide in his ways, when we listen closely to his voice and directions.

Gracious God, thank you for speaking your promises to me. Thank you for giving directions, help me today to follow closely to your voice.

Moses lifted his hand and hit the rock twice with his stick. Water began pouring out, and the people and their animals drank it.

NUMBERS 20:11 NCV

The water came out abundantly. Moses messed up. He didn't follow God's instructions. Yet God, in his graciousness, still allows water to flow from the rock. Not just a trickle but enough for the whole of Israel and their livestock to drink. There are ramifications to Moses' decision for himself but God is still gracious and allows water to flow.

Thankfully, God is still gracious to us today. We can rest assured that He will continue to honor his promises to us. He is a gracious God who provides even when we don't deserve it. God provides abundantly.

Gracious Provider, you are gracious to me in providing abundantly for what I need. Thank you for reaching beyond my mistakes and still providing for me.

How has God provided for you today? In what ways was that provision abundant?

Content with God

Not that I was ever in need, for I have learned how to be content with whatever I have. I know how to live on almost nothing or with everything. I have learned the secret of living in every situation, whether it is with a full stomach or empty, with plenty or little. For I can do everything through Christ, who gives me strength.

PHILIPPIANS 4:11–13 NLT

It could never be said that Paul had it easy. Maybe you can relate to what he went through: His life was riddled with ups and downs. He faced hardships and successes; agony and abuse; rejection as well as acceptance; shame but also joy. Paul had made huge mistakes and caused tremendous pain that scarred his past. His life changed dramatically after he met Jesus. He began to help others and learned to share himself vulnerably. Instead of bullying his way to victory, he would sometimes go hungry. Instead of being celebrated, he would sometimes suffer loss.

Yet, because of Jesus, Paul found contentment. He learned that no matter his circumstances, he was grounded in who he was because of who Jesus was in his life. He found confidence in what he was called to do because of what Jesus was calling him to do.

God, help me find my sense of worth, my sense of peace, my sense of identity in you. Let me trust you fully for the contentment I so desperately seek in my life.

Not that I speak from want, for I have learned to be content in whatever circumstances I am. I know how to get along with humble means, and I also know how to live in prosperity; in any and every circumstance I have learned the secret of being filled and going hungry, both of having abundance and suffering need. I can do all things through Him who strengthens me.

PHILIPPIANS 4:11–13 NASB

Hopefully, you found your inner strength today in the life and power of Jesus Christ. During your difficult moments, Jesus was ready to strengthen you. During your exuberant moments, Jesus was ready to focus you.

If you had a typical day, it was probably much too easy to get distracted by your circumstances and lose focus on the source of your true life.

No matter the circumstances you had today, and no matter the ones you will face tomorrow, may the Lord be your unwavering source of confidence and peace.

Savior Jesus, you are truly all that I need. Right now, give me a deep breath, a calm heart-beat, and a contented soul.

What are the biggest things at the forefront of your mind? How could you entrust these to Jesus?

Better Together

Let us not neglect our meeting together, as some people do, but encourage one another, especially now that the day of his return is drawing near.

HEBREWS 10:25 NLT

We were created to be in community with others. From the time of our birth to the time of our death and all the time in between we need community. In Europe, the churches of old are often filled with tourists looking for the camera angle for the perfect photo; there are few people there who are seeking community or to encourage one another.

We have an amazing opportunity in our local churches to be involved in so many things that can foster community and encourage one another. We weren't meant to be alone. Today be thankful for the community of believer's around you.

Heavenly Father, thank you that I do not have to live the Christian life alone. Thank you that I am surrounded by people who care about me and encourage me

You should not stay away from the church meetings, as some are doing, but you should meet together and encourage each other. Do this even more as you see the day coming.

<small>HEBREWS 10:25 NCV</small>

Introverts often push back on this verse, but this is not a meeting to fear or shy away from. The author encourages believers to gather together to encourage and exhort one another. He shows the importance even now as we see the day of Christ's return approaching. We need other believers to help us in challenging times.

We need to lean into those who are on the same journey with us who can share their story and life with us so we can be encouraged to hold onto our faith even as the world around us tries to discourage us. The community of faith is there to build us up. Lean in because we are better together.

God, thank you for your church. Thank you that I am loved by you and your people. May we be the encouragement to each other and others in these challenging times.

How have you gathered this week to encourage other believers? Have you been encouraged by others this week?

Taking the Hill Country

"Give me this hill country of which the Lord spoke on that day, for you heard on that day how the Anakim were there, with great fortified cities. It may be that the Lord will be with me, and I shall drive them out just as the Lord said."

JOSHUA 14:12 ESV

Caleb was well into "the golden years" at this point in the story. He could have taken the easy land. Maybe he could have used his old age as a reason to sit back and let others fight the battles to take the land. He deserved it, right? Eighty years he had been following God. Forty of those years he had wandered through the desert following God. Can't he just take it easy this once? Nope! Caleb had seen God work each day of those eighty years and he wasn't going to stop following God just because he was getting a little older.

No matter what our age, God will continue to act according to his word. God had promised Caleb the mountain and Caleb was going to follow that promise. Today God has promised to never leave us or forsake or forsake us, even if we are old.

God, you love me and have been with me. Thank you for your promises and that you are always with me. Help me today to follow you even if I have to walk uphill.

"Give me the mountain country the Lord promised me that day long ago. Back then you heard that the Anakite people lived there and the cities were large and well protected. But now with the Lord helping me, I will force them out, just as the Lord said."

JOSHUA 14:12 NCV

There is no hesitation in Caleb's request. He did not hesitate to claim the promise of God. Sure, the people of Anak were still there living in large, fortified cities. Caleb had spent 40 years following God in the desert. He didn't have an army, catapults or any real means of taking the cities. What he did have was God's promise from forty years earlier; the hill country was going to be his. Caleb boldly asked for it.

God kept his promise to Caleb, brought him through 40 years of desert wandering and then lead him and gave him the hill country. God continues to act in our lives in similar ways. What has been promised, will come to be. You can boldly ask for it.

God, your promises are good. I may currently be in the desert wandering, but I trust your promises and will continue to boldly ask you to fulfill them in my life. Thank you for your promises.

Are you currently wandering in the desert waiting for the promises of God? Have you asked God boldly to continue to give his promises to you?

God Is Speaking

The boy Samuel served the Lord in Eli's presence. In those days the word of the Lord was rare and prophetic visions were not widespread.

1 SAMUEL 3:1 CSB

Samuel's mother, Hannah, had committed him to the service of God because God had moved and given her the miracle she had asked for. It did not matter to Hannah that the word of the Lord was rare or that prophetic visions were not widespread. What mattered to her is that God heard her prayer.

God heard her prayer and even though he wasn't revealing himself in the ways he normally did, he had spoken to her through his actions. Go is still reacting to our prayers, even if he is not speaking in the ways we are used to him speaking. He hears our prayers!

God, it seems like I have not heard from you in a while. Help me to trust that you are responding even if I don't hear your voice or see how you are working.

In those days, when the boy Samuel was serving the Lord under the direction of Eli, there were very few messages from the Lord, and visions from him were quite rare.

1 SAMUEL 3:1 GNT

How young is too young to serve the Lord? Samuel was just a boy when his mother left him at the temple to work with Eli. This was the promise that Hannah had made and even though she had longed for this child, she kept her promise to God.

Samuel started serving the Lord under the direction of Eli. It's an important thing to see young children involved in the service of the Lord. There is no greater thing than seeing a young child serving next to a seasoned veteran in ministry.

Heavenly Father, thank you for involving your children in your plan and you church. Help me to see where I can train up children to serve the you in the church.

Where are you serving that you can involve younger people? Are you training young people to serve the Lord?

Like the Others

Then all the elders of Israel gathered together and came to Samuel at Ramah, and said to him, "Look, you are old, and your sons do not walk in your ways. Now make us a king to judge us like all the nations."

1 SAMUEL 8:4-5 NKJV

The elders asked Samuel to make them like everyone else. They didn't want to be different. Yet this difference was made this unique and different. They wanted a king, God was their ruler. They wanted a man to lead them, God already was. It is hard to be different, but being different is what sets us apart as we follow God. It makes us different.

Today we might not be asking for a king but maybe we have asked to blend in a bit more and not stand out as a Christ follower. We are different and that's a good thing.

God, help me to see how being different is part of your plan. Help my light to shine through my difference.

*One day the nation's leaders came to Samuel at Ramah and said,
"You are an old man. You set a good example for your sons, but
they haven't followed it. Now we want a king to be our leader,
just like all the other nations. Choose one for us!"*

1 SAMUEL 8:4-5 CEV

They didn't ask God's plan or seek the wisdom of Samuel.
They simply demanded that Samuel choose them a king to
lead them like all the other nations. Looking around at other
nations caused them to desire what they didn't have. What
they did have was the creator of the universe leading them.
God who had spoken the universe into creation was leading
their nation. But they wanted a king.

The Creator of the universe is still leading us today and often
we still want a king. It seems better to be like everyone else.
But we have the opportunity to be different and have God as
our leader. Be different with God.

*Heavenly Father, I want to be different. I want you to be my leader
and king. Help me to follow you.*

How have I fallen into wanting another king? How can I be
different with God at my side?

Like David Danced

David danced before the Lord with all his might,
and David was girded with a linen ephod.

2 SAMUEL 6:14 JUB

The roar of the crowd is almost unbearable when a grand slam is hit in the bottom of the ninth to win the come from behind Cinderella story game. Jumping up and down, cheering, high fives and hugs are all part of the experience. What would a worship service look like if we were as emotionally involved as we are at a sports game?

God created us as emotional beings, meant to feel and express feelings. David danced with all his might before the Lord. We can worship with all our might, whether at church or at home, God wants all of ourselves to be involved.

Gracious Father, my heart is over flowing with worship, let me express it to you in the ways that honor you.

David danced before Jehovah with all his might;
and David was girded with a linen ephod.

2 Samuel 6:14 ASV

It was a bit beyond the norm and it was probably the talk of the town for several weeks. The king danced with abandon. He danced like no one was watching. But in fact, David knew that Jehovah was watching and that was the only person who mattered. He was dancing for joy, praising God that the ark had returned. Surrounded by people, the only thing that mattered to David was dancing for the king.

Let out a shout for joy and dance a happy dance for what God has done. Do not worry about who is watching.

God, thank you for allowing me to dance with joy in front of you. Help me to focus only on you as I worship.

How can I express my gratefulness to God? What am I dancing for today?

Whispering His Words

After the earthquake there was a fire, but the Lord was not in the fire. And after the fire there was the sound of a gentle whisper. When Elijah heard it, he wrapped his face in his cloak and went out and stood at the entrance of the cave.
And a voice said, "What are you doing here, Elijah?"

1 KINGS 19:12-13 NLT

Elijah was desperate to hear from God. He was feeling alone in his service to God. He needed to hear from God. As a loving Father, God is near when he is needed. He promises to pass by and speak to Elijah. A fire, a great wind and an earthquake all take place in front of Elijah, and he doesn't move.

God had spoken to the people of Israel through those means in the past. But it wasn't until the whisper that Elijah moved and knew God was ready to speak. God is often a God who whispers to us, when we are listening for him to yell.

Gracious Father, help me to hear your whisper.

After the earthquake a fire, but the Lord was not in the fire. And after the fire the sound of a low whisper. And when Elijah heard it, he wrapped his face in his cloak and went out and stood at the entrance of the cave. And behold, there came a voice to him and said, "What are you doing here, Elijah?"

1 KINGS 19:12-13 ESV

You need to lean in pretty close to hear a still small voice. Like when must get down really close to the young child to hear them ask for a cookie or say they love you. Here the booming voice that created the universe, was whispering to Elijah.

That voice is still whispering it's love for you. Still whispering because he wants us close to him.

God, thank you for whispering and brining me in close to your side. Thank you that that you are a loving God who whispers your words to me.

Am I hearing God's whispering voice? What areas of my life are causing noise to block our his still small voice?

God Restores

Then I will teach your ways to rebels,
and they will return to you.
Forgive me for shedding blood, O God who saves;
then I will joyfully sing of your forgiveness.

PSALM 51:11-12 NLT

You can hear the desperation in his voice. David is crying out to be restored. He has been confronted with his many sins. Grievous sins that racked David with guilt. With perhaps little hope left, David cries for restoration. Cries out to be again experience joy from when he first encountered God.

We know, despite his sin, that God heard David and restored his soul. You too can be restored from any sin if you cry out to God, he will restore your soul to rejoicing!

Heavenly Father, forgive me and restore my soul, that I may rejoice in your deliverance of me and give me desire to obey you.

Then I will teach your ways to those who do wrong,
and sinners will turn back to you.
God, save me from the guilt of murder,
God of my salvation,
and I will sing about your goodness.

PSALM 51:13-14 TLV

Do you remember the day of your salvation? Perhaps it was a day long ago as a young child or perhaps it was only a few weeks ago. Do you remember the joy that salvation brought? To know that death had been brought to life. What an overwhelming joy to feel!

Often living life day to day can rob us of that joy. Sin may be blocking us from that joy. But we can ask God to restore that joy in our lives. He wants us to have joy and will graciously give it when we ask.

God, restore to me the joy of your salvation. May your joy remain in me even during the hardest of times. Restore your joy to me.

What keeps me from being joyful? Have I asked God to grant me joy in every circumstance?

Wondrous Law

Open my eyes, so that I may behold
wondrous things out of your law.

PSALM 119:18 NRSV

In Minnesota, it is illegal to cross the state line with a duck on your head. This may be one of the dumbest laws ever written. First because for it to be written someone must have walked across state lines with a duck on their head, and second that it was enough of a problem that a law had to be created.

The Psalmist writes a prayer that desires to see the wondrous things of God's law. How can a law be wondrous? Because the law of God is right and just and is there for our good and protection. God has placed his law for our good.

God, may I see your law as good and as a protection for me and
those around me. Help me to rejoice in your law.

Open my eyes that I may see
wonderful things in your law.

PSALM 119:18 NIV

Sometimes it takes a prayer to see how God's law can be
wonderful. We see those who do not follow God seeming to
enjoy life and prosper in many ways, while we follow God's
laws and seem to struggle. Yet God has given his law and it is
wonderful.

There are things that we can only understand and fully
appreciate as wonderful when God gives us open eyes to see.
When we see his ways, they are wonderful.

God, let me see your laws as wonderful. May my eyes be opened to
your ways. May I see them as you see them, wonderful.

How have I seen God's law as wonderful? What areas of his
law are hard for me to understand and see as wonderful?

Wrong Focus

"Should I not have concern for the great city of Nineveh, in which there are more than a hundred and twenty thousand people who cannot tell their right hand from their left—and also many animals?"

JONAH 4:11 NIV

Jonah was upset because his shade tree had been destroyed and he was hot. God had to remind Jonah that he had just spared 120,000 people because they repented and cried out to him. Jonah was so focused on himself throughout this whole encounter that he was having a hard time seeing beyond his own comfort. Even as the town and heaven rejoiced, Jonah sulked.

When we are focused on ourselves it is hard to see the joy all around us. Look out and look up to see what God is doing around us for his glory!

God, help me to take my eyes off of me and place them on the work you are doing all around me. Help me to understand your compassion and mercy not just for me but for others.

"Nineveh has more than 120,000 people living in spiritual darkness, not to mention all the animals. Shouldn't I feel sorry for such a great city?"

JONAH 4:11 NLT

We love to see justice doled out—to others. We want the people who wronged us to have the book thrown at them but we desire clemency when it comes to ourselves. When others who have wronged us are shown grace we don't often know how to respond.

The great news is that God doesn't treat us or anyone else as our sins deserve because his grace is abundant for those who call on his name. Rejoice that your sins are forgiven. And rejoice that the sins of those who have wronged you can be forgiven also. God's grace is available to all.

Gracious God, thank you for your grace in my life. Thank you for forgiving me. Help me to rejoice that others have been forgiven also.

How have I benefited from God's grace today? How have I seen God's grace in others lives?

When God Says No

Going along the borders of Mysia they headed north for the province of Bithynia, but again the Spirit of Jesus said no.

ACTS 16:7 TLB

No is a word that parents use often for the good of the child. Nine times out of ten, if a child asks to do something dangerous a parent is going to say no. The child doesn't understand why there is a no. They just know the funny looking hole in the wall is not supposed to have a fork in it, or that little bead does not belong in their nose.

Sometimes that is what God's no to us is like also. We may not understand it but we can rest knowing it really is for our good and part of God's great plan for our lives and his story in all of humanity.

God, may your no be something I accept for my own good. May your no be welcome in my life for my good and your glory.

When they reached the border of Mysia, they tried to go on into
Bithynia, but the Spirit of Jesus did not let them go there.

ACTS 16:7 ERV

They didn't know why the spirit of Jesus would not let them go
to Mysia. But they were blocked from going. They could have
pressed on and disobeyed because they felt called to go there
or they could allow their plans to be changed and follow the
path the Jesus laid out for them. They chose to follow.

We must choose to follow even when we don't know the
reason why God said no. But even his no is for his glory and
for our good as we follow him.

Jesus, help me to understand you no in my life. But even more than
understanding help me to follow you and accept your no.

Have I kicked back against your no and followed my way
instead? Have I followed God in spite of a no?

Trust in God Alone

I didn't speak my message with persuasive intellectual arguments.
I spoke my message with a show of spiritual power so that your
faith would not be based on human wisdom but on God's power.

1 CORINTHIANS 2:4-5 NOG

Most of us tend to pull back from someone who is giving us
a hard sale. Our defenses come up and we try to get out as
soon as we can. We don't want to end up buying something we
didn't need. This is the opposite of how Paul presented the
gospel to the people in Corinth.

God's message is strong enough without a hard sell. The Holy
Spirit will speak to and guide those who need to hear the
message as we speak. We can trust in God's power to help us
communicate his message to those around us.

God, help me to speak your message to those around me. May
I rely only on your power and not on fancy words or persuasive
arguments.

My speech and my message were not in plausible words of wisdom, but in demonstration of the Spirit and of power, so that your faith might not rest in the wisdom of men but in the power of God.

1 CORINTHIANS 2:4-5 ESV

Maybe you remember the message or the speaker who gave the message, on the day you became a Christ follower. Maybe you have used almost the same message as you shared the gospel with someone and they didn't follow Jesus that day. What was the difference? Was it the way you said something or how passionate you were or weren't? Nope, man's response is up to the Spirit, otherwise it would be our words that people placed their hope in and not in the power of God.

Rejoice today that you can share the message and trust God for the results!

Jesus, help me to trust you for the results in sharing your story. Let the Holy Spirit speak through me and speak to those who are listening.

Am I trusting in God's power or my words? Have I asked the Holy Spirit to guide me?

One Body

*You are the body of the Anointed One, and each of you is a unique
and vital part of it.*

1 CORINTHIANS 12:27 TPT

It's nice to be needed, to know that because of your unique
efforts and skills a task was accomplished. It is actually
beyond nice, it is part of who we are. We were created to be in
community to be part of other people's lives. To have people
rely on us and us rely on them. Eve was created because it was
not good for Adam to be alone.

We are a vital part of the body of Christ. We can find
community in the people of Christ and each of us needs the
other to complete the body.

*God, thank you for creating me for others and others for me. Help me
to live in community and be there for people as I serve your church.*

Together you are the body of Christ, and each one of you is a part of that body.

1 CORINTHIANS 12:27 NCV

Together is a very key word here. We can not be the body of Christ alone. Alone we might be the nose or the ear or some other part of the body. But the part is not the whole. Alone the part functions and can survive but only together does it find and live its true purpose. Together the nose can offer a sense of smell that aides the tongue in sense of taste that causes the body enjoyment when ice cream is eaten.

Together the body of Christ functions to bring the kingdom of God to earth and each of us has a part to play. We are better together because God has given each of us a unique way to serve.

Jesus, thank you for including me in your body. Thank you for creating me to fill a unique role in the church. Help me to understand that role.

How am I a part of the body? Am I fulfilling my part fully?

Wholly Devoted

"So, my dear brothers and sisters, be strong and immovable. Always work enthusiastically for the Lord, for you know that nothing you do for the Lord is ever useless."

1 CORINTHIANS 15:58 NLT

Have you ever volunteered for an event at church only to have no one show up? You spent hours upon hours on preparation, hours in prayer ahead of time. All for nothing. Disappoint comes easy in this situation. It seems like all your time was spent in vain. Yet we can claim this verse!

Nothing you do for the Lord is ever useless. You may never know what kingdom impact your actions may have had but they were not in vain. Keep working enthusiastically for the Lord! You can rest assured that your efforts are not in vain. Keep strong and immovable!

God, thank you for redeeming my work. Thank you for being able to replace the disappointment with joy, knowing that there is a kingdom work that you are doing.

Stand strong. Do not let anything move you. Always give yourselves fully to the work of the Lord, because you know that your work in the Lord is never wasted.

1 Corinthians 15:58 NCV

Paul reminds the Corinthians that Christ gives victory over death through his sacrifice on the cross. And then reminds us to be strong and not let anyone change their mind. It is easy to keep strong and press forward, when reminded that Christ has given us eternal life. Discouragement comes in when we take our focus off the promise of eternal life.

As a Christ follower, everything is brighter in the light of eternity. Be strong and do not let anyone change your mind. Christ has called you, and your call will not be destroyed.

Jesus your death conquered death for me and can encourage me to be strong and hold firm to my belief. May the light of Christ keep me firm in my faith and my call secure.

Am I fully holding firm to teachings of Jesus? Am I trusting Christ that my work is not in vain and working well because of that?

What's Inside Matters

We have this treasure in jars of clay to show that this all-surpassing power is from God and not from us. We are hard pressed on every side, but not crushed; perplexed, but not in despair; persecuted, but not abandoned; struck down, but not destroyed.

2 CORINTHIANS 4:7-9 NIV

It is a juxtaposition between a treasure and fragile jars of clay. Who would put treasure in jars of clay that easily break and crack? Paul calls us jars of clay, fragile vessels to hold the Word of Christ.

Unless we are talking about works or art usually the jar is not as important as the contents inside. The jar has a role to play but what the jar holds is what people want. This is a great picture of Christ in us. We bring Christ will all of us everywhere we go and Christ changes people's eternity!

Jesus, thank you for filling my life with your love. I want to share you with others and bring you with me as I go through the day.

We now have this light shining in our hearts, but we ourselves are like fragile clay jars containing this great treasure. This makes it clear that our great power is from God, not from ourselves. We are pressed on every side by troubles, but we are not crushed. We are perplexed, but not driven to despair. We are hunted down, but never abandoned by God. We get knocked down, but we are not destroyed.

2 CORINTHIANS 4:7-9 NLT

Troubled, frustrated, persecuted, and captured. If we only read those words we would be beyond discouraged. Yet the sustaining power of Christ is changing these words into testimony of Christ at work in us! Troubled but not crushed, frustrated but not giving up, persecuted but not abandoned, captured but not killed. It is always good to hear the rest of the story.

The treasure inside of us changes the bad from good. It is enough to keep up through all things. We can overcome hard times when Christ is inside us.

Heavenly Father, thank you that even through tough times and persecution on all sides you are here with me. Thank you for trusting me with the treasure of Christ.

How have I been trusting Christ in the difficult times?
How have I seen the faithfulness of Christ in difficulties?

For the Cause of Christ

It is for freedom that Christ has set us free. Stand firm, then, and do not let yourselves be burdened again by a yoke of slavery.

GALATIANS 5:1 NIV

It only takes one sip is what the recovering alcoholic says. One sip and the freedom of sobriety is exchanged again for the yoke of slavery. That is the extreme case of slavery. There are times when our slavery is called something else.

Consumerism, perfectionism, bigger, better, faster more expensive, these are all things that can lead to slavery. But Christ has set us free to be free. He has set us free so that his cause can go forth. So that our freedom can help other people to be free through the love of Christ. Freedom is a much better place to live than slavery. You are free to live the cause of Christ!

Jesus, thank you for setting me free from the things that have been yoke of slavery in my life in the past. Please help me to continue to live in freedom and a freedom bringer to those around me.

Christ has liberated us to be free. Stand firm then and don't submit again to a yoke of slavery.

GALATIANS 5:1 HCSB

In the history of slavery, most slaves did not submit to the yoke of slavery. Here the followers of Christ were set free and yet they were tempted to go back into slavery to the law that was comfortable to them. It is like the Israelites, who, when hungry in the desert, looked back longingly to their slavery in Egypt because food was abundant.

We often forget the slavery when there we are uncomfortable in our freedom. We look back to life before freedom and gloss over the slavery to sin or addiction, and look back through rose colored glasses. This wrong view of the past can tempt us to return to slavery. Stand firm then and don't submit. Don't look back thinking everything was rosy, it was slavery and you have been set free for the cause of Christ.

Heavenly Father, help me to stand firm. I want to continue to be free and trust you to give me strength to continue in this freedom.

What am I tempted to turn back to? How can God help me to stand firm?

Cut Off

You were running the race so well. Who has held you back from following the truth?

GALATIANS 5:7 NLT

You hear Paul's heart breaking in this verse. He was remembering the faith of the Galatians. The things they had done, the ministry of their love for each other and for others around them. But something happened, something changed and Paul was devastated. Paul could not continue his sorrow and asks what happened? Who stopped you?

Perhaps you have hit a bump in your relationship with Jesus and someone has stopped your from doing right. The good news today is you can start again where you are. God is not far off. He is as close today as he was yesterday. When you reach out to God he is near and reaches back to you. No pause in the journey has to stop your journey with Christ. You can start again right where you are!

God, help me start again. I know my relationship with you has been paused, but I want to start again. Help me to know you more. Help me to believe your words and walk this journey with you.

You were running a good race. Who stopped you from following the true way?

GALATIANS 5:7 NCV

During a motorcycle road test, the test taker must perform a procedure where they get up to speed and, without braking, swerve around an obstacle and continue in the same direction. If the driver applies the brake there is risk of laying the bike down. If they do not continue at the current speed they risk deduction of points. The obstacle must be avoided and the course continued. The maneuver is referred to as "swerve and continue."

This should be the way a Christian approaches obstacle or people attempting to dissuade them from following Christ and obeying the truth. We do not have to let the obstacle stop us from following Christ and doing good. God had provided a plan to allow for us to follow him. Swerve and continue; don't stop and get cut off from following Christ.

Heavenly Father, I want to swerve and continue in the right direction. Help me to avoid the obstacles and continue to follow you with all my heart in your direction and plan.

What obstacle is approaching that I need to swerve around and continue?

Flip the Switch

The lovers of God walk on the highway of light,
and their way shines brighter and brighter
until they bring forth the perfect day.
But the wicked walk in thick darkness,
like those who travel in a fog
and yet don't have a clue why they keep stumbling!

PROVERBS 4:18-19 TPT

Have you ever walked through your home at night, thinking that you could make it without turning a light on, only to stumble on something unexpectedly set in your path? When you cannot see where you are going, you are likely to get tripped up. On the other hand, your way is obvious when you simply turn on a light.

Are you choosing the light? Is your path brightly lit? Or are you standing in total darkness? If so, then flip the switch. Pray that you will make wise choices. Seek his wisdom for your life. He wants to shine brightly for you. Let him in, and he will gladly be your eternal light, illuminating your days.

God, give me wisdom so that I walk in your light today. Keep my feet from stumbling.

The path of the just is like the shining sun,
That shines ever brighter unto the perfect day.
The way of the wicked is like darkness;
They do not know what makes them stumble.

PROVERBS 4:18-19 NKJV

The Bible tells us that walking in righteousness is just like
walking in the bright light of day. But choosing rebellion is
like stumbling around in a deep darkness. You never know
what hit you until it's already too late.

When you walk in the light, you expose the darkness, even in
the lives of others around you.

Lord, let your light in me be a positive influence on the life of others
around me. I often see darkness in the world around me and I get
discouraged. Holy Spirit, encourage my soul tonight as I prepare to
bring your light to the world in the morning.

How can you bring light in a world of darkness?

Doing Good to All

When we have the opportunity to help anyone, we should do it.
But we should give special attention to those who are in the family
of believers.

GALATIANS 6:10 NCV

Loving those we are closest to can be both the easiest and
hardest thing to do at the same time. Easy in that they are
those we are close to and have invested deeply in. Hard in
that they do not always act as we expect them to act and yet
we need to love them and do good for them anyway. It is often
easier to do good for the stranger because they are far off.
Paul reminds the Galatians to do good to everyone. Those far
off and those in the household of faith.

Doing good does not have to be a grand act of kindness, it
may just be a smile or hug. It may be a listening ear. It may be
having the same conversation with the same person for the
tenth time because that person needs a listening ear and a
loving heart. Do good to all, particularly to the household of
the faith.

Gracious Father, help me to see those in need. Help me to do good
to all. As long as I can, in any way I can.

As we have opportunity, let us do good to all people, especially to those who are of the household of faith.

GALATIANS 6:10 MEV

If you have ever watched parents teach their children how to interact with others you may have seen this verse played out in real life. "Timmy, you know it would be good to share your ten trucks with Johnny who doesn't have anything to play with." From the birth to death we need these reminders.

Do good to all people. Not to some, not to those we choose to do good to, but to all people. It is what parents teach their children, what Paul reminds the Galatians and what we must remember as we encounter people. Do good to all. Sometimes people think that sounds strange or odd, but that is the Christian call. Do good to all.

Loving God, help me to be a person who does good to all. Help me to share the resources that God has given me with those around me. God, thank you for others who have done good to me.

Who are those who are around me that I have opportunity to show the love of Christ? Where can I do good today?

Ask or Imagine

Glory be to God, who by his mighty power at work within us is able to do far more than we would ever dare to ask or even dream of— infinitely beyond our highest prayers, desires, thoughts, or hopes.

EPHESIANS 3:20 TLB

It took God no more or less effort to speak the universe into creation than it did for him respond to your prayer request. There is nothing beyond his power. Even in our wildest dreams we can't begin to see the limit of his power.

Yet this all-powerful God has chosen to work gently in us. His voice boomed at the creation of the universe. Yet to us he chooses to act gently within us. Some might say this limits his power, but instead we can see it as a controlled use of his power in us, deep within us so we know we are changed for eternity.

All powerful Father, thank you for working gently and deeply inside me to reveal your infinitely great power in my life. Thank you for your gentleness.

All glory to God, who is able, through his mighty power at work within us, to accomplish infinitely more than we might ask or think.

EPHESIANS 3:20 NLT

The concept that God is able to work and accomplish in us infinitely more than we can understand, is a tough concept to fully understand. It does not simply mean just a little bit beyond what we can understand.

Imagine trying to buy a car that is infinitely beyond what you could afford. You get all the money and yet the price of the car is still infinitely more than all the money that you can have or imagine. The distance between your ability to pay and the price never gets smaller.

God's power at work in and through us is like that. We can ask or think we are asking something big of God, that might test his power at work. Yet our imagination, our dreams are not closer to the limit of his strength than before we started.

All powerful God, let me rest in the knowledge that your strength is never ending. Your power is never diminished by my thoughts or requests. You are a mighty God.

In what way areas have I held back thinking God isn't powerful enough to react in that area? What dream have I thought was beyond God's power?

We All Have a Part

He gave some to be apostles; and some, prophets; and some,
evangelists; and some, pastors and teachers; for the perfecting of
the saints, unto the work of ministering, unto the building up of
the body of Christ.

EPHESIANS 4:11-12 ASV

God provides what is needed for his church to be built up.
Apostles, prophets, evangelists, pastors and teachers are
the five areas needed to see the body of Christ built up. By
this if some are called to be pastors, then some are called to
do things other than pastor. So, while it might seem that the
pastor can accomplish all these roles, we are each given a role
in building up the body of Christ.

If you are a teacher, teach in the body of Christ. If you are
prophet, prophecy for the building up of the body of Christ.
We may often think that our gift is not needed in the body, but
it was given for the building up of the body of Christ.

Great giver of Gifts, thank you for giving me my gift for your body.
Help me to understand it more fully and use it more completely.

*He Himself gave some as apostles, and others as prophets, and
others as evangelists, and others as shepherds and teachers, for the
equipping of the saints for the work of ministry, for the building-
up of the body of Christ.*

Ephesians 4:11–12 dlnt

Often these five labels might cause us a bit of fear. But these
are things we are by the gift of God, whether we like them or
not. Often an evangelist is very good at evangelizing without
evening thinking about it. There are people around us that
can describe the best restaurant that they have ever visited
or can tell us about the best customer service they received at
the local store. They encourage you to go to that restaurant or
that store; this is the evangelist heart.

The gifts are God's gifts to be used for his kingdom. We all
have a part to play in the building up of the body of Christ.

*God, help me to use my gift for the building up of your body. I am
grateful for the opportunity I have to use this gift and who I am for
your glory.*

What area is my gift? How am I using it for the building up of
the kingdom?

Imitators of God

Be imitators of God, as beloved children; and walk in love, just as Christ also loved you and gave Himself up for us, an offering and a sacrifice to God as a fragrant aroma.

EPHESIANS 5:1-2 NASB

They say that imitation is the sincerest form of flattery. How that plays out in the copycat game between kids in the backseat of a long drive, doesn't seem to fit that definition. Imitation is more than just copying outward appearance or words. To be an imitator of God requires a deep heart change. The imitation is not simply a service imitation but comes from within. The service imitation is like veneer that may look okay for a while but easily cracks and fades and reveals what is deep within. Real imitation comes from within and changes the outside from the inside. We are called to be deep imitators of God, changed at our core and it's God who does the changing!

Heavenly Father, help me to imitate you in real and authentic ways. Change me from the inside out as I follow you.

Do as God does. After all, you are his dear children. Let love be your guide. Christ loved us and offered his life for us as a sacrifice that pleases God.

EPHESIANS 5:1-2 CEV

Like father like son. That phrase can be used to explain a good action or a bad. When a son follows his father in good deeds it is a good thing. When a son falls victim to the same sin of his father it is a negative thing.

As children of God, we want to reflect his goodness and have it said of us, like father like child. No matter who our earthly father is we can rest assured that, as Christ followers, we are children of the king and can do as God does because we are his children. God is love. If we want to do as God does, we need to love and let love, real love, be our guide.

Father God, thank you for calling me your child. Thank you for giving me the example of Christ of what love and a pleasing sacrifice is. Help me to imitate you in all I do.

How am I imitating God? In what areas of my life do I need to better respond in love?

Grumbling and Mumbling

Do everything without grumbling and arguing so that you may be blameless and pure, innocent children of God surrounded by people who are crooked and corrupt. Among these people you shine like stars in the world.

PHILIPPIANS 2:14–15 CEB

It is so easy to get into the bad habit of grumbling about things. We quickly see grumbling in others, but it is often harder to see it in ourselves. We are not grumbling we are just suggesting new ideas. We are not grumbling, we just think there is a better way. We don't mean to grumble but _____ (fill in the blank with your own reasoning).

Paul was writing this letter from prison. If anyone had a reason to grumble it was him. Yet instead he not only did not grumble but encouraged others to not grumble or argue also. He saw the bigger picture. He saw that for the glory of God, we must not grumble. So we can be blameless and pure!

Christ Jesus, help me to have the right attitude in everything. Help me not to grumble or argue. Help me to see each situation as a way to be content and know that you are at work.

*Do everything without complaining or arguing. Then you will
be innocent and without any wrong. You will be God's children
without fault. But you are living with crooked and mean people all
around you, among whom you shine like stars in the dark world.*

PHILIPPIANS 2:14-15 NCV

The simple act of not complaining or arguing can be a great
testimony to the people around you. This is not an invitation
to be a doormat for people but instead allows us to be
content in all circumstances. The right understanding of our
circumstances keeps us from complaining and grumbling or
arguing that we deserve to be treated differently.

True contentment in our lives is something not often seen
in the world. Paul says that when we are content and we will
shine like stars among them. Our contentment with God
allows the world to see our life and joy comes from places
other than things or people.

*Thank you for where you have placed me in life. Whether in rich or
poor help me to be content in you.*

In what areas have I been grumbling? How am I reflecting
contentment in life?

Just Passing Through

Our homeland is in heaven, and we are waiting for our Savior, the Lord Jesus Christ, to come from heaven.

PHILIPPIANS 3:20 NCV

After traveling internationally, there are few things better than getting back on your native land and walking up to the passport control with our passport and having someone say, "Welcome home." Those two simple words mean so much when it comes to a variety of things, but most of all it means you have arrived where you belong.

As Christ followers, our citizenship is in heaven and there will be no greater joy than when we arrive in heaven and we are welcomed home. As eternity has been placed in our hearts, everything we long for will be completed. All that has been wrong will be made right. All that we have waited to be fulfilled with be completed. Welcome home.

God, thank you for my citizenship in heaven. Thank you for the hope beyond the current situation.

[We are different, because] our citizenship is in heaven. And from there we eagerly await [the coming of] the Savior, the Lord Jesus Christ.

PHILIPPIANS 3:20 AMP

There have been times that Christians have been called so heavenly minded that they are no good on the earth. Some Christians have taken this verse to mean that there is no reason to be concerned about things on this earth.

However, even while we wait in eager anticipation for Christ's return, we have a role to play here on earth, even if we are just passing through. We have the role of bringing others into the citizenship of heaven. We have the role of alleviating injustice and allowing the world to have a glimpse of the kingdom of God as we live on the earth. Even as we are just passing through we are called to be ambassadors of Christ in this foreign land!

Heavenly Father, as I eagerly await your return help me to also be a good ambassador of your kingdom here on earth.

Do I long for the kingdom to come through me to the earth? Am I being a good representative of Christ?

Joy in Trials

Consider it pure joy, my brothers and sisters, whenever you face trials of many kinds, because you know that the testing of your faith produces perseverance.

JAMES 1:2-3 NIV

In training to run long distance, normally one does not just lace up their running shoes and having never run before, run a marathon. There are a variety of different ways to make it happen but basically to go from the couch to marathon is a long series of shorter runs that allows the runner to build up endurance so when the day of the marathon comes they will have the perseverance to finish the 26.2 miles.

The Christian life is often like that also. We are in it for the long haul and need faith to hold on through the hard times. We face trials of many kinds so our perseverance is built up so we can have a faith that lasts!

Christ Jesus, thank you for the trials that build in me an endurance and perseverance to continue in faith and my relationship with you. Help me to find joy in the trials.

When you have many kinds of troubles, you should be full of joy, because you know that these troubles test your faith, and this will give you patience.

JAMES 1:2-3 NCV

This command really does seem contradictory. How can it be a joy to face temptations of all kinds? What is so good about perseverance that we should rejoice in temptations and trials? Is it really worth it? Yes, it is. Because the kingdom is a bigger reality than we can see and understand. Joy in temptations doesn't mean we enjoy the temptations; rather, it means we understand that the trials and temptations are serving a greater purpose, a purpose that has eternity in mind.

God wants us to preserve to the end so that we may experience eternity of joy and be with him forever. This is worth any trial.

Heavenly Father, help me to understand temptations and trials in light of eternity. May I see the bigger picture as you call me to be joyful. Help me God to be have joy in the trials.

Have I viewed my trial in light of eternity? What keeps me following God during temptations?

Good Gifts

Every good action and every perfect gift is from God. These good gifts come down from the Creator of the sun, moon, and stars, who does not change like their shifting shadows.

JAMES 1:17 NCV

Have you ever seen the kid at the birthday party wanting a particular gift and passing through all the other gifts like they are not worthy of their time? The child misses the amazing gifts that their friends purchased for them. With anticipation of the gift they want they are unappreciative of the gifts they received.

The gifts of God in our lives are often like that. God knows us better than we know ourselves. He created us unique with unique needs and desires, so when receive from him the things he offers they are the perfect gift. Often times we miss his gifts in our lives because we are focused on what we think we want, instead of what God has already given us. He has given us good and perfect gifts.

God help me to see your gifts as good and perfect. Help me to focus on what you have given me and not on what I think I am missing.

Whatever is good and perfect is a gift coming down to us from God our Father, who created all the lights in the heavens. He never changes or casts a shifting shadow.

JAMES 1:17 NLT

The gifts of God in our lives are often brought by the others around us. Not just birthday or Christmas presents, but the gift of friendship, the gift of love, the gift kindness, the gift of a long conversation, the gift of coffee, the gift of time in nature, the gift of time with friends, the gift of time alone, the gift of a new job, the gift of family, the gift of life, the gift of a home, the gift of an unexpected financial blessing, the gift of walking hand in hand with someone you love, the gift of holding a newborn baby, the gift of breath, or the gift of a joyful heart.

And the list goes on and on and on. These are the perfect gifts that our Father has given to us and will continue to give to us.

Father God, thank you for all your gifts.

What gifts did God give me today? How can I bring God's gifts to others?

Slow to Anger

Let every man be swift to hear, slow to speak, and slow to anger.

JAMES 1:19 MEV

Most of us have that one friend who is known for his temper. The cartoon image of the person with steam coming out of their ears and face redder than a tomato. The person who, it seems, goes from zero to ten on the anger scale in a blink of an eye. James encourages us to be quick to listen and slow to speak and become angry.

As we listen swiftly we understand the other person or situation better. The better we understand the less anger we have. Take time to listen. It will keep anger at bay and our testimony to our friends will not be tarnished by anger.

Help me to listen quickly, speak slowly and keep anger far from me. Forgive me for the times my anger has been too quick.

Know this, my dear brothers and sisters: everyone should be quick to listen, slow to speak, and slow to grow angry.

JAMES 1:17 CEB

Very few good decisions have been made when someone is angry. In the history of mankind there have been no peace treaties signed when one side was angry at the other. Anger can usually be avoided as we listen more and speak less. The proverb says we have been given two ears and one mouth, to listen twice as much as we speak.

Often, we listen to respond instead of listen to understand. God wants us to live at peace with others as much as it is up to us. To do that we need to listen more and try to understand. This allows us to love the other person deeper than we did before and to pray more specifically for them.

Prince of Peace, help me through listening to be a bringer of peace. Help me to understand those who speak and respond in love.

How am I listening? Where have I been a peace maker today?

Shut Their Mouths

It is God's will that your honorable lives should silence those ignorant people who make foolish accusations against you.

1 PETER 2:15 NLT

There is a reason courtroom dramas are a popular tv genre. We like to see justice be served. We like things to be set right when there has been a wrong. We like to see the good people get good things and the bad people get punished. We love the big build up to when they innocent person is set free.

Peter goes beyond the courtroom drama to say an honorable life silences foolish accusations It shuts the mouths of those who would accuse us. We are called to live lives above reproach so when those accusations come we can stand in the light of our right choices both before God and man. It is a great comfort to know that in the long run right living will silence all accusations.

Father God, help me to live an honorable life. Thank you that you are there to bring justice and silence those who accuse me.

It is God's will that by doing good you should silence the ignorant talk of foolish people.

1 PETER 2:15 NIV

There are many reasons to do good and this one stands out as pretty big reason. Gossip and slander can easily spread. God's will is that we can silence gossip and foolish talk by doing good and living upright lives.

We are given opportunities every day to lower our standards. To tell a little white lie. No one will get hurt. Just a little one. But yet that is not the standard that will help shut the mouths of our accusers. Stand firm and do good. God is on your side helping to fight your battle.

God, you are calling me to the right choices to do the right thing. The promise you make me is that it will silence foolish accusations against me. Help me to do right to be a testimony to you.

Am I doing good? How has God revealed himself to others through my actions?

What God Has Done

I was so happy when some Christians arrived and told me how faithful you are to the truth—just as you always live in the truth.

3 JOHN 3 GNT

There is something about hearing another person's story of redemption. It fills the fellow believer with joy as they hear the story of God. Each testimony of God at work is a unique story of how God works in our lives.

Stories of redemption, faithfulness, death to life are refreshing to the believer's ears. This is one of the reasons as Christians we are called to meet together, so we can share stories of what God is up to in our lives. God is at work in our lives, share the story with others to encourage them and then take time to hear their stories and be encouraged.

Abba Father, thank you for your work in my life. Help me to share your story with others and may I hear stories from others to be encouraged.

Some of the brothers traveling by have made me very happy by telling me that your life stays clean and true and that you are living by the standards of the Gospel.

3 JOHN 3 TLB

Telling the testimony of what God has done is our lives and the lives of those we know is a powerful tool of encouragement. There is power in sharing what God is doing. When we forget to share testimony of God at work we miss opportunity to encourage those around us.

Gather with others and share the story of Christ at work in your life over a meal, around a campfire or while you walk through the woods. God has a plan of meeting our emotional needs through the stories of others. Don't hold your testimony of God's faithfulness in your life to yourself but instead use it to encourage those around you.

God, you are doing a work in and through me. I want to tell your story to others around me. I want my friends to know your good deeds. Help me be brave to share of your goodness.

What can I say about what God is doing in my life? Who can I share it with?

Happiness Is Overrated

Wounds from a friend can be trusted,
but an enemy multiplies kisses.

PROVERBS 27:6 NIV

What if we rethought something culture regularly says? It's the whole "Do whatever makes you happy." line people often tell others. Maybe it comes from a good place, such as us knowing people who are worn out and haven't smiled for years. But how many problems in the world all come down to at least one person insisting that everyone else should let them do whatever makes them happy?

Goodness far exceeds happiness as a value. When the opposite attempts to be true—if we live in a society that makes the pursuit of happiness its national creed—we get an "opposite" society. And if we let the people we care about head off in this "opposite" direction because we're afraid of saying something they don't want to hear we miss an opportunity to speak out something they need to hear.

Lord, there are so many advertisements and ideas in the world that tell us what we "deserve." Show me what the healthier perspective is, and then help me show it to others.

The slap of a friend can be trusted to help you,
but the kisses of an enemy are nothing but lies.
PROVERBS 27:6 NCV

Why wouldn't we want our loved ones to feel good and get what they want? You actually already know the answer. Our motives to encourage our friends or to not be intrusive may seem productive, yet blindly cheerleading them or pulling back does very little for someone who is running in the wrong direction. You may have to step on their toes to point this out, but in doing so you anchor them down versus letting them run off a cliff.

Still feeling tentative about speaking up, though? Think about it. Do you want "yes people" around you who only pat you on the back with sugar-coated affirmation, or do you want friends who lovingly say, "You do a lot of great things, but can I point out a bad pattern in your life so I can help you do something about it?" How is your answer any different than the ones the people you know would love you to give?

Tough love is tough to do, God. Yet somehow you do it with me every day. Thank you for fighting for what I need even when it gets in the way of what I want.

What is the difference between being a "happiness wisher" versus a "goodness coach?"

Permission to Prod

As iron sharpens iron,
so people can improve each other.

PROVERBS 27:17 NCV

You probably know a few people who don't take no for an answer. They show up at your door when you're sick insisting their chicken noodle soup will help you out. They text you when you don't show up for a workout and expect you show up for the next one. They dare you to give to cause by explaining, "You don't have any money on you? I'll wait while you go find some loose change in the couch."

People like this can be a gift if they use their stubbornness for our good. They keep us from settling into a funk by nudging us into the future. Purposefully giving people who "get" you and love you permission to prod you is something God uses to grow you.

Lord, thank you for truths I can't shake through people I can't ignore. In addition to your written Word and Holy Spirit, show me who in my life will hold me accountable to keep growing.

As iron sharpens iron,
So a man sharpens the countenance of his friend.

PROVERBS 27:17 NKJV

Butter doesn't sharpen butter. That seems obvious, right? So why is it so tempting to surround ourselves with others who will only butter us up with their words? That's not to say we don't need encouragement but that soft relationships don't create solid people.

Proverbs 27:17 shares another obvious truth: just as two blades mutually benefit by rubbing together, so can we sharpen one another into the life God invites us to claim. So, look around and ask yourself, "Who won't just butter me up but actually spur me on when I'd rather sit down?" Start in one area of your life and build out from there into every other area. It moves you from just talking about change you want to have happen to you by challenging you into the change that needs to happen in you.

Holy God, may I never lose by edge, and I may never resist the people you send into my life to sharpen me.

When was the last time you let another person show you who Jesus saved you to be?

The Family of God

"These commandments that I give you today are to be on your hearts. Impress them on your children."

DEUTERONOMY 6:6-7 NIV

You're invited. This is the message God wants his people to catch and impart to the next generation. That there is hope and we are each invited into it. Moreover, whether we are parents we are all charged to make sure kids and teenagers catch this. For every person who says that the only real way to help kids learn about God is to not force it on them, God himself says to "impress" faith into children. Why would we tell them nothing about the greatest opportunity in the universe while freely teaching them about money, politics, driving, art and more?

So you're invited—not only to receive but to give. Presenting it doesn't mean forcing it but being intentional with it. Tell your story and make sure all ages can understand it. Offer the next generation your best understanding of Jesus and the Bible, taking them alongside of you as you imperfectly live it all out. From God himself, you are invited.

Father, you have allowed me to learn from others. In turn, I open up my life as a way to teach and impart truth, too.

"Always remember these commands I give you today. Teach them to your children, and talk about them when you sit at home and walk along the road, when you lie down and when you get up."

DEUTERONOMY 6:6-7 NCV

The Bible, in multiple places, mentions that kids are to honor their parents, but also that parents need to honor their kids. Such mutual respect is lived out in the context of grace and love so that homes don't stifle any freedom to share thoughts and feelings. Practically, it might mean forming boundaries that nurture encouraging language.

Faith is more than morality and mission statements, though. As the family of God, we don't introduce each other to principles but a person—Jesus Christ himself. Let them make a choice, but cheer on the choice you want them to make. You can never be so good at this that God is obligated to make those kids Christians, but you can never be so messed up that God can't reach into their lives through you.

You are my father and I am your child. Let's get some more kids into this family, Lord.

Who are five kids or teens that you have some kind of relationship with God can leverage to reach them through you?

Name Calling

The angel appeared and spoke to Gideon, "The Lord is helping you, and you are a strong warrior."

JUDGES 6:12 CEV

Everyone is a leader, whether they realize it or not. This is the message the Lord sent to a young man named Gideon as he was working in secret one day to avoid being seen by his enemies. Instead of the angel appearing before him and calling him a coward, God named Gideon brace and spoke about a calling he had in mind for him.

Any of the Bible's notable leaders similarly had to let the Lord speak through their perspective and excuses so they would surrender whatever they had at their disposal to the higher cause they were created for. Whether it's your time up to bat, you're sitting on the bench or standing outside the stadium you have the ability to influence others if you'd first let yourself be influenced.

Holy Spirit, put into me the right "names" and "calling" others around me need to hear. I am available to speak it into them as you lead me.

The angel of the Lord appeared to him and said to him, "The Lord is with you, O mighty man of valor."

JUDGES 6:12 ESV

Leadership is commonly thought of as a position or influence over large crowds, like speaking in meetings, running a team or commanding an organization. We can overlook the power of speaking life into our loved ones during dinner, how we handle an issue in the neighborhood, or the relentless grace we offer toward someone who has caused us hurt. Every person can bless every person by naming them with truth and encouragement that draws them into a deeper connection with God.

This is something you can join into right now, wherever you're at. No matter if you're above someone, below someone or right next to someone, you have some influence as to how they see life and make their decisions. It can be as simple as sharing the "name calling" God has done in your life and as detailed as coaching them into a relationship with him and his words so they can be inspired, too.

Who am I really, Lord? Beyond what I have already learned, what else is there to know and claim? I invite you to name me and call me more deeply.

What is one thing God has told you about who you are that has surprised you?

No Reason to Fear

He will not fear evil tidings; His heart is steadfast,
trusting in the Lord.

PSALM 112:7 NIV

Do you struggle with what to teach children about Halloween?
You're not alone. The alluring costumes, the candy, and even
the public television offerings make this holiday seem
friendly, benign. Plastic skeletons smile from the store
aisles, and puffy ghosts decorate the windows.

And yet, as followers of Jesus, we know the darkness that's
underneath the mask. But explaining that darkness and
its source is just as difficult as watching a child's growing
interest in it.

Halloween bears evil tidings; yes, even saccharine-coated
greetings from our adversary. Do not give in. Claim your
steadfast heart, trusting in the Lord who has conquered death.

Father, protect the minds and hearts of the generations we are
charged with teaching today. Help us to give them strong and true
answers, and reorient their faith toward you.

He shall not be afraid of evil tidings:
his heart is fixed, trusting in the Lord.

PSALM 112:7 KJV

Some churches host alternatives to Halloween events. They are usually incredible offerings to their communities for safe, Christ-centered opportunities to allow children to celebrate their imagination and creativity without fearing for their safety.

These events are a great example of the church and community stepping into the culture and taking something that the enemy meant for evil, and turning it into good.

Not that we lose vigilance, or that evil can't infiltrate and attempt to take back what it meant as a gateway for destruction. No. Holding tight to our steadfast faith gives us a means to be in the world, not of it.

Father, help us build a wall of prayer around Halloween, fortifying our families, friends, and communities with your steadfast truth. We do not have to fear the enemy's evil tidings, because we trust your strength and your goodness.

What evil tidings can I pointedly ignore tomorrow in light of who I trust?

Wonder-Full

And the wolf will dwell with the lamb,
And the leopard will lie down with the young goat,
And the calf and the young lion and the fatted steer together;
And a little child will lead them.

ISAIAH 11:6 AMP

Remember when the world used to be wonder-full? You got excited seeing snowflakes fall instead of calculating how much time it would take you to shovel them. People asked you what you were going to be when you grew up and you knew that whatever came out of your mouth was completely possible. You didn't consider what you were qualified for or how your resume looked. You just said whatever sounded extra-ordinary, because somewhere deep inside you knew you were more than ordinary.

All these experiences when you were younger weren't perfect but they were wonder-full. Each one hinted at how life is full of more possibilities than we give it credit for. The life God offers you in eternity and even now is like that where enemies embrace each other and peace is possible. Maybe it's been a while since you've seen that, but are you willing to trust that God still does?

This world can make even the greatest optimist a pessimist, Lord. Fill me with wonder again. Fill me with you.

Then wolves will live in peace with lambs,
and leopards will lie down to rest with goats.
Calves, lions, and young bulls will eat together,
and a little child will lead them.

ISAIAH 11:6 NCV

Sometimes we think the greatest thing we can do is live spontaneously, dancing in the streets until odd hours while capturing it on our camera phones to prove how zany we are. Other times we think the greatest thing we can do in life is have every moment planned, tidied up and folded down. Living in either extreme either makes life so practical that we forget how to live or so carefree we forget what we're supposed to care about.

Remember that Jesus Christ came to this earth as a baby versus showing up as a man. Don't skip over relating to the wonder he took the time to experience by growing up as a toddler, child, pre-teen and teenager. Just as kids don't see things as they are but as what they can be, our Savior offers us to receive and embrace some wonder through his eyes.

The responsibilities of life try to tell me what to think and how to live. I don't want to ignore them, Jesus, but I'd rather not let them lead me. So, lead me instead.

What was the last thing you were pleasantly surprised by?

615

Eat It Up

Why do you spend money on what is not food,
and your wages on what does not satisfy?
Listen carefully to Me, and eat what is good,
and you will enjoy the choicest of foods.

ISAIAH 55:2 HCSB

Overspending. We've all done it, right? Perhaps you blew
your budget on a vacation or special occasion and had to
face a tough financial reality afterward. Maybe you bought
a vehicle or home for its size only to feel cramped by the
upkeep. We could easily write out a list of our missteps yet
miss the larger issue of treating wants like needs. We fall for
the pitch in front of us because of the itch inside of us, but
nothing we've spent can make us content.

God's alternative offer is clear: listen to him to learn what's good
so you can then enjoy good things! It's simple and loving despite
how complicated and commanding we make it out to be, as if
spending intentional time with him each day is a stiff activity we
do to be religious. Your heavenly father loves you and wants to
show you what's worth your time and resources. Eat it up!

Father, I'll never be perfect at managing money but I know your
wisdom makes a huge difference. I'd love to spend the whole day open
to you today so that I can sense your leadership and follow you.

Why spend your money on food that doesn't give you strength?
Why pay for groceries that do you no good? Listen and I'll tell you
where to get good food that fattens up the soul!

ISAIAH 55:2 TLB

Just thinking about state fair food probably makes your
body want to change its oil. No matter where you live, these
annual savory spectacles host some of the weirdest stuff to
eat. Beyond corn dogs and cheese curds you can munch on
deep fried cookies, deep friend licorice, deep friend bacon
and deep fried butter. Somehow seeing it on a stick makes us
think, "Well, why not?"

Culture tempts us to pursue taste over substance, but God
reveals that life in him is healthy, filling and succulent. The
next time you reach for a funnel cake filled with macaroni
and cheese, pause and consider what it symbolizes in how you
live and what you entertain yourself with.

God, there are so many things that could easily distract me.
Instead, show me what's incredible and guilt-free because it's
rooted in you and what you're up to.

When do you tend to let your guard down when it comes to
falling for something that doesn't truly satisfy?

Reference Point

More than anything else, a person's mind is evil
and cannot be healed.
Who can understand it?

JEREMIAH 17:9 NCV

Something extraordinary happened when you were born. The world was given "you"—a gift that never before existed, and never will again. You were created with a purpose that is just as unique as your fingerprint. The problem is that purpose is often stuffed down by our feelings or reactions to life. We've all been duped into thinking something that sounded good for a moment was actually good for us.

Every story has a beginning, and you can through Jesus decide what yours will be—either it starts with how you're feeling, or it starts with your God-given identity that leads to freedom. Maybe you're tired of the way things are. Perhaps you can tell that flying by the seat of your pants in life isn't working anymore, and it never really did. It's time for a new reference point beyond your heart.

God, instead of playing games I want to get serious about the freedom and transformation you offer me. Let my true identity emerge as I seek you out.

The heart is deceitful above all things
And it is extremely sick;
Who can understand it fully and know its secret motives?

JEREMIAH 17:9 AMP

How different could life would be if each of us stopped justifying our actions and became more teachable about our faults? We want to feel loved, so we run out after anything that looks like it and watch it turn to ashes once we embrace it. We want to feel appreciated, so we guilt others into applauding for us. We want to be in control of something, so we tell people to listen to us because of our resume instead of having integrity that draws people toward us.

Our hearts are where the change we want to see around us begins in us. Nothing in the world can cure our hearts, but God can give us a new one. Instead of our hearts making us miss what we see, the Lord helps us see what our hearts miss. Doesn't a new reference point sound great right about now?

Lord, I have so many feelings that want to take into situations and relationships that aren't good for me. Put a new heart into me.

So, what do you want, and why do you want it?

Forgiving Forgiveness

*"Forgive us our debts, as we have forgiven our debtors
[letting go of both the wrong and the resentment]."*

MATTHEW 6:12 AMP

Among the many true and powerful thoughts or slogans
about forgiveness, we get it. We inherently know forgiveness
is a healthier response than bitterness. Still, the pain we've
experienced can feel like something we won't ever get over
(or want to get over). While smiling to hide the hurt, we're
dying deep inside.

Have you ever considered forgiving forgiveness? Specifically,
the version of it where you're not allowed to be angry or
honest? What Jesus teaches us isn't a denial of the wrong but
a journey with it. He invites us into a fresh perspective that is
only one step away, and then another fresh perspective that
is one more step away, and so on. Forgiveness is you saying,
"I'm looking for something different than how angry I've
been at you, but I have been angry at you. I'll start by taking
my cue from what Jesus has done for me."

*Lord, my anger alone will only amplify problems and cause new
ones. So I ask you to teach me how to forgive through my emotions
so that I'm not handcuffed to them.*

"Forgive us our debts,
As we forgive our debtors."

MATTHEW 6:12 NKJV

Why choose forgiveness? Why not? Forgiveness cancels
a debt. Have you ever had a debt canceled? Forgiveness
removes someone's ability to control your feelings. Have
you ever shaken someone's grip? Forgiveness reminds you
that you are not the judge. Have you ever appreciated God's
wisdom over your own? Forgiveness reminds you that there
may be good in someone. Have you ever needed someone to
know this about you? We could go on and on, but the benefits
are obvious.

A caution is in place too. In "The Lord's Prayer," Jesus taught
us to pray essentially states, "God, only forgive me in the same
way I've forgiven others." Yikes! Why would Jesus want us to
pray that? Again, it may be for us to move past our hesitancy
with forgiveness and get going with it. Forgiveness is a key
Jesus hands you to unlock that otherwise slammed door.

I'm not sure what to make of the prayer you've asked me to pray,
Jesus. But I do know that the way you've forgiven me is meant to
help me forgive others. Give me the courage to do this today.

When have you seen forgiveness change someone's life?

I'm Rubber, You're Glue

"When they hand you over, don't worry about how or what you should speak. For you will be given what to say at that hour, because you are not speaking, but the Spirit of your Father is speaking through you."

MATTHEW 10:19-20 HCSB

Children are notorious for taunting each other in the name of "fun." Firing back something sarcastic never seems to help, but it sure comes easy to kids at home, in school and on the playground. Then again, even as adults we sometimes come across would-be bullies who enjoy feeling better about themselves by making others feel horrible. Chances are you've either been the bully, the victim or a nearby audience member while the show went on. Too bad we can't settle what happens in the office, our neighborhoods or extended family with a good old fashioned game of kickball.

Jesus says that it's always possible to be proactive, though. We do this not through clever comebacks, petty venting or passive-aggressive social media posts but by pausing for words from God himself. What you pause and allow him to speak into you in just a few seconds can change the trajectory of every moment the rest of your life. When we're rubber, he's glue.

Mighty God, please keep me tender to you in this tough world. May your words and thoughts always mature and transform my own.

"When you are arrested, don't worry about what to say or how to say it. At that time you will be given the things to say. It will not really be you speaking but the Spirit of your Father speaking through you."

MATTHEW 10:19-20 NCV

Friendly fire is a brutal and heartbreaking component of war. As soldiers fire away at their enemy, weapons that were intended to take out the bad guys can end up harming the good guys. You'd think this only happens on accident as there's no practical reason why two people on the same side would quit fighting the enemy to fight each other. History has sadly shown us that friendly fire sadly can happen on purpose.

Maybe we need a dramatic example like this to consider the friendly fire in our lives we're either a recipient or instigator of. Rather than coming alongside of each other, we can be people who fire away and nitpick others with rubbery comments that unglue others. Thankfully, letting the Holy Spirit speak through you not only helps you settle tension but also helps you not start it up in the first place.

Holy God, I care about you and others. Focus my mind and heart so that I always have something life-giving to say to others.

What would your last three conversations with people have been like if you'd paused to let the Holy Spirit speak through you?

Wherever You Are

"Nothing is covered up that will not be revealed, or hidden that will not be known."

LUKE 12:2 ESV

You know something's up when you see someone lie to a treadmill as they're entering information into it. Maybe it's a guy claiming his age as 29 when he clearly isn't, because the attractive gal next to him clearly is. Or it could be someone who thinks they can handle the toughest setting despite not having set foot in a gym in months. It's easy to want to keep up appearances when reality is something we'd rather not face.

Jesus invites you into a life of authenticity that is more freeing than a life of imitation. Living and telling the truth frees you up from having to keep track of all the lies you've told or cover-ups you've created. Doesn't that sound better than unrealistically maintaining an unrealistic life? Instead of impersonating yourself you can choose to become yourself.

I know I can't lie to you without you seeing through it, God. Reach me on this in how I live among others.

"There is nothing concealed that will not be disclosed, or hidden that will not be made known."

LUKE 12:2 NIV

According to the pitch, whatever you post on a particular website or app will only stay online until you no longer want it there. Whether the post automatically deletes itself or you manually eliminate it, you allegedly don't have to worry about anything you've said coming back to you. Unfortunately, it's all a lie. People take screenshots and companies can legally archive all kinds of data. What we think is hidden can absolutely be discovered.

Similarly, whatever seems hidden in our lives really isn't. Jesus says that every personal thought, secret attitude and undiscovered sin will one day in this life or eternity be exposed in such a way that all will see. That is, if you don't confess your sins and turn from them. A pathway into grace awaits by telling the truth to Jesus, inviting him to forgive you and sharing it with others so that true healing may take root.

Lord, I have some things to tell you. Where do I start?

What are some specific things you feel you've gotten away with because they haven't been discovered? How might Jesus be challenging you on these today?

Heavenly Hoopla

"Just so, I tell you, there will be more joy in heaven over one sinner who repents than over ninety-nine righteous persons who need no repentance."

LUKE 15:7 ESV

Calling oneself a "sinner" isn't easy. We're a little more inclined to say "I make mistakes" or "I'm not perfect" than to confess, "I'm an offending lawbreaker who is guilty of missing the mark before a holy God." Strangely, it can be just as hard to call ourselves "redeemed" or a "new creation" once we've come to Jesus and asked him for forgiveness. Maybe it's just easier to keep our head down than lift it up.

How strikingly marvelous that in contrast we find that all of heaven erupts in heavenly hoopla when someone is saved. As we respond to Christ (since Christ has responded to us), angels join in. As perspective, those who regularly live in the breathtaking wonders of God find what's happening inside of you and others who choose Jesus so important that they throw a party over it! So own it out loud: "Heaven says that I'm worth celebrating!"

God, thank you for every heavenly party that has been thrown for every person. Help me to hear your cheers for me as I keep growing with you.

"In the same way, I tell you there is more joy in heaven over one sinner who changes his heart and life, than over ninety-nine good people who don't need to change."

LUKE 15:7 NCV

Among the many, many things you can be encouraged by in your journey with God, know that his love for you isn't up for debate. There is nothing that you can do that will make him love you any more and nothing you can do that would make him love you any less. Seriously take a moment to soak this in.

Now go a step further, because there are times when he's especially excited about a decision you've made to trust him and be obedient. Every time you do this you invite him to shed the sin that could have defined you. Can you understand why your heavenly father is eager to cheer for you in this? Not only does your growth bless you but it reveals who he originally made you to be—the amazing person underneath that he wants to help bring forth and show the whole world!

Father, I praise you for who you are and not just for what you do. Your character is amazing and inspiring. Show me who you made me to be.

Think about a time you felt appreciated by others. How is God's cheering for you similar or different?

I've Got a Feeling

As Jesus came to the city and observed it, he wept over it.

LUKE 19:41 CEB

Our first experience with crying usually has something to do with pain. We skin our knees as kids or get pushed down by someone else and all we can do is cry until someone pulls us out of it. Isn't that interesting, though? As we let the outside world experience the raw ache we're experiencing on the inside we're taught to bottle it back up. There's certainly some wisdom in this, but consider the long-term effects of biting your lip and never weeping publicly.

During his years on the earth, Jesus wasn't shy about showing a full range of emotions. As he saw the brokenness of others around him he'd pause and let himself be moved. On one instance he literally wept over a whole city before entering into it. Following in his footsteps means doing the same, letting ourselves pause before and weep over "our own city." Chances are you've got a feeling you may not even have given yourself a moment to feel, until you give yourself a moment to feel.

Jesus, how did you do it? How did you look at so many broken people and care for all of them while still staying on mission? Teach me to follow in your footsteps.

As He approached Jerusalem, He saw the city and wept over it [and the spiritual ignorance of its people].

LUKE 19:41 AMP

Kids may roll their eyes when they hear it, but the average mom or dad really does mean it when they say, "This is going to hurt me more than it hurts you." It's our way of communicating that whatever tough response we make toward our sons and daughters isn't without feeling. Even if what went wrong happened out of ignorance, the discipline has to be on purpose. Perhaps the discomfort of being firm is why some parents end up being soft on consequences or emotionally cold.

One of the biggest dangers of shutting down the painful parts of your heart is you can end up also shutting down the good parts. Jesus' example shows us the value in feeling the letdown or rebellion others set forth into our lives. Him pausing to weep cries out to us, "Don't run from the tough stuff. Feel what you need to feel. And then let's keep going forward." Keeping our hearts open to him keeps our hearts open like him.

Lord, I invite you to break my heart for specific people but also all people. By weeping for them I hope to care for them.

Who are the people in your circle you might be tempted to not feel anything for? What might happen if you began pausing and weeping for them?

White Noise

"This is the verdict: Light has come into the world, but people loved darkness instead of light because their deeds were evil."

JOHN 3:19 NIV

A classic psychological exercise prods a person to look at a piece of paper with a drop of ink on it. After being asked about what they see most people tend to focus on the ink, assuming it's a miniature Rorschach test. The person testing follows up by asking, "Why did you overlook all of the 'white' on the page?"

Take that in and consider if the "white" we're looking for is right in front of us, but we tend to focus on the "darkness." You'll see it when a business wrongs someone and that person endlessly blasts them on social media or a person is letdown by a church and tells everyone not to go there. What would it look like to "do something" about how we "do something" instead of becoming a cynic and critic?

God, in the middle of all the white noise in my day may I see you and see all things through your light.

"The light has come into the world, and people who do evil things are judged guilty because they love the dark more than the light."

JOHN 3:19 CEV

There are moments in life when we feel like we have nothing to say. It could literally be a project with a blank screen or workspace that we have no idea how to fill up. Other times we wonder if we're healthy enough to say something productive. Maybe we feel like all there is to say has been said or you're not sure how to put into words what you feel. It may be that something is so fragile that you're apprehensive to speak about it or so spoken about that you fear your thoughts will merely blend into the chatter.

Remember that this world without light is by nature dark. Pressing through the awkward moments before you shines hope into others who also may feel like they have nothing to contribute. Instead of shutting down and hiding, humble let God use you. The possibility of light is a reality in this dark world. How brightly and often it shines is up to us.

God, when I feel tongue-tied, untie my tongue. When I believe I'm just noise, inspire me to speak up anyway.

Who is someone you admire who doesn't seem to hold back from inspiring others?

Whatever

Whatever you do, whether in word or deed, do it all in the name of the Lord Jesus, giving thanks to God the Father through him.

COLOSSIANS 3:17 NIV

Everyone juggles, even if poorly. A ball enters one hand, is traded off to another and tossed into the air in the hope it'll be caught again. We do this not as a circus act but in how we spend our time. Every day you toss one thing in the air hoping to gain something else, like sacrificing a hobby to be at home or investing in certain relationships at the expense of others. At times you'll feel the satisfaction of pulling it off while other times watch it all come crashing down.

There's no permanent solution to all the juggling on this side of heaven, but you can invite God into every toss. This is what it means to do it all in the name of the Lord for in faith you trust that he's going to be God in ways you can't. "Whatever" you've released for a moment may not have your hands on it but it does have his.

The pressures of life can push me into juggling more than I know how to, God. Help me not to let it all drop but instead find your hands ready to help.

Whatever you say or do should be done in the name of the Lord Jesus, as you give thanks to God the Father because of him.

COLOSSIANS 3:17 CEV

The whole world is holding its breath today, hoping you will be incredible. That's more than the bare minimum we expect they expect of us. If you're employed, there's a supervisor, board or customers who anticipate you'll get the job done. If you "stay-at-home" your family desires a certain level of upkeep. Yet in the midst of all of that minimalism the world is salivating for extravagance.

That's what God says is possible through every moment you're on the clock at work or folding laundry at home. You have a great purpose that is deeper than getting by and wider than self-importance. You were made for raw, untamed greatness that instills fully-alive living in you and through you because it isn't really whatever you do but whomever you do it for.

Humble me, Lord. If there is anything in how I spend my days that is holding me back, release me from its grip. I don't need to control life but will trust you with it.

If you were able to see the birth of Jesus and could only bring an item from your home as a gift, what would you pick?

Label Gun

We do not think of anyone as the world does. In the past we thought of Christ as the world thinks, but we no longer think of him in that way.

2 CORINTHIANS 5:16 NCV

Give yourself a little grace on this: we all label other people. It's a survival tool God put into our brains so we can have a coherent thought about others in the middle of all the unending complexities of life. That thought could be as simple as "I know her" or as complex as "He feels dangerous," for these quick summaries help us grapple with who they are, how they're a part of what's happening and which ones we're drawn to connect with.

Give yourself a little growth in this too. Our labels about someone can become we always see them, like adding one drop of food coloring to a glass of water. Try as you may to ignore it, that one drop will taint how you see the rest of the water. God invites us to give others the same clean slate we want from them each day.

Holy Spirit, examine me and draw my attention to any patterns in my thought life that aren't accurate. Use all that I am learning from you to help me live with an openness toward truth instead of stuck in my opinions.

We regard no one according to the flesh. Even though we once regarded Christ according to the flesh, we regard him thus no longer.

2 CORINTHIANS 5:16 ESV

Let's say you had a time machine and could go back to physically meet Jesus Christ. Picture yourself standing before him, but at the same time ponder what you're pondering. Does the "Jesus" you'd picture meeting resemble the Caucasian-European "Jesus" of famous art, the pastel "Jesus" of a children's Bible, the good-looking "Jesus" of movies or something else? Have you ever considered how you consider Jesus?

A huge question like this can check our blind spots toward others. Just as Christ is more than our favorite Bible stories about him, so are others more than our stories of them. Their potential isn't defined by what we know of them but of what Jesus says of them. To see past the natural we consider the supernatural—the most powerful way to see others for who they really are is to first see Jesus for who he really is.

Jesus, you tell me things about who I really am that I have yet to grow into. I know you say similar things about others. Help me put my label gun down so I can pick up your perspective instead.

When have you felt misunderstood by others? How might you be misunderstanding others?

Happiness Is Overrated

Be kind and compassionate to one another, forgiving each other,
just as in Christ God forgave you.

EPHESIANS 4:32 NIV

Let's face it: relationships take work and can be exhausting
even when there isn't conflict. Throw in an actual issue and
soon we're trying to figure out how to deal with how others
treat us through their personalities: the labelers who don't
take the time to get to know you, the pokers who justify their
jabs as "kidding around," the pretenders who pull away but
act like they haven't, and so on. Then there is the crowd
watching who doesn't want to get caught up in the drama so
they start treating you differently.

In those moments when you want to throw in the towel, there
is another option. Being kind toward someone you have
tension with and forgiveness them simply means choosing
to not let the last thing that happened have the final say.
Consider that for a moment — do you want the funk to define
things, or would you rather have it refine things?

I know that with you, God, all things are possible. May I always
remember the forgiveness that you have given me to motivate me to
share something similar with others.

Be kind to each other, tenderhearted, forgiving one another, just as God has forgiven you because you belong to Christ.

EPHESIANS 4:32 TLB

Picture your two index fingers trying to pull away from the other inside of a rubber band. The tension would obviously increase and break the band, causing extreme pain from the whiplash. In contrast, if each finger came toward the other then the tension would decrease. As an analogy, which approach symbolizes the kind of relationships you'd like to have?

Hang onto that thought, because it's easy to hit walls and feel bruised living out God's wisdom. Sometimes when we've decided to "try" to work things out what we mean is, "I'll try as long as it's easy and quick." When things don't pan out in our timeline our "trying" may become our excuse to quit. Again, there is another option: care about the other person the way Jesus cares about you by allowing for freewill on their side but always working good on your side. You don't need to "agree to disagree" but can commit to "work it out."

Lord, help me dream about where forgiveness and bridge-building kindness in my relationships could lead!

If you could fix a relationship with someone right now who would it be?

Speak Up

Take no part in the unfruitful works of darkness, but instead expose them.

Ephesians 5:11 ESV

It's incredibly difficult to ignore all the ranting in the world. Between politicians campaigning, celebrities complaining, and social media inflaming it's all quite frustrating. In reaction, we start abstaining. That sounds like a good idea, only often in our effort to say, "I don't want to be like that" we can end up indefinitely holding our tongues. Our fear of becoming a negative stereotype keeps us from becoming a positive example.

How important is your silence? God asks us to be straight on what's crooked so we can shine his light into the dark. It means, instead of getting excusing the sin in movies, TV, books, and online as "common," we remind everyone what Jesus says is normal. We do this not only in what we say but in how we live.

Jesus, I don't want to get used to what bothers you. Renew my heart and mind today so that I am more willing to stand for what you died for.

Do not participate in the worthless and unproductive deeds of darkness, but instead expose them [by exemplifying personal integrity, moral courage, and godly character].

EPHESIANS 5:11 AMP

What if the real enemy of whatever is "best" isn't whatever is "worst" but whatever is "good enough?" For example, most people don't reject God by intentionally running toward evil but by getting distracted doing fun things that seem harmless. These activities or hobbies may be some of our favorite things to do, but they likely aren't worth all the time we give to them. They are "worth less"—something that's hard to own because it sounds like we're saying they're "worthless."

But what if we stopped spending so much money and time on pursuits we hope God's okay with and started making a deeper investment into what he's actually told us to do?

God, I like having fun, but I want to honor you and change this world. So change my world first, even if it means a shift in my hobbies and interests.

When God asks you to make a sacrifice, do you feel he's for you or against you? Why?

Glory Story

I expect and hope that I will not fail Christ in anything but that I will have the courage now, as always, to show the greatness of Christ in my life here on earth, whether I live or die.

PHILIPPIANS 1:20 NCV

Everything you say or do is a choice to be whole or broken. Choosing the former isn't about our willpower but us willfully embracing the power of Christ; defaulting into the latter means we've let the hurtful, cheating, lying and misleading ways of the world win out over God. While some might argue that it's impossible to avoid being overwhelmed by life, God says freedom is possible in him.

Paul claimed this while in jail for his faith, noting that he wouldn't just wait to be released by was able to live a life of impact already. You are able to do this too! You don't have to wait to be released from whatever is holding you back to claim the territory in front of you. But before you do the work, do the worship. Claim the glory in your story.

Lord, you're not done and I'm not done either. Whatever I think is a wall you tell me is a staircase. I'm trusting you and stepping up.

My eager expectation and hope is that I will not be ashamed about anything, but that now as always, with all boldness, Christ will be highly honored in my body, whether by life or by death.

PHILIPPIANS 1:20 HCSB

Pretend that you're invited to a family reunion full of relatives you don't particularly get along with except for your grandma. While you'd like to avoid going, you think, "I'll go and make the most of this for the one person who gets me." Having a purpose in the chaos because of a relationship with clarity helps you claim life in a dead situation.

Life is like that with opportunities to focus your heart, soul, mind, body and relationships on Jesus for a greater benefit. We live one story made up of chapters with each one affected by the other, but you're not the only one scanning these "pages." Other people may not read the Bible as much as they'll read you. By choosing to honor Jesus in every moment you can become fully present to what he's doing in the people around you and help them become fully present to him.

Your glory is in my story, Lord. And you are also at work in people who frustrate me. Open my heart to them as I open my heart to you.

When has a setback in your story turned into a setup for glory?

Questions Are Welcome

Test everything. Keep what is good, and stay away from everything that is evil.

1 THESSALONIANS 5:21-22 NCV

Everybody has an opinion about truth, including if it's truth at all. Keep in mind that none of that actually affects truth for truth always is what it is regardless of what we think of it. Some people seek it without a loving, biblical community (creating blind beliefs) while others only ask safe questions so they won't hear unlikable answers (creating subjective conclusions). There are those who decide truth can't be found (creating elusive agnosticism) while others find that truth can inform spirituality (creating a reasonable faith).

To simplify, what do you do with the questions you have about God? The Bible itself encourages us to ask questions about "everything" so we can discover truth, and the word everything means everything. We do this not to become gunslingers who figure out what to destroy but greenhouse attendants who figure out what's worth growing. Questions are welcome.

You know everything, Lord. I only know some things. Teach me what to do with my questions so I know you and life in the clearest way possible.

Test everything that is said to be sure it is true, and if it is, then accept it. Keep away from every kind of evil.

1 THESSALONIANS 5:21-22 TLB

A classic bumper sticker says "God is my co-pilot." It's a bit ironic, isn't it? If you had the choice to do surgery on yourself or have a master surgeon do it for you, wouldn't you want the expert? Likewise, if you were going to journey through life wouldn't you want the one who sees all things and knows all things to be the one behind the wheel?

It's easy to take God out of the driver's seat when we look at his truth and say, "Yeah, but…" or "The Bible may say that, but I just feel…" and try to have the final word. Letting God be "God" means letting God be "God." This is to our joy and not to our detriment. As you're on the journey of trying to figure out what is credible God is present with you. Ask him what it means for him to practically be behind the wheel of your life. You are not alone.

Father, I want to trust you more than all the experts in the world. Be the leader of my life in every area of my life.

If you could ask God five questions, what would you ask him?

Bigger than Everything

The Spirit God gave us does not make us timid, but gives us power, love and self-discipline.

2 TIMOTHY 1:7 NIV

Wouldn't it be great if you could immediately fall asleep on command? It just doesn't work that way, though. You can't order your body to instantly snooze any more than you can will away the stress that wells up inside of you before great fears or opportunities. Whatever the biggest thing in your life is will make you feel that it's the biggest thing in your life.

The good news? You get to choose what the biggest thing in your life will be! If it's God, then whatever could've been a big thing automatically becomes smaller in comparison. That's what it means to be led by the Spirit, for he doesn't just give spiritual pep talks from the outside but actually works inside of you after you receive Jesus Christ as your Savior. It's a big spiritual truth that is bigger than everything big, because he is bigger than everything big.

Lord, I call you that for a reason. I want you to be the Lord over my life, including the things I worry about. I will trust you with what I can't see by looking for ways to see you. Show me in your Bible what I need to know in my heart.

The Holy Spirit, God's gift, does not want you to be afraid of people, but to be wise and strong, and to love them and enjoy being with them.

2 TIMOTHY 1:7 TLB

Once upon a time, you and someone else were super close. You're not sure when it all changed, because they now live in a tall tower of a castle called "silence" or "busyness." Everything that once felt like a fairytale relationship has changed into you trying to get a drawbridge down. Even then, you're not sure if what awaits you on the other side is a royal friendship or a dragon who will bite your head off.

Following God helps you see the castle for what it is—not a big fortress made out of impenetrable brick, but a small fort made out of movable cushions. The Holy Spirit makes you "wise and strong" so you can "love them and enjoy being with them." That's the key, because it's not about reproducing tales from the past but Jesus authoring a new chapter through you in the present.

God, I never want the walls other people put up to define my relationship with them. Just as you pursue me when I block you out, show me how to do the same for others. The front door of my heart is wide open to you on this.

What is a situation or relationship that has made you feel timid?

645

A Thousand Words

The word of God is alive and active. Sharper than any double-edged sword, it penetrates even to dividing soul and spirit, joints and marrow; it judges the thoughts and attitudes of the heart.

HEBREWS 4:12 NIV

It's said that every picture is worth a thousand words. If so, consider how photographs have changed over time. We once used film that limited our chances to capture an image, know how it turned out or change it. The digital era then made it possible to take unlimited shots to capture the "perfect picture" as we reviewed it on the camera and edited it on a computer. In our social media era, we've all become amateur photographers carrying cameras around to make anyone and anything globally famous (with or without a filter).

Amidst all these "advances" to help us capture and present life, nothing can sum up people or things like God can. His words dissolve all the filters and edits the world tries to use to sell us on who we're supposed to be or what the perfect life looks like. The blessing of reading God's Word is the way it helps you read the world.

You see through everything, Lord. I'm so thankful that I don't have to hide from you but can be honest with you. Show me the good, the bad and the ugly in this world and in me so I can grow.

The word of God is living and effective and sharper than any double-edged sword, penetrating as far as the separation of soul and spirit, joints and marrow. It is able to judge the thoughts and intentions of the heart.

HEBREWS 4:12 CSB

We all struggle for the right words to comfort someone in a crisis. Parents and mentors may feel useless around young people who claim "Nobody understands me!" Spouses can feel tongue-tied when their loved one says, "I hate my job and want to quit." Telling someone to "buck up" or "it gets better" doesn't work the kind of magic we hope it does.

Be encouraged, for as you struggle you're actually doing amazing - not because of what you may or may not say, but because you haven't left. You are representing God and his words in doing so, for his words never leave us but are always available to give the perspective that's needed. Life is full of inconsistencies but the Bible is always reliable. Reminding others of this as you stick with them is like a thousand words of hope to get through the rough waters ahead.

I know your words are not just for me, Lord. So as I take them in would you show me how to share them and who needs to hear them?

If everyone could have access to a thousand words of the Bible, what parts would you want them to read?

Spurs and Sparks

Let us consider how we may spur one another on toward love and good deeds.

HEBREWS 10:24 NASB

If you had to symbolize the level of honesty you want from others, would you ever consider a "spur" as a word? These little metal circles on the backs of riding boots have historically been a way to move a horse while riding it. These days we're a bit cautious about it to appropriate avoid animal abuse, and yet the tool remains a part of modern-day equestrian events for a reason.

Getting back to the point, do you want people in your life who "spur" you on toward love and good deeds. Specifically, are you willing to be jabbed at in love to get you past "status-quo" and into "let's help each other grow?" It's definitely a challenge to maintain this kind of friendship, but the good news is if we do we gain the ability to help our friends (and have our friends help us) avoid huge missteps in life.

Holy Father, I know you are speaking into my life through the people and situations around me. Spur me on through it all into a greater love and goodness.

Let us consider each other carefully for the purpose of sparking love and good deeds.

HEBREWS 10:24 CEB

If you live in the dark long enough, you lose the ability to see colors for what they are. Not only is this true physically but in all other ways. When you're lonely, you'll assume the first grey-option you see is a rainbow of hope; when you're angry you'll punch at a moving object you assume is an enemy when it is actually a friend. The list of possible points of confusion is endless.

It's why those closest to us need us to set off some light for them to see, even if it means creating sparks to do it. Just as in the physical realm, these quick shots of illumination happen when we cause friction like saying, "Whoa! You're drifting and I'm going to help you get back on track" or "Nice job! Keep that up!" God uses the heat of friendship to shape us all into the people he made us to be. Get fired up!

As I speak truth into others, Lord, use my sparks to offer light that helps them see instead of blinding them. Just as you have done this for me, may I do it for them.

What is something in your life that would have gotten worse if someone hadn't spoken truth into you?

Listen In

They were put to death by stoning; they were sawed in two; they were killed by the sword. They went about in sheepskins and goatskins, destitute, persecuted and mistreated—the world was not worthy of them.

HEBREWS 11:37-38 NIV

No need to pretend on this. We all eavesdrop on others. Even when you try not to it's difficult to shut off that part of your brain. At times eavesdropping helps us learn important information about the world that we'd otherwise miss, but often your secondary exposure to the direct thoughts of strangers can plant a disastrous thought or negative gossip that's hard to shake.

You may experience both in Hebrews 11 as you eavesdrop on the faith of Christians who experienced dramatic persecution. Listening in is both inspiring and perspiring, and in light of what's written about them, you may wonder if your relationship with God measures up. Perhaps the issue isn't eavesdropping but who you're listening to. These people are not our role models (for many reasons) but their faith in God is worth hearing about.

I can't imagine what some of my brothers and sisters have gone through, Lord. May their faith inform mine, but may I always hold you up as my one and only example.

They were stoned to death, they were cut in half, and they were killed with swords. Some wore the skins of sheep and goats. They were poor, abused, and treated badly. The world was not good enough for them!

HEBREWS 11:37-38 NCV

At extended family gatherings, you'll typically find an assortment of card tables and random chairs thrown together so the kids (and consequently, the grown-ups) can have a place of their own. Sometimes a stray parent or college-aged adult ends up sitting there if there's a shortage of available seats among the senior family members. It can leave that person feeling a bit belittled. Strangely, the adult table can have its own hiccups if opinions fly, politics are debated or miscommunication abounds.

Which table represents how you feel about your spiritual journey? Both tables are a part of the same family of God. May you never waste your chance to listen in to anyone relative to where you're at or at the next table over. We are family.

You are Father over all of your children, Lord. I want to keep growing but I also want to celebrate how far I've come. Lead me by your grace.

In what ways has comparing your faith to others been both a good thing and a bad thing?

Open Court

My dear children, I write this to you so that you will not sin. But if anybody does sin, we have an advocate with the Father—Jesus Christ, the Righteous One.

1 JOHN 2:1 NIV

A metaphorical story is told of a woman in open court who had to answer for the laws she'd broken. The righteous judge before her had to hold her accountable for her choices, so he declared her guilty and pronounced an enormous-yet-appropriate fine. The kicker was that after the gavel was slammed the judge stood up, walked down to the woman, put his arm around her and offered to pay the cost. While he was a righteous judge, he was also her loving father.

This parallels God's heart and our hope. We crave a righteous Lord who will hold the wrong in the world accountable and can receive the payment for our sins Jesus offers us on the cross. Like it or not, God won't impose himself upon you and make you go to heaven. Thankfully, he doesn't desire for you to go to hell and offers to pay your fine. Let him be your "dad."

Father, your righteousness and justice are needed in this world and in my life. I praise you for your goodness, too. You're exactly what we need and what I need.

My dear children, I write this letter to you so you will not sin. But if anyone does sin, we have a helper in the presence of the Father— Jesus Christ, the One who does what is right.

1 JOHN 2:1 NCV

Let's face it. We love the idea of heaven. But hell? No way! People commonly wonder, "Why would a loving God create hell?" It's an honest question and God can handle it along with other questions we ask like, "What can I away with doing or not doing and still be a Christian?" or "Is God really keeping track of everything?" Meanwhile, Jesus essentially proposes, "How can I offer you so much LIFE that the very idea of life apart from me isn't something you'd consider?"

Hell is not a declaration that God does not love us but a declaration that God will not force us to love Him. Maybe you know what it's like to seek out a relationship with someone who says, "Nah, not interested." Every second of every day God feels this from millions of people, yet He hasn't given up on us but openly courts us. You may need to read that again.

I'm in, Jesus! You offer me eternal life even though I can choose eternal death. The choice is obvious. The choice is you!

Would you still choose to follow God if hell didn't exist?

Wake Up Call

*This is all the more urgent, for you know how late it is; time is
running out. Wake up, for our salvation is nearer now than when
we first believed.*

ROMANS 13:11 NLT

That energetic guy spinning a sign near the pizza place. The
smiling girl selling lemonade on the sidewalk. The woman
ready to take your coffee order. Each is ripe with enthusiasm
that inspires others. At least, that's what we hope for. Any one
of them could be contagiously grumpy because of the routine.
Some may be working an angle until the next thing comes along.

We have an opportunity each day to receive and give a
spiritual wake up call to others. It's also possible for our
grumpiness to discourage others or our agenda to make them
guarded. What if our homes become spiritual lighthouses in
the darkness? Could the places we work become less about
paychecks and more about making a difference in the life of
another? Instead of being a breaker or a taker, what about
being a waker?

*You are the one who inspires me, O God. Whether or not I find joy in
what I'm doing, may I always find joy in what you're doing in me.*

You know what time it is, how it is now the moment for you to wake from sleep. For salvation is nearer to us now than when we became believers.

ROMANS 13:11 NRSV

It's commonly thought that it's dangerous to wake up someone who's sleepwalking. That may be true in some situations, but the truer danger has less to do with the disorder and more to do with disorientation. Rousing sleepwalkers typically confuses or distresses them to the point that they lash out. Still, it's possible to properly wake them up so they don't end up in dangerous situations.

The analogy couldn't be clearer. It's possible for any of us to appear as if we're awake to God when we actually aren't. Our culture tells us to leave others who are "sleepwalking spiritually" alone — as if spiritual tolerance is a greater value than spiritual life-saving. Meanwhile God invites us to wake up (and wake others up) to Jesus.

Lord Jesus, examine me to see if I tend to be awake or asleep to you. May all that I am learning from you help me to stay alive with conviction.

What "alarms" has God set off recently as your own personal "wake up call?"

A Long Story Short

They triumphed over him
by the blood of the Lamb
and by the word of their testimony;
they did not love their lives so much
as to shrink from death.

REVELATION 12:11 NIV

It's hard to think about the supernatural realm without feeling like we're out of our league. The unending opinions out there through special-effects-filled movies, speculative TV shows, doomsday prophets, and conspiracy theorists prompt us into silence. "I know what I don't know," we reason, "which makes me wonder about how much I actually do know."

This analysis paralysis is a tool that God's enemy loves because it keeps us from speaking up. Maybe you don't know the whole story of God backward and forward yet, but you do know what he's done in your life. Saying that out loud is your story-within-the-story, but it's also God's Story-within-your-story. Don't sell yourself short on this because it's one of the amazing tools he uses to defeat Satan. Claim who you know in what you know to face what you don't know.

God, thank you for every heavenly party that has been thrown for every person. Help me to hear your cheers for me as I keep growing with you.

*They overcame and conquered him because of the blood of the
Lamb and because of the word of their testimony, for they did not
love their life and renounce their faith even when faced with death.*

REVELATION 12:11 AMP

For all of the ills that social media has brought into our lives,
one possible good thing is the digital footprint—whatever you
post online today is archived and can be read in the future.
Just imagine what it would be like for somebody down the
road to get to know you based solely on the things you post.
That probably makes you wonder if what you're putting out
there is worth reading.

But what if it is? What if you don't just post silly things or
political nonsense but are a beam of light in a dark world?
Can you imagine getting a random email from a stranger who
said that they stumbled across what you put out there and how
it affected them? Just as the lives of people in the Bible have
inspired you, God is ready to use your life to make his long
story short and inspire others!

*Eternal Lord, you are not bound by time and yet you use it. Teach
me how to share whatever you're doing in me today so others can see
you more clearly. Use my turning points to turn them toward you.*

Would you be willing to share your testimony online? What
would it look like?

It's the Little Things

Catch for us the foxes,
the little foxes
that ruin the vineyards,
our vineyards that are in bloom.

SONG OF SOLOMON 2:15 NIV

"Can I keep it? I promise I'll take care of it." Some kids are master negotiators at talking their parents into keeping a stray animal as a pet (while other kids just feed it so it won't go away). It takes a sharp mom or dad to resist out of a commitment to the big picture. No matter how cute an animal looks up front, someone has to remember what will come out its behind (and if it's a burden worth taking on).

Some animals clearly don't belong in the house, though. God invites us through a poetic conversation between two lovers to consider how a tiny fox can be destructive to an entire vineyard. This challenges us to consider what in our lives and relationships is sneaking in and nipping at things. Rather than calling it cute and ignoring its wild nature, we need to "catch" these "foxes."

Father, I trust you and know you see so much that I don't. Thank you for telling me "no" to something I want that isn't good for me in the long run. Show me my role in this.

Catch all the foxes, those little foxes,
before they ruin the vineyard of love,
for the grapevines are blossoming!

Song of Solomon 2:15 NLT

Investing into a garden means facing natural challenges year-round. The climate may work against you; rabbits or deer may nibble at what's growing; moles will mess with things underneath; kids could trample over things by accident. Whatever you're trying to see "bloom" will need some kind of protection.

It's all an interesting analogy for relationships. When a friendship is growing or a romance is alive, all potential threats to what's beautiful must be addressed. This specifically includes the "little" things that are often overlooked—be it the "climate" of attitudes around you, people who "nibble" at what's growing, busyness that messes with things "underneath," or how even kids can "trample" a very good thing by accident. Little things add up and keep big things from blooming.

Lord, you were the first Gardener. Teach me what it means to invest into and protect the good things you're growing in the people around me.

What one thing could have a dramatic impact on your relationships, one way or another?

No = Yes?

The grace of God has appeared, bringing salvation to all, training us to renounce impiety and worldly passions, and in the present age to live lives that are self-controlled, upright, and godly, while we wait for the blessed hope and the manifestation of the glory of our great God and Savior, Jesus Christ.

TITUS 2:11-13 NRSV

It's a simple truth: every time you say yes to one thing you are simultaneously (at a level you can't fully comprehend) saying no to other things. So if you say yes to eat at one restaurant for dinner or vacation in a particular city, you're in that same moment saying no to all the other locations everywhere else in the world you could be. Make sense?

Because God invites you into this truth at the deepest, most freeing level possible. When you say yes to Jesus, you simultaneously (at a level you can't fully comprehend) are saying no to every sin that's every existed controlling you. Through Christ, you no longer are who you once were.

God, I know I can't see all that you can. I'm in faith going to thank you for the commands you give me because I trust that it's so I can say YES to something greater you have planned for me.

The grace of God has appeared, bringing salvation for all people,
training us to renounce ungodliness and worldly passions, and to
live self-controlled, upright, and godly lives in the present age,
waiting for our blessed hope, the appearing of the glory of our
great God and Savior Jesus Christ.

TITUS 2:11-13 ESV

If every time you say yes to one thing you are saying no to other
things, is the opposite true? Unfortunately, not always. It's
possible to try to resist sin in your own willpower without ever
saying yes to Jesus.

But the opposite can be true! It's possible to say no to sin
with power because you're at the same time saying yes to
Jesus and all he offers you. Consider an analogy about food.
It's possible to turn down a piece of baloney even when we're
incredibly hungry, but there's definitely more excitement and
conviction behind it when we're saying yes to a gourmet meal
later. When temptation tries to serve you up something when
your life feels empty, say your big no by saying a greater yes.
There's no baloney about it.

Holy Spirit, remind me of all that I say YES to every time I say NO
to sin. May the joy you give me in those moments be contagious
and inspire others.

What is one God-thing you said YES to the last time you said
NO to sin?

Day and Night

I will bless the Lord who guides me;
even at night my heart instructs me.
I know the Lord is always with me.
I will not be shaken, for he is right beside me.

PSALM 16:7-8 NLT

At night while sleeping, we are completely checked out from the outside world. Our bodies and brains finally find rest and refreshing after a full day's activities. We have ceased from "doing." And in this place God continues to watch over us, speak to us, love on us and guide us.

Find comfort today in the truth that God never ceases to keep his eye on you. All day and all night. While you're intentionally focused on him or sleeping. While you're actively producing something or resting from doing anything. You can rest assured that the earth continues to turn without your help. You have no reason to be shaken. God's got it.

Heavenly Father, thank you for watching over me even in the night. I can truly rest in your peace knowing that you are always by my side.

I praise the Lord because he advises me.
Even at night, I feel his leading.
I keep the Lord before me always.
Because he is close by my side,
I will not be hurt.

PSALM 16:7-8 NCV

If you need wisdom, you can ask God for it, assured that he'll show you the way ahead. Do you need God's guidance on something right now? He wants to give you wise counsel and show you the way to go. You don't have to stumble around in darkness. You can trust him.

Consider the words of the hymn "Be Thou My Vision": "Waking or sleeping, thy presence my light."

Know tonight that as you rest, God is your light and he wants to speak to you. Choose to trust him and rest firmly in his loving arms tonight, knowing that he doesn't ever let you go.

Lord Jesus, as I fall asleep tonight, I set my heart on you. I ask that you speak to me in my sleep and show me the way ahead. I trust that you want to speak to me.

In what areas of your life do you need God's guidance?

Pleasures Forevermore

You will show me the path of life;
In Your presence is fullness of joy;
In Your right hand there are pleasures forevermore.

PSALM 16:11 AMP

Human beings are pleasure seekers. We fill our minds, bodies and souls with things that make us feel good. It can be so easy to fall into the trap of thinking that earthly things will finally fulfill our deepest hungers. But we were fashioned to find the greatest of pleasure in the one who created us. We were made to be fully satisfied by our God.

Where have you sought to fill the longings of your heart apart from God? Fullness of joy is available to you, in this moment, right now because God's presence is with you and his very nature is joy. Seek pleasure in God's presence today, knowing that the path of life is found in Jesus, who offers you true life in him.

Jesus, thank you that I don't have to run to things of this world to fully satisfy the hunger in my heart for pleasure. Life is found in you. Help me to seek you with all my heart today.

You will show me the path of life;
In Your presence is fullness of joy;
At Your right hand are pleasures forevermore.

PSALM 16:11 NKJV

How do you know if you are going in the right direction or doing the right thing? With so many options of which way to go, it's easy to get trapped into worrying that you'll miss God's plan for you. The truth is, God's guidance in your life is stronger than your ability to wander. If your heart's desire is to follow in God's ways, you can trust that you won't miss it. He won't abandon you along the way.

He is faithfully with you on the journey. He is shining his face on you, radiant with his overflowing love, grace, and kindness towards you. He sees you and he knows your heart. You never have to worry you'll miss the way forward. He has taken your hand, guiding you along the life path.

Lord Jesus, you are so good in your faithfulness towards me. I can trust I am on the right path because you are with me.

Do you need to allow Jesus to take your hand and guide you?

Life and Death

"Today I have given you the choice between life and death, between blessings and curses. Now I call on heaven and earth to witness the choice you make. Oh, that you would choose life, so that you and your descendants might live."

DEUTERONOMY 30:19 NLT

Have you ever felt like you didn't have a choice or a say in the circumstances around you? Like you were helpless to do anything about your situation? In reality, you always have a choice, in every circumstance or situation. You can choose your attitude. You can choose what you focus on and think about. You can choose whether you do something or don't do it. You can choose how you respond.

We oftentimes think about it as a decision between right and wrong. But what if we started thinking about it as the choice instead between life and death? God pleads with us to choose life. Choose him. Don't turn your back away from him today. Choose the path that leads to the fullness of life he desires for you.

Heavenly Father, I ask you today to show me the areas of my life where I am choosing death. You long for me to choose life and I say yes to life today Lord.

"I call heaven and earth to witness against you today, that I have set before you life and death, blessing and curse. Therefore choose life, that you and your offspring may live, loving the Lord your God, obeying his voice and holding fast to him, for he is your life and length of days, that you may dwell in the land that the Lord swore to your fathers, to Abraham, to Isaac, and to Jacob, to give them."

DEUTERONOMY 30:19-20 ESV

A lot of people view God like the "Big Angry Guy in the Sky," just waiting for us to screw up or make a mistake so that he can smite us from heaven. They view him as a God who is poised ready to curse us for our disobedient behavior. In reality, he is life itself!

God loves you with an unsurpassable, immeasurable love, and he simply asks you to respond with love in return. God's heart cry is for you to love him, obey him and embrace him. Why? He is the source of all good and beautiful things. He is life itself and the fullness of life is found firmly in him. Choose life today. Choose Jesus today. He longs for you to cling to him and find your life first in him above everything else.

Lord, I want to love you, listen obediently to you and embrace you with all my heart. Help me to choose life today.

How can your life be changed by the truth that God is life itself?

Action Word

God so loved the world that he gave his one and only Son, that whoever believes in him shall not perish but have eternal life.

JOHN 3:16 NIV

That word *so*: we often read it like it means "so much." It actually means "in this way." The way God showed us was by giving up his Son Jesus so that we could be made right with him. Jesus made it clear that when we look at him, we look at the Father (John 14:9). Jesus has shown us what God is really like and he came into this world showing us the love of God through his actions.

He took on himself the punishment for our brokenness and all the ways we fall short. Jesus took our place and we are made right with God because of what he did for us. God's immeasurable love for you isn't just empty words. It didn't passively sit back. Love did something. It did everything. Reflect on that earth-shaking love today, knowing that Jesus' love for you is an action word.

Lord Jesus, thank you for your love for me expressed in your sacrifice on the cross. I give you praise for that love. Open my heart to receive more of your love today.

God so loved the world that He gave His only begotten Son, that whoever believes in Him should not perish but have everlasting life.

John 3:16 NKJV

We can easily set our focus mainly on what the death and resurrection of Jesus accomplished. But what about his life? What did love look like when Jesus was here? He healed the diseased. He freed people who had been demonized and cast out of their community. He brought the Good News of his kingdom, and radically loved and embraced all people. He called us friends, we who were far away from him.

God's love is something that is meant to be experienced. And felt. Not just words on page or an idea we hear. Love is experienced. It is active. And God wants you to experience his love in a real and tangible way here and now. He sees you and knows you and he wants you to find life in him.

Lord Jesus, I want the whole and lasting life you offer me in you. I choose to trust and believe in you.

How might you express love as an action word in your life?

Here I Am

When the Lord saw Moses coming to take a closer look, God called to him from the middle of the bush, "Moses! Moses!" "Here I am!" Moses replied.

EXODUS 3:4 NLT

Moses, the faithful patriarch who led the Jewish people out of slavery, has a surprisingly sordid history. After taking matters into his own hands, murdering an Egyptian slave driver, he flees to the desert and ends up in the wilderness tending to sheep. In this distant land, far away from his people, the living God speaks to him.

God speaks in strange ways sometimes. This time it was through a bush. God had to get Moses' attention and when he had noticed he captured it, he called his name from the bush. Has God been trying to get your attention? Has he been calling your name? Has he been speaking in an out of the ordinary way? If so, respond with "Here I am" and trust that he'll show you what's next.

God, thank you for speaking to me. Give me the eyes to see you and the ears to hear your voice.

When the Lord saw that he turned aside to look, God called to him from the midst of the bush and said, "Moses, Moses!" And he said, "Here I am."

EXODUS 3:4 NASB

It can be easy to wonder if Moses had lost hope of his life amounting to anything. Tending to sheep, the lowest of the low jobs, had to have been very humbling for this man. After years and years of wandering with smelly sheep he must have wondered if God had forgotten about him or the plight of his people.

Maybe you can relate to Moses and the feeling of being forgotten. Or not knowing how it's possible for God to take your mess and do something out of it. Rest assured, God will get your attention when the time is right. Moses couldn't miss God's calling. And just like Moses, God is a good shepherd to his sheep. You can trust that He has not forgotten you. Your name is on his lips. Keep your ears and heart open to respond when he calls.

Heavenly Father, I am right here! I want to hear your voice. I trust that you're leading me.

How might God be trying to get your attention right now?

Gateway of Hope

I will win her back once again.
I will lead her into the desert and speak tenderly to her there.
I will return her vineyards to her
and transform the Valley of Trouble into a gateway of hope.

Hosea 2:14-15 NLT

We all have the propensity to wander away from Jesus. We falsely think we can do life better without him. We turn our hearts away out of our shame, sin, or rebellion. Whatever the reason, we have a God who still faithfully pursues us.

God's heart towards you is tender and loving. He longs to have your whole heart. He sees you. He calls out to you and speaks tenderly to you. If you are walking through a dark valley of trouble unsure of where God is, trust that he promises to turn your trial into a gateway to hope. He will take your broken mess and make it beautiful. Return to him with all your heart today.

Jesus, I pray that you would "bind my wandering heart to thee."
I return to you today.

I am going to attract her;
I will lead her into the desert
and speak tenderly to her.
There I will give her back her vineyards,
and I will make the Valley of Trouble a door of hope.
There she will respond as when she was young,
as when she came out of Egypt.

HOSEA 2:14-15 NCV

The thought of God pursuing us like a man pursuing a woman may feel a little unsettling. Courting? Dating? Bouquets of roses? It might make us blush. But this passage in Hosea truly reveals the heart of God towards his people. He loves us with the kind of passionate all-consuming love that overpowers, captures and enraptures. God has the heart of a lover towards his church.

This same passionate pursuit is directed at you, beloved. His eyes are squarely on you. And he longs to bind up your broken heart and flood you with renewed hope. Let him in. Open your heart to him today. There is always hope when you're in the gaze of the lover God.

Lord, increase my heart's ability to receive your love. Take my heartbreak and turn it into hope.

What are God's words of hope and love for you today?

673

God's Artwork

We are God's masterpiece. He has created us anew in Christ Jesus,
so we can do the good things he planned for us long ago.

EPHESIANS 2:10 NLT

If you have every found yourself wanting to grow in who God created you to be, but found yourself paralyzed, overwhelmed and confused, welcome to the club. But there's good news. That confusion, that uncertainty, that desire for perfection, is all part of the journey of becoming who God created you to be. And the Creator, is incredibly patient. He is committed to the process. He takes joy, not only in the final product, but the journey as well.

You may need to hear that you are in process! You aren't done yet! You're on a journey and that's ok. Because there is something beautiful about the process. God is an expert artist fiercely committed to what's he's doing in you. You are God's art piece in the process of being created into the image of Christ. Take joy today in the process.

Thank you, Jesus, that you're with me every step of the journey,
and you're committed to transforming me into the image of Christ.

We are God's handiwork, created in Christ Jesus to do good works, which God prepared in advance for us to do.

Ephesians 2:10 NIV

What is the Artist doing in you right now? Sometimes it's hard to see the big picture, but choose to trust that he is working something in you, even in the process. Where is he taking your rough places and smoothing them out? What is he doing with the things you would label as "accidents"? Where have you questioned or judged the work of the Artist in you by labeling his work as bad, or out of order? What areas do you need to invite him into, because you've made a mess on your own?

God is doing a master work in you, that will lead to a beautiful overflow of good deeds he has prepared for you to do. Trust the Artist.

Heavenly Father, thank you that you're shaping my life into a masterpiece.

What are you being made into?

Actions Matter

What good is it, dear brothers and sisters, if you say you have faith but don't show it by your actions? Can that kind of faith save anyone?

JAMES 2:14, NLT

We love to proclaim the words of "Amazing Grace." We find security in the truth that we are saved by grace through faith in Christ. We can't earn our salvation by the good deeds that we do. So the words of James might feel a little unsettling. There's no mincing words here. Faith without good deeds is simply dead.

James is speaking a convicting truth to us. Has your faith in Christ resulted in a lifestyle that lines up? Because the truth is when God gets a hold of your heart, you can't help but love others and serve others. When the living God comes and dwells in you, he changes your motivations. He transforms your priorities. True faith inevitably leads to good deeds. How is God calling you to put your faith into action today?

God, I want a faith that results in actions. Thank you for your transforming work within me.

*My brothers and sisters, if people say they have faith, but do
nothing, their faith is worth nothing. Can faith like that save them?*
JAMES 2:14 NCV

Nothing irks us more than the hypocrisy we see in others.
We're annoyed at the person spouting their opinions on
social media about social justice issues, but never doing
anything to fix the problem. We're bothered by our friends or
family saying "sorry" but then continuing in the same hurtful
behavior. But do we hold ourselves to that same standard?

Take a minute to look in the mirror today. Can you fall into the
trap of talking without doing? We've all heard the old phrase,
"If you want to talk the talk, you've gotta walk the walk."
Simply put, having faith in Christ means your actions will
line up with your words. Internal transformation needs to be
expressed externally. What action is God calling you to take
today in response to the work Christ has done inside you?

*Heavenly Father, I don't want to fall into hypocrisy. Strengthen me by
your Holy Spirit to respond with actions that line up with my words.*

How has your faith impacted your actions?

Boldly Enter

We can boldly enter heaven's Most Holy Place because of the blood of Jesus. By his death, Jesus opened a new and life-giving way through the curtain into the Most Holy Place.

HEBREWS 10:19-20 NLT

"The Most Holy Place" was a sacred and set apart place in the tabernacle where the fullness of God's presence dwelled. Anyone who entered carrying the guilt of sin would surely die. But Jesus' death and resurrection was a cataclysmic shift. Everything changed by this reality and we can now walk right into God's presence with no fear.

Reflect on this truth today. You don't have to be cowardly or ashamed as you approach God. The beautiful and holy God, who is completely perfect, says "Come right up on my lap! Come right into my presence! Not because of the good things you have done. Not because you have tried harder. And in spite of your flaws and failures, simply come!"

Don't allow anything to hold you back. It is because of the precious shed blood of our Jesus, who has made a way for you.

Jesus, I rejoice in the truth that you have made a way for me to get close to God without fear. I boldly enter your presence today assured of your glad welcome.

Since we have confidence to enter the Most Holy Place by the blood of Jesus, by a new and living way opened for us through the curtain, that is, his body,

HEBREWS 10:19-20 NIV

God stands with his arms open wide to you, simply saying, "Come." Is there any hesitation in your heart when you ponder this truth? What stands in the way of you walking straight into God's presence?

Is it your shame? Are you afraid that God won't accept you in your brokenness? Do you wonder how could God possibly love you or forgive you? Have you been wounded at the hands of others and that has affected your view of what God is like? Jesus' blood covers all that. Fear and shame have been broken in the name of Jesus. He wants to show you what He is really like. He is a loving father. He does not condemn you. He sees all your failures and still says you are beloved. Enter boldly, right into God's presence.

Heavenly Father, I want to come right into your presence with no hesitation. I trust that Jesus has cleared the way for me!

Can you imagine what God's face look like when he sees you?

The Good Shepherd

"The thief's purpose is to steal and kill and destroy. My purpose is to give them a rich and satisfying life. I am the good shepherd. The good shepherd sacrifices his life for the sheep."

JOHN 10:10-11 NLT

In the midst of challenges that life throws at us, we are quick to point fingers at the people who hurt us. And at ourselves for our mistakes or failures. Its critical we keep the perspective that we have a very real adversary who doesn't want to see our success. Worse than that, the devil has one aim alone; destruction. There is no good in him.

Sometimes the finger gets pointed firmly at God for the troubles we find ourself in. Why didn't he protect us? Why did this terrible thing happen? Where was God? While there are not always clear answers to these questions, the words of Jesus must ring in our hearts; his purpose for us is entirely clear. He is only good. And a satisfying life is what he wants for us. Proclaim the truth over your life and your problems today that Jesus wants a rich and satisfying life for you.

Heavenly Father, I'm sorry for the times I've questioned your goodness. I believe the truth today that your plans for my life are good.

"The thief comes only to steal and kill and destroy; I came that they may have life, and have it abundantly. I am the good shepherd; the good shepherd lays down His life for the sheep."

JOHN 10:10-11 NASB

Sheep are very foolish animals that are quick to wander off. And isn't that true about us too? One minute we are walking close to Jesus, the next we're going our own way. Sometimes it's blatant rebellion, but most of the time it's a subtle turning away from God in the hidden places of our heart. It's truly good news that Jesus calls himself a Good Shepherd to his sheep.

But the threat of a thief or a wolf is real out in the wilderness where sheep graze. Have you listened to the voice of the thief in your life? Have you allowed him to steal from you? Have you wandered off down a path that leads to destruction? You can trust that Jesus will look for you when you wander. But not only that, his heart is to lavish you in good, fulfilling, real, true, and eternal life, better than you could ever dream of! Come back to the Shepherd if you have wandered off on your own way.

Good Shepherd, I want the abundant life you have for me and I trust that you are good.

What does the rich and satisfying life Jesus has for you look like?

Safe in His Hands

*"My sheep listen to my voice; I know them, and they follow me.
I give them eternal life, and they will never perish. No one can
snatch them away from me, for my Father has given them to me,
and he is more powerful than anyone else. No one can snatch
them from the Father's hand."*

JOHN 10:27-29 NLT

We all have the capability of wandering off, down the wrong
path. This can be out of our own rebellion, or just plain
foolishness. We can find ourselves in situations that we know
are not good for us. Or maybe there's fear we might end up on
the wrong path, making the wrong decisions. The voice of the
Shepherd calls out for his sheep to listen to him and follow
him. And this Shepherd knows each of his sheep personally.

Do you consider yourself a follower of Jesus? If so, he calls
you his sheep. He promises you eternal life in him. And he
holds you safely in his hands. No one has the power to snatch
you out of the hands of the loving Father. Find peace in this
truth today, that God's powerful hand in holding you.

*Heavenly Father, thank you that you are the Shepherd of my heart.
Help me to rest today in the truth that you hold me securely in your
hands.*

"My sheep hear my voice. I know them, and they follow me. I give them eternal life, and they will never perish. No one will snatch them out of my hand. What my Father has given me is greater than all else, and no one can snatch it out of the Father's hand."

JOHN 10:27-29 NRSV

Satan works through the schemes of man to steal life from you. It may be in the form of fear, shame, or insecurity. Maybe you're finding yourself in the place of fear and shame more than you'd like to admit.

There is great news in the truth that you are under the divine and gentle care of Father who knows you and loves you just as you are. He wants to bless you with fullness of life now, and also forever. We must remember, however, that satan has been defeated by the precious blood of Jesus. You can rest in the confidence assurance that real life is available to you in Jesus.

Lord Jesus, thank you for your divine protection. I rest tonight in that truth that no one can snatch me from you.

What work of the Thief is defeated in your life because you're in the hands of the Father?

Deep Roots

Let your roots grow down into him, and let your lives be built on him. Then your faith will grow strong in the truth you were taught, and you will overflow with thankfulness.

Colossians 2:7 NLT

What is your life built on? Is it on your accomplishments? Is it in how much stuff you own, or how many friends you have? Is your life built on the praise or rejection of people? We can fall into the cultural pressure to build our lives on a lot of other things, but Jesus calls us to build our lives on him. Simply, Jesus wants to be our rock, cornerstone, and anchor. The source where all life comes from.

Do you ever feel tossed around by the cares or concerns of life, not sure where to be grounded? Let your roots grow deeper into the soil of God's love. Put down roots in Jesus. Draw up nourishment from him. Stronger faith that can sustain the storms of life come from a life grounded in Christ.

Lord Jesus, I want to build my life on you. Help me to grow deeper roots in you, that I would remain strong in all of life's challenges.

Keep your roots deep in him and have your lives built on him. Be strong in the faith, just as you were taught, and always be thankful.

<small>COLOSSIANS 2:6 NCV</small>

If you have been following Jesus for awhile, it can be easy to get a little comfortable with where you're at. You might need a little nudge to get you to step out. If your life is built on Jesus, how might God be challenging you to take action? If you know your way around the faith, it's probably time to start doing something with it.

A plant with good healthy roots, will produce good and healthy fruit. What kind of fruit are you seeing in your life? According to this passage, thankfulness is a natural outpouring of a life rooted deeply in Christ.

Jesus, I pray for a life deeply rooted in you and for the grace to live out my faith in my actions.

How is God calling you to start living out your faith in this season?

The Cry of the Soul

How long must I struggle with anguish in my soul,
with sorrow in my heart every day?
But I trust in your unfailing love.
I will rejoice because you have rescued me.
I will sing to the Lord
because he is good to me.

PSALM 13:2, 5-6 NLT

Every soul has experienced sorrow and sadness. It's part of what makes us human. In those dark times, we can find great comfort in the words of the psalmists who cry out for God to hear and answer. We are not alone in our struggles. But more than that, there is something gloriously beautiful about praising God in the midst of pain and sorrow. Singing and rejoicing when our soul is hurting is an act of faith. This kind of praise touches the heart of God and his unfailing love will carry us through the sorrow.

Do you need to cry out in anguish today and acknowledge your sorrow or pain before God? He wants to hear it. Then allow your outcry of pain turn into an outcry of praise. Choose to trust in God's unfailing love today.

Lord God, thank you that you hear the cry of my soul and that you love me with an unfailing love. I rejoice in you even in my pain.

How long must I take counsel in my soul,
Having sorrow in my heart day after day?
But I have trusted and relied on and been confident in Your
lovingkindness and faithfulness;
My heart shall rejoice and delight in Your salvation.
I will sing to the Lord,
Because He has dealt bountifully with me.

PSALM 13:2, 5-6 AMP

The psalmist models something very beautifully for us in this passage. While he cries out in pain, he also cries out in trust. He reminds his soul of God's faithfulness and goodness to him. While he may not see it clearly manifested in his circumstances, he boldly declares in this passage that God's always been good.

You may need to remind your soul of this truth today. It's easy to rejoice when everything is great. It is an act of faith to proclaim God's goodness when you are in the darkness. Rejoice and delight in the goodness of God, even if you're filled with sorrow. God will meet you in your exact place of need.

Lord Jesus, I choose to trust today that you are always good.

What does your soul need to say to God today?

Reviving the Soul

The instructions of the Lord are perfect,
reviving the soul.

PSALM 19:7 NLT

Traditionally, Christians view the soul as our thoughts, will, and emotions, a necessary and important part of what makes us human. God also gave us a spirit that works together with his indwelling Holy Spirit. As followers of Jesus we want to live by the Spirit's power. But sometimes we focus so much of our attention on growing in our spirit that we can forget to take care of our soul.

How is your soul doing today? What's going on in your emotions that you need to acknowledge before the Lord? What about your thought life? Are there old patterns of thinking that you slide into that you know are not good for you? What about your will or desires? Do they line up with God's desires for you?

Maybe your soul is weary and needs some reviving. The perfect Word of God, Jesus, wants to tenderly care for your soul today. He is the lover of your soul and his instructions are perfect.

Lord Jesus, thank you for your care and concern for the wellbeing
of my soul. Help me to listen to what my soul needs today.

God's laws are perfect.
They protect us, make us wise, and give us joy and light.

The full revelation of what God is like came in the person of
Jesus Christ. If we ever wonder what God is really like, we
can look to Jesus. Jesus had a human soul, with emotions,
thoughts, and desires. He felt sadness and anger, joy and
pain. This was God incarnate, God with us.

Jesus also modeled for us what a life fully dependent on the
Father could look like. Jesus said he only did what he saw his
Father doing. Jesus was our model for what it looks like to live
fully alive. Our lives are pulled together in Christ. Our lives
have meaning, purpose and our souls can be revived.

Do you need God to pull your life together? Do you need
clarity of purpose and calling? Peace in your soul or healing
for your heart? Invite him in tonight to do the restoration
work only he can do.

Lord Jesus, you have shown me what God is really like. I give you
permission to work in my life however you want to.

What does your soul need from God today?

Deepest Longing

O God, You are my God; with deepest longing I will seek You;
My soul [my life, my very self] thirsts for You,
my flesh longs and sighs for You,
In a dry and weary land where there is no water.

PSALM 63:1 AMP

The words of thispPsalm were penned by David while he was fleeing for his life in the Judean wilderness. You can hear the longing in this prayer, welling up from a deep place of physical and spiritual need. He understands physical thirst, very likely searching for water to preserve his life in this dry wilderness.

And he allows his external circumstances to inform his cries to God. To pray for literal water was probably not too far fetched. But David is desperate for God not just what God can provide him. He cries out for God himself. He knows at his core he needs God more than the blessings God can give him.

You may have a deep physical need right now, and you're longing for God to break into your circumstance. Pray the words of David, asking God to give you a greater thirst for him alone. Desire God more than the blessings he can give you.

Lord Jesus, I want more of you in my life. Stir up a greater thirst in my heart for you today.

O God, you are my God; I earnestly search for you.
My soul thirsts for you; my whole body longs for you
in this parched and weary land where there is no water.

PSALM 63:1 NLT

It may seem at times your prayer for more of him is not being answered. It may feel like you're in a dry land with no water, no answers and prolonged thirst for God to respond. You were created to be satisfied by God. You were made to have your thirst quenched by him. Allow your prayer to rise up to God tonight that your soul thirsts for more of him.

A cry for more of God in your life will always be answered. It may not be immediate but God hears your cry. God wants to meet your deepest longings and needs in himself. Jesus says that he is Living Water and that when we drink of this water we will never thirst again (John 4:14).

Lord Jesus, I know that my deepest longings are satisfied in you.
I cry out for more of you.

What thirst does God want to satisfy in you today?

Light of the World

"You are the light of the world—like a city on a hilltop that cannot be hidden. No one lights a lamp and then puts it under a basket. Instead, a lamp is placed on a stand, where it gives light to everyone in the house. In the same way, let your good deeds shine out for all to see, so that everyone will praise your heavenly Father."

MATTHEW 5:14-16 NLT

Think about living in Jesus' time with no electricity. Once night fell, there was great importance of a lamp to guide your way in a house. And the very purpose and nature of one of these lamps was to shine. It would be absolutely ridiculous to take this light and hide it under a bowl. Light is meant to shine!

For Jesus to say that you are the the light of the world is to say that you are to be the light that guides people wandering in darkness. You are to be God's' representatives on this earth and point people to Jesus!

The world is going to look to you. Your good deeds are to point them to God.

Lord Jesus, I want to be a light to those wandering in darkness. Shine your light through me.

"You are the light of the world. A city set on a hill cannot be hidden. Nor do people light a lamp and put it under a basket, but on a stand, and it gives light to all in the house. In the same way, let your light shine before others, so that they may see your good works and give glory to your Father who is in heaven."

MATTHEW 5:14-16 AMP

Jesus also called himself the Light of the World (John 8:12). Jesus is the very substance of light. And the amazing thing about Jesus' death on the cross is that he willingly entered into the pit of darkness and he rose victoriously. Death and darkness could not hold him down. Light is more powerful and it pushes back all darkness in its presence.

When the love of God transforms you from the inside out, you can't help but share that love and light with the world. At the moon reflects the light from the sun, we are called to reflect the light that comes from him into a world that doesn't know there is light.

"This little light of mine, I'm gonna let it shine."

Lord Jesus, you are the light of the world. Help me to reflect that beautiful light to a world wandering in darkness.

How might God be calling you to shine your light?

Strong Tower

The name of the Lord is a strong tower;
The righteous runs to it and is safe and set on high [far above evil].

PROVERBS 18:10 AMP

Sometimes, it can be a cold world out there that is insensitive to our need for safety. A lot of things in this life can threaten our safety. We have all found ourselves in situations where our emotions feel battered or bruised. People have the capacity to hurt us. But God never will.

You can trust that God is always a safe place for you. He will always gladly welcome you into his strong arms. Your fight or flight instincts don't have to kick in in God's presence. He can be your strong tower and your place of safety. Ask Jesus to show that he is a safe place for you today. He cares about you and you can trust him with everything. He will tenderly watch over you and give you his peace.

Heavenly Father, thank you that you are stronger than any challenges I may face in life. Help me to trust that you are a safe place for me.

The Lord is like a strong tower;
those who do right can run to him for safety.

Maybe you know that God is a safe place but something
is holding you back from running towards him without
hesitation. What are the things that stand in way of you
trusting that God is place of protection? Maybe the wounds
inflicted on you by people make it hard to see that God is
trustworthy. Or you have falsely thought that God wasn't there
when you needed him. What lies are you believing about who
God is that prevent you from trusting?

Ask him to show you what he is really like. Ask God to show
you a picture of the place of safety and protection you can
enter into in him. Ask him to show where he was in your
place of pain. He is your strong tower.

God, I ask you to reveal any lies I am believing about you that prevent
me from trusting you are my protector. I ask for an encounter with
you and a heart that desires to walk in righteousness.

What does your place of safety with God look like?

Don't Worry

Don't worry about anything; instead, pray about everything.
Tell God what you need, and thank him for all he has done.
Then you will experience God's peace, which exceeds anything
we can understand. His peace will guard your hearts and minds
as you live in Christ Jesus.

PHILIPPIANS 4:6-7 NLT

The troubles that we face in this life threaten to shake and dislodge us from peace. We are so quick to first go to the place of worry, over thinking and anxiety over the things in our lives that are not as they should be. Paul's words in Philippians are truth that our anxious souls need to hear. Our first reaction to the troubles we face must always be to go straight to God in prayer.

This passage acts a promise to you. Peace is always available in Christ, regardless of the challenges you face. You can walk in a radical peace that cannot be shaken by the concerns of this world, peace that comes from an honest and thankful heart before God. Seek God first today and experience his peace as you live in him.

Lord Jesus, I choose to pray about the things troubling me today
instead of worrying. I ask for a tangible sense of your peace as
I trust you today.

Do not be anxious or worried about anything, but in everything [every circumstance and situation] by prayer and petition with thanksgiving, continue to make your [specific] requests known to God. And the peace of God [that peace which reassures the heart, that peace] which transcends all understanding, [that peace which] stands guard over your hearts and your minds in Christ Jesus [is yours].

Philippians 4:6-7 AMP

When facing trials, nothing hurts more than a friend dismissively telling you to "just pray" or to "get over it." That is not Paul's intent in these loving words to the Philippians. Instead he is giving us truth for our weary souls to be able to move forward. The natural human response to challenges is anxiety or worry. Rather than to stay stuck in this place, we must actively invite God into our struggles and bring our specific requests and petitions before God.

Peace that reassures the heart is for you tonight as you rest. Wait for God to respond with his peace, which will be your strength in the challenges. As you cry out to God, may you walk in a radical peace that cannot be shaken by the concerns of this world.

Lord Jesus, I ask for your peace to stand guard over my heart and mind tonight as I rest.

How might God's peace change things for you?

Trust before Understanding

Trust in the Lord with all your heart;
do not depend on your own understanding.
Seek his will in all you do,
and he will show you which path to take.

PROVERBS 3:5-6 NLT

In this post-enlightenment era, we humans really like to take pride in all the wisdom we have gained about how the world works. As science and technology continue to advance, our human understanding can start to take a front seat in our approach to the world. We highly value our minds, their ability to think, reason, and understand. While this human capacity is not a bad thing, sometimes God works in ways that human reason is simply unable to grasp.

Are you resting too heavily on your ability to think and reason through a situation? Has that drawn your heart away from fully trusting God? Set your heart today to trust in him with everything, even if you can't make sense of what he's doing in your life right now.

Father God, it truly is my desire to trust you fully, and to not rest too heavily on my ability to understand what you're doing. Help me to trust you.

Trust in and rely confidently on the Lord with all your heart
And do not rely on your own insight or understanding.
In all your ways know and acknowledge and recognize Him,
And He will make your paths straight and smooth [removing
obstacles that block your way].

PROVERBS 3:5-6 AMP

The writer of these words isn't telling us to fully throw out
your capacity for reasoning. He's telling us to not rest in it, or
place or our trust, dependence, or confidence in our ability
to understand. Instead, we are to continue to keep our hearts
fully fixed on God, seeking him in every single thing we do.

God can be trusted to show you the right way to go and take
down the barriers that are preventing you from moving
forward. God wants to show you the way, even if the way
ahead doesn't make sense. Ask for a heart that fully trusts
him and desires to submit to his leadership in your life. He is
making your path straight. Choose to trust in him.

Lord Jesus, I ask you to reveal your amazing plans for me and
deepen my ability to trust you, in all areas of my life.

What would a straight path look like in your life?

Through the Wilderness

Listen! It's the voice of someone shouting,
"Clear the way through the wilderness for the Lord!
Make a straight highway through the wasteland for our God!"

ISAIAH 40:3 NLT

There are seasons of our lives when we feel like we are
wandering in the desert, unsure of what's ahead and where Jesus
may be taking us. We can find ourselves weary or confused,
hurting and maybe even angry at what God may be doing.
We're not alone in this. Israel experienced the challenges of
wandering in the desert waiting on God to break in.

If you're in one of those seasons, these are words of hope
for you. God is doing something, even in the wilderness.
He is making a way in your life for a greater release of God's
presence. The wilderness is a time of preparation that, while
painful, increases your capacity to trust God. God is making
a straight path ahead for his coming into your life in a greater
measure. LIsten to the voice crying in your wilderness that
the Lord is coming.

Lord Jesus, I ask you to make a clear path in my life for your
coming. I will trust where you lead me.

A voice of one is calling out,
"Clear the way for the Lord in the wilderness [remove the obstacles];
Make straight and smooth in the desert a highway for our God."

ISAIAH 40:3 AMP

If you have found yourself in the wilderness, what are the obstacles you're seeing, preventing the fulfillment of God's promises to you? Maybe it's a lie you're believing about yourself or God. Maybe it's a person standing in the way of your advancement. Maybe it's a self-inflicted obstacle you have put up between you and God. Whatever the obstacle may be, God has something to say about it: "Clear the way!"

He is with you and he is taking you through the wilderness. Not around it, but through it. Restoration and blessing is on the other side. And his presence is with you now in it. You can trust he is making a way where there seems to be no way. A straight and smooth path is ahead. There is an open invitation for more of God in your life.

Lord Jesus, I ask you to remove any obstacles from my life that are preventing me from receiving more of your presence.

What are the obstacles in your life that God wants to remove?

Close to His Heart

He will feed his flock like a shepherd.
He will carry the lambs in his arms,
holding them close to his heart.
He will gently lead the mother sheep with their young.

ISAIAH 40:11 NLT

The illustration of God as a Shepherd is all over the scriptures. It must be a picture that captures what his heart is really like. Listen to the tenderness of God's heart towards his people in this passage. We have a God who is rich in love and care for us. And these are God's words towards you today.

You don't have to worry about having your basic needs met. He promises to ensure his flock has enough food to eat. He will provide for you. If your legs are tired from walking, if you're weary in body or soul, he will pick you right up. He will wrap his arms around you. He holds you near and dear to his heart. Think about God as your Shepherd today, leading you and tenderly caring for you. Imagine him holding you close to his heart. Simply receive his love today.

Lord Jesus, thank you for your tender care for me. Hold me close to your heart today.

He will protect His flock like a shepherd,
He will gather the lambs in His arm,
He will carry them in His bosom;
He will gently and carefully lead those nursing their young.

ISAIAH 40:11 AMP

The words of Isaiah are penned in a time when the people of God were in exile. They were far away from home, suffering the consequences of their rebellion against God. They had chosen to go their own way, turning their hearts away from the Good Shepherd. In this place, God reveals himself as a tender-hearted God who longs to gather his people and hold them close to his heart.

God's love for you perseveres even through your rebellion and hardness of heart. He wants to carry you in his bosom even if you are far away from home. He is a Good Shepherd and his love and care are not dependent on you and anything you need to do to earn it. Open your heart to the Good Shepherd tonight and allow him to carry you close to his heart.

Lord Jesus, I'm sorry for any rebellion in my heart towards you.
I turn my heart towards you tonight and rest in you.

How does the idea of God holding you change things for you?

Remember the Cross

Just consider and meditate on Him who endured from sinners such bitter hostility against Himself [consider it all in comparison with your trials], so that you will not grow weary and lose heart.

HEBREWS 12:3 AMP

Life is filled with trials, challenges and setbacks. We all know the agony of defeat and the disappointment of loss. It can be easy to fix our attention on our troubles and find ourselves deeper in the pit of despair. The early church suffered too, and much of their struggle surrounded the persecutions they endured at the hands of those standing in opposition to the Lordship of Jesus.

The author of Hebrews gives us a simple yet profound instruction for when our hearts are weary; meditate on the cross. Think of all that Jesus endured at the hands of hostile people who thought they knew better. Remember his sacrifice. Set our minds on his response towards those who beat and whipped him; His response was steadfast love and forgiveness.

If you're weary, set your mind on Jesus on the cross. Remember what he did for you and be strengthened.

Lord Jesus, I remember all that you endured on the cross. May this truth strengthen my heart today.

Think of all the hostility he endured from sinful people; then you won't become weary and give up.

Why would mediation on the cross strengthen us and prevent us from giving up? There is power in recognizing that we are not alone in our suffering. We have a God who came into the darkest, dirtiest recesses of humanity and suffered at the hands of those who didn't recognize who he was. He did not run away or cower from the suffering he knew was coming. Instead, In this place of great suffering, the Holy Spirit strengthened him.

And this same Holy Spirit that filled and strengthened Jesus, and raised him from the dead, now dwells in you! You have access to that enduring strength available in the Holy Spirit. Do not give up or grow weary. Instead remember the cross. Remember Jesus' endurance to finish what God called him to do. Remember he is with you.

Holy Spirit, thank for you filling me with your presence. Please strengthen me!

When you remember the cross, what stands out to you today?

Just Keep Going

Lift your drooping hands and strengthen your weak knees, and make straight paths for your feet, so that what is lame may not be put out of joint but rather be healed.

Hebrews 12:12–13 ESV

Have you ever wanted to just throw in the towel and call it quits in your faith? Maybe you've been faithfully serving God for some time and still not seeing the blessing or breakthrough you've been praying for. Or maybe obstacles keep getting in your way or you're plagued by one disappointment after another. Whatever the challenge, Hebrews 12 is a chapter encouraging us to endure in following Jesus.

In our weakness, we can get sucked into running down crooked paths that only lead to more pain. If you're already limping from an existing injury or affliction, ensure you're running on the right path, with Jesus by your side. If you want the injury to heal, don't keep running back to the same things that cause you hurt and pain. Instead, fix your eyes on Jesus and follow him.

Lord Jesus, I want to run down the straight path with you by my side. Heal my existing wounds and strengthen me for the race ahead.

[Strengthen the hands that are weak and the knees that are feeble, and make straight paths for your feet, so that the limb which is lame may not be put out of joint, but rather be healed.

Hebrews 12:12-13 NASB

Running the race of faith can be challenging at times, and exhilarating at other times. Marathon runners will tell you the same. There are moments where it's hard to think of even taking one more step, and times when the "runner's high" renews your strength. But the best motivator is having other people cheering you on or even running with you.

God created us for relationship and we need each other to continue running the race with endurance. Do you need to invite someone else into your life to run the race with you? Do you need to help someone else out in their journey of faith? Ask God for direction and just keep going!

Lord Jesus, help me to keep running with endurance and encourage others on their journey too.

Who is God calling you to encourage in their journey today?

The Word

In the beginning the Word already existed.
The Word was with God,
and the Word was God.
He existed in the beginning with God.

JOHN 1:1-2 NLT

These words penned by John are some of the most beautiful, poetic words of the New Testament that speak to the supremacy of Christ. While the other Gospel writers begin the story of Jesus at his earthly birth or miracles, John heads right to the beginning of all creation. Jesus Christ embodies the Word of God. While we often like to think of the Bible as the Word of God, in reality, the Word is a person. And this person, Jesus Christ, shows us what God is really like. Jesus is the unchanging one, God in the flesh.

Reflecting on the eternal existence of Christ has the power to put our little lives into perspective. The God who has always been and always will be, sees you, knows you, and loves you to the depth of your being. The Creator God, Jesus Christ, who spoke the earth into being and hung the stars knows you by name.

Lord Jesus, I confess that you are God. Thank you for coming to the earth to show us what God is like.

In the beginning [before all time] was the Word (Christ), and the Word was with God, and the Word was God Himself. He was [continually existing] in the beginning [co-eternally] with God.

JOHN 1:1-2 AMP

Jesus Christ was the Word at the beginning, in perfect unity with God, the Creator. He existed before time began as we know it. This is a difficult reality to wrap our finite minds around. The unity that exists with God in three persons, Father, Son and Holy Spirit, is a reality that he invites us to join in with!

How does reflecting on this truth tonight change the way you approach Jesus in prayer? If he has always been, and always will be, that means he is present with you in this exact moment. He comes right into your messes and dwells with you. Worship him tonight as the eternal one. Sing your praises to the God who has always existed, and yet he sees and knows you.

Lord Jesus, I praise you tonight for your eternal existence and eternal presence. Help me to be more unified with you.

What is the Word, Jesus, saying to you tonight?

Through Him

God created everything through him,
and nothing was created except through him.
The Word gave life to everything that was created.

JOHN 1:3–4A NLT

The Word is translated from the Greek word Logos, which
carries with it a few meanings. For the Jewish audience, the
Logos was the spoken word of God, which had the power
to set creation into being. For the Greek philosophers, the
Logos was the cosmic power that brought order and meaning
out of chaos at the creation of the world. John plays on both of
these understandings to speak a profound truth about Jesus
Christ: It was through the true Word, Logos Jesus, that all
things on heaven and earth were brought into being.

Jesus brought meaning and purpose out of chaos. If he did
it at creation, and continues to do it now, he can do it in
your life too. Reflect on the truth today that God created you
through Jesus, and that Jesus put the very breath in your lungs
that you now breathe. Life came through him, and true life
exists only in him.

Lord Jesus, thank you that you are the divine Word of God and all
things were made through you, including me.

All things were made and came into existence through Him; and without Him not even one thing was made that has come into being. In Him was life [and the power to bestow life].

JOHN 1:3-4A AMP

Many people go through life thinking of Jesus as just another religious figure who had some good things to say. Yes, he started a movement, but they can dismiss him as just another good man, teacher, or prophet. Yet the words of John demand a higher honor of Jesus--literally everything that has ever come into being was through divine power of Jesus Christ.

This includes all living creatures. The person who cut you off in traffic today, your angry boss, or cranky teenager. All are people who Jesus breathed life into. The power to give and bestow life rests firmly in the hands of Jesus. And as Jesus' follower you have the power to speak life into people through your words. Agree with Jesus today by proclaiming life over all of God's creation.

Lord Jesus, all people were made by your hands. Help me to speak life over those who need your hope.

Who is God calling you to speak life into?

The Light

The Word gave life to everything that was created,
and his life brought light to everyone.
The light shines in the darkness,
and the darkness can never extinguish it.

JOHN 1:4-5 NLT

We all know and understand the power of light. If you have ever been in a dark room when a light switch suddenly turned on, you know what light does. You can suddenly see things you didn't know were there before. You squint as your eyes adjust to the brightness. Any fear of what may be lurking in the darkness is quickly dismissed.

God is compared to light all over scripture. This poem about Jesus, the True Light, proclaims a profound truth about him that brings hope to our hearts. When he came to the earth, it was like a light switch suddenly turned on. His presence is a gloriously light and the darkness stands no chance against it. If you're battling darkness in your life, take courage in the truth that the light of Jesus is more powerful than any darkness you may be facing.

Lord Jesus, you are the light and you are more powerful than any
darkness around me. Help me to walk in your light.

In him was life, and that life was the light of all mankind. The light shines in the darkness, and the darkness has not overcome it.

JOHN 1:4-5 NIV

When we look back on our lives, we can all see spots of darkness, despair and defeat. There are times when things didn't go as planned and we were left distraught and confused with what God might be up to. In these times the darkness may feel overwhelming and it can be easy to feel like giving up.

They say that it's always darkest right before the dawn. You are on the verge of the light of Christ shining into your darkness. The light of Jesus is always more powerful. It will always persevere, and blaze forth. Set your gaze on Jesus if you're in one of those dark seasons. Don't give up on hope. The light will always find a way. Light can not be put out or boxed in. It will always triumph over the darkness in the end.

God, I give you permission to search my heart and shine your light into any darkness in my life.

What darkness in your life is the Light of Christ pushing back?

In the Highest

"Glory to God in the highest,
and on earth peace among those with whom he is pleased!"

LUKE 2:14 ESV

The angels sang of the glory of God and they didn't ask us for any help. This is a declaration, not an invitation. It is a performance, not a sing along. God is the highest glory! How do we know? The heavenly choir sang it to us on Christmas Eve and the people of God have been singing it back every Advent since then.

As you prepare your heart for the celebration of Christmas, look no further than the angels. God, the Almighty left all the heavenly glory to take on an earthly humility so that you could see his heavenly glory. The one who created mankind became a man on Christmas Day and the glory came close enough for you to see it. Look to him today! Look to Christ to see the glory of God in the highest!

Glory to you, eternal God! You have shown us your heavenly glory
in your earthly humility and we sing praise to you with the angels.

"Glory to God in the highest,
And on earth peace, goodwill toward men!"

LUKE 2:14 NKJV

How has seeing the glory of God in the Christ brought peace to your earthly life? Have all the enemies in your life been brought to peace? Maybe not, but one has and it is the one that matters most.

You were the enemy, and God was on the other side of the battle line. You were sinful like your father Adam and a liar like your father the devil. You were by nature a child of wrath. The last thing in the world that you wanted was for the God of glory to come near to you. But he did. He came in humility in order to show you his glory. The glory of God in the birth of Christ has led to the glory of God in the death of Christ where all of your enmity was removed, bringing peace on earth to all who believe. Glory to God in the highest!

Gracious God, as I lay down to sleep, I sleep in peace because of the goodwill you have shown me in Christ Jesus.

How can seeing the glory of God in the humility of Christ bring peace to your earthly life?

Unexpected Messengers

When they had seen this, they made known the statement which had been told them about this Child. And all who heard it wondered at the things which were told them by the shepherds.

LUKE 2:17-18 NASB

In the ancient world, a shepherd is a step below blue collar—maybe a few steps. A shepherd is gruff, uneducated, sleeps with the sheep, and probably hasn't groomed themselves in quite some time. When you think of a powerful God wanting to get a message across about a coming king who's going to save the world, you'd think it would be wise to go to your influencers, leaders, and upper echelons of society. They are the ones that get things done, they are the ones that everyone respects—or at least has to—for better or worse.

Why would God choose to reveal this message to a dirty stinky shepherd? Is it possible that God is trying to set a precedent for the kind of Messiah that's about to enter the world? Dwell on that kind of Messiah today.

God, thank you for coming to me in unexpected ways and saving even me.

*When they saw it they made known the saying which had been
told them concerning this child; and all who heard it wondered at
what the shepherds told them.*

LUKE 2:17-18 RSV

One characteristic that often leaves us in awe of God is
the fact of his unexpected revelation and goodness to the
people who are least deserving of it—at least by our culture's
perspective. Jesus has been revealed to even you. When you
are feeling your most unworthy, that's perfect; because that's
when is God is most worthy. Another biblical writer says that
his power is made perfect in your weakness.

You may have felt undeserving of God's great message of love
today, and yet he comes to you anyway. Allow that to put you at
ease as you sleep.

*God, thank you showing up over and over and sharing good news
with me.*

What unexpected thing has God done in your life recently?

Among Us

The Word became flesh and dwelt among us, and we have seen his glory, glory as of the only Son from the Father, full of grace and truth.

JOHN 1:14 ESV

The Creator of all living and breathing things, of all things seen and unseen, and all things that have ever existed. He who set the earth into motion, and hung the stars in the sky, the divine maker who knew and loved you since the beginning of time. He left the perfection and joy of heaven to come crashing into our broken world.

If you ever worry that your life is too broken or too messy for God to come close, remember that Jesus took on human form. Think about what he left behind to be with you. He was born in a dirty stable, surrounded by the mess. He took residence with sinful people. And extended to them the unconditional love of God. He suffered and died on a cross, and rose again that you might be reconciled to God. The good news of Christmas is that Jesus is Immanuel, God with us. God with you.

Lord Jesus, I invite you into my mess today. Thank you that you are with us.

The Word became a human and lived among us. We saw his glory—the glory that belongs to the only Son of the Father—and he was full of grace and truth.

JOHN 1:14, NCV

Imagine rubbing shoulders with Jesu, seeing him heal people with his touch, multiple food by his word, and walk on water by his power. This is an indescribable glory that the disciples witnessed first-hand in their time with him. And John is proclaiming this was the Father's glory manifested in and through Jesus.

As followers of Jesus, you carry a measure of glory too. Just as the Holy Spirit empowered Jesus in everything he did, that same Holy Spirit dwells in you and manifests the Father's love and power through you to a world that needs hope. God with us, also means God in us, working through us.

Lord Jesus, may I be more aware of your presence dwelling in me and walk more fully in the power of your Spirit.

What areas of your life need to be touched by the truth that God is always with you?

In the Air

"On coming to the house, they saw the child with his mother Mary, and they bowed down and worshiped him. Then they opened their treasures and presented him with gifts of gold, frankincense and myrrh."

MATTHEW 2:11 NIV

Your Christmas Nativity scene is likely inaccurate. Consider the "Three Wise Men." The Bible only states that three gifts were given but doesn't cite how many of these scholars actually visited Jesus. The other hiccup is that Matthew 2:11 shows these visitors not visiting Jesus in the manger when he was a baby but meeting Christ the "child" with His mother in a "house."

The point? Christmas can be based on traditions more than based on truth. That's not necessarily evil, but it is confusing. In the air there's a feeling of how snow should fall on Christmas morning as we exchange the perfect gifts with loved ones who never argue. These expectations mimic how we imagine our lives should look a certain way based on what we've experienced in the past. What if this year God wants to show you something in his story to help you better understand your story?

Do you see what I see? Do you hear what I hear? Lord, reset my winter wonderland so that I might recognize the difference between what I expect versus what you have already given.

"Going into the house, they saw the child with Mary his mother, and they fell down and worshiped him. Then, opening their treasures, they offered him gifts, gold and frankincense and myrrh."

MATTHEW 2:11 ESV

As hard as it may be to reconsider your Christmas Nativity, there is incredible hope in it if you do. The fact that the magi didn't show up for weeks if not months after the birth of Christ highlights that Christmas doesn't end the day after we celebrate it. Just as his time on earth continued, so can we move past something traditional or "religious" in order to claim something that's ongoing and relational.

Mary and Joseph had to go through this same journey. Their life didn't turn out the way they planned it when they first got engaged, but as they followed the Lord in obedience he continued to show them how he was providing for them. The gift of the Magi was a part of that. In what ways might God want to continue to gift you with blessings beyond the holiday season?

Lord, in the air there's a feeling of hope and joy. I enjoy this, but I'd rather seek you than the feeling. Prepare me for the year ahead, wherever it leads.

If you were able to see the birth of Jesus and could only bring an item from your home as a gift, what would you pick?

In Plain Sight

*"Today in the city of David a Savior was born for you, who is the
Messiah, the Lord. This will be the sign for you: You will find a
baby wrapped tightly in cloth and lying in a manger."*

LUKE 2:11-12 CSB

The Christmas season and hinting seem synonymous with
each other. Whether it's others casually letting us know what
they'd like as a gift or you walking into a store and hearing
someone ringing a bell for charity, we're surrounded by little
prompts and reminders meant to get our attention. The bigger
question is why is hinting even needed in the first place?

Consider the first Christmas when the angels appeared to
shepherds and clearly proclaimed that the Savior had been
born and was in plain sight. While we may avoid speaking
clearly because we fear the awkwardness it may cause, God
chases after us to clearly invite us back into a relationship
with Him. Christmas is one of those times when we
remember how through Jesus new life is absolutely accessible
to you. God came down so you can take him up on that!

*Father, you care for me and sent me your son so I wouldn't have
to guess about it. I choose today to trust in Jesus as my Savior,
whether it's the first, fiftieth or five-thousandth time. Thank you
for your assurance.*

"Unto you is born this day in the city of David a Savior, who is Christ the Lord. And this will be a sign for you: you will find a baby wrapped in swaddling cloths and lying in a manger."

LUKE 2:11-12 ESV

Jesus wasn't born onto a gold hospital bed filled with bouncy cushions and the best medical care possible. He certainly was worthy, but instead was birthed as a rather "plain sight" into a smelly animal area into the hands of an awkward couple. In this putrid ugliness of a manger in the shadows God proclaimed, "Look at me. I'm the most accessible to you than I ever have been before. Take me up on it!"

Often the Christmas season becomes what we don't want it to be amidst strangers elbowing each other in stores and people closest to us letting us down. What if twenty centuries ago it is in these less-than-beautiful moments that Jesus is most beautifully found? And what might happen if when you or I stand in the midst of chaos we recognize it as an opportunity to be a gift instead of demand one?

Savior Jesus, I know your presence is where I often least expect it. I invite you to make yourself seen through me as one of those places for others to find you.

What is one thing about Jesus you don't have to guess or wonder about?

God Revealed

No one has ever seen God. But the unique One, who is himself God, is near to the Father's heart. He has revealed God to us.

JOHN 1:18 NLT

Many people can get tripped up on the God of the Old Testament, who sometimes appears angry and judgmental. While Theologians have debated this seemingly conflicting picture of God, one thing is unmistakable. Jesus came to the earth with a crystal-clear mission: to show us what God the Father is really like.

Any understanding of God must be put through the lens of Jesus. Any reading of the Old Testament text must have Jesus at the center. Any debate about the nature of God must point first to Christ Jesus. If you have ever wondered if God was angry, or disappointed with you, look to Jesus. He laid down his life to free you from the power of sin. He loves you with an everlasting love. Rest firmly in the truth that Jesus shows you the heart of the Father.

Lord Jesus, thank you for showing us the Father's love for us.

No one has seen God [His essence, His divine nature] at any time; the [One and] only begotten God [that is, the unique Son] who is in the intimate presence of the Father, He has explained Him [and interpreted and revealed the awesome wonder of the Father].

JOHN 1:18 AMP

It has been said, the most important thing about a person is how they view God. If God is angry, it's easy to walk in fear. If God is a pushover, it's easy to continue to live in sin. If God is distant, it's easy to live a prayer-less life.

What are your conceptions of God? If Jesus reveals to us what God is like, do you have any conceptions of God that need changing? Jesus is in the intimate presence of the Father, and he want you to have greater intimacy with the Father too. Ask God to show you if you have an inaccurate view of him. Ask him to reveal the truth of what he is really like.

Lord Jesus, show me if there are inaccurate perspective I have of what you are really like. I want to know you more.

Are you holding onto any misconceptions of God?

Living by the Spirit

Those who belong to Christ Jesus have nailed the passions and desires of their sinful nature to his cross and crucified them there. Since we are living by the Spirit, let us follow the Spirit's leading in every part of our lives.

GALATIANS 5:24–25 NLT

Whether you have just started your journey walking with Jesus or you've been following him for some time, you know there are passions and desires within you that stand in opposition to the way of Jesus. When we start our walk with Jesus, there are some times when things may change instantly for us. Other times, it's a journey to learn from Jesus' example and allow the Holy Spirit to change us. Either way, we are always being transformed into the image of Jesus, more and more each day, as we seek him.

The writer of Galatians is speaking of your position before God, and it's quite the striking image! This is a new reality. The parts of you that live in opposition to God have actually been crucified along with Christ. That is no longer who you are. You may struggle with sin, but it's not your identity.

Lord Jesus, thank you for taking upon the cross the desires of my sinful nature. Help me to follow the Spirit's leading.

Those who belong to Christ Jesus have crucified the flesh with its passions and desires. If we live by the Spirit, let us also keep in step with the Spirit.

GALATIANS 5:24-25 ESV

If you are a follower of Jesus, you are now living by the Spirit. The Holy Spirit has taken up residence within you and he is transforming your desires to line up with God's desires. The thing is, this isn't always an instant change. It is a daily, moment by moment decision, to keep in step with the Spirit.

How do we keep in step with the Spirit each day? Ask him to help you. Set aside time in your day to position yourself to hear from him. You're learning how to listen and obey the Spirit's leading each day. Live by the power of the Holy Spirit, trusting that he is working in you. All of this is possible because you belong to Christ Jesus.

Lord Jesus, I belong to you. Help me to keep in step with the Holy Spirit's leading each day of my life.

What would change in your life if you daily walked in step with the Holy Spirit?

Rejected

He came into the very world he created, but the world didn't recognize him. He came to his own people, and even they rejected him.

JOHN 1:10-11 NLT

Think about the heartbreak that Jesus probably felt. The soldiers who nailed him to the cross? He knew before the foundation of the world. The religious leaders who plotted for his execution? He formed in their mothers' wombs. His friend who betrayed him and every man, woman, and child who scoffed at him, threw insults at him, or even crucified him? He loved beyond measure. The extravagant love of God, came to this earth in the bodily form of Jesus, and he was not wanted. He was not seen for who he was. They turned their backs on him and went their own way.

If you have ever experienced the heartbreak of rejection, you know it can crush the spirit. Take great comfort in knowing that our Lord Jesus understands. He sees and knows how it feels. And while he was rejected himself, he will never reject you.

Lord Jesus, you understand the heartache of rejection more than anyone. Give my heart peace when I am rejected by people.

He was in the world, and the world was made through him, yet the world did not know him. He came to his own, and his own people did not receive him.

JOHN 1:10-11 ESV

We can read this verse from the book of John and quickly jump to thinking of all the low-life, foolish people who rejected Jesus when he was here on the earth. How could they have missed it? How could they not have seen who he was? How could they have crucified him?

The reality is that all humanity has blood on our hands in some regard. We have all gone astray from God and done things our own way. The beautiful truth in Jesus' story is that he laid down his life for us, even when we were the worst of sinners, in rebellion against God. This earth-shattering love was extended to each of us, unconditionally, even when we reject him. You can turn your back on God but he will never turn his back on you.

Lord Jesus, forgive me for the times I have rejected you. Even when I turn my back on you, you have never turned away from me.

How does the truth that Jesus doesn't reject you change things for you?

Children of God

*To all who believed him and accepted him, he gave the right
to become children of God. They are reborn—not with a physical
birth resulting from human passion or plan, but a birth that
comes from God.*

JOHN 1:12-13 NLT

We deeply value our rights; our right to freedom of speech,
right to opinion, and the right to life, liberty and the pursuit
of happiness. But in the kingdom of God, we are often called
to lay down our rights, and instead cling to Jesus' Lordship.
We are called to turn the other cheek, to pray for our enemies,
and love the unlovable. Yes, God's kingdom is very different
from the kingdoms of this world.

And yet, one area where we have an irrevocable right given
directly from God himself, is our right to become the
children of God, simply through faith, and acceptance of
Jesus as Lord. This is a right that cannot be stolen by any
person, enemy, government, or worldly system. It is a right
not shaken by borders or difficulties. If you have accepted
Christ, you are a child of God, period.

*Lord Jesus, thank you that you have given me the irrevocable right
to be God's child.*

To all who did receive him, who believed in his name, he gave the right to become children of God, who were born, not of blood nor of the will of the flesh nor of the will of man, but of God.

JOHN 1:12-13 ESV

What are the benefits that come with being adopted into God's family? You are loved beyond measure. Your life has a greater purpose. You are never forgotten or forsaken. You have access to unspeakable joy that will strengthen you in hard times. You have been re-born, alive in Christ, with the Holy Spirit living inside you.

Your identity is God's child. The world will always speak lies trying to convince you that God could never love you that much, or forgive you for your wrongdoings. But the person you are, right now, flaws and all, has been adopted into God's own family. He doesn't just love you, he likes you! You have a new life in Christ that cannot be snatched away by the enemy's schemes. Rest firmly in the truth that you are a beloved child of God.

Lord Jesus, open my heart to receive the truth about what I have access to as your child.

How might things change if you more fully embraced that you are a child of God?

Set Your Sights

Since you have been raised to new life with Christ, set your sights on the realities of heaven, where Christ sits in the place of honor at God's right hand. Think about the things of heaven, not the things of earth.

COLOSSIANS 3:1-2 NLT

We live in a world bombarding us with the sights, sounds, and images of a broken world around us. Political tensions alone have a way of sending us off kilter and into despair. Wars and famine, people hurting other people; this is the narrative of our culture. The writer of Colossians knew that our hearts could easily be distracted by the pain around us.

How can you persevere and not lose hope? Set your sights on heaven! Fix your thoughts and your gaze towards things above. Think of Jesus seated on the throne. You have new life in Christ that defines your present reality on this earth. Allow God's perspective to inform your perspective on the world around you.

Lord Jesus, thank you for the new life I have in you. Help me to fix my thoughts on heaven rather than just the things on the earth.

If you have been raised with Christ [to a new life, sharing in
His resurrection from the dead], keep seeking the things that
are above, where Christ is, seated at the right hand of God. Set
your mind and keep focused habitually on the things above [the
heavenly things], not on things that are on the earth [which have
only temporal value].

COLOSSIANS 3:1-2 AMP

If you have said yes to Christ, you have a new life in him. You get
a do-over, a fresh start on life. But not just once. Each moment
of every day, you are sharing in Jesus' resurrection. He is
perpetually raising you to newness of life. The best way to stand
firm in this new reality is to recognize what gets your attention.

Are you worried about the problems around you?
The solution is to set your mind on heaven. Are you
overwhelmed? Remember God's perspective. He sent Jesus
to restore this world back into right relationship with him,
and the restoration work is still in progress. Think from the
perspective of heaven, which is always hope.

Lord Jesus, you are perpetually raising me from the dead. Help me
to set my focus on you.

What is God's perspective on the broken things in your life?

Like Him

We are already God's children, but he has not yet shown us what we will be like when Christ appears. But we do know that we will be like him, for we will see him as he really is.

1 JOHN 3:2 NLT

The Word *Christian* means "little Christ." The aim of a Christian's life is to made more like Christ. You are called to love like Christ, walk in the same power as Christ and respond like Christ in the face of trials. He truly is your model for life. At the final revealing of Jesus to the world, we will see him fully as he really is. And in seeing him, we are transformed to be like him.

But what if this is true today in our journey towards Christ-likeness? The more we see and know him the more we are made like him. May this reality, stir up a greater hunger in your heart to know him here and now.

Lord Jesus, I want to be more like you. Help me to see you as you really are in this life that I may become even more like you.

Now we are children of God; and it has not yet been revealed what we shall be, but we know that when He is revealed, we shall be like Him, for we shall see Him as He is.

1 JOHN 3:2 NKJV

There may be conflicting voices coming at you trying to tear you down. Remember today who you are really are: God's child. There's nothing that can negate this reality. But there's even more available to you in Christ Jesus! God is doing a beautiful work in you making you more and more like Jesus every day. And this same Jesus will one day be revealed to the world as the Christ.

Your journey towards Christ-likeness will be completed. In seeing Jesus, you'll be transformed to be more like him. May this truth inspire your heart today. God is committed to you and the work he is doing in you. He's not finished yet. But you will someday look just like Jesus.

Lord Jesus, thank you for calling me your child! I rest in the truth that you will someday make me just like you.

How would your life change if you became more like Christ?